W9-AWD-118

AnandTech

Contents at a Glance

201 W. 103rd Street
Indianapolis, Indiana 46290

The AnandTech Guide to PC Gaming Hardware

Copyright© 2002 by Que® Publishing

All rights reserved. No part of this book shall be reproduced, stored in a retrieval system, or transmitted by any means, electronic, mechanical, photocopying, recording, or otherwise, without written permission from the publisher. No patent liability is assumed with respect to the use of the information contained herein. Although every precaution has been taken in the preparation of this book, the publisher and author assume no responsibility for errors nor omissions. Nor is any liability assumed for damages resulting from the use of the information contained herein.

International Standard Book Number: 0-7897-2626-2

Library of Congress Catalog Card Number: 20-01090313

Printed in the United States of America

First Printing: October 2001

05 04 03 02 4 3 2

Trademarks

All terms mentioned in this book that are known to be trademarks or service marks have been appropriately capitalized. Que cannot attest to the accuracy of this information. Use of a term in this book should not be regarded as affecting the validity of any trademark or service mark.

Warning and Disclaimer

Every effort has been made to make this book as complete and as accurate as possible, but no warranty or fitness is implied. The information provided is on an "as is" basis. The author and the publisher shall have neither liability nor responsibility to any person or entity with respect to any loss or damages arising from the information contained in this book.

Associate Publisher
Greg Wiegand

Executive Editor
Rick Kughen

Acquisitions Editor
Rick Kughen

Development Editor
Todd Brakke

Managing Editor
Thomas F. Hayes

Project Editor
Tricia S. Liebig

Production Editor
Candice Hightower

Indexer
Aamir Burki

Proofreader
Plan-It Publishing

Technical Editor
Mark Reddin

Interior Designer
Alan Clements

Cover Designer
Alan Clements

Reviewers
Steve Kovsky
Josh Norem

Contents

About the Author

Anand Lal Shimpi has turned a fledgling personal page on GeoCities.com into the world's most visited and trusted PC hardware site. Anand started his site in 1997 at just 14 years old and has used his uncanny hardware knowledge and writing ability to transform his site into a site that industry heavyweights turn to daily. Anand has been featured in *USA Today*, *48 Hours*, and *Fortune Magazine*. He also has appeared on *ZDTV* (now *TechTV*) and CBS. His site—`www.anandtech.com`—receives more than 50 million page views and is read by more than two million readers per month.

About the AnandTech Team

Brandon Hill is the Web news editor for AnandTech. He scours the Net for all of the latest hardware and software news to keep the AnandTech readers up to date on current events. Brandon is currently attending North Carolina State University and can be found posting frequently on the AnandTech Community Forums (`http://forums.anandtech.com`).

Debbie Barber is an instrumental part of the AnandTech sales team. Debbie gets us fed by managing the sales and marketing for AnandTech. Prior to AnandTech, she was a founder and head of the sales team for SharkyExtreme. She started her Internet activity with *Tom's Hardware Guide* as sales account management. Prior to this, she was a pharmaceutical representative. Debbie, a true California native, lives and works in Silicon Valley.

Henry Kuo, the motherboard editor for AnandTech, is in charge of all the individual motherboard reviews as well as scheduled roundups. He obtained both his bachelor's and master's degrees in electrical engineering.

Jason Clark is the president and CEO of e-Zone Media, Inc., an Internet solutions company based in Canada. Jason, along with his partner Dominic Plouffe, has developed many widely used Web applications such as FuseTalk, FuseAds, and FuseMail. FuseTalk powers discussion boards from those at AnandTech to Macromedia's latest acquisition, Allaire Corporation. Jason is an avid computer enthusiast and has been AnandTech's Senior Webmaster/developer since 1998. You can read about his accomplishments at `www.e-zonemedia.com`.

Jeff Brubaker is the Linux guru behind the AnandTech team, often putting in late hours to include a bit of Linux performance/compatibility exposure in AnandTech's articles. You can find his work at `www.anandtech.com`.

Jim Warren has a well-trained ear for audio, which makes him the perfect addition to AnandTech's staff as the official audio editor. Jim is also an electrical engineering major at the Massachusetts Institute of Technology. Jim Warren contributed considerably to Chapter 6, "Sound: Waking Up the Neighbors."

Kiran Venkatesh is a Web news reporter for AnandTech as well as the author of the *Weekly Memory and Motherboard Price Guide*. He is attending North Carolina University majoring in biomedical engineering. Kiran's *Price Guides* and *News Stories* are read by millions at `www.anandtech.com`.

Lalchand Shimpi is a member of AnandTech's Board of Directors and has provided Anand with immeasurable inspiration and advice. Dr. Shimpi is a Professor of Computer Science at St. Augustine's College. He shares the same passion for technology as the rest of the AnandTech staff while bringing his vast experience in the programming and mathematical worlds to the table.

Larry Barber heads up the AnandTech business team. Before AnandTech, Larry was president of Tyan Computer followed by founder and publisher of SharkyExtreme.com. He collaborated with Tom Pabst on the book *Tom's Hardware Guide*, also published by Que. From an early career of Flying B-52's in the Air Force to a President of a motherboard company, to the Internet, he brings many years of business experience to the AnandTech team. He currently resides in Silicon Valley where he is also our eyes and ears to the valley.

Manveer Wasson is the editor of *AnandTech's Weekly CPU and Video Card Price Guide*. Also attending North Carolina University and majoring in electrical engineering, Manveer helps with a lot of the behind-the-scenes testing for AnandTech while cooping for IT companies such as Tekelec in the Raleigh area. You can read his guides at `www.anandtech.com`.

Matthew Witheiler started writing for AnandTech in early 2000 and has since been promoted to the level of senior hardware editor. His specialties include 3D graphics performance and quality analysis. Matthew's overclocking guides and 2D image quality testing have earned him a solid reputation at AnandTech.

Mike Andrawes is a graduate of Duke University's Electrical and Biomedical Engineering program in North Carolina. He has been working in the computer industry for over a decade, starting out as most did with a hobby and eventually working at a PC repair shop before finally becoming AnandTech's first senior hardware editor.

Razieh Shimpi is the vice president of AnandTech, Inc. and is key to the advancement of the corporation. A graduate of the University of Massachusetts, Razieh has brought her years of experience in the business and real estate worlds to AnandTech. She is currently leading up the development of AnandTech's new headquarters in Morrisville, North Carolina.

Tillmann Steinbrecher is AnandTech's German correspondent that specializes in cooling. He was a major contributor to Chapter 9, "Cases and Cooling: Living in Style and Keeping Your Cool." Tillmann also runs his own Web site, *The Heatsink Guide* (`www.heatsink-guide.com`).

About the Technical Editor

Mark Reddin is president of Trinity Microsystems, Inc., a computer reseller and repair center in Indiana. He is a Microsoft Certified Systems Engineer (MCSE) and A+ Certified PC technician who has enjoyed using computers, as well as breaking and fixing them, since the days of the early Commodore and Atari machines. Mark still enjoys being involved with computers and networks at a hands-on level and can often be found in the trenches, configuring hardware and running cables. He has been involved with several Que publications, providing technical verification as well as development. You might reach him through the contacts page at `www.trinitymicrosystems.com`.

Dedication

To Lal and Razieh:

The best leaders in this world don't run countries, they raise children.

Acknowledgments

Although I have written hundreds of reviews, totaling thousands of pages for AnandTech, this book is my entry into the hardcopy arena. I must say that the process was definitely an education, but as is the case with my normal review schedule, a number of people helped me get through it all.

First and foremost, my parents, Lal and Razieh Shimpi, to whom I dedicate this book, receive my greatest thanks. It is rare that I get to see either one of them much because of my seemingly endless work, yet they are always on my mind and in my heart. My parents are the inspiration for much of my work; my father having come to the United States with less than $27 in his pocket and truly living the "American Dream"; and my mother having proven on countless occasions that there are no limits to what one can achieve, other than those that are self-imposed.

In spite of the fact that I don't even know 1% of them by name, the two million readers of AnandTech (`www.anandtech.com`) that have supported me for the past four years and counting are worthy of my undying appreciation. The hundreds of e-mails that fill my box every day along with the millions of posts that populate the AnandTech Community Forums are some of the best examples of what makes this endless work seem less like that and more like a fun blessing. To them, I thank for dealing with the somewhat decreased stream of articles during the three months I was working on this book.

A very special thanks goes out to all of those who have helped me with AnandTech over these past few years—the entire AnandTech staff that I listed earlier, thanks for always being there for me and being the dependable friends I've always been able to come to.

There are those that I've met through my work at AnandTech who have also earned my respect that I'd like to mention as well. I'd like to thank Alex "Sharky" Ross and Joan "Mango" Woods formerly of `www.SharkyExtreme.com`, for the advice and support they have given me. Dr. Thomas Pabst of Tom's Hardware Guide (`www.tomshardware.com`) was my original inspiration to get on the online hardware enthusiast committee and for that I extend to him my continued respect and gratitude. Of course I cannot forget Kyle Bennett of HardOCP (`www.hardocp.com`) who has truly been an honest and kind friend to me, two characteristics that are seemingly increasingly rare. Anders Hammervald designed the face of today's AnandTech and he has definitely earned my respect as a very talented artist.

I must thank my very good friends that have put up with the fact that what started out as a hobby took me away from them for so very long. This is the project that has kept me at home instead of going out with you all, so to all of you I hope you enjoy it although the majority of you aren't too interested in the advantages of one motherboard over another. Aubrey, Amy, Ben, Dana, Danielle, Dave, Douglas, M. Downey, Jon, Joy, Kiran, Manny, Sarah, Shawna, Thakker and all of those that I have failed to mention but always carry you in my mind and in my heart—thanks.

The countless English teachers and professors that have had a great impact on my life and my desire to write also played a large part in the writing of this book. Mrs. Ayscue, Ms. Larsen, Ms. Woodbury, Dr. Bauso, and Dr. Leaker—thank you.

Then there is the Que staff that has helped me tremendously with turning my content into the book you see in front of you today. Thanks to Rick Kughen, the Executive Editor of this book, for not only giving me the opportunity to pursue this project, but also for putting up with my hectic schedule. My continued thanks and appreciation goes to Todd Brakke and the rest of the members of the edit and graphics team that helped put this book together.

The final and most important acknowledgment I'd like to make here is to you, the reader, for purchasing this book. I'm hoping that this will be the first of many and your support will help turn that dream into a reality. Thank you.

Tell Us What You Think!

As the reader of this book, *you* are our most important critic and commentator. We value your opinion and want to know what we're doing right, what we could do better, what areas you'd like to see us publish in, and any other words of wisdom you're willing to pass our way.

As the publisher for Que, I welcome your comments. You can fax, e-mail, or write me directly to let me know what you did or didn't like about this book—as well as what we can do to make our books stronger.

When you write, please be sure to include this book's title and author as well as your name and phone or fax number. I will carefully review your comments and share them with the author and editors who worked on the book.

Fax: 317-581-4666

E-mail: `hardware@mcp.com`

Mail: Greg Wiegand
Que Corporation
201 West 103rd Street
Indianapolis, IN 46290 USA

If you'd like to contact the author directly, you can do so via e-mail sent to `anand_shimpi@anandtech.com`.

I always appreciate any comments or suggestions you might have. I'll do my best to answer as much e-mail as I can, but unfortunately there's no way for me to respond to it all. So please don't be offended if I cannot get to your e-mail. I do make an effort to read every message, so your words won't go unread.

Introduction

The AnandTech Guide to PC Gaming Hardware is your on-ramp to the high-speed highway of hardware enthusiasts. PC gaming hardware enthusiasts not only want to go fast but they also want to win. It is no secret that you win with information and knowledge. Keeping up with the latest information is quite difficult without a solid foundation of knowledge, and that foundation is exactly what this book is designed to do. It's very rare that you find a print publication, whether a magazine or a book, dedicated to the hardware enthusiast. This book is such a book.

What is a hardware enthusiast? A computer hardware enthusiast is someone that is beneath the hood of their PC, much like they would a car, except with a much more delicate touch. The true computer hardware enthusiast knows the internals of their PC like the back of their hand, and more importantly, the hardware enthusiast knows how to separate the truth from the marketing b.s. the manufacturers give them. The hardware enthusiast knows how to take a look at a piece of technology and take from it what its true worth is, leaving the fluff behind. The hardware enthusiast has a passion for computer hardware and is on an ever-expanding journey to broaden their knowledge of hardware in the computer industry.

This book is for hardware enthusiasts. It doesn't discuss which processor is faster, the AMD Athlon or the Intel Pentium 4. It teaches you what makes one faster than the other. A major shortcoming of a lot of books is that by the time they hit the store shelves, the majority of the content is obsolete. Although the material in *The AnandTech Guide to PC Gaming Hardware* isn't completely immune to becoming obsolete, by focusing on the underlying architecture of today's technology you are left with a resource that doesn't tell you "what," but it explains "why."

The "why" is very important as it applies to 3D gaming because gamers often upgrade their systems much more than regular computer users. The reason is simple, games are much more demanding than running a Word Processing application or browsing the Internet. Because of this constant upgrading, understanding what is the fastest today isn't as important as knowing how to determine what is the fastest tomorrow. Becoming a more intelligent buyer is one of many very positive results of journeying down the path of the computer hardware enthusiast, in this case, the computer gaming hardware enthusiast.

Fortunately, this knowledge is easily extendable to other areas so you'll not only be able to understand how technology relates to gaming, but also how it relates to other application areas as well.

The AnandTech Guide to PC Gaming Hardware covers the most relevant technology of today and tomorrow. CPU coverage includes AMD's and Intel's latest solutions, the Athlon 4, the Pentium 4, and the future of both platforms; NVIDIA's first entry into the chipset market with their nForce, as well as competing solutions from AMD, ALi, Intel, SiS, and VIA, comprise the chipset coverage in this book. The true use for AGP as well as current and future interconnects such as PCI, PCI-X, and HyperTransport. Storage technologies include IDE, SCSI, Serial ATA, as well as memory technologies such as cache, RDRAM, SDRAM, DDR SDRAM, and the future of system memory. The world of peripherals is brought to life with discussion of USB 1.0 and 2.0 as well as FireWire (IEEE-1394). The best OS for gaming, Windows Me, 2000, or XP, is crowned. Peripherals and monitors are also explained in greater detail than you've ever seen before.

The bottom line is with *The AnandTech Guide to PC Gaming Hardware* you don't only learn what is the best out there, but you gain the knowledge to continue to pick the best hardware out there as time goes on. It's an education that you can't gain in any class.

Why Build a PC?

The AnandTech Guide to PC Gaming Hardware focuses on building your own gaming PC. By "building" I mean purchasing the individual components you want in your PC, assembling them inside your case, and going from a pile of parts to a finished product that is your PC. On the other end of the spectrum you have a ready-made PC. These are the PCs that you find in retail stores and contrary to popular belief, they are also the PCs that are "built to order" by a lot of the major manufacturers. Just because you can choose how much memory and storage space is in your system doesn't mean that it's "custom built."

Each end of this PC ownership spectrum, whether it is building your own PC or purchasing one from a store, has its pros and cons. Since it is by far the most popular way of obtaining a PC, I'll start off by addressing the pros and cons of going retail.

The biggest advantage to purchasing a ready-made PC is that it's truly as "plug and play" of a system as you're going to get. The most work you have to do in order to get it running is to unpack the box and plug it into your wall outlet. For many, this is a major benefit since PCs can be very intimidating to those that aren't familiar with them. The everlasting fear of breaking something especially when you're talking about a "something" worth $1,000–$3,000 is quite difficult to overcome.

Another advantage is that if something does break, it's not your problem. Obviously pouring water inside your PC is going to void your warranty quicker than you can imagine, but if anything does go wrong with your PC, the manufacturer will generally take care of it. If you've purchased from a reputable manufacturer, their warranty and support benefits will minimize the amount of downtime you have.

Software and peripheral costs are often very low when dealing with ready-made PCs. The bundled software and peripherals that come with the system rarely increase the average system cost much at all. This is especially beneficial for those people that were going to buy the software that they're being given with their PC anyways.

I just introduced you to three of the most popular reasons to purchase a ready-made PC: no hassle operation, warranty, and software/peripheral bundle savings. However, there are even more reasons not to purchase a ready-made PC.

To put a common myth to rest, you rarely save a tremendous amount of money when building your own PC versus buying a ready-made system.

Generally speaking, once you add in the costs of software and all of the extra benefits you get with a ready-made PC, as well as take into account your time and efforts, you rarely end up saving a ton when building your own PC.

Just because you're not saving a lot doesn't mean that what you're getting for your money isn't worth more. When building your own PC, you control what goes into your system. All too often I have seen incredibly fast processors coupled with two-year-old hard drives and video cards. Retail systems are first and foremost sold based on CPU speed. As you'll learn in this book, microprocessor speed does not always translate into greater performance. Not every single 1.5GHz computer is faster than a 1GHz system, and I'll show you why. When building your own PC you get the final say in what parts make it in. You'll be able to not only pick the fastest microprocessor but the fastest video card, memory, and hard drive. Even if you're not entirely familiar with all of those terms, you will be by the end of this book.

Higher performance is a major benefit of building your own PC but so is the knowledge you get from actually undertaking such an endeavor. Understanding how the components inside your PC work with one another will make you much more knowledgeable about what technologies you should look for in the future.

Future upgradeability is another major pro to building your own PC. In the past, retail systems were often not very upgradeable. While it was always easy to stick in more memory or a new peripheral card, more performance-oriented upgrades were often difficult to perform. If you look at it from the PC manufacturer's standpoint, they don't want you to upgrade. They want you to go out and buy a new PC when you want more performance so they will do whatever is necessary to make their systems attractive enough for you to buy, but crippled enough that your idea of an upgrade will end up being a new system. With your custom built PC, you can easily upgrade your processor, video card, and even motherboard. Today's retail PCs are a bit better, but because most of them choose components that look good on paper but not necessarily perform/upgrade well in the real world, you're still better off building your own.

The final thing I must mention here is that building your own PC isn't hard at all. Granted, you lose the warranty and technical support that a ready-made PC would give you, but what you gain in performance, upgradeability, and most importantly, knowledge more than makes up for it. This book will show you how to do it.

Gamers Are Users Too: The Gamer's PC

Computers are for work. Computers are for business. Computers are not toys.

You've heard it before; there's no way someone would pay $2,000 to play games. If that were true, then there'd be no way that someone would pay $200,000 to drive a Ferrari. The truth of the matter is that games are some of the most demanding applications you can run on a PC. Running a word processor application like Microsoft Word, or a spreadsheet application like Microsoft Excel, can be done on hardware that is three years old at acceptable speeds. If you try and run *UnrealTournament* or *Quake III Arena* on a three-year-old PC you'd be lucky if you can get the game to run, much less get any enjoyment out of it.

Building a gaming PC isn't much different from building any other type of PC. All of the components install the same and you still face the same compatibility and troubleshooting issues. Where a gaming PC differs from just about every other type of PC out there, is in the performance requirements. Gamers, especially if you're going to be playing any 3D games, require some of the fastest, most powerful hardware available on the market.

The perfect example of this is in video card requirements. For surfing the Web, typing up documents, and responding to e-mails, you just need an entry level video card that is compatible with your hardware and supported by your software. This video card will probably be capable of processing on the order of millions of operations per second. That may seem incredibly fast, but now take a look at what kind of power is necessary to run today's games at high performance levels. The latest video cards for gamers can perform over 900 billion operations per second and will soon be capable of processing over one trillion operations in a single second. From millions to billions and trillions, that's the difference between a gaming machine and most other PCs.

It's the gaming PC that this book is made for. Although the knowledge here can be applied to much more than just gaming PCs, the recommendations are gaming oriented.

Book Objectives

The AnandTech Guide to PC Gaming Hardware is your boot camp to becoming a true PC hardware enthusiast and an expert when it comes to PC gaming hardware. The tools and knowledge provided for you in this book cannot be found anyplace else—they are timeless resources that will provide you with the stepping stone you need to become the guru of the hardware world you've always wanted to be.

You'll learn about the inner workings of microprocessors and cache and the way to tell whether a motherboard is solidly constructed or not. You'll learn what's important about one of the most neglected parts of the PC, the chipset, and how it interacts with the rest of your system. This book focuses on teaching you how to benchmark and properly test your machine to measure performance, and how to measure performance after you tweak and overclock your PC to the max.

A major benefit of the knowledge provided within this book is the ability to increase the performance of your system with a few simple tweaks and an introduction to the world of overclocking. You'll learn how to persuade your 1.5GHz CPU to run faster, maybe as high as 2.0GHz, for no extra cost; or how to make your $100 video card perform in the league of $300 cards. These are the tricks of the enthusiast trade that *The AnandTech Guide to PC Gaming Hardware* will teach you.

The main areas that this book focuses on are the key gaming performance areas of your PC: the CPU, the chipset, the memory, the motherboard, and the video card. These five components, if chosen wisely, can provide your system with performance that completely dominates much more expensive store-bought machines. With less than $1,500, you can own one of the fastest machines on the planet and this book will show you how.

The rest of the PC is not left neglected, as *The AnandTech Guide to PC Gaming Hardware* allows you to pick the best peripherals and components to make your PC a very solid overall machine. With a heavy focus on mass storage devices, such as hard drives and CD/DVD burners, you'll gain all the knowledge you need to know of what to put into your system.

The buck doesn't stop there; *The AnandTech Guide to PC Gaming Hardware* gives you step-by-step instructions on how to build your winning gaming PC, and in the unfortunate event that something goes wrong, this book will also show you how to troubleshoot and fix your PC.

When you're done with this book, you'll know more, you'll be able to do more, and you'll be able to put together one killer system for little money.

Is This Book for You?

If you've ever felt lost when reading or talking to someone that knew a lot about computers—or if you've ever wanted to know more but can't seem to find exactly where to learn it—this book is definitely for you.

The AnandTech Guide to PC Gaming Hardware will teach you the skills necessary to not only build the perfect winning gaming PC but it'll provide you with the knowledge required to understand and discuss future technologies. For example, You will be able to understand and dissect exactly what allows the Intel Pentium 4 to reach higher clock speeds than the AMD Athlon. You will be able to understand rather than just relying on the "higher clock speed means faster" mentality that is too commonly thrown around the industry.

This Guide is for those that want to learn and broaden their computer knowledge bases. Anand has been explaining the most complicated hardware for years to two million readers every month on AnandTech (`www.anandtech.com`); he has consistently separated the manufacturer fluff from reality and provided an honest, unbiased view of the computer hardware world to his readers. He has been doing it on the Web for years, and now he's bringing the foundation to you in this book.

Is this book for you? Yes.

Chapter-by-Chapter Breakdown

The AnandTech Guide to PC Gaming Hardware is organized in chapters of order of importance to gamers. The first half of the book deals with the components that truly improve the gaming experience whether in performance or in visual/audio effects. The latter half is the icing on the cake, discussing getting the most out of your system as well as completing the package.

Chapter 1, "The Central Processing Unit: The Heart and Soul of the PC," begins with a discussion of CPU architecture and how it affects performance. Topics such as cache memory, front side bus interfaces, branch prediction units, FPU vsersus ALU performance, and operating frequencies are covered among others. This chapter includes detailed information about every CPU from the Intel Celeron and Pentium III, to the AMD Athlon and Intel Pentium 4.

Chapter 2, "The Chipset: The PC's Crossing Guard," explains the role of the chipset in today's high performance PC. This chapter introduces NVIDIA's nForce and what its incredible feature set will mean to the PC gaming world. It also discusses the vast importance of the chipset in a gaming PC and the benefits of properly choosing a chipset. A thorough listing of today's high performance and not so hot chipsets is provided as well as a detailed explanation of the benefits and unfortunate downsides to these labors of love.

Chapter 3, "The Motherboard: Low Rent Housing for the CPU and Chipset," serves as an introduction to the wide world of motherboards. Often one of the culprits of an unstable system, choosing the right motherboard is key to the success of your gaming system and it is critical to the overclocking and tweaking potential of your machine, as well. Discussion includes identifying 4-layer versus 6-layer motherboards as well as information about all of the major manufacturers and their track records. There's a reason that this book gives so much attention to the board everything plugs into.

Chapter 4, "Memory: Your PC's Scratchpad," dispels the myth that all memory types are created equal and that the only thing that matters is size. Memory is indeed very different and the types of memory that are currently available can either give you the time of your life, or make you wish you never spent so much money on a couple of sticks before.

Chapter 5, "The Video Card: A Gamer's Heart and Soul," is quite possibly one of the most important chapters in this book. It covers the architecture behind today's video cards that breathe life into our games. Truly understand how math can turn a bunch of triangles and curvy shapes into beautifully immersive 3D environments on your PC, and at very high frame rates.

Chapter 6, "Sound: Waking Up the Neighbors," is just as important as the performance chapters because the key to a great gaming system is a great set of speakers. Consider this chapter to be audio technology 101, you'll learn about the decibel and the true meaning of wattage when it comes to speakers. Decipher the differences between 2.1, 4.1, and 5.1 speaker setups.

Chapter 7, "Storage: The Slowest Part of Your PC," provides an in-depth look at how mass storage devices work. The internal architecture of hard drives and differences between magnetic and optical storage devices are covered in great depth in this chapter. Learn how a hard disk works, the importance, and keys to obtaining high disk performance. Also, competing optical storage standards such as CD-R, CD-RW, DVD-RW, DVD+RW, and DVD-R are discussed. An introduction to RAID and its usefulness as a gamer's tool is also addressed.

Chapter 8, "Networking: Gamers Unite," serves as an introduction to networking and the protocols that are associated with it. Explanations of DHCP, CAT5, Switches, and Hubs precede detailed instructions on how to set up your own network for some of the best LAN parties you could ever imagine. This chapter concludes with discussion on getting online and the competing broadband standards of today and tomorrow.

Chapter 9, "Cases and Cooling: Living in Style and Keeping Your Cool," serves as a guide to the truly important aspects of cases and cooling. Dispelling myths about how to achieve effective cooling and what to look for in a case, from the perspective of not only looks but functionality, are covered in this chapter. The often overlooked power supply is addressed very thoroughly here, explaining how a power supply can be the difference between a rock solid system and one that constantly crashes.

Chapter 10, "Monitors and Input Devices: Your Sense of Sight and Touch Restored," begins with an explanation of how monitors work. Both conventional analog CRTs and newer digital displays are covered. The section ends with specifics on what to look for in a monitor and a few recommendations. The second half of the chapter revolves around input devices such as keyboards, mice, and gamepads. Discussion of interfaces, ergonomics, and drivers comprise this part.

Chapter 11, "Putting It All Together: Break Out the Hammers and Duct Tape," is one of the most useful items in the book because of its timelessness. This chapter serves as a guide to building your first computer and will even be useful to you if you have had some experience in the past by providing you with a few tricks of the trade that you may not have known before. This chapter is entirely hardware-centric, dealing with every step from unpacking your components, to what screws you need to use and what order to put things together, to the final strike of the power button.

Chapter 12, "Upgrading: Feeling the Need for Speed," is a how-to diagnostic chapter that will help you decide if/when you need to upgrade and what part(s) of your system need upgrading. It's all to often that you upgrade and you don't feel like you got what you paid for—this chapter will help prevent that situation from occurring.

Chapter 13, "Operating Systems and Device Drivers: Making Your Hardware Work," picks up where Chapter 12 left off with a software-centric discussion of setting up your new computer. In-depth discussion of the benefits versus drawbacks of the most popular OSes are provided, as well as a crowning of the best overall gaming OS: Windows Me, Windows 2000, or Windows XP. How to install your OS, drivers, and program updates are also covered.

Chapter 14, "Tweaking and Overclocking: Turbo-Charging Your PC," dispels the myth that there is no such thing as a free lunch. Pay for a 1.5GHz CPU and get a 2.0GHz CPU, and this chapter will show you how. An introduction to what overclocking is, why it works, how to do it, and the drawbacks are explained in great detail. Other performance tweaking is addressed such as BIOS tweaking and OS/program tweaks to improve performance. A benchmarking primer concludes the chapter, allowing you to find out if your overclocks/tweaks were successful or not.

Chapter 15, "Troubleshooting: Something Is Wrong with My Baby," rounds off the book with easy to follow step-by-step instructions on how to troubleshoot hardware and software problems.

AnandTech.com

One of the biggest drawbacks of print media is that it's very difficult to keep up to date. Luckily, with the education you've received from *The AnandTech Guide to PC Gaming Hardware* you'll be more than ready to get a much larger dose of the same information that was covered here at my Web site `www.anandtech.com`. AnandTech is updated frequently with the most in-depth articles covering all technologies.

Reviews, editorials, news, and comparisons are among the most popular features at AnandTech, but you can also join our online community with over 70,000 registered users to seek help, ask questions, or simply relax after a tough day among some of the most knowledgeable and friendly users on the Web.

Our extensive review section includes hundreds of reviews covering the latest in CPUs, video cards, chipsets, motherboards, memory technologies, as well as roadmaps so you know what AMD, Intel, NVIDIA and the rest of the computing world are planning for the future. Find out when to upgrade and what to upgrade to by visiting the site.

The rest of the AnandTech staff and myself will be eagerly waiting for you at `www.anandtech.com`. Hope to see you there!

Chapter 1

The Central Processing Unit: The Heart and Soul of the PC

Introducing the CPU

Although the majority of the population isn't surgeons, we all know where our brain is. And although many of us aren't automotive mechanics, if one asked you where your engine was, you wouldn't be hard-pressed to point it out. Today, computers are much more commonplace than they were 30 years ago. However, if you ask an average or a novice user where the "brain" or the "engine" of his PC was located, most of the time you'll probably get a puzzled look in response. Building a no-compromises gaming PC pretty much requires that you also become a hardware enthusiast with a fundamental understanding of how PCs work. The best way to gain that understanding and prepare yourself to be an educated hardware enthusiast is to start at the brain of the computer: the central processing unit (CPU).

The central processing unit of a computer is its brain. This is where all the computation takes place, such as calculating the damage the slash of a sword has on an enemy in *Diablo 2* or how that enemy reacts to your advancing attacks. Because of this, the CPU is a component for which the rest of your computer's parts are constantly fighting to get a minute of its time. In actuality, the rest of your computer is fighting for much less than a minute of its time in fact, fractions of a second. But what the CPU can do in a fraction of a second is quite amazing when you consider that it can understand only two numbers, 0 and 1.

The CPU is colloquially referred to under a few different titles, just like the human brain (or noggin, think-tank, gray matter, and so on). Getting those titles out of the way first is best because they are often used interchangeably by most hardware enthusiasts. Thus, it makes sense for you, on your quest to become such an enthusiast (or more of one if you already put yourself in that class), to become familiar with some of the different forms of the term central processing unit.

The first is CPU. It is merely an acronym that stands for the words central processing unit. If you are easily overwhelmed with memorizing acronyms, you'll need to get used to dealing with them, because the computer world is full of them. Not only that, but just when you think you've remembered them all, they change and you have to start the process all over again. Luckily CPU is one of those acronyms that will be with us for quite some time, simply because it is so critical to the foundation of today's PC (and many other common devices, like cell phones and even VCRs). The CPU is also often referred to as a processor or a microprocessor as well as just a chip. Be careful when using any of these terms in various contexts because as you will soon learn, the CPU we are talking about now isn't the only "processor" in your PC.

It is very easy for something as complex as a CPU to overwhelm the uninitiated. Imagine trying to comprehend the inner workings of an object that costs hundreds of dollars, took three to five years to develop, and contains hundreds of millions of "parts." Remember how difficult it was to make sure you didn't break the 10 parts that made up your train set when you were young? Well, now you're being asked to compare, contrast, purchase, install, and tweak a "toy" with 160 million parts. Don't worry, the bark is a lot worse than the bite in this case.

A Brief Lesson in Counting

Keep in mind that the CPU is a computational workhorse; it performs quite a few mathematical calculations at any given moment. You've probably heard the first computers referred to as being less powerful than today's calculators, but how can you compare a computer to a calculator? Essentially, they are the same. A calculator has a CPU that takes a number of inputs, performs a set of internal functions, and outputs a result. This is exactly what the CPU in your computer does, except on a much larger scale.

Earlier, I mentioned that the CPU understands only two things: the numbers 0 and 1. At this extremely low level, all that is being described is a switch, such as the one you use to turn your lights on and off. If you flip the switch up, you complete the circuit and electricity is allowed to flow through, thereby giving power to your light. The value of this "on" position is 1. Turning the light off consists of doing the exact opposite; breaking the circuit by restoring the switch to its original position, thus removing electricity from the circuit and effectively shutting off the light. For the sake of simplicity, let's give the switch in the "off" position a value of 0.

Why bother assigning numbers to such basic concepts as "on" and "off"? Well, it's much easier to deal with two numbers than it is to deal with two words. Numbers are universal, holding up a single finger is very rarely mistaken for two and holding up no fingers is generally not misinterpreted as meaning 10. On the other hand, words are much less universal. There are language barriers that must be dealt with and your CPU doesn't want to bother with that kind of stuff. Instead it's much happier understanding the difference between a 0 and a 1. We normally deal with a base 10 number system, meaning that for every placeholder in a number there are a total of 10 possibilities (0–9) that placeholder could assume. A CPU, only capable of understanding a 0 and a 1, deals with numbers in what is known as a binary number system, meaning that for every placeholder in a number, there are only two possibilities (0 and 1) that the placeholder could assume.

Imagine for a moment that you had a row of eight light switches in various modes of being "on" (1) or "off" (0). Each one of these switches represents one bit of information. With all the switches (bits) in the off position, you have a series of eight zeros (any series of eight bits is known as a byte in the computer world). This relationship will come in handy later, but for now let's just concentrate on this 8-bit arrangement of switches.

Because each bit has a total of two possible positions, 0 and 1, and there are 8 bits in this setup, the total number of unique arrangements of 0s and 1s offers 256 (2^8) possibilities. So by using no more than two numbers, 0 and 1, this byte is capable of representing any number from 0 to 255. This byte is also capable of representing more than just numbers, because these numbers could represent the 26 letters of the English alphabet. A collection of bytes could be used to represent the 6,500 most commonly used Chinese characters. The point of this is to show you exactly how powerful having a switch that can only distinguish between two positions, off and on, 0 and 1, can be if used in large enough quantities.

Obviously, you cannot use millions of light switches in a box and expect that to be the most efficient CPU. You'd end up having a very large, impractical device. Actually, this light-switch analogy might sound a little off-the-wall, but in reality, this was the way computers used to work. They used very large mechanical switches that took up a considerable amount of room and were prone to failure because of the fact that they were made of moving parts. When a device is made of moving parts, not only is the smallest size of the device restricted to that of the moving parts of which it is composed, but reliability is also limited. The mean time between failures of such a device is governed by the failure of any one of its individual parts. This is where the old stories of computers—such as the Eniac (the first computer), which took up entire rooms and used vacuum tubes—come from; the vacuum tubes were the switches I just discussed.

This is where the transistor comes in (see Figure 1.1). Invented in 1948, the transistor is nothing more than a switch, like we've been talking about thus far, except its "position" is determined by the electricity that is fed to it. What makes the transistor so unique and so desirable for use in modern day CPUs is that not only is it electrical (meaning there are no moving parts), but it also can be extremely small. Being able to pack a large number of these electrical switches, or transistors, into a very small space is the foundation for the types of CPUs that are found in any PC you purchase today.

So, just what is considered a "large number" of transistors? The majority of today's CPUs use tens of millions of transistors, whereas some of the higher-end CPUs, especially those in the high-end server and workstation world, use hundreds of millions of transistors.

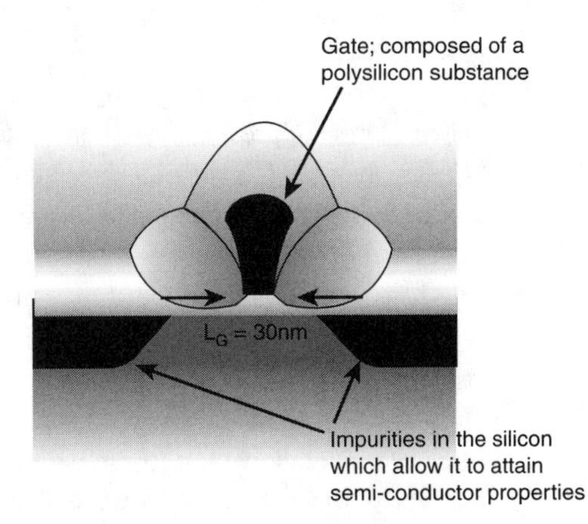

FIGURE 1.1
The top picture is of a transistor with a gate width of 30 nm. In the presence of a low voltage, the gate "closes" and electricity is conducted through the capacitor.

Millions of Anything=Heat

Very few people understand how small these transistors are and how small the actual "CPU" is. The chip you can pick up and look at when you're holding a CPU isn't a collection of transistors; you are actually handling the packaging of the chip. Generally the center of the chip is home to the actual CPU. This is usually referred to as the *core* or the processor's *die*. The CPU core is often no bigger than the size of your thumbnail, and it is the core that is home to these millions of transistors. Having this many transistors packed into such a small space obviously has some downsides, one of the biggest being heat. As you can probably imagine, if you have millions of *anything* constantly switching millions of times, over and over again, and packed into an area about the size of a fingernail, things are bound to get hot.

There are a number of ways CPU manufacturers can combat this problem of heat from a design standpoint.

The first and most obvious method is what is commonly known as a process or die shrink. This is a physical reduction in the circuit size of the CPU's core. The smaller the circuit size, the cooler running the core is going to be. A die shrink also frees up a considerable amount of space, which is quite expensive when it comes to manufacturing CPU cores. The more space you save, the more you save in terms of manufacturing costs, the higher your yields are (number of *working* processors that are manufactured compared to the *total* number produced), and the greater the ability for you to include even more features on a processor.

As a CPU manufacturer continues the production of its CPU, often it discovers methods of improving and making the design of the processor more efficient. These improvements are introduced in things called *steppings*. A particular stepping is a revision or version of a processor core. For example, if you had an Intel Pentium 4 2.0GHz processor that was Stepping B and another identical Pentium 4 processor that was Stepping A, the former would be a later revision of the chip. This is akin to revisions of software. For example, the difference between Windows 98 and Windows 98SE or if you remember back to the older days of Windows, the difference between Windows 3.0 and 3.1. New steppings can decrease the power requirements of the processor, allowing it to run with less electricity being fed to it. In other words, the voltage of the current being fed to the processor can be decreased without adversely affecting performance or reliability. The voltage fed to the processor is known as the *core voltage*, for obvious reasons.

Clock Speed: The Horsepower of CPUs

Wanting to quantify things is human nature; we love to measure. We measure the weight of our bodies, the size of our muscles, and the amount of power in our cars. It is through these measurements that we can do what we love to do most—compare. Just as much as we want to know how much horsepower the Italian-bred 3.6L V8 produces at 8500rpm, we want to know how to compare different CPUs based on their specifications.

A term you are all undoubtedly familiar with is *clock speed*. The clock speed of a CPU is its operating frequency and like all frequencies, it is measured in cycles per second whose unit happens to be hertz (Hz). You are probably more accustomed to seeing clock speed measured in millions of cycles per second, megahertz (MHz) or billions of cycles per second, gigahertz (GHz).

When comparing two processors of the exact same type and specification, such as two Intel Pentium 4s, a higher clock speed translates into higher performance. The greater the operating frequency of a CPU, the more the processor can accomplish every second. As many users don't realize, this does *not* apply to processors of different families, because there are a number of architectural differences outside of clock speed that can influence the performance of various CPUs. But for the sake of simplicity, we will restrict our current discussion to comparing processors of the same type.

The CPU generates its operating frequency by taking a multiple of another clock frequency that is fed to the processor. If you consider the CPU the brain of the computer, it must have a connection to the "outside world" or the rest of the computer (as the brain connects to your spinal column). This connection is known as the Front Side Bus (FSB). A bus, as depicted in Figure 1.2, is nothing more than a pathway or a road between two or more points in a system. A bus isn't something that you can touch or buy, it is a system level component that is quite critical to proper operation of a system. Much like the roads we're constantly comparing these buses to, you don't purchase them, but you use them all the time.

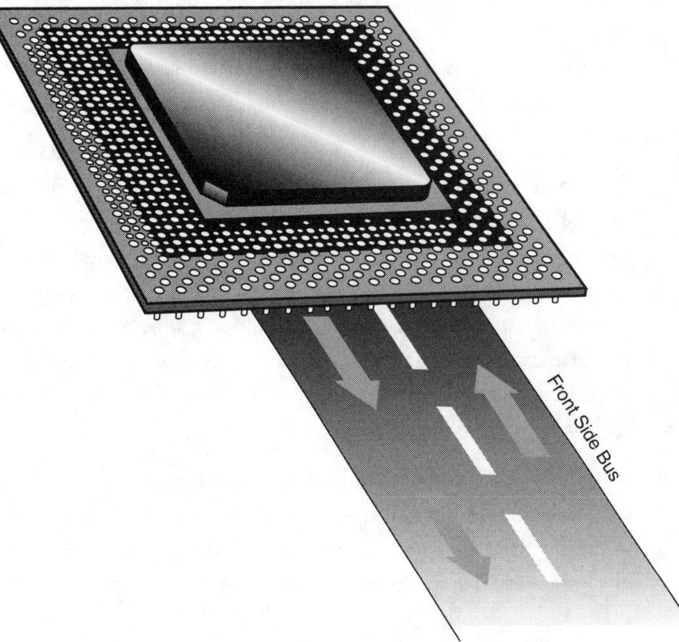

FIGURE 1.2
The CPU sends and receives data via its Front Side Bus.

Because the FSB is a data path that represents the only connection from the CPU to the rest of your system, it is the only incoming/outgoing path connected to your CPU. However, it isn't entirely contained within the CPU, rather it actually depends on an external chip for complete functionality. The specifics of this chip are discussed in Chapter 3, "The Motherboard: Low Rent Housing for the CPU and Chipset."

The FSB has an operating frequency much lower than that of your processor, generally on the order of 100MHz–200MHz in a typical Pentium III or Athlon-based system. This clock, however, is multiplied by a factor known as

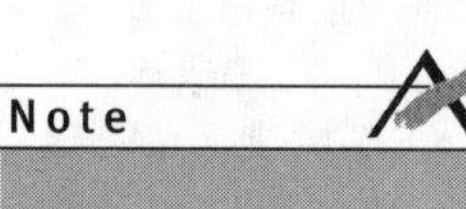

Note

If you've been pricing components for a Pentium 4, and are used to seeing FSB speed listed as 200MHz or 266MHz, the previous 100MHz example might sound odd. However, the numbers you see associated with FSB speeds often have more to do with *effective* speed rather than *actual* speed. This is explained in more detail in Chapter 3.

the *clock multiplier*, which results in your CPU's operating frequency, or clock speed. For example, an Intel Pentium 4 2.0GHz uses a 100MHz FSB; dividing that 100MHz FSB frequency into the 2.0GHz (2000MHz) results in a factor of 20—meaning the Pentium 4 2.0GHz runs with a clock multiplier of 20.0x the FSB frequency.

Unlike the FSB, the clock multiplier is controlled entirely within the CPU's core. In the case of all Intel processors manufactured after August 1998, the clock multiplier of a given CPU cannot be changed after it is set during the manufacturing process. The same is true for AMD processors. However, there are ways of getting around that limitation in the more recent CPU releases. We'll cover these limitations in more detail in Chapter 14, "Tweaking and Overclocking: Turbo-Charging Your PC."

Why would you want to change the clock multiplier of your CPU? We won't get too far into the reasons now, but if you can control the clock multiplier of your CPU, you can control the operating frequency of it as well. This means that a Pentium 4 at 1.7GHz could conceivably be set to a 20.0x multiplier (up from its 17.0x multiplier) and just as easily become a 2.0GHz processor. Anyone looking to eek out just a few more frames per second of performance when playing *Tribes 2* can see why overclocking can be useful. That being said, there are obviously limitations to the effectiveness of this approach, but I'll get to those in Chapter 13.

Be careful when looking at clock speeds, though. Just as horsepower isn't necessarily an indication of the overall performance of a car (other factors such as weight, torque, suspension, and so on contribute), clock speed isn't always as big of a contributor to the overall performance of your system as many people think.

This brings up the question of "What limits clock speed?" The only explanation you have at this point is heat, which we have already described as a major problem for these CPUs. We have also examined a couple of workarounds for this problem, such as a die shrink or other manufacturing improvements. But those are, unfortunately, quite impractical to undertake much of the time because of the sheer cost of moving to a smaller production process (die shrink) and outfitting fabrication plants with the tools necessary to produce chips of a smaller circuit size. As we explore the architecture behind these CPUs and see what the tricks of the trade are when it comes to designing the CPUs of today as well as those of tomorrow, things will get interesting.

Moving In: A Look Inside the CPU

So far, we know that CPUs are extremely complicated devices that are not capable of any more than counting between zero and one really fast (see Figure 1.3). We also know that the CPU itself is much smaller than a chip you can hold in your hand and the chip is fed current at a specific voltage, known as the core voltage. CPUs run at a certain clock frequency determined by a factor known as the clock multiplier, multiplied by the frequency of its road to the "outside world," the FSB. But what really makes the CPU tick—not on the lowest level in regard to transistors switching between 1s and 0s, but on an architectural level in regard to what the various groups of transistors actually do?

FIGURE 1.3
Inside Intel's Pentium 4 Processor. The large blocks on the right of the die are the Pentium 4's L2 cache and above them is the bus interface that transfers data through the FSB. (*Photo courtesy of Intel Corporation.*)

With a device as complex as a modern day microprocessor, there must be some degree of organization in place to keep the millions of transistors running efficiently and thus allowing the processor to actually be of some use instead of being an expensive hunk of silicon.

We'll start at what is known as the CPU's *pipeline*. The pipeline is a set of steps or stages that a command sent to the CPU must go through before actually being executed. These stages are quite important as they perform all the necessary logic to ensure not only that the command is executed, but also that it is done so in an efficient manner. You can consider the CPU to be a very fast-moving and fast-working person, depending on the co-workers around him who provide him with the data he needs to keep his efficiency high.

When the program you are running, whether it is an Internet browser window, a game, or maybe just Microsoft Word, gets input from you, the user, to carry out a task, the command keeps on traveling through your system until it reaches the level of your CPU. At this point, you must realize that the CPU has no clue what "Copy and Paste" means or what "Click on the Start Menu" entails. What the CPU does understand however is its own language, known as an Instruction Set Architecture or ISA for short. The CPU's ISA is the language it understands and operates on, just like English is the language you are reading now. The ISA this book primarily focuses on is known as *x86*, which is what both Intel and AMD processors use. Variations on x86 exist, as well as completely different ISAs that we will discuss throughout the course of this book. But for our purposes, we should be concerned only with the x86 ISA.

Note

Knowing that your CPU uses an x86 ISA and the basics of how it works is important because the x86 ISA currently is supported by the vast majority of programs and game titles you run on your new PC. If the processor is not compatible with it, most of your games won't be compatible with your processor.

So, your CPU gets a command from you, the user, and the first thing that must happen upon receiving this command is that it must translate it into its own language, something it can understand. This is one of the earliest stages in the pipeline, known as the decoding stage. This stage is handled by part of the core known as the decoder. The decoder, depicted in Figure 1.4, is one of the most complicated parts of the processor core. Quite a bit of time is spent decoding instructions into more "bite-sized" operations the processor can execute.

The instructions sent to the decoder based on your actions—equipping a new shield in *Baldur's Gate II*, for example—are sent to the CPU, where they are then decoded into smaller operations. These operations are known as *macro-operations (macro-ops)* to the AMD Athlon processor and *micro-operations (micro-ops)* to the Intel Pentium 4 processor. Even though the specifics of the decoder in both of those processor architectures are different, the basic principle is the same.

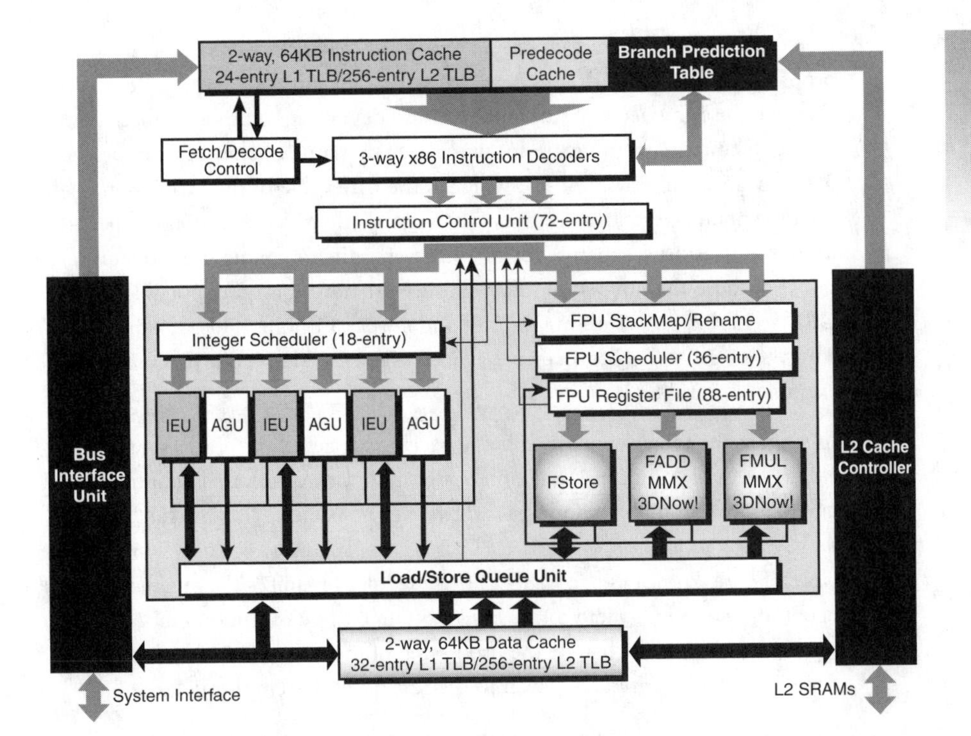

FIGURE 1.4
In this AMD Athlon block diagram, you can see how data flows through the Athlon processor during its operation.

After the instructions are decoded, the next major stage in the pipeline is taking the decoded operations and sending them to the appropriate execution units. As the name implies, the execution units actually execute the instructions that were just decoded. However not all operations are created equally. On the most basic level you have two types of operations, Integer and floating-point.

Integer operations deal with whole numbers, or integers. Such operations would consist of things like 3 + 5 or –19/6, however the answers are always computed as whole numbers. This unfortunately results in a loss of precision because there is a significant amount of truncation done because all the numbers are whole. For example, 6/4 as an integer operation would result in an answer of 1 although we all know that the real answer is 1.5. That is 33% error, which might be acceptable in some situations, but if you're calculating the length of a beam to be used in a bridge, you don't want that kind of error. For this reason, Integer operations are generally much less taxing than floating-point operations and are generally used in business/home office applications such as Word Processing, Presentation or even Internet browsing applications.

The other type of operations are *floating-point operations* which, as you can probably guess, deal with numbers that have a decimal or "floating point" in them because the decimal can move around depending on the number. These operations are much more precise, as the same operation from before: 6/4 now gives an answer of 1.5, which is the true value of the expression. floating-point operations are thus much more intensive than Integer operations and thus use a separate set of execution units to handle these operations. Because the integer and FP units are separate it is quite possible for a CPU to have a powerful integer unit and a weak FP unit. This was the case with the original Cyrix processors as well as some older AMD processors (for example, K5 and K6).

As soon as the type of operation being executed is determined, it is sent to either the integer unit or the floating-point unit for execution. The integer unit is more commonly known as *arithmetic logic unit (ALU)*. The ALU (and there can be more than one in a CPU to accomplish more at once) contains a piece of logic known as a *scheduler*. The scheduler organizes the incoming operations and sends them to the execution units. The execution units, as their name implies, actually handle the processing of the operations. After they are done, the data is retired and given to the rest of the system through the FSB.

The process is very similar for floating-point instructions, except they are set off to the FPU (again, there can be more than one) and are executed by the floating-point execution units.

As you can tell, the pipeline is mainly present for organization and an improvement of efficiency. Much like Ransome E. Olds's invention of the automotive assembly line (and Henry Ford's later improvement on it), the idea of pipelining makes a lot of sense; unfortunately, it does have its drawbacks. The biggest fear with a pipelined CPU is that if a break or stall occurs in normal activity between the start and end of the pipeline, the performance and efficiency of the pipeline are completely thrown to waste.

One way around this is to have multiple pipelines, promoting *parallelism* because two or more pipelines are operating in parallel. A multipipelined CPU is referred to as a *superscalar* CPU. The concept of parallelism is one that you'll see repeated quite often in many of the technologies that we're going to be looking at throughout the course of this book.

However, having multiple pipelines is useless if they are not being used efficiently. The goal is to get instructions from the start to the finish of the pipeline as quickly as possible. Obviously a shorter pipeline would be able to fit this requirement quite well; a CPU with a 6-stage pipeline could perform the same type of operations a CPU with a 20-stage pipeline could. So, why bother with longer pipelines? One drawback of having a short pipeline is that you are accomplishing a lot in a very small amount of time. Although this would normally be thought of as a pro for shorter pipelines, it is actually a con in disguise. Doing a lot in a short amount of time can actually limit the clock speed your CPU is capable of reaching. Without building the CPU on a smaller process (via a die shrink), a CPU with a 6-stage pipeline might be limited to 600MHz, whereas one with a 20-stage pipeline built on the same process could be capable of 2.0GHz.

Obviously, at lower clock speeds, CPUs with shorter pipelines are capable of accomplishing more instructions per clock (IPC) than those with longer pipelines and might end up outperforming them. This is one reason the first generation of a new CPU architecture often shows little, no, or even a negative performance improvement over its predecessor. A 1.0GHz Pentium III would actually be faster than a 1.0GHz Pentium 4 in a lot of cases (if the latter existed); however, the Pentium III will never reach the 2.0GHz+ clock speeds the Pentium 4 currently can.

Keeping One Step Ahead

With pipelined architectures, assuming data is moving along fast enough, there comes a point where the CPU is waiting for the results of one calculation before it can continue with another calculation already present in a pipeline. This could cause a break or stall in the normal operation of the pipeline. An example is if you were working on a car assembly line and you could not install a steering wheel in the car coming down the line because the steering wheel from its manufacturing area was not yet ready. This would completely halt the assembly line and result in a great deal of loss in efficiency.

Never fear, the CPU has a way of working around issues like this by using a technique called Branch Prediction. As the name indicates, Branch Prediction is a tactic used by the CPU to predict the outcome of a particular calculation before the actual outcome is known. Many complex algorithms can be employed to improve the success rate of the Branch Prediction Unit (BPU) in the CPU, but we won't get too far into those. It turns out that most of today's processors are capable of predicting these branches with their BPUs with about 95%–98% accuracy. That is quite high; however, the 2%–5% of the time that the BPU is wrong, the penalties can be disproportionably large.

Remember the downsides we mentioned to having an extremely large pipeline? Well, if the CPU finds itself in the middle of a calculation at the 15th stage of a 20-stage pipeline and mispredicts a branch, the penalty is that the calculation must start all over again. Obviously the penalty is much lower when you have a shorter pipeline. However, shorter pipelines restrict clock speed so that's not a good solution. The only good solution here is to make sure that these CPUs with extremely long pipelines have very good BPUs. Generally speaking, Integer code is more likely to result in mispredicted branches than FP code because of the size of datasets. (It is easier to predict large and repetitive code). Because 3D games rely on a lot of FP calculations, having a high mispredict penalty isn't necessarily much of a downside. As long as a strong FPU and a good branch prediction unit are present, there shouldn't be much of a concern for a longer pipeline. Many other factors have a greater impact on 3D game performance.

Raking in the Cache

I have already pointed out that your CPU runs at a pretty high multiple of its front side bus frequency. However, even if CPU speed is, in some ways, limited by the FSB, the reality is that no components within your system run as fast as your CPU. As you can guess, the CPU doesn't like waiting—that's why it goes to such great lengths as attempting to predict branches and so on. Another thing the CPU hates waiting on is data to be fed to it through the FSB.

As was mentioned earlier, the Pentium 4 running at 2.0GHz has an FSB that runs at 100MHz (it actually performs at about four times the speed of a 100MHz FSB, but we'll get into that in the next chapter). If the processor had to wait to get data over that relatively slow bus all the time, it would be a much poorer performer because a lot of those clock cycles would have gone to waste.

Luckily, the Pentium 4 and all today's CPUs have a good portion of their die dedicated to something called cache (see Figure 1.5). Cache is essentially a very high-speed storage area that the CPU can use to store frequently used data. Cache generally has multiple levels and in most of today's CPUs those two levels are referred to as Level 1 and Level 2 cache (L1 and L2, respectively). The lower the "level" of the cache, the closer it is to the CPU. This means that the CPU will first attempt to find frequently used data in the L1 cache, then the L2 cache. Finally, if it isn't present in either, it will traverse the FSB to find it elsewhere in the system.

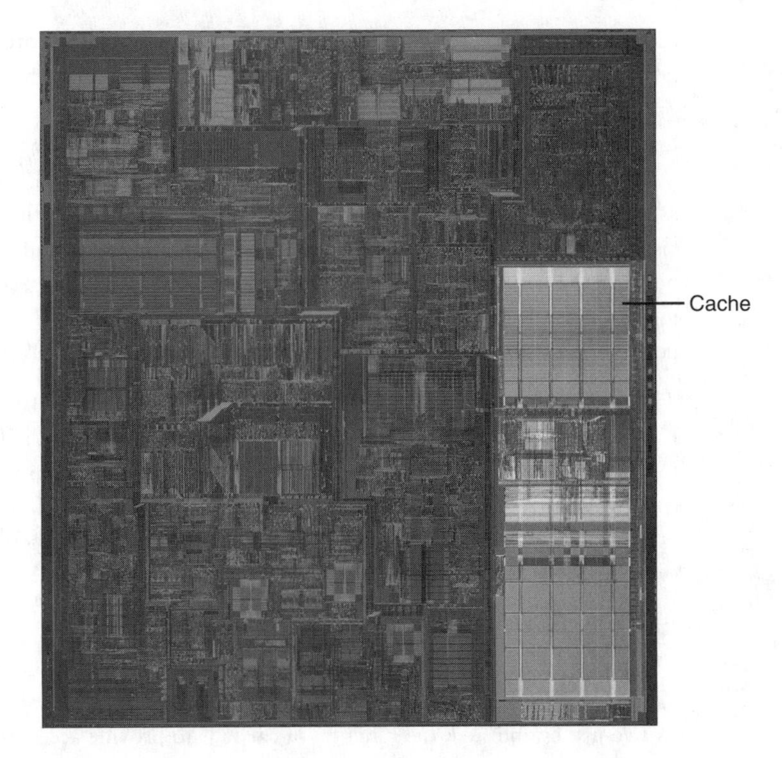

FIGURE 1.5
L2 Cache on the Pentium 4 Die. (*Photo courtesy of Intel Corporation.*)

This type of design makes L1 cache much more desirable, but the size is limited because the CPU wants to be able to access data from it quickly. The smaller the size of the cache, the more quickly data can be accessed from it. The L1 cache is usually split into two different parts, an instruction set cache (this caches instructions before they are decoded into micro/macro-ops) and a data cache (this caches actual data that is frequently used). The L1 Data and Instruction caches are usually the same size. As you might already be aware, the L1 Instruction cache has a flaw in that it compounds the penalties of a mispredicted branch. Not only must the CPU start over from the beginning of the pipeline, but it must also re-decode all instructions used. The ways around this are discussed later.

To compensate for the relatively small size of the L1 Data cache, L2 caches are generally much larger and thus take more time to access. The amount of time required to access data from either the L1 or L2 caches is referred to as latency. Latency is measured in terms of time, in this case, CPU clock cycles, so the lower the latency, the better.

Although caches are relatively easy to implement on the CPU core, they do take up a lot of die space; this unfortunately limits the amount that can be put on. One solution is to place the L2 cache off-die, somewhere else in the system. Unfortunately, that not only increases latency, but it also means the cache won't be capable of operating at the clock speed of the CPU's core. And as we've already discussed, that speed is generally much higher than anything else in the system. In fact, manufacturers have tried having an off-die L2 cache in the past that ran at a fraction of the processor's clock speed (including the Pentium II and first-generation Athlon, also known as the K7), but if possible, it is almost always best to keep it on-die running at full speed.

The problems with off-die L2 caches primarily include higher latency to the L2 cache (it's further away from the CPU now) and cost of finding high performing L2 cache chips because third parties must make the chips (Intel/AMD aren't memory manufacturers). Additionally, the slower your L2 cache is in comparison to your clock speed, the less scalability you get from every boost in clock speed.

Cache Mapping Techniques

As I've just established, the function of cache is to provide access to frequently used data at very high speeds. It does so by essentially mapping the lines of the cache to multiple addresses in the computer's system memory (the number of which is defined by the cacheable memory area of the cache).

A number of methods can be used to dictate how this mapping occurs. To keep things simple I refer to mapping techniques in regards to L2 cache, although the same applies to L1 cache. On one end of the spectrum is a *direct mapped cache*, which divides the system memory into a number of equal sections, each one being mapped to a single cache line in the L2 cache.

> **Note**
>
> In this example, we stick to L2 cache because it's easier to illustrate. With L1 cache, you want to get different types of things out of your mapping technique, such as lower latency versus higher hit rate, and so on, which complicate the scenario.

The beauty of a direct mapped cache is that it can be searched relatively quickly and effectively (low latency) because everything is organized into sections of equal size. This benefit, however, forces the sacrifice of the cache's hit rate. The *hit rate* is the percentage of data being looked for that is actually found in the cache; the higher, the better. A direct mapped cache loses in hit rate because it does not optimize access for more frequently used data, which is most likely to be repeatedly accessed.

On the other end of the spectrum is a *fully associative cache*, which is the exact opposite of a direct mapped cache. Instead of equally dividing up the memory into sections mapped to individual address lines, a fully associative cache acts as more of a dynamic entity that enables a cache line to be mapped to any section of system memory.

This flexibility enables a much greater hit rate because allowances can be made for the most frequently used data. However, because there is no organized structure to the mapping technique, searching through a fully associative cache is much slower than through a direct mapped cache (higher latency).

Establishing a mid-point between these two cache-mapping techniques, we have a *set associative cache*, which is what the current crop of processors use.

A set associative cache divides the cache into various sections, or sets, with each set containing a number of cache lines. With an 8-way set associative L2 cache, each set contains 8 cache lines. In a 16-way set associative L2 cache, each set contains 16 cache lines.

The beauty of this is that the cache acts as if it were a direct-mapped cache—except that, instead of the 1-cache-line-per-memory-section requirement, we get *x* number of cache lines per section of memory addresses.

This helps sustain a balance between the pros and cons of a direct mapped and a fully associative cache (see Table 1.1).

Table 1.1 The Latency and Hit Rates for Various Types of Cache

	Direct Mapped	Set Associative	Fully Associative
Latency	Very easy; quick to search through	More associations; higher latency (slower searches)	Searching is slow
Hit rate	Low hit rate	More associations; higher hit rate	High hit rate

Players Betting Chips in the CPU Game

There is much more to CPU architecture than what you've learned thus far. However, at this point you know enough (and possibly more than enough) to actually understand the premise behind many of today's and tomorrow's CPU architectures. Understanding the architecture can help you recognize the good gaming CPUs from those that couldn't push a polygon across a screen with two hands and a flashlight.

What better way to test your knowledge at this point than to introduce you to some of the most popular architectures of today? Later, in the section, "Tomorrow's CPUs: What to Look For," I prepare you for what is to come.

Intel's P6 Architecture

Intel's P6 architecture had been with Intel for about five years before finally being replaced. A microprocessor's architecture (sometimes referred to as a *microarchitecture*) can be considered the foundation for a microprocessor. The architecture dictates things such as bus interface, cache types, number and power of integer and FP units, and so on. These architectures can take years to create, but because they last a few years in implementations, the development time is usually worth it. Unfortunately, because of the amount of time invested in designing such an architecture, it's difficult to recover if a poor design decision is made at this stage. This is one of the reasons the CPU design industry is so difficult to get into.

Multiple processors can use a single microprocessor architecture. For example, the Pentium Pro used the Intel P6 Architecture, as did the Pentium II, and later the Pentium III. Although all those CPUs did have some architectural improvements (for example, the Pentium II improved 16-bit application performance over the Pentium Pro, and the Pentium III added SIMD-FP instructions to the ISA), they were all based on the same microarchitecture. The processors varied in cache speed and size, yet the basic cache structure remained the same (although a bit of maturing did occur during the Pentium III lifetime). The FSB was kept constant except for increases in operating frequency, which was also the case with the CPUs. The microarchitecture and manufacturing improvements were leveraged to enable the P6 architecture to go from 150MHz with the Pentium Pro to over 1GHz with the Pentium III.

Processors that share the same microarchitecture generally share the same pipeline characteristics, but improvements occur when necessary.

Pentium Pro

The first CPU based on Intel's P6 Architecture got its roots in 1995 with the introduction of the Intel Pentium Pro processor. Mainly an attempt by Intel to gain entrance into the high-end workstation and server markets, the Pentium Pro failed to be an effective desktop or gaming PC solution. At the time of its introduction, most gamers were playing under Windows 3.11/DOS where the Pentium Pro did not perform well at all. There were a number of architectural issues that hampered its performance there, but it truly shined under Windows NT, which was Microsoft's first 32-bit OS core. The Pentium Pro simply had poor 16-bit performance, although there was much more to it than just that. So, even though Intel's first CPU in the P6 architecture family had its warts, at the same time, some very interesting benefits of the Pentium Pro allowed the P6 architecture to last as long as it did.

The oversimplified P6 pipeline used on the Pentium Pro was a 10-stage pipeline and was double the size of its predecessor's pipeline (the P5 pipeline used on the Pentium MMX was 5 stages long). Because of this, the P6 featured a much improved branch prediction unit and algorithm from its predecessors that helped lower the frequency of performance killing mispredicted branches.

The P6 architecture was also the first from Intel to bring the L2 cache onto the processor. In the case of the Pentium Pro, the L2 cache was not placed on the CPU's die itself, rather in a separate die but still on the same chip. This was considered to be off-die L2, but on-package because it shared the same packaging as the Pentium Pro processor itself. The Pentium Pro's design caused it to be quite expensive simply because the entire processor had to be manufactured before it could be tested. If the L2 cache failed, the entire thing would be thrown out. The L2 cache did run at the same clock speed as the CPU core itself, in spite of it being off-die. This gave the Pentium Pro incredible performance because of its high-speed L2 cache. (At its release, most processors had off-chip L2 cache that resided on the motherboard and operated at no faster than 66MHz, whereas the Pentium Pro's L2 cache was on-package and ran at 150MHz–200MHz.)

Illustrating the idea of maturing manufacturing processes, the Pentium Pro chip was manufactured on a 0.35-micron (circuit size) process and eventually reached speeds of 200MHz; the previous Intel flagship, the Pentium (P5), was introduced on a 0.8-micron process and ran at 60/66MHz. The 150MHz and 180MHz Pentium Pro processors used a 60MHz FSB, and the bus itself was known as the GTL+ bus. The 166MHz and 200MHz parts ran on a 66MHz FSB and simply used a higher clocked version of the GTL+ bus.

The Pentium Pro featured a 32KB L1 cache. 16KB of that was dedicated to a data cache, and 16KB was an instruction cache. The on-package L2 cache was offered in 256KB, 512KB, and 1MB versions.

The CPU itself was quite large compared to previous Intel CPUs; after all, it housed a complete 256KB–1MB of L2 cache. The CPU used a Socket-8 interface (the socket it plugged into) and featured a total of 387 pins.

With 3D games depending on FPU performance, the Pentium Pro, with its powerful FPU, could have been a huge success in the gaming market. Then, there were no 3D accelerators to offload 3D floating point calculations from the CPU onto dedicated hardware, requiring a very powerful FPU to get good 3D gaming performance. Remember that in 3D games, almost all the mathematical calculations performed are floating point (decimals) in nature so a strong FPU is necessary. Unfortunately, because of an incredibly high price tag and relatively poor 16-bit Windows/DOS performance, most gamers ignored the Pentium Pro and stuck to their Pentium MMX processors.

Over time, this changed because, historically, the technology being used in the high-end servers and workstations today eventually filters down to the level of tomorrow's desktop systems. This was the case in the evolution of the P6 Architecture, as the desktop version of the Pentium Pro was released in 1997 as the Pentium II.

Pentium II

The Pentium II offered a number of architectural advancements over the Pentium Pro that resulted in improved 16-bit Windows/DOS performance, making the processor much more desirable for home users. But by that time, Windows 95 had pretty much replaced Windows 3.11. In addition, Windows 95 had considerably more 32-bit optimized code than Windows 3.11, making even the old Pentium Pro a much happier processor.

One of the major changes Intel made to the Pentium II was to take the L2 cache from the Pentium Pro and pull it off the CPU packaging completely, thus helping to reduce costs. Unfortunately, this was a step back in terms of performance because it not only increased latency to the L2 cache, but also ended up decreasing the initially available L2 cache speeds. Remember, the on-package L2 cache running at up to 200MHz gave the Pentium Pro a big performance advantage. Instead, Intel did the next best thing; it mounted the Pentium II's core on a card that inserts into a slot instead of on a chip that is placed into a socket.

By placing the Pentium II on a card they could put external L2 cache chips on the card with the processor and at the same time implement a 512KB L2 cache size by default (versus 256KB on the Pentium Pro). The Pentium Pro featured a technology Intel called their Dual Independent Bus (DIB) that connected the Pentium Pro core to its on-die L2 cache.

Note

The Dual Bus comes from the fact that this is a second bus for the L2 cache instead of using the FSB for an external L2 cache.

This DIB was on the Pentium II as well; however, it connected the processor's core to an external set of L2 cache chips. This L2 cache operated at half the core speed of the Pentium II processor, meaning that the Pentium II running at 233MHz had a 116.5MHz L2 cache. This also meant that the first Pentium IIs were less attractive than the Pentium Pro for a lot of high-end users because it actually had a slower L2 cache—that is, until the Pentium II broke the 400MHz barrier the year following its initial introduction.

The fact that the processor was mounted on a card meant that the CPU interfaced in a slot. Intel called this interface Slot-1 or SC242, which was a 242-connector slot interface (see Figure 1.6). This was the first slot interface Intel had used for a CPU; in the past they had used socket-style interfaces.

FIGURE 1.6
Without the worry over bending CPU pins upon installing them, Intel's Slot-1 Interface made installing CPUs much easier than previous socketed designs. Intel eventually went back to socketed CPUs after they could move the L2 cache back onto the die.

The Pentium II was introduced on a 0.35-micron process at a 233MHz core speed, but later received a die shrink down to 0.25-micron at 333MHz. This 0.25-micron Pentium II core carried the Pentium II up to 350MHz where it received an upgrade of another kind in that it could now operate off of a 100MHz FSB, which carried it up to 450MHz.

Upgrades such as the Pentium II's upgrade from a 66MHz to a 100MHz FSB require very few modifications, if any, on the processor side. However, they generally take place whenever clock speeds increase dramatically. The reason for this is as you increase the clock speed of a CPU while keeping the rate at which it can receive data the same (for example, keeping the FSB frequency static), the FSB will eventually become a bottleneck. When this happens, your system is "FSB limited." I discuss these limitations throughout the book, as a good understanding of them will help you figure out why your game performance is suffering and what type of PC upgrade is required to make it scream with the banshees again.

Note

Currently the CPU controls very little with regards to game performance. A faster CPU does ensure data gets to the video card faster, but only handles AI (the importance of which depends on the game) and some light bits of triangle setup. Honestly, it's difficult to say how big a difference a particular processor will make.

Right now it's the graphics hardware that needs continued improvement so that developers can push the limits. As AI becomes more advanced, CPU dependency will increase.

Celeron

After the release of the Pentium II, Intel quickly realized that they could segment the Pentium II line easily by controlling the size and speed of the processor's L2 cache. Because the L2 cache was not a part of the physical CPU core, it was easy to remove or add more cache as necessary. The first time Intel tried this was with a highly criticized processor known as the Celeron.

The Celeron was in fact no different than a 0.35-micron 66MHz FSB Pentium II. It debuted at 266MHz and was available at two clock speeds, 266MHz and 300MHz. The Celeron was a low-cost version of the Pentium II, but because it shared the same core, the only thing that made it low cost was the fact that the Celeron had no L2 cache.

With no L2 cache, the Celeron had no place to store frequently used data, but it was a great, low-cost CPU for gamers because it had a strong FPU (the same as the Pentium II). However, it was still a highly controversial part because its lack of any L2 cache hurt its performance in a lot of business applications such as Microsoft Word and Excel. Such applications generally fit their data within the L2 cache of most of today's processors, making the cacheless Celeron a very poor match for everyone but gamers. Unfortunately, gamers don't make up the majority of Intel's market so they had to change the design.

Just as the Pentium II received a die shrink, so did the Celeron (see Figure 1.7). However, Intel gave the Celeron a little more when they did this, than what they gave the Pentium II. The 0.25-micron, 66MHz Celeron, was given a 128KB on-die L2 cache. Because it was on-die, the L2 cache ran at the core clock speed of the Celeron. It was smaller than the Pentium II's 512KB L2 cache, but it was also much faster.

FIGURE 1.7
Because of its on-die L2 cache, the 0.25-micron Celeron could outperform an equivalently clocked Pentium II.

This made gamers even happier as the CPU continued to have the computational power of the Pentium II, but now it also had an on-die L2 cache that kept the business/home office users content as well. The market segment Intel went after with the Celeron was a relatively new one for the chip giant, and they referred to it as the value market segment. This segment originally targeted the sub-$1,000 PC, meaning the PC could be purchased for less than $1,000 USD. However, it has because evolved to include the sub-$600 market as well and will continue to move towards lower and lower price points.

This new 0.25-micron Celeron with on-die L2 cache started at 300MHz. To differentiate it from the first 300MHz Celeron this one was referred to as a Celeron 300A. Celeron 300A made its way all the way up to 566MHz, never gaining an FSB speed boost. By giving the chip high multipliers and making it suitable for only 66MHz FSB operation, Intel made sure that its high-performance buyers didn't want the Celeron. Segmentation based on cache sizes, clock speed, and FSB frequency are common tactics Intel has used in the past and will continue to use.

Note

Gamers got a great bargain out of the cacheless Celeron because this was, as some might remember, during a time when 3D acceleration was still much less advanced than it is today and CPUs were not fast enough to place the bottleneck on 3D graphics cards.

In this case, having a strong FPU offered a tremendous performance incentive because the previous generation of processors (for example, Pentium MMX) as well as competing solutions (for example, AMD K6 and Cyrix 6x86MX) had very poor FPUs compared to what the Pentium II could offer.

The Celeron, in particular, had some very high yields during its initial run because it was manufactured using a very similar core to the Pentium IIs that were shipping at 400MHz+ at the time. Although it was released at 300MHz (for the first on-die cache version) those chips were often able to run at 450MHz–500MHz without much work. Because of this, many Celeron 300A users increased their FSB from 66MHz to 100MHz and ended up running unofficial Celeron 450A parts.

➤ ***For more information on overclocking your CPU, see Chapter 14, "Tweaking and Overclocking: Turbo-Charging Your PC."***

Because the Celeron didn't need the processor card that the Pentium II used (it's L2 cache was either not present or on-die), the Celeron was introduced in both Slot-1 form as well as in a cheaper socketed package known as Socket-370 (see Figure 1.8). Over time this further reduced production costs, making the Celeron line synonymous with high-performance, low-cost processors at least among the knowledgeable hardware enthusiasts.

FIGURE 1.8
Intel's Socket-370 Interface was first introduced with the socketed Celeron processors. The lever on the left is lifted to enable the CPU to be inserted into the ZIF (Zero Insertion Force) socket, and then lowered after the CPU is placed in the socket.

Pentium III

Where the Pentium II left off, the Pentium III picked up. However, the upgrade from the Pentium II to the Pentium III was not nearly as dramatic as the name change would imply. From an architectural standpoint, Intel did make some fairly major changes as they amended the x86 instruction set and added a total of 70 new instructions that they called their Streaming SIMD Extensions (SSE). These instructions can be viewed as a follow-up to MMX. MMX is an integer version of SSE that was originally introduced with the Pentium processor. In Figures 1.9 and 1.10, you can see a Pentium III cartridge and what the actual processor card inside it looks like.

FIGURE 1.9
The Intel Pentium III Processor, pictured here inside its cartridge, was the last Slot-1 processor from Intel. (*Photo courtesy of Intel Corporation.*)

FIGURE 1.10
The actual Intel Pentium III Processor Card found inside the Slot-1 cartridge.

Single Instruction Multiple Data (in this case SIMD-FP as it applies to FPU instructions, whereas MMX offered SIMD-Int for Integer instructions) enables a single command (or instruction) to be applied to multiple sets of data simultaneously. The key to understanding the benefits of SIMD-FP instructions is the emphasis on the simultaneous execution of commonly used instructions such as multiplication, division, and addition. The perfect example would be in the transfer of a simple cube in mathematical space to a 3D world as is illustrated in Figure 1.11.

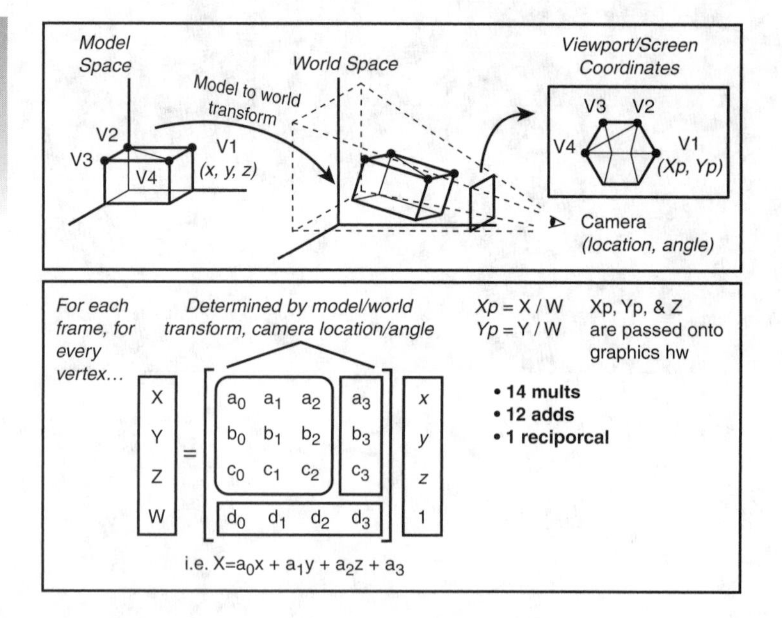

FIGURE 1.11
The need for SIMD can be illustrated in how a CPU renders a three dimensional cube. (*Photo courtesy Intel Corporation.*)

The 14 mults, 12 adds, and 1 reciprocal function of the previous transfer from model space to world space (mathematical space to 3D world space) could benefit greatly from the Pentium III's SSE. You're essentially executing the same instruction and applying it to multiple forms of data over and over again. The nature of SIMD-FP instructions allows for these instructions to be applied to multiple data structures processed by the CPU in a more timely manner, offering an actual improvement in performance.

Although MMX did the same thing for Integer values (whole numbers, 1, 2, 3, and so on), most complex software such as 3D games, 3D rendering programs, image editing software, and even speech recognition software make use of Floating Point values (numbers with decimals, for example, 0.0001). Therefore there was a very tiny real-world performance improvement that Intel's MMX instructions brought to the table. At the same time, floating point calculations already take an incredible amount of time to process, even on today's fastest x86 processors (relatively speaking, from the point of view of the CPU not the user). Because of this, the application of SIMD to floating point operations, as the Pentium III's SSE provides, offers a greater tangible performance improvement than the application of SIMD to integer operations, which are already quite fast on x86 systems.

The trick here is that to take advantage of SSE's benefits, the software being run on an SSE enabled system must have support for it. So for the majority of the introductory months of the Pentium III processor, it was nothing more than a higher clocked Pentium II. Still based off of a 0.25-micron process, the Pentium III eventually made its way up to 600MHz without receiving a dieshrink. Before it did however, a few interesting things happened.

Although the Pentium III continued to use a 100MHz FSB, after Intel released the Pentium III 600MHz they went back and released a Pentium III B clocked at 533MHz and 600MHz. These two CPUs used a 133MHz FSB, a 33% increase from the 100MHz FSB that the Pentium III started on, and a 100% increase from the 66MHz FSB that the Pentium II started on. This is also on a processor that is clocked at over 2.5x the speed of the first Pentium II. From this point on, the "B" extension onto the Pentium III name denoted a 133MHz FSB version. There were no other differences between the Pentium III and the Pentium III B other than the fact that the Pentium III B used lower multipliers. For example, a Pentium III 600 ran at 6.0 × 100MHz, whereas a Pentium III 600B ran at 4.5 × 133MHz (it is actually 133.3333MHz). This meant if you put a Pentium III 600B in a system that only supported the 100MHz FSB, it would run at 450MHz.

Note

Theoretically, this would also mean that a standard Pentium III could be made to run on 133MHz FSB. Unfortunately, doing so while maintaining the certified 600MHz clock speed was impossible because the processor's multiplier is locked at six.

The other interesting thing to happen was that for the entire life of the Pentium III, the 0.25-micron core ran at a core voltage of 2.00V. However the 600MHz part, reaching the limits of the P6 Architecture on the 0.25-micron process, required an increase in operating voltage to 2.05v. This 2.5% increase in core voltage wasn't accidental; it was an attempt to increase yields on the 600MHz CPUs. By increasing the core voltage of a CPU, you increase its tolerance for operation by giving it more power. This can be dangerous for the CPU if the core can't deal with the increased voltage, however in this case it could. Increased core voltages are important things to look for when trying to see how much life is left in a particular microprocessor architecture. Luckily for Intel, the Pentium III was finally ready for a shrink down to a 0.18-micron process.

Enter the Coppermine

Toward the end of 1999, Intel made its first 0.18-micron desktop processor public. The reason I make a point of saying the first 0.18-micron *desktop* processor is because Intel generally debuts its dieshrinks on mobile platforms, simply because they are much lower demand than desktop platforms. This way it can work out all the kinks with the new process in a low-demand area and prepare it for the limelight in a later debut for the higher-demand sectors.

The 0.18-micron Pentium III went under the codename Coppermine (the original Pentium III carried the codename Katmai), and it was more deserving of the Pentium III name than the very first Pentium III 500 was. The Coppermine debuted at 500MHz and was available in both 100MHz and 133MHz FSB versions; again, the two were separated by the "B" denotation. To separate Coppermine core Pentium IIIs from regular Pentium IIIs, the letter "E" was added as well (see Table 1.2).

Table 1.2 Coppermine Confusion: Outlining the Various Iterations of the Intel Pentium III Coppermine CPU

	Core	FSB	Clock Multiplier	Clock Speed
Pentium III 600EB	0.18μ Coppermine	133MHz	4.5x	600MHz
Pentium III 600E	0.18μ Coppermine	100MHz	6.0x	600MHz
Pentium III 600B	0.25μ Katmai	133MHz	4.5x	600MHz
Pentium III 600	0.25μ Katmai	100MHz	6.0x	600MHz

One very important characteristic that determines not only yield, but overall cost of the CPU is the size of the processor's die or core. The larger the core the more expensive it is to produce and the greater the potential for lower yields on the CPU. The original Pentium III core had an area of 128 mm_, while the Coppermine core had an area of 106 mm_ (the later Coppermines had a slightly smaller core). However, the more impressive statistic was that although the original Pentium III had approximately 9.5 million transistors, the new Pentium III had 29 million transistors and was still smaller because of its dieshrink. This brings up the next question: What were these ~20 million new transistors doing in the Coppermine Pentium III?

When we introduced the P6 Architecture, we mentioned that one of the strengths of the Pentium Pro was that its L2 cache was on-package, and as close to the actual CPU die as possible. At the same time we mentioned that the ideal location for a processor's L2 cache would be on the processor's die itself; well, guess where Intel put the L2 cache of the Coppermine Pentium III? That's right, it had an on-die L2 cache. This brings up an interesting point about adding L2 cache on-die; it takes up quite a bit of space and accounts for the skyrocketed transistor count we just discussed.

The cache's move on-die reduced the L2 cache latency noticeably, and also increased the performance of the cache. To save space, Intel only went with a 256KB L2 cache, but it did operate at the core clock speed, which was an immediate improvement over the 512KB off-die L2 running at half the core clock speed. The Pentium III has an internal 256-bit wide bus to the L2 cache, which is actually four times wider than the 64-bit FSB that connects the Pentium III to the outside world.

Because of the fact that the L2 cache was moved on-die, there was no longer a need for the Slot-1 processor cartridge that the Pentium III was placed on. So Intel began phasing out the Slot-1 interface in favor of a socketed chip design known as FC-PGA 370 (see Figure 1.12). The FC-PGA stands for Flip Chip Pin Grid Array. Flip Chip refers to the method in which the core is packaged so that the back of the die actually makes contact with the base of the cooling device placed on top of the CPU. The 370 stands for the 370-pin interface that the CPU used. This interface was also known as Socket-370.

FIGURE 1.12
The FC-PGA 370 Pentium III used the same physical Socket-370 interface as the first socketed Celerons, but had some slightly more specific voltage/electrical requirements preventing it from working in previous Socket-370 motherboards.

The Coppermine core took the Pentium III up to a speed of 1.0GHz (1000MHz) before finally reaching its architectural limits. Intel did attempt to release a 1.13GHz Pentium III; however, they had to recall the CPU after it was found that the processors were not exactly up to Intel's high quality standards. Intel proceeded with the recall after less than 200 CPUs had been shipped.

Coppermine128

With a new 0.18-micron Pentium III core, Intel was ready to provide a new 0.18-micron Celeron to the public. By this time, the limits of the 66MHz FSB were truly being seen as the Celerons were performing noticeably lower than their 100MHz FSB Pentium III counterparts. Remember, as clock speed increases, the dependency on a high-speed bus increases. As time goes on, the software that these CPUs are running stress the CPUs even more, also requiring a high-speed bus. When it comes to many 3D games such as *Quake III Arena*, the demand for a high-speed FSB and memory bus definitely outweighed the need for an incrementally faster FPU. In this case, the Celeron still performed underpar because it was not able to deliver on either of those points despite its high clock speed.

From a manufacturing standpoint, Intel had a very cost-effective idea. When producing CPUs, not all the Pentium III processors (Coppermine) would have fully functional 256KB L2 caches on-die. There might be cases when only 206KB was functional, or possibly even less. At the same time, it didn't really make sense to design a completely different core for the new Celeron and have to produce two cores at their production facilities. Intel's solution was to create a new core known internally to Intel as the Coppermine128 core (see Figure 1.13). This core, as the name implies, has exactly half of the cache of the regular Coppermine core (128KB vs. 256KB) and uses a 4-way set associative cache vs. the 8-way set associative L2 cache that is present on the Pentium III's Coppermine core. Another interesting fact was that the Coppermine128 core had exactly the same die size and transistor count as the regular Coppermine core, indicating that the new Celerons were nothing more than Pentium IIIs with half of their on-die L2 cache disabled. These could either be processors that didn't have a fully functional 256KB L2 cache, or they could also be fully working Pentium IIIs with only 128KB L2 enabled. And because it used the same Pentium III core, the new Celerons had SSE support.

FIGURE 1.13
The Coppermine128 Celeron looks a lot like the first FC-PGA Pentium III Coppermine processors. They are almost identical except for the fact that half of the cache is disabled on the Coppermine128.

This core started at 600MHz and made its way up to 766MHz with a 66MHz FSB. However the 66MHz FSB had, by this point, already begun to show its age and the performance delta between the Pentium III Coppermine and this new Celeron (sometimes unofficially referred to as the Celeron 2) grew even larger. It turns out that the fact that the Celeron's L2 cache was only a 4-way set associative compared to the Pentium III's 8-way set associative L2 cache resulted in quite a significant performance penalty as well. This made the Celeron much less attractive, from a performance standpoint, than the Celeron was when it originally launched with an on-die L2 cache (as a Pentium II alternative). Times do change, and as the applications you're running continue to get more intensive, performance gaps between processors increase tremendously as well.

To breathe more life into the aging Celeron processor, Intel finally gave it a 100MHz FSB when they released a Celeron CPU at 800MHz. This increased its performance tremendously, but its smaller 4-way set associative L2 cache still held it back in comparison to the Pentium III Coppermine.

Table 1.3 looks at the significant milestones in the development of the Celeron line of processors.

Table 1.3 Specifications for the Celeron Family of CPUs

	Core	FSB	Clock Multiplier	Clock Speed
Celeron 300*	0.25-micron Covington	66MHz	4.5x	300MHz
Celeron 300A	0.25-micron Mendocino	66MHz	4.5x	300MHz
Celeron 600	0.18-micron Coppermine128	66MHz	9.0x	600MHz
Celeron 800	0.18-micron Coppermine128	100MHz	8.0x	800MHz

* *This Celeron had no L2 cache; every other Celeron had 128KB on-die.*

AMD's K7

For some time, AMD had taken great pride in their successes in the value market segment with processors such as the K5 and K6. However, with Intel's Celeron release, AMD could not compete with Intel's lucrative performance figures and very competitive prices.

For gamers, Intel was even more attractive because AMD's CPUs at the time didn't have fully pipelined FPUs; they were slow and inefficient when it came to game performance.

This all changed near the end of 1999 when AMD released their Athlon microprocessor based on the AMD K7 architecture (see Figure 1.14). The Athlon offered advancements over the Pentium III in almost every category.

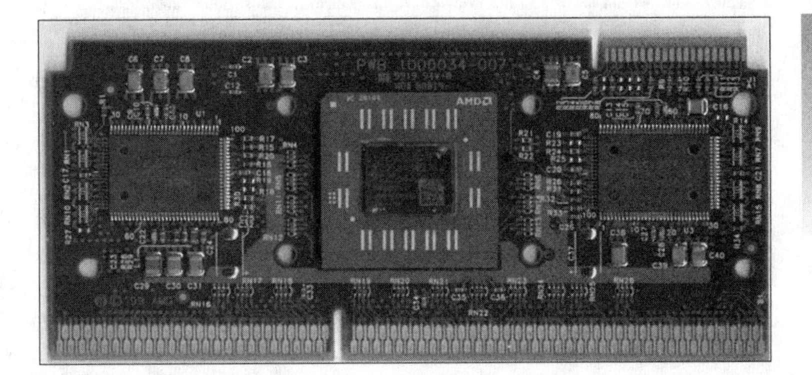

FIGURE 1.14
The AMD Athlon K7 looked a lot like the Pentium III in that it was mounted on a similar size card, but there's definitely more than meets the eye.

AMD's K7 core was the long awaited successor to the K6. The first seventh-generation x86 processor ever made was based on the K7 core because it was a 7th generation microarchitecture (at least from a technology standpoint).

From a performance standpoint, the K7 didn't outperform the Pentium III, but it remained competitive. The K7 microarchitecture was better suited for higher clock speeds than the Pentium III, enabling it to run at much higher frequencies on the same manufacturing process than the Pentium III.

The benefits of the K7's architecture included a very powerful FPU, strong execution units, and very solid performing design. Like Intel's P6 architecture, the K7 architecture is the basis for more than one AMD processor. The Athlon, Duron, and all variations of those two processors are based off the same K7 architecture.

Athlon: Death of the Pentium III

The first Athlons were built on a 0.25-micron process under the codename K7. These processors had no on-die L2 cache because of their already large die, and instead implemented a slot-based interface much like the Pentium II and Pentium III Katmai processors. In fact, the Athlon's Slot-A, as it was called, was mechanically nothing more than a backward Slot-1 (see Figure 1.15).

FIGURE 1.15
Only orientation separates the mechanical differences between the interface of a Slot-1 and that of a Slot-A.

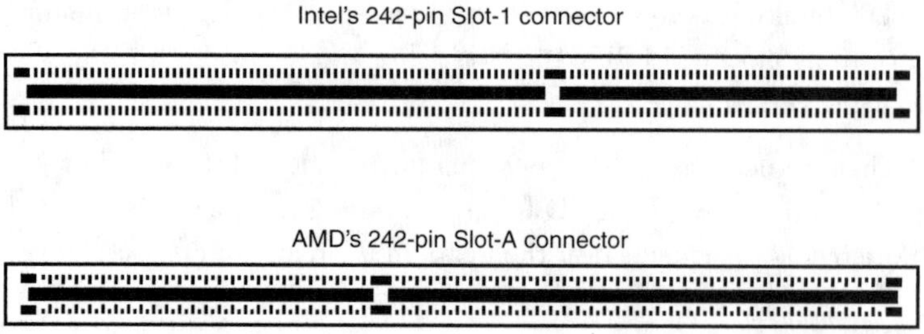

The Athlon had a 64-bit bus connecting it to its external L2 cache, and this bus operated at 1/2 or 1/3 the core clock speed of the CPU. The clock speed of the CPU determined which L2 cache divider would be used. AMD always made an effort to keep the L2 cache speed at or around 300MHz, the only exception being the Athlon 700 whose L2 cache ran at 350MHz (1/2 core speed). You can already begin to see a bottleneck in the original Athlon's design as there would come a point where the processor was waiting on its "slow" L2 cache for data. The Athlon featured a 512KB L2 cache again, much like the original Pentium II/III processors from Intel.

Moving on to the Athlon's core, we'll find that the processor was designed for high clock speeds, higher than those of the Pentium III at least. The processor featured an 11-stage pipeline and now featured a fully pipelined FPU as well (AMD's previous processors lacked this feature). This unfortunately increased the branch mispredict penalties over AMD's previous processors which used a 6-stage pipeline. The branch mispredict penalties held back the performance of the Athlon significantly. Its branch prediction unit was always argued to be inferior to other units, even some that AMD had implemented in past chips.

The K7 has an incredibly large 128KB L1 cache split evenly into a 64KB instruction cache and a 64KB data cache. This 128KB L1 cache allowed the Athlon to last quite a while without having an on-die L2 cache. The L1 cache is 2-way set associative, meaning it has a very low latency, whereas the Athlon's L2 cache is 16-way set associative translating into a higher latency but much higher hit rate as well.

The large caches of the K7 enabled many programs and games to fit most of their execution code into the processor's cache, which is much faster than going to main memory to fetch data all the time. The high hit rate of the L2 cache translates into a greater likelihood of finding that game execution code/data in the large L2 cache, which improves performance considerably.

The Athlon's decoders are quite powerful in comparison to the Pentium III's as well. Both the Athlon and Pentium III can simultaneously decode three x86 instructions into smaller operations; however, the Pentium III's decoders have some stipulations on what type of instructions can be decoded simultaneously. The Athlon's decoders have no such stipulations, offering the Athlon much more flexibility than the Pentium III. As you'll remember from our architectural discussions earlier, the decoding stage is quite possibly one of the most important parts of the entire pipeline and the Athlon's superiority here definitely helps when the translation is made to real-world performance.

Although the Athlon's Branch Prediction Table (the processor's scratchpad for predicted branches) enables more entries than that of the Pentium III, the BPU is actually using an oddly simple algorithm that actually hurt the Athlon's performance considerably.

The Athlon's FPU is also noticeably more powerful than that of the Pentium III and is capable of executing many more instructions than the Pentium III's FPU. Upon its release the Athlon offered a huge performance advantage over the Pentium III in all categories.

Continuing the impressive list of features, the Athlon's FSB became another feather in AMD's cap. The FSB for the Athlon processor is called EV6 and operates at 100MHz. This might not sound any better than a Pentium III, but this bus operates at a Double Data Rate (DDR) frequency. This means that, although the clock frequency is 100MHz, data is transferred twice per clock cycle, yielding transfer rates equivalent to that of a 200MHz FSB. Such a high-speed FSB kept the Athlon fed with data constantly and removed a bottleneck before it even became one.

The Athlon debuted at 500MHz and made its way to 700MHz on the 0.25-micron process, each CPU having a half-speed L2 cache. At 750MHz–1GHz, the Athlon was on a new process (0.18-micron) and thus a new core, codenamed the K75 (see Figure 1.16). Although this was a 0.18-micron CPU with a significantly smaller die size than the original K7 core, AMD failed to include any on-die L2 cache. In fact, AMD dropped the L2 cache divider from 1/2 down to 1/2.5, meaning that the L2 cache on the 750MHz–850MHz processors ran at 0.40 x the core clock speed. At 900MHz–1GHz AMD dropped the ratio even further so that the L2 cache ran at a third of the speed of the CPU. These reductions were mainly an attempt to keep the L2 cache frequency at or below 350MHz, because finding faster L2 cache chips at the time was considerably more costly.

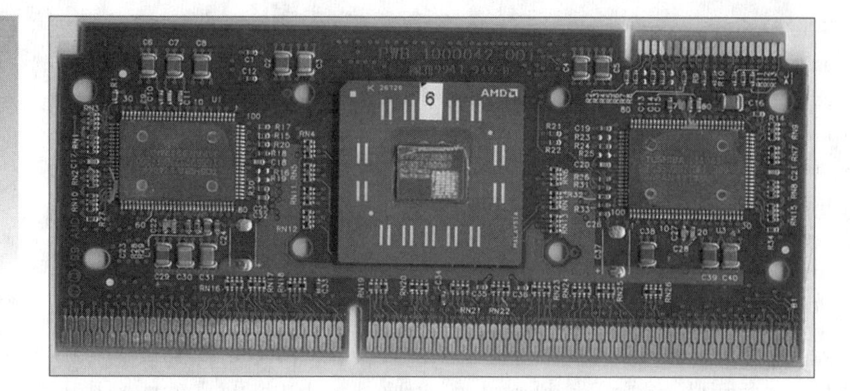

FIGURE 1.16
The AMD K75 looked identical to the AMD K7 Athlon processors with the exception of a noticeably smaller core (center) due to its 0.18-micron fabrication process.

Thunderbird

It wasn't until June 2000 that AMD gave the Athlon what it so greatly desired, an on-die L2 cache. This was done with the Thunderbird core; a socketed version of the Athlon that used a 0.18-micron process (like the K75 core) yet featured an on-die L2 cache (see Figure 1.17). The on-die L2 cache enabled AMD to rid itself of the Slot-A card because there was no longer a need for the extra space it provided. AMD did make a Slot-A version of the Thunderbird, but it was in much smaller quantities and really only targeted at OEMs and system builders that couldn't upgrade their Slot-A systems quickly enough.

FIGURE 1.17
The AMD Athlon (Thunderbird) eventually made its way to a 462-pin socketed interface that is known as Socket-A. This mainly helped to reduce cost.

Moving the L2 cache on-die decreased the L2 cache latency tremendously because the Athlon didn't have to travel nearly as far to grab the data it needed. More specifically, the K75 core had a 21-cycle latency when accessing L2 cache, whereas the Thunderbird features only an 11-cycle latency.

However, aside from the Thunderbird's L2 cache being on-die, it is still quite different from the Coppermine's on-die L2 cache.

If you've ever read AMD's press releases on the Thunderbird, you'll likely notice that they refer to the Thunderbird as having a total of 384KB of cache. This figure is derived by adding the 128KB of L1 cache that the Thunderbird still has from the original Athlon to the 256KB of L2 cache that is now on-die with the Thunderbird.

So what's different about the caching system of the Thunderbird versus that of the Intel Pentium III Coppermine? AMD is employing an exclusive cache architecture on the Thunderbird instead of the more conventionally used, inclusive cache architecture, which is what Intel uses on the Coppermine.

Basically with an inclusive cache, all the data that is stored in the L1 cache is duplicated in the L2 cache. Although the Pentium III (Coppermine) features a 256KB on-die L2 cache, the data contained within its 32KB L1 cache is duplicated in the 256KB L2 cache.

An exclusive cache, which, as you can tell by the name, is the opposite of an inclusive cache, doesn't duplicate L1 data in the L2 cache area. The L2 cache only contains the copy-back cache blocks that are to be written back to the memory sub system (basically everything that doesn't fit in L1 and would normally go to the system memory if there was no L2 cache). Therefore, when AMD claims that the new Thunderbird core has a total of 384KB of on-die cache, they aren't lying; any data in the Athlon's (Thunderbird) 128KB L1 is *not* duplicated in its 256KB L2 (see Figure 1.18).

The Thunderbird still features a 64-bit data path to and from its L2 cache, which is unchanged from the original Athlon. This is a narrower data path than the Pentium III Coppermine's L2 cache has (256-bit vs. 64-bit), which poses a limitation, although not enough to cripple the Thunderbird's performance.

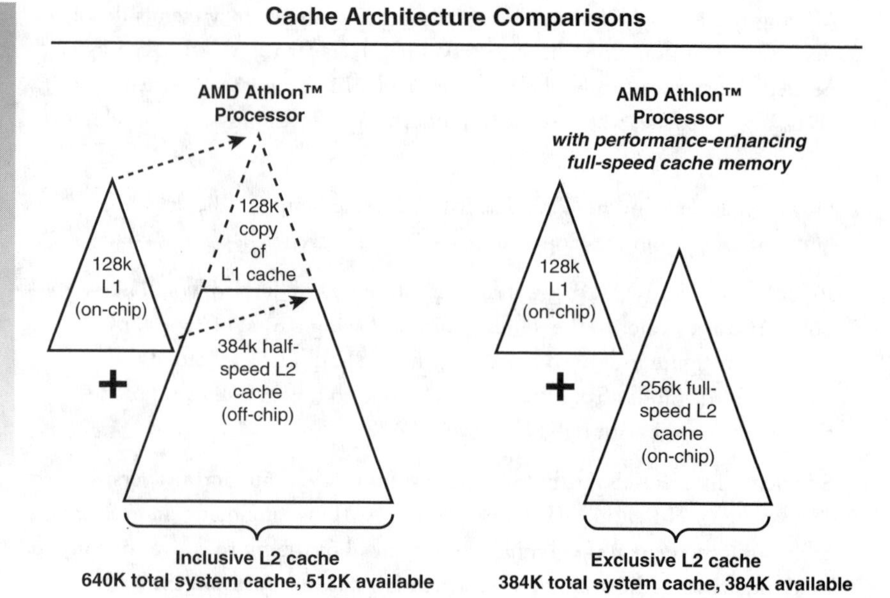

FIGURE 1.18 Comparing the Cache Architecture of the K7 with that of the Thunderbird core, which implemented an exclusive cache architecture. This meant that the data in the L1 cache was not duplicated in the processor's L2 cache, increasing latency somewhat while also increasing the L2 cache's usable size. *(Original picture courtesy of AMD.)*

The Thunderbird core was originally paired up with a 100MHz DDR FSB, however, AMD soon initiated a transition to 133MHz DDR FSB processors. The only way to tell the difference between an Athlon that was intended to be run at the 100MHz DDR FSB and one that was supposed to run at the 133MHz DDR FSB was the fact that the latter was referred to as an Athlon-C. The difference between an Athlon and an Athlon-C was that the latter featured a lower clock multiplier to deal with the increased FSB.

The Thunderbird core was introduced at 700MHz and eventually made its way up to 1.4GHz before being replaced by another core, the Palomino core.

Palomino: Faster and Cooler

Technically speaking, the Palomino core does mark the fourth AMD Athlon core since the release of the original K7 core in 1999. If we begin counting at the K7 core, there was the 0.18-micron Athlon which was based on the K75 core, followed by the 0.18-micron Thunderbird with on-die L2 cache, and then the fourth Athlon core would be the 0.18-micron Palomino core (see Figure 1.19). Because of this quirk (and mostly because of the fact that the chip's chief competitor was the Pentium 4), AMD introduced the first Palomino-based processor as the mobile Athlon 4 CPU.

As the name implies, the mobile Athlon 4 was an entry into the notebook market. AMD's plan was to start there, bring the Palomino core to the server/workstation market, and then to the desktop market. This was the plan because it is always easier to get all the kinks out of producing a new chip, with a new core design in smaller markets (for example, notebook and server markets) than it is to go ahead and mass produce them for the largest market (desktop).

The server/workstation part was known as the Athlon MP and was identical to the mobile part. The desktop version, which carries the Athlon XP name, is identical to the server/workstation and mobile chips.

FIGURE 1.19
The Palomino core (right) has a much different appearance than the Thunderbird core (left), but the improvements are far from just cosmetic.

When designing a microprocessor you don't use the same type of transistors all over the core. The Athlon (Thunderbird) core had 37 million transistors of various types, but it was AMD's first shot at an Athlon core with an on-die L2 cache. The Athlon XP takes the same Thunderbird core and further optimizes the core by using more optimized transistors for various portions of the core. When you are dealing with the 37.5 million transistors that make up the Athlon XP, such optimizations can result in quite a bit of power savings. According to AMD, these improvements to the Athlon XP result in a 20% decrease in power use compared to an equivalently clocked Athlon using the Thunderbird core. The die size hasn't changed much either; a small increase from 120 mm^2 to 128 mm^2.

Part of this optimization process included a change in layout of the core which is why the Athlon XP core does in fact look different than the older Athlon (Thunderbird) core. The change wasn't cosmetic; it was for further performance and power optimizations.

There are three features that the Athlon XP offers over its predecessor outside of the power reduction. These features are all performance enhancing.

The first advantage the Athlon XP offers is an increase in the number of L1 translation lookaside buffer (TLB) entries. When a processor accesses main memory it doesn't directly reference the physical addresses in memory. Instead there is a set of virtual addresses that map onto these physical addresses in memory. The process of translating virtual addresses to physical addresses is necessary for actually getting to data in main memory. Unfortunately, your CPU doesn't like to have to go to main memory. The reason is that when your CPU must go to main memory, it has to travel down the FSB, through the North Bridge, and down the memory bus before it can actually get there. A way of avoiding this long trip is by caching.

You are aware of two particular types of processor caches, the L1 and L2 caches. Well, there is also another type of a cache known as the Translation Lookaside Buffer or TLB for short. The TLB caches the translated addresses that result from this virtual address to physical address translation process. The probability of a CPU finding the address it needs in its TLB is extremely high, usually around 99%; this is known as the processor's TLB hit-rate. This is quite good because in the event that the CPU cannot find an address it needs in the TLB, the penalty can be incredible and the CPU's performance suffers in turn. To resolve a single address, the penalty can be 3 clock cycles. Multiply that by the number of addresses that must be looked up in main memory and you can see where the CPU would end up slowing down considerably because of this. Upon a hit to the TLB, this lookup can be done in 1 clock cycle, improving performance by 200%.

The TLB for the L1 cache on the Athlon XP has received an increase in the number of entries, which increases the hit rate for the Athlon's TLB. The Thunderbird only had a 24-entry L1 TLB compared to the 32-entry L1 TLB on the Pentium III for the instruction cache and a 32-entry TLB for the L1 data cache as opposed to the Pentium III's 72-entry L1 D-cache TLB. Unfortunately AMD did not have the exact number of L1 TLB entries of the Athlon XP at the time of this writing. We simply know that they did increase the number.

This increase actually only amounts to a marginal real-world performance increase for the Athlon XP over the Athlon (Thunderbird).

The Athlon XP's L1 and L2 caches size and mapping remain unchanged. As a refresher, the Athlon 4 has a 2-way set associative 64KB L1 instruction cache and a similarly associative 64KB L1 data cache. The Athlon's L2 cache is a 16-way set associative exclusive 256KB L2 cache. The fact that it is an exclusive architecture means that the L1 addresses are not duplicated in the L2 cache allowing AMD to claim a total on-die cache of 384KB for the Athlon 4. That part of the equation remains unchanged. What did change was that the Athlon XP now has an automatic data prefetch mechanism that works alongside its cache.

This is similar to the Pentium 4's hardware prefetch which predicts what data it will need before it is requested and fetches it from main memory into its cache. This process obviously increases FSB and memory bandwidth usage and it does tend to show more of a performance improvement on higher clocked/higher bandwidth FSB/memory platforms. This does translate into DDR SDRAM being much more useful for the Athlon XP than it was on the Athlon (Thunderbird).

The data prefetch that is now a part of the Athlon XP's core has actually been around for quite a while with desktop microprocessors. The Athlon XP's data prefetch is simply an evolution of previous prefetch designs. The data prefetch functions can also be software initiated which will take precedence over the Athlon XP's own data prefetch mechanism.

This is where the bulk of the Athlon XP's performance increase does come from, and although it isn't an incredible boost in performance, it is respectable nonetheless.

The Athlon XP also adds the same SSE instructions with which the Pentium III was introduced. This support is an indication of AMD standardizing on SSE instead of 3DNow! as the preferred SIMD-FP instruction set. Most developers have echoed support for this, stating that SSE is superior to 3DNow!. Don't get the fact that the Athlon XP supports SSE confused with being able to run SSE code as fast as a Pentium III. That is determined by how well the Athlon 4's architecture can execute SSE code which is still a question that has yet to be fully answered.

> **Note**
>
> When there are answers to these questions you can be sure that they will appear on the AnandTech Web site (www.anandtech.com).

For the most part, the Palomino core is between 0%–20% faster than an equivalently clocked Thunderbird core based Athlon. For games, the Palomino core's data prefetch comes in handy and usually offers a 5%–10% boost in performance over the Thunderbird core. The fact that it is cooler running is a plus as well.

The Athlon XP differed itself from its predecessors (including the mobile Athlon 4 and the Athlon MP, although they are based on the same core) through a new packaging and naming system.

There are two main parts to the majority of socketed CPUs like the Athlon XP and Pentium 4. These parts are the silicon that makes up what we call the core and the actual chip, which is called the processor substrate or packaging. The job of the packaging is to take the signals generated on the core itself and transmit them to the rest of the system through the motherboard. Remember that no direct connections are made to the core because the core is so small. The core is connected to the outside world through wires in the packaging. For AMD, all their socketed CPUs have used ceramic packaging, which can easily be identified by the ceramic surface of the majority of their CPUs. Intel on the other hand has been very advanced in their packaging technologies in the later days of the Pentium processor with an organic-based package that felt more like plastic than ceramic. The benefits of this organic package are a better ability to deal with higher clock speeds and the denser routing of wires going from the core throughout the package. With the Athlon XP, AMD has a similar organic-based packaging, enabling even higher clock speeds and more headroom on its CPUs. Unfortunately, AMD's packaging technology is still an area in which it lags behind Intel. You can tell the difference between the Athlon XP's organic package and older ceramic packages by the color of the package (brown versus purple) and the light weight of the package.

Another area in which AMD lags behind Intel is clock speed. If you've read sequentially through this chapter you know the performance equation has two parts: how much work you can do in a single clock cycle and how many clock cycles you can go through in a single second.

While the Pentium 4 was under 2GHz, AMD had a clear lead in the performance equation because the "how much work" part of the equation was tilted in the Athlon's favor and Intel hadn't gained the clock speed advantage to offset that. However, as the Pentium 4 hit 2GHz and is journeying to 2.2GHz and beyond the processor will be much more competitive in terms of its total performance.

With the Athlon's current architecture however, AMD will not be able to raise clock speed up to the level that the Pentium 4 can reach as quickly. Yet in many cases, lower clocked AMD Athlon CPUs can outperform Pentium 4 processors at higher frequencies because of the two parts to the performance equation.

The problem AMD runs into is that the average Joe (no offense to you if you're named Joe) going into a Best Buy or a CompUSA equates clock speed with performance and doesn't understand the fundamentals of CPU architecture that invalidate this comparison. To deal with this population AMD is introducing a model rating system for their Athlon XP processors to replace the conventional MHz/GHz ratings that are assigned to processors.

The rating is based on performance relative to other processors. Although AMD claims that the relative performance is to other Athlons, it's clear that the relative performance is supposed to be compared to the Pentium 4. I am not a fan of this solution at all because it can end up confusing the consumer more than anything, but for your information, AMD's model numbering system for the Athlon XP is in Table 1.4.

Table 1.4 AMD Athlon XP Chip "Ratings" and Their Actual Clock Speeds

Processor Name	Clock Speed
AMD Athlon XP 1800+	1.53GHz
AMD Athlon XP 1700+	1.47GHz
AMD Athlon XP 1600+	1.40GHz
AMD Athlon XP 1500+	1.33GHz

All Athlon XP processors use the 133MHz DDR FSB (effectively 266MHz) and boast what AMD calls their "QuantiSpeed architecture." AMD's justify their modeling system by saying that the QuantiSpeed architecture enables their Model 1800+ processor to only run at 1.53GHz while offering the performance of a 1.8GHz CPU. What can I say—marketing at its finest.

Duron: AMD Learns the Ropes

With the P6 core Intel was eventually able to create an entire line of processors out of one core by simply varying the FSB frequency and amount of cache. With the Athlon core AMD was finally able to do the same.

The natural progression indicated that AMD should next concentrate on a cost-effective CPU to compete with the Intel Celeron, and they did with their release of the Duron.

The Duron was no different from the Athlon except that it had a 64KB L2 cache instead of the 256KB L2 cache of the Athlon. Because the Duron had such a large L1 cache, however, its 64KB L2 cache was much less of an issue. Again, the Duron used the same exclusive cache architecture as the Athlon giving it a total of 128KB of data cache.

The Duron used only the 100MHz DDR FSB and ended up offering performance approximately 10% lower on average than that of the Athlon. From a performance standpoint, the Duron truly put the Celeron to shame because its architecture was identical to that of the Athlon, with the exception of a slightly smaller but similarly associative L2 cache.

Pentium 4 and the NetBurst Architecture: The Culmination of Five Years of Work

With the Pentium III stuck at 1GHz on a 0.18-micron process, it was clear that the 5-year-old P6 architecture was not going to be able to carry Intel much longer. Luckily, as they had done so many times in the past, Intel planned ahead. In fact, during the five years that the P6 architecture was in the eyes of the public, Intel was working on its successor behind the scenes. The successor to the P6 architecture didn't become the P7 architecture; rather it went under the name of NetBurst. And the first processor to use the NetBurst architecture was the Intel Pentium 4 (see Figure 1.20).

FIGURE 1.20
The Pentium 4 processor is yet another socketed processor from Intel, but instead of being based on the old P6 architecture, it implements Intel's latest microarchitecture known as NetBurst.

The NetBurst architecture consists of what Intel calls its Hyper Pipelined Technology. The Hyper Pipelined Technology behind NetBurst is a marketing term for the 20-stage pipeline the architecture revolves around. You'll notice that at 20-stages, the NetBurst pipeline is significantly longer than any other pipeline we have discussed thus far (see Figure 1.21). This does mean that the NetBurst architecture is geared toward high clock speed CPUs, but at the same time, it also means the penalty for a mispredicted branch can be devastating to the Pentium 4's performance.

Basic P6 Pipeline

1	2	3	4	5	6	7	8	9	10
Fetch	Fetch	Decode	Decode	Decode	Rename	ROB Rd	Rdy/Sch	Dispatch	Exec

Basic Willamette Pipeline

1	2	3	4	5	6	7	8	9	10	11	12	13	14	15	16	17	18	19	20
TC Net IP		TC Fetch		Drive	Alloc	Rename		Que	Sch	Sch	Sch	Dsp	Dsp	RF	RF	Ex	Flgs	Br Ck	Drive

FIGURE 1.21
The Pentium 4's (codename Willamette) pipeline is clearly much longer than that of a basic P6.

Another feature the Pentium 4 boasts is a Rapid Execution Engine. In an over-simplified manner, this means that two of the Pentium 4's ALUs are "double-pumped" or running at the clock speed of the CPU but can transfer twice as much data per clock, effectively giving a Pentium 4 clocked at 1.5GHz a set of ALUs that run at 3.0GHz. This would seemingly give the Pentium 4 a huge performance advantage in integer applications—mainly those related to business and office work, such as word processors and presentation software. However, that is not the case. It turns out that the Rapid Execution Engine is a necessity of the architecture to combat the grave branch mispredict penalty I just discussed.

The Pentium 4 has a very advanced branch predictor that can help to avoid any mispredicted branches that might occur in the later stages of its pipeline. The Pentium 4's branch predictor is actually much more advanced than the Athlon's. Unfortunately, regardless of how advanced it is, you can't predict something that is generally unpredictable. This is the case when it comes to integer instructions.

The nature of integer instructions is that predicting branches when dealing with these types of operations is quite difficult. In many cases, when dealing with these integer instructions as you would when running many business/office level applications, the Pentium 4's branch predictor will mispredict a branch sending the instructions back to the start of the 20 stage pipeline. This penalty is huge compared to what it would be on the Pentium III because it only has a 10-stage pipeline. By double pumping the ALUs, the penalties associated with the long pipeline are further reduced and the latency of such operations is dramatically minimized.

Apparently, other portions of the Pentium 4 are also double pumped; when combined with the double-pumped ALUs, you can see a clear trend toward achieving lower latencies in certain parts of the CPU.

The low-latency motif of NetBurst and the Pentium 4 continues with the fact that the Pentium 4 only has an 8KB L1 data cache. This is exactly half the size of the L1 data cache of the Pentium III (16KB), so why the reduction in size? Smaller caches have lower latencies so in part it was an attempt to decrease the latency of the L1 cache. In comparison, although the Athlon's 2-way set associative 64KB L1 Data Cache has a better hit rate (larger caches have better hit rates) it has a 50% higher latency (3 clocks versus 2 clocks). The goal behind such a small data cache was to, again, keep latencies low thus allowing for even higher clock speeds to be reached. As you are probably beginning to notice, NetBurst is designed with high clock speed CPUs in mind.

To make up for the small size of the L1 data cache, the Pentium 4's L2 cache is significantly improved. The size still remains as 256KB; however, data can now be transferred on every clock from the L2 cache instead of every other clock in the case of the Pentium III (Coppermine). The Pentium 4 still has a 256-bit datapath to its L2 cache. These two factors combined give the Pentium 4 a huge advantage over the Athlon (Thunderbird) in terms of how much data it can transfer from its L2 cache at any given time. However, the gap won't translate into a real-world performance gap until the processors dramatically increase in clock speed.

The one thing we have failed to mention thus far is the Pentium 4's L1 instruction cache, mainly because it does not have one. Instead, Intel introduced a very interesting feature known as an Execution Trace Cache (see Figure 1.22).

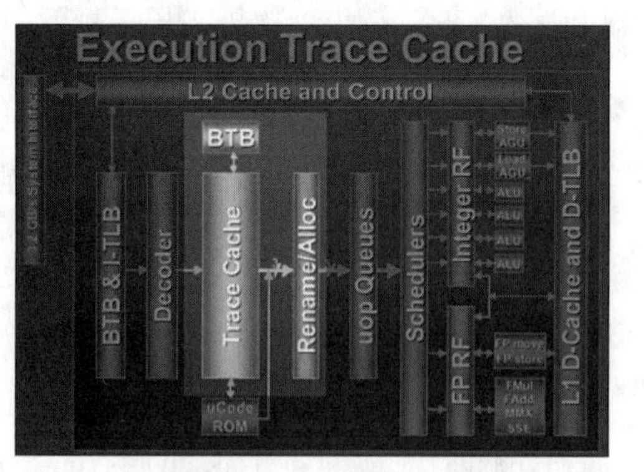

FIGURE 1.22
The Execution Trace Cache lies between the decoding stage and the first execution stage.

The decoder of any x86 CPU has one of the highest gate counts of all the pieces of logic in the core. This translates into quite a bit of time spent in the decoding stage when preparing to process an instruction either for the first time or after a branch misprediction.

The Execution Trace Cache acts as a middle-man between the decoding stage and the first stage of execution after the decoding has been completed. The trace cache essentially caches decoded micro-ops (the instructions after they have been fetched and decoded, thus ready for execution) so that instead of going through the fetching and decoding process all over again when executing a new instruction, the Pentium 4 can just go straight to the trace cache, retrieve its decoded micro-op and begin execution. On the Pentium 4, the 8-way set associative Trace Cache is said to be able to cache approximately 12K micro-ops.

This helps to hide the penalties associated with a mispredicted branch later on in the Pentium 4's 20-stage pipeline. Another benefit of the trace cache is that it caches the micro-ops in the predicted path of execution. So, if the Pentium 4 fetches three instructions from the trace cache, they are already presented in their order of execution. This adds potential for an incorrectly predicted path of execution of the cached micro-ops. However, the probability of this happening should be reduced because of the Pentium 4's highly advanced BPU.

One of the more interesting features of the Pentium 4's NetBurst architecture is its Hardware Prefetch that allows the processor to predict what it will need next and place it into cache before it is even requested. Keep this feature of the Pentium 4 in mind as we talk about the Pentium 4's platform in Chapter 2, "The Chipset: The PC's Crossing Guard."

Of course, the Pentium 4 features the same SSE instructions that were added to the Pentium III but it also supports a total of 144 new instructions that Intel calls SSE2. SSE2 enables the Pentium 4 to handle two 64-bit SIMD-INT operations and two double precision 64-bit SIMD-FP operations. This is in contrast to the two 32-bit SIMD operations the P6 architecture used to handle. The benefit of being capable of handling two 64-bit operations through SSE2 is greater performance and in the case of SIMD-FP instructions, the ability to handle greater precision floating point calculations which is very important when dealing with more professional level applications. For gamers, this won't be an immediate concern; however, in the future, as developers begin designing games with SSE2 in mind, this might change.

I've mentioned throughout this chapter that as clock speeds increase, the CPU's FSB must increase as well to meet the demands of the processor. With the Pentium 4 and NetBurst built to scale well above 2GHz, a high-speed FSB is a necessity. At the same time, when discussing FSB frequencies I mentioned that the Pentium 4's FSB operated at 100MHz. The one tidbit of information I left out was that the 100MHz FSB was "quad pumped" meaning that data is transferred four times on every clock, giving the Pentium 4's FSB the performance of a 400MHz FSB.

The Pentium 4's extremely high bandwidth FSB helps tremendously in newer 3D games, which depend on high-speed memory/FSB interactions. Likewise the hardware prefetch function of the processor aids in improving 3D gaming performance as well.

Tualatin: The Rebirth and Death of the Pentium III

When manufacturing on a new process, such as the 0.13-micron process, yields never start out at their highest during the initial production cycles. It takes months of perfection to increase yields, making it ideal to debut such new manufacturing processes on processors that ship in lower volumes. The desktop CPU market is unfortunately the largest CPU market for AMD/Intel, making it the worst market in which to debut a new technology. This is why AMD/Intel generally debut newer technologies in lower-volume segments, such as the server or mobile market. Historically, Intel has favored introducing such technological enhancements in the mobile market, as was the case with its first 0.13-micron CPUs.

Intel took the Mobile Pentium III (virtually identical to the desktop Pentium III, but with some power saving features) and put their 0.13-micron capabilities to use, shrinking the CPU, which was previously on a 0.18-micron process. This provided a die savings of about 50% and also enabled the Pentium III to run a lot cooler and reach much higher clock speeds. This core is known as the Tualatin core, but the processor carries the Pentium III-M designation (see Figure 1.23).

Intel also introduced this technology to the dying Pentium III desktop market. Because the Pentium III was being replaced aggressively by the Pentium 4 at the time, it made little sense for Intel to actively promote the Tualatin as a desktop solution. The Tualatin was really a mobile part brought to the desktop sector for introduction and will likely be brought to the Celeron later. The Tualatin was introduced to the desktop with two major improvements over the previous Coppermine-based Pentium IIIs. The 0.13-micron process enables the processor to run much cooler and reach even higher clock speeds (it was introduced at 1.13GHz and 1.2GHz). The smaller core decreases the surface of the core with which the heatsink comes in contact. This requires the use of an Integrated Heat Spreader (IHS), such as the Pentium 4. The second improvement is the addition of Data Prefetch Logic (DPL) to the Tualatin core, which gives it a 0%–5% increase in performance over an equivalently clocked Pentium III in most applications.

FIGURE 1.23
A Tualatin Pentium III processor (middle) compared to a Pentium 4 processor (left) and a Coppermine Pentium III processor (right).

Unfortunately, the Tualatin is held back by the 133MHz FSB of the platform which nothing can be done about. Remember that the DPL uses FSB bandwidth to prefetch data into the processor's cache; this is why it works so well on the Athlon/Pentium 4 platforms which have between two and three times the bandwidth of the Pentium III's FSB.

The real beauty of the Tualatin core is that it finds its way into the next-generation Celeron, making that platform much more competitive than the previous cores.

Northwood: 0.13-micron Goes Mainstream

The Northwood core is the first 0.13-micron Pentium 4 processor, implementing the same manufacturing process that was used to shrink the Coppermine Pentium III core. The beauty of the Northwood is that it dramatically reduces the cost of the Pentium 4's production because, again, the shift from a 0.18-micron process to a 0.13-micron process cuts die size by about 50%. Some of this die savings is lost because Intel outfitted the Northwood with a larger 512KB L2 cache which improves performance, 10%–15% over the 256KB L2 cache models (Willamette core).

The Northwood core is also able to pave the way for increased Pentium 4 clock speeds. This is obvious by its 2.2GHz launch speed and hitting 2.4GHz just a quarter later.

For more information on the Northwood core update to the Pentium 4 as well as its other performance enhancing features, visit `www.anandtech.com`.

The Gamer's CPU

Now that you know everything you could possibly want to know about the CPUs currently available, what should you, as a gamer, look for in a CPU?

The majority of today's games are 3D titles, and as a result, they deal with a good amount of floating-point calculations. Thus the first requirement for The Gamer's CPU is a strong FPU. What makes a strong FPU? By now you should be pretty familiar with what the basic requirements are. A fully pipelined unit that is properly optimized for the software you're going to be running is what you'll want to be looking for. But with AMD and Intel as the only major players in the market right now, you will rarely find either of them releasing a new CPU without a pipelined FPU or with an unusually slow FPU. This was much more of a concern in the days of the Cyrix 6x86 and the AMD K5/K6, which had poorly performing FPUs.

Cache, cache, and cache. A low latency, high-speed cache subsystem is definitely something you'll want to look for. Your new CPU doesn't necessarily have to have enough cache to store everything you possibly imagined in it. However, it must have enough to deal with the footprint of the applications and games you will be running. By today's standards, a 256KB L2 cache is commonplace, but in the future cache sizes of 512KB will be much more common. You will want to look at the architecture behind the cache subsystem of these CPUs and put yourself in the CPU manufacturer's shoes. What was AMD shooting for when it outfitted the Athlon with a 16-way set associative L2 cache? Or does the fact that the Athlon has only a 64-bit path to its L2 cache mean that higher–clock-speed Athlons will be L2 cache bus limited (in other words, the CPU-cache bandwidth is the bottleneck)?

A high-speed FSB is definitely a must when buying components for your new system. If you were to purchase a Pentium III EB (133MHz FSB) today with the hopes of it offering superb performance in tomorrow's titles, chances are that you're going to be FSB limited (held back by the performance of your FSB) somewhere down the line. In comparison, the Pentium 4's quad-pumped 100MHz FSB or the Athlon's 100MHz DDR FSB are much more attractive when looking at performance from a long-term standpoint. A higher speed FSB is also necessary when you have features such as Hardware Prefetch. Because the processor is requesting much more data to be sent over the FSB than normally would be, which is part of the reason why the Pentium 4 has such a high-speed FSB.

With today's CPUs running as high as 2GHz and those of tomorrow promising speeds two and three times faster, manufacturing processes must get finer and pipelines must get longer. Be careful of being an early adopter of a new technology when one of the main improvements is a longer pipeline. Although this longer pipeline will help guarantee future performance, it actually can penalize the technology upon its introduction. The best example of this is the Pentium 4. In quite a few cases, the Pentium 4 running at 1.5GHz was slower than the Pentium III at 1GHz, simply because the Pentium III was doing more while running at 1GHz (shorter pipeline = more work being done in a shorter period of time). In the long run, the Pentium 4 would win over the Pentium III because the Pentium III already had troubles running at 1.13GHz, but you should always beware when adopting such dramatically new technologies.

Another example of why being an early adopter can hurt you is the 0.13-micron Northwood-based Pentium 4 processors. They use a new type of socket known as Socket-478. This means early Pentium 4 adopters could not upgrade their Socket-423 processors to the Northwood Socket-478 processors without also replacing their motherboard. Obviously if you're running on a 5-year-old system and need to get a new system today, being an early adopter might be your best choice. However, if you upgrade regularly, this is something you should stay away from.

With pipelines growing in length with every major architecture change it is a necessity that your next CPU have a strong BPU (Branch Prediction Unit). Do your research, find out how accurate the BPU can predict branches and compare that to the penalty of a mispredict. Features like Intel's Execution Trace Cache are quite useful in negating the penalties of an extremely long pipeline, so keep an eye out for those as well. A lot of this information is available directly from the manufacturers, and also at the AnandTech Web site (`http://www.anandtech.com`).

Bandwidth- and latency-enhancing features, such as hardware prefetch and even integrated memory controllers, are also key features to look for in terms of finding a CPU that offers good gaming performance—especially 3D gaming.

Pay attention to how dependent CPUs are on the success of their SIMD instruction sets because these extensions to the x86 ISA require proper software support to be taken advantage of. Generally speaking, the best optimization for one architecture's SIMD instructions does not come until the architecture has been available for a while and the particular CPU has been in the hands of application/game developers long enough for them to optimize their software for the instructions. Because most games have a two-year development cycle, a CPU released today would take a while to gain support in games. Most developers, however, do work closely with the CPU manufacturers to implement architecture- and instruction-specific enhancements into their games as quickly as possible.

Finding Low-Cost Wonders: The Search for the Holy Grail

AMD and Intel both love to segment their product lines. They love to take one product, change the cache size or FSB, and market it as an inferior and cheaper solution for the cost conscious market. You, as an educated gamer, should learn to ignore the marketing of some of these solutions as "value chips" and find one that does most of what its older and more expensive brother will do, but at a lower cost.

The first requirement for finding a low-cost wonder is that it shouldn't be any different architecturally from the high-performance CPU on which it was based. The Celeron would never have been a good buy if it didn't have the strength of the Pentium II's FPU. Although it is rare that a manufacturer would change some major part of the architecture to make a low-cost variant, be wary of such a part should one appear on your radar.

Accepting a smaller L2 cache size is acceptable when looking for a lower-cost variant of a high-performance CPU, but there are a few things to look for here, as well. For starters, be sure the type of cache remains the same. This was a major issue when the Celeron got up to speed and everyone noticed that the Celeron's performance, even with a 100MHz FSB, wasn't able to approach that of the Pentium III. The reason for this performance disparity was because of the fact that the Celeron's L2 cache was not only smaller than the Pentium III's but it was also only a 4-way set associative L2 cache vs. the 8-way set associativity of the Pentium III's L2 cache. This is something you want to stay away from, because you will definitely not get the same performance as the more expensive CPU; and remember, the goal is to get the same performance or very similar performance without spending the extra money on the more expensive chip.

It is okay to sacrifice FSB speed for a lower-cost CPU, which was the case of some of the earlier Celerons that boasted only a 66MHz FSB while 100MHz FSB Pentium IIs had just been released. However, you will definitely want to *stay away* from solutions that have too great of a clock speed to effective FSB frequency ratio. By effective I mean that the Pentium 4's FSB is effectively operating at 400MHz, so the previous ratio would be 1500:400 or 3.75 for a Pentium 4 running at 1.5GHz. Keeping this ratio as low as possible will ensure that your CPU's performance won't be limited by your FSB. You will want to stay away from low-cost CPUs that have this ratio at 10 or above.

Another thing to keep in mind is that clock speed isn't the final determinant of the performance of your gaming PC. In fact, chances are that with a high-enough clocked CPU you will end up being limited by other components in your system before you find yourself needing a new CPU. The highest clocked CPUs almost always command a premium over those that are sometimes no more than 100MHz lower in speed. Although having the highest clocked CPU on the block will give you bragging rights, saving an extra $100 could buy you a better video card. What you quickly find out is that today's CPUs are really fast enough to run most of the games you play; it's your graphics card that often needs upgrading. For example, the Xbox, Microsoft's gaming console, has only a 733MHz Pentium III processor. However, it also has one of the most powerful graphics processors available, making it a killer gaming system.

➤ ***For more information about video cards, see Chapter 5, "The Video Card: A Gamer's Heart and Soul."***

What to Buy: Today's CPUs

You've just graduated from Anand's College of CPU Architecture, now it's time to actually put that knowledge to use. Keep in mind that the recommendations I'm going to make in this section are very time sensitive and they can change. For the most up-to-date information, I strongly suggest you take a look at AnandTech (`http://www.anandtech.com`), which enables you to get even more up-to-date information on a regular basis.

The main thing I want you to get out of this chapter is not which of today's CPUs are the best, but a true understanding of the intricacies of CPU architecture and what all the marketing jargon actually means. However, I do realize that you want a recommendation. Now that you know what to look for in a CPU, let's pick out the best buys in today's CPU market.

Cheap Upgrades

The king of the cheap upgrade CPU will have to be, without a doubt, the AMD Duron. You will want to pick up a Duron based on the core AMD has dubbed "Morgan." Luckily, these aren't hard to identify. All Durons boasting speeds faster than 900MHz use the Morgan core, so finding one won't be a problem.

The Duron is the ideal value CPU because the architecture and FSB are identical to its bigger brother (Athlon). The only difference is that the Duron has a smaller cache. The performance difference between the Duron and the Athlon at any given clock speed ranges from 0%–10% in the majority of games currently available.

High Performance/High Price Monsters

Because of its high-speed FSB and memory bus, as well as its hardware prefetch mechanism, the Pentium 4 has the greatest potential to deliver the absolute most in gaming performance. Especially above 2GHz, the Pentium 4 can truly shine in games.

Even at its introduction, the Pentium 4 was the fastest solution under *Quake III Arena*. Keep in mind, however, that CPU speed is only part of the equation. A good graphics card is also necessary for true gaming performance.

Price Versus Performance

The AMD Athlon continues to offer the best bang for your buck. AMD introduced a very aggressive pricing structure with the Athlon to gain market share. With approximately 30% desktop market share now, the Athlon has definitely done well in that respect. By continuing to price the processor competitively, AMD is able to offer quality performance at a reasonable price.

Tomorrow's CPUs: What to Look For

The one beautiful thing about the way the hardware industry works is that the high-performance, high-priced monsters of today are the ultra-cheap upgrades of tomorrow. But, of course, by the time that is true you don't want the ultra cheap upgrades, you want the monsters of tomorrow. So, how do you figure out what technology to watch for in your future PC?

It turns out that a good deal of the hardware that goes into the extremely high-cost servers eventually trickles down to the desktop markets in a matter of years. Provided that this continues to hold true, we can make some make some assumptions about what your future PCs will be running in terms of processors.

The current crop of processors we've been talking about thus far are all 32-bit processors. However, in the enterprise server markets we have actually seen 64-bit processors in use for a while now. With the introduction of Intel's Itanium and the upcoming introduction of AMD's 64-bit processor, code-named SledgeHammer, it is clear that 64-bit processors are on the horizon.

There is no doubt that we will see 64-bit architectures come down to the level of the desktop gaming PC. Remember when 4MB of memory was a lot to have on a computer? Well, there will come a time when 4GB is not thought of as a lot of memory much like how we laugh at 4MB having ever been a reasonable amount of memory for a respectable PC. A 64-bit CPU will allow for memory addressing beyond the ~4GB limit of today's 32-bit processors. This combined with 64-bit software, such as 64-bit Windows XP and other such applications will truly make 64-bit CPUs well suited for the gaming PC. However that reality is still a while away.

Multiprocessing: Are Two Heads Better Than One?

One server technology that might not necessarily be such a great move for a gamer to pursue is SMP, or Symmetric Multi Processing. The idea behind SMP is to have two or more CPUs in a system, thus increasing the processing power of the system significantly.

The problem with this is that to take advantage of the power of SMP, software support needs to be there. Although I won't get into the specifics of this, it comes down to the fact that very few games can take advantage of SMP, thus making it a waste of money for gamers.

Because of the generally high cost of implementing SMP in systems (two CPUs always costs more than one), developers are generally not seeing the return on the investment of time. It has always been theorized that eventually SMP will be a widespread technology used by everyone on a daily basis. If that day does come, it's still a while away. Another solution might be a bit more compelling, however.

SMT: A Better Way?

One of the biggest advantages SMP provides is that your system can now simultaneously process two "threads." On the most basic of levels, a single CPU can only work on one "thread" at a time, given to it by your software/OS. With a two-processor SMP system, your computer can now work on two threads at once. However, the performance improvement associated with going to two processors is far from the doubling you would expect. In fact, the performance improvement can be as little as 10% or 20% in many cases. There are obvious overheads such as calculating which processor gets what, that limit the performance improvement. One of the problems you often run into is that the efficiency of one processor running code isn't all that great to begin with, so having two doesn't mean that much.

In terms of efficiency, a technology known as Symmetric Multi Threading (SMT) is supposed to improve that. The beauty of SMT is that it allows the processor to execute more than a single thread at once. The theoretical number of instructions a processor can execute in a given clock cycle (IPC), compared to the processor's actual IPC, during real-world usage is generally a very high ratio indicating low efficiency or low usage of the architecture's potential. This is simply because the processor is not always kept "busy" and a good portion of its execution power is wasted.

Being able to concurrently execute, on a hardware level, multiple threads on a single processor dramatically increased the processor's efficiency—a tangible benefit of SMT technology.

You can expect SMT technology to filter down into a few desktop processors in the near future. Rumor has it that the desktop Pentium 4 will eventually get SMT, but we are unlikely to see that until sometime in mid to late 2002.

Chapter 2

The Chipset: The PC's Crossing Guard

Introduction to the Chipset

If the Central Processing Unit (CPU) is analogous with the brain of your computer, then it goes without saying that it must have some sort of neural network to connect to the rest of your system. In fact it does; in Chapter 1, "The Central Processing Unit: The Heart and Soul of the PC," you were introduced to the Front Side Bus (FSB), which is the CPU's only connection to the outside world. But where does that path lead? This chapter deals with just that in discussing what is known as the chipset.

The chipset is an interesting piece of hardware since it isn't something you can go out and buy like you can a CPU or a monitor. Instead, your chipset is already chosen for you when you purchase your motherboard (the board that your CPU, memory, and expansion cards plug into).

➤ ***For more information on motherboards, see Chapter 3, "The Motherboard: Low Rent Housing for the CPU and Chipset."***

So why study it? What role does it play in making your games (whether you're playing *High Heat Baseball* or *Warcraft III*)? Since your chipset is essentially what connects the CPU to the rest of the components in your system, as well as what connects those other components in your system to one another, there is quite a bit of performance-affecting technology that is contained within the confines of the chipset. Making a poor chipset selection could be deadly for your frame rates and you definitely don't want that.

Diagnosing a chipset limitation is much harder than doing so with a CPU, since you can't really "upgrade" your chipset once you buy your motherboard. Again, this is not a component you can go buy. The closest thing to a "chipset upgrade" is a relatively major upgrade of your system by replacing your motherboard. As time waits for no processor or motherboard, you will eventually have to do this, but we want to make sure that you make the best decision the first time around so you can hold off on that upgrade until it is absolutely necessary.

One thing to keep in mind before digging into any discussion on chipset functions and features is that there are a lot of acronyms to throw around (that are used quite frequently in this chapter). In Table 2.1, I've included a listing of the most common ones you should log in your mental Rolodex.

Table 2.1 Common Chipset Acronyms

Acronym	Meaning	Description
AGP	Accelerated Graphics Port	A dedicated port for graphics cards that offers up to 1.06GBps of bandwidth to the graphics card.
ACR	Audio and Communications Riser	Riser standard supported by Intel. Looks like a small AGP slot.
AMR	Audio and Modem Riser	Precursor to the ACR standard; supported by Intel. Looks like a small AGP slot.
BIOS	Basic Input/Output System	The first program to load when your PC boots, the BIOS contains settings about your hardware and provides hands-off control to your OS.
CNR	Communications and Networking Riser	Riser standard supported by VIA. Looks like a backwards PCI slot.
FSB	Front Side Bus	Connection between the North Bridge and the CPU.

Table 2.1 Continued

Acronym	Meaning	Description
FWH	Firmware Hub	A fancy name for the BIOS in chipsets that implement IHA.
ICH	I/O Controller Hub (Revisions: ICH1, ICH2, ICH3, ICH4)	The equivalent of the South Bridge in Intel 8xx series chipsets. Controls the PCI bus, IDE channels, USB, and so on.
IGP	Integrated Graphics Processor	The equivalent of the North Bridge in NVIDIA nForce chipsets. Features an integrated NVIDIA graphics core.
IHA	Intel Hub Architecture	Intel's chipset architecture. Features three "hubs": an I/O Controller Hub, Memory Controller Hub and a Firmware Hub, all connected by an interlink bus.
MCH	Memory Controller Hub	The equivalent of the North Bridge in Intel 8xx series chipsets. Has the FSB interface, memory controller, AGP Controller and sometimes integrated graphics (this is known as the GMCH).
MCP	Media and Communications Processor	The equivalent of the South Bridge in NVIDIA nForce chipsets. See ICH for more information on features.
PCI	Peripheral Component	A bus used for connecting Interconnect peripheral devices.

Bandwidth—Keep It Moving Folks

In Chapter 1, I introduced two very important concepts: latency and frequency. Basically, the amount of time it takes to get a piece of data from one point to another is known as latency and the speed at which it travels is relative to the frequency of the medium (in most cases a bus) on which it is traveling. The one metric that I haven't introduced is the amount of data that can get from point A to point B. We know how long it takes to get there, and how quickly it can get there, but computers don't deal with one piece of data at a time. They deal with massive amounts. This is where we run into a concept known as bandwidth.

Simply put, bandwidth is the amount of data that can get from one point to another in a certain amount of time. Bandwidth is generally referred to in Megabits (1,000,000 bits), Megabytes (1,000,000 bytes or 8,000,000 bits), or

Gigabytes (1,000 Megabytes) per second. The common representation of these units is Mbps (Megabits per second) or MBps (Megabytes per second) or for short, MBps (Megabytes per second or GBps for Gigabytes per second). Be careful when looking at bandwidth figures for hardware components since the difference between Mbps and MBps can be huge.

Bandwidth is also very easy to calculate. It is simply the product of the width of the bus, the frequency at which the bus operates, and the amount of data that is transferred on every clock. For example, as discussed in Chapter 1, the later series of Pentium III processors ran at a 133MHz FSB frequency. This bus happens to be 64-bits wide and data is transferred once on every clock. Plugging these three facts into our bandwidth calculator results in the following equation:

Note

Bandwidth is critical to performance, especially 3D game performance. For the most part, every day applications don't require much bandwidth. That's because these applications normally involve editing a document or browsing the Internet, two very low bandwidth actions. When playing a 3D game however, you've constantly got triangle information to send, AI and physics calculations to make, and all that requires bandwidth. The more bandwidth you have between any two components that are being used such as your CPU and your system memory, the faster your gaming performance will be.

(Bus Width) × (Frequency) × (Data Transferred per Clock) = Bandwidth in Mbps

For a Pentium III EB (E = Coppermine core; B = 133MHz FSB):

(64-bit bus width) × (133MHz FSB frequency*) × (Data Transferred 1x every Clock) = 8533.3Mbps FSB bandwidth

This shows us that the Pentium III's FSB has a *peak* available bandwidth of 8533.3 Megabits per second. This means that every second the bus can transfer, at *most*, 8533.3 Megabits of data to/from the CPU. Now I mentioned before that bandwidth is generally referred to in terms of MBps, so let's do just that. As discussed in Chapter 1, there are 8 bits in 1 byte, so to convert Megabits per second to Megabytes per second, simply divide by 8.

For a Pentium III EB:

(8533.3Mbps FSB bandwidth) / (8 bits in 1 byte) = 1066.6 MBps or approximately 1GBps FSB bandwidth

So in a much more illustrative number, the Pentium III's 133MHz FSB can transfer at *most*, 1066.6MBps to/from the CPU, which we round off to approximately 1GBps. While it will always depend on the game in question, this kind of performance is good enough for most of today's games to get by. However, most games are hungry for even more bandwidth, and that hunger will continue to increase. Let's look at one more example where data is transferred more than once on every clock. This is the case with the AMD Athlon's EV6 FSB which, as we mentioned before, operates on a Double Data Rate (DDR) basis where data is transferred twice per clock.

**Note: This number is actually 133.33333... but by convention it is rounded to 133MHz.*

For an AMD Athlon-C (C = 133MHz FSB):

(Bus Width) × (Frequency) × (Data Transferred per Clock) / 8 = Bandwidth in MBps

(64-bit bus width) × (133MHz FSB frequency*) × (Data Transferred 2x every Clock) / 8 = 2133.3 MBps ~ 2.1GBps FSB bandwidth

So as you can see, thanks to its DDR implementation, the Athlon's FSB has twice the FSB bandwidth as the Pentium III. What you'll also notice, from either of these examples, is that FSB bandwidth is *independent of CPU clock speed.* This should illustrate to you why it is common practice to increase FSB speed as clock speed increases. At 450MHz the Pentium III had the same FSB as a Pentium III at 600MHz. Although the CPU was running 33% faster, it was still being fed data at the same rate. The reason this happens is that the processor's clock speed is, as discussed in Chapter 1, a function of the FSB frequency. The clock multiplier, multiplied by the FSB frequency, yields the processor clock speed.

Manufacturers also don't like to wait to boost FSB bandwidth until it's immediately necessary; instead they plan ahead. The difference in performance between a Pentium III 600 with a 100MHz FSB and a 133MHz FSB was relatively small, but at 1GHz the difference in performance is noticeably larger. Table 2.2 shows a cross-section of different processors and how the design of their FSB effects their performance.

Table 2.2 Front Side Bus Bandwidth Greatly Depends on the FSB Width, Its Frequency, and the Number of Times Data Is Transferred in Each Clock Cycle

	FSB Width	FSB Frequency	Data Transfers per Clock	Theoretical FSB Bandwidth
AMD Athlon	64-bit	100MHz	2	1.6GBps
AMD Athlon-C	64-bit	133MHz	2	2.1GBps
Intel Pentium III	64-bit	100MHz	1	0.800GBps
Intel Pentium III B	64-bit	133MHz	1	1.06GBps
Intel Pentium 4	64-bit	100MHz	4	3.2GBps

Don't Believe the "Peak Bandwidth" Hype

Every time I referred to the bandwidth we calculated in the previous section I referred to it as "peak" available bandwidth or the "most" you could transfer at any given time. The reason I say this is because those numbers are only somewhat useful in getting an idea of how well "fed" your CPU is. Granted a FSB with 2.1GBps of available bandwidth will probably offer more real-world bandwidth than one capable of transferring at 800MBps. However, it is very rare that you actually see 100% bus bandwidth utilization in a real-world scenario. If you are seeing 100% bandwidth utilization, it could mean that you are in fact FSB limited.

Although you have no sure fire way to know if you're FSB limited, you can always compare performance between two of the same processors, clocked at different speeds with all other factors held constant (FSB, memory bus, and so on) and see what kind of scaling you get between the two CPUs. If you test a 1.4GHz CPU and a 1.0GHz CPU and note that the increase in performance from 1.0GHz to 1.4GHz is only 5% in spite of the 40% clock speed increase, then there is definitely a limitation somewhere. By choosing your benchmark properly and by eliminating as many bottlenecks as possible, you might be able to identify whether the culprit is indeed an FSB limitation. For more information on benchmarking, look at Chapter 14, "Tweaking and Overclocking: Turbo-Charging Your PC."

There are a number of different types of overhead that reduce the amount of utilized FSB bandwidth including the type of applications or games you are running. The more complex your game happens to be, the more data your CPU has to crunch, thus resulting in greater FSB bandwidth utilization.

Other parts of your system can limit the performance of your FSB as well. If your memory is not capable of taking up the full bandwidth of the FSB with data being sent to the processor, your FSB never has a chance to approach 100% bandwidth utilization. This introduces the idea of memory bandwidth, which I discuss in greater detail in Chapter 5, "The Video Card: A Gamer's Heart and Soul."

The key point to remember here is that the moons definitely have to be in alignment to get 100% bandwidth utilization not only in respect to your FSB, but in respect to every other bus present in your system. There are always limitations to overcome and there are always weak links in your system. The goal, obviously, is to be able to identify those weak links and reduce their effects as much as possible.

It's Okay to Want to Be the Same

Just as your FSB operates at a certain clock (sometimes multiplied by the amount of data transferred per clock), other parts of your system operate at their own clock frequencies. While none of these components match the frequency of your CPU, quite a few of them operate at frequencies close to that of the FSB.

One thing you notice is that manufacturers like to make these various components, and particularly buses, run synchronously with the FSB. There is good reason for this; one of the pros is that you decrease the number of situations in which your FSB cannot be supplied with enough data from another bus (assuming that they are all of the same width). Another very important thing to take into consideration is that when the frequency of a bus that interacts with the FSB is operating at a synchronized frequency with the FSB, the latency of data transferred between the two is at a minimum. If the two are operating out of sync, an additional latency penalty is incurred.

The best way to think of this is as the difference between having a conversation with someone when you're placed face to face across a table versus being offset by a few seats and trying to hold the same conversation.

Keep this idea of synchronizing buses in mind as we discuss the various buses that are controlled by or interact with the chipset in the coming sections.

North Versus South

I started out this chapter introducing the chipset as the hardware that lies on the other side of the FSB; however that isn't entirely true. The term chipset usually encompasses a handful of chips (hence the name chip*set*), all of which lie on the other side of the FSB but only one of which directly connects to the FSB.

Note

The first Athlon chipsets used the PCI bus to connect the North and South Bridges. AMD's 760MPX chipset (a high-end server/workstation chipset) used a 64-bit PCI bus to connect the two chips, however with the advent of NVIDIA's nForce, future AMD chipsets will use Hyper Transport technology to connect the bridges.

In modern day technology there are actually two major parts to any chipset, these two parts have historically been called the North and the South Bridges. Both of these chips act as traffic controllers. None of the instructions in your games are calculated by these chips. They merely take the instructions and data being executed and send them on their merry way.

The North Bridge is by far the more important of the two chips. The North Bridge is the actual chip that lies on the other side of the FSB opposite the CPU. This means that the North Bridge does also contain some bus logic that is used to communicate with the CPU. It also means that CPUs with different types of buses (not necessarily different frequencies, although the same does apply there in some cases) require different North Bridges. The general trend is that for every new CPU architecture there will be a new North Bridge (for example, one for the P6 architecture, one for the NetBurst architecture used in the Pentium 4, and so on) from a chipset manufacturer. During the period of the architecture's reign the chipset manufacturer will provide different versions of the North Bridge, often times offering new features while keeping most of the North Bridge core the same. This is akin to what CPU manufacturers do in various successors to a particular processor, such as the differences between the Pentium III Katmai and the Pentium III Coppermine. Both processors shared the same basic core, but as the technology became available Intel was able to move the L2 cache on-die giving the Coppermine version a considerable performance boost. Likewise, with chipsets, as the technology becomes available for higher performing features to be implemented, chipset manufacturers do just that.

The bus width and frequency (bandwidth) of the FSB is identical on both ends of the bus, the end that interfaces with the CPU as well as the end that connects to the North Bridge.

In addition to making the connection to your CPU, the North Bridge makes three other connections with other components. In Figure 2.1 you can see how the North Bridge connects to these other components.

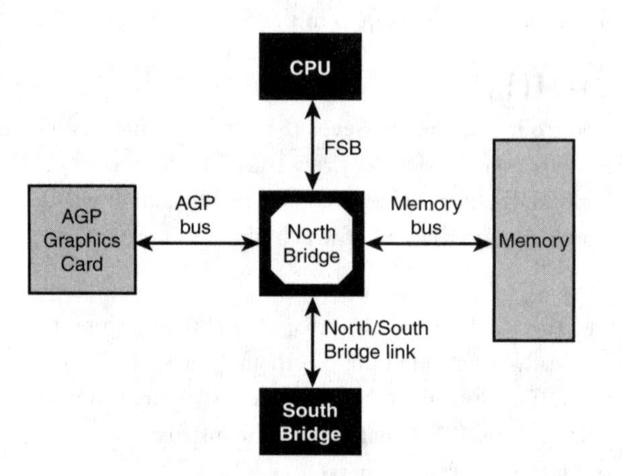

FIGURE 2.1
The role of the North Bridge is to connect all of the major components in your system together.

In current chipsets the North Bridge has a bus connecting it to your graphics card; this bus is known as the AGP bus. Some low cost North Bridges have an integrated graphics core eliminating the need for an external AGP bus; however these integrated graphics cores are generally poor performers when it comes to games and are generally avoided.

➤ ***For more information about integrated graphics, see Chapter 5, "The Video Card: A Gamer's Heart and Soul."***

The third connection the North Bridge makes is via another bus to your system's main memory. This is known as the memory bus.

The final connection that the North Bridge makes is with the South Bridge. This connection used to be made via a bus known as the PCI bus. However, this bus has since been replaced with one that is much more specialized for the task. In most chipsets this bus has a peak bandwidth rate of 266MBps. For a look at the actual motherboard locations for each of these components, see Figure 2.2.

While the North Bridge handles the juggling of traffic to and from the "main" components in your system, the South Bridge handles more of the peripheral responsibilities. The South Bridge features provisions for peripheral expansion cards as well as your USB/keyboard/mouse controllers. The South Bridge also has an integrated IDE (Integrated Drive Electronics) controller which is a hard drive controller for your storage drives.

The South Bridge, unlike the North Bridge, is CPU independent. Notice that it simply features a connection to the North Bridge and never directly interfaces with the AGP or memory buses. This means that manufacturers

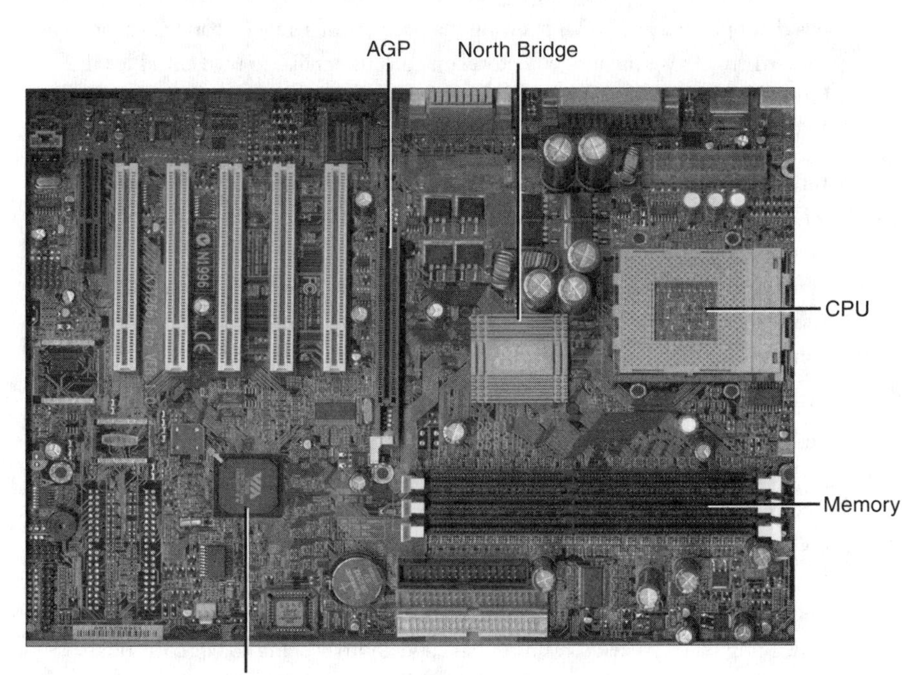

FIGURE 2.2
As you can see, the North Bridge of this MSI motherboard does indeed connect all of the major components that it houses. The traces going to/from the North Bridge are its means of communication with the components it's connecting.

Note

Being *pin-compatible* means that the two chips can be used in the same design with relatively minor changes or sometimes none at all.

can often choose one South Bridge for an entire line of motherboards regardless of for what processors the motherboards are built. This helps to reduce the cost of manufacturing since only one part needs to be designed around and the chipset manufacturers do whatever is possible to make sure that their different South Bridges are as *pin-compatible* as they can be.

Intel's Hub Architecture

In 1999, Intel made an effort to do away with the North/South Bridge architecture and introduced what they called the Intel Hub Architecture (IHA). Since then, all Intel chipsets have followed this Hub Architecture philosophy and although the name is different, IHA is really no different from the North/South Bridge chipset setup we just discussed.

Originally IHA set itself apart from the conventional North/South Bridge chipset architecture in that the connection between the two "bridges" was not the PCI bus as it was in the case of previous architectures. The problem with using the PCI bus as a connection between the two bridges was simply that it does not offer enough bandwidth. The PCI bus, at the time, was a 32-bit wide bus that operated at 33.3MHz giving it a peak transfer rate or bandwidth of 133.3MBps. As we mentioned before, manufacturers like to plan ahead for the future so buses don't become bottlenecks. Eventually, this meant that the existing 133MBps connection between the two bridges had to offer more bandwidth.

Intel went about it by introducing a special "interlink" bus (see Figure 2.3). This bus was 8bits in width and operated at 133MHz, yet it enables data to be transferred twice on every clock giving it an effective peak bandwidth of 266MBps. The PCI bus, which is used for many peripherals such as Sound Cards, became an extension of the South Bridge instead of being used to connect the North and South Bridges.

An interesting thing to note is that Intel went for a narrower, yet higher speed bus as opposed to simply widening the bus to increase its transfer rate. This is an increasingly common trend that you see later in this book. The trend is towards more serialized operation (sending data bit by bit in a long, but very quick stream) versus the more conventional parallel operation that we are used to (the wider is better mentality). There are a number of reasons for Intel's drive in this direction, one being because of their vision of the future of computers as depending on serialized streams of data and another being to cut costs (it all comes back to the almighty dollar). We will get into greater detail regarding this topic in the next chapter. For now, just remember that the width of a bus directly translates into the number of pins necessary on a North Bridge.

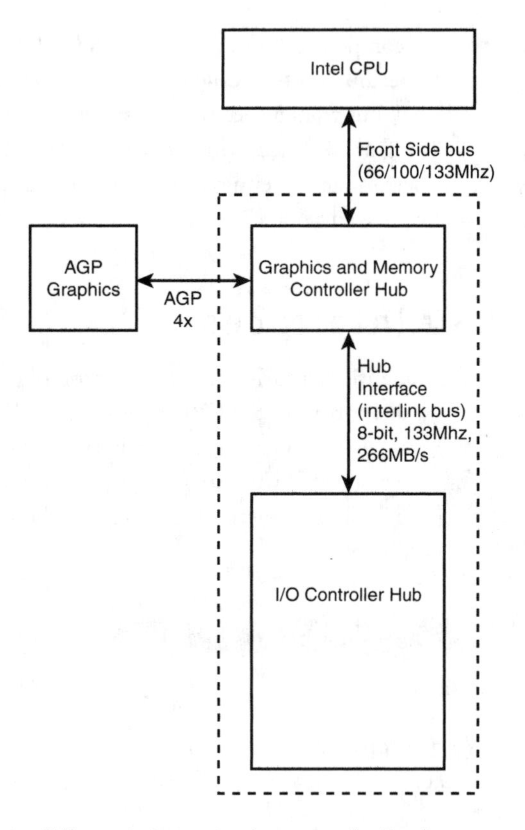

FIGURE 2.3
Intel's Hub Architecture improved upon the conventional North/South Bridge design by introducing "hubs" connected by a high speed interlink bus.

This interlink bus was the main differentiating point between the Intel chipsets of the past and the Intel chipsets of the present. All previous Intel chipsets (for the P6 architecture) went under the i4xx series (such as the i440BX sometimes just referred to as the BX chipset), while all Intel Hub Architecture chipsets were labeled as i8xx (such as the i815) series where the xx varied according to different chipset models.

The name Intel Hub Architecture comes from the fact that Intel essentially renamed the North Bridge and South Bridge to the Memory Controller Hub (MCH) and the I/O Controller Hub (ICH). The new names made much more sense than just North Bridge and South Bridge, as you can probably tell. There is actually a third component in the IHA, the Firmware Hub (FWH). This "hub" is basically an IHA name for the BIOS.

➤ ***For more information on the BIOS, see Chapter 3, "The Motherboard: Low Rent Housing for the CPU and Chipset."***

The MCH still connects to the AGP (Accelerated Graphics Port), memory and front side buses and the ICH still maintains the same duties as the South Bridge did.

A competing chipset manufacturer, VIA Technologies, later adapted a similar interlink bus they called V-Link. In fact, V-Link is identical to Intel's interlink bus from a specification standpoint in that it is an 8-bit wide bus, running at 133MHz, with a transfer rate of 266MBps. In terms of real-world performance, neither of these bus types seems to have a significant performance advantage.

FSB Interfaces

I mentioned earlier that the first job of the North Bridge/MCH is to provide a direct path to the CPU by way of the Front Side Bus (FSB). You should also, by this point, be relatively familiar with the different FSB interfaces that are associated with the various processors. If you need a refresher, though, see Table 2.3 where I briefly review the various interfaces that pertain to chipsets.

Table 2.3 A Comparison of Front Side Bus Interfaces

FSB	Bus Width	Operating Frequencies	CPU Compatibility Interface
GTL/GTL+/AGTL/ AGTL+	64-bit	66–133MHz	Intel Pentium Pro, Pentium II, Pentium III, Celeron
AGTL/AGTL+	64-bit	100MHz+ (Quad-Pumped)	Intel Pentium 4
EV6	64-bit	100–200MHz (DDR)	AMD Athlon, Duron

The Pentium II, Pentium III, and Celeron all use Intel's GTL+ FSB interface. This bus is 64 bits wide and operates at 66MHz, 100MHz, or 133MHz and transfers data once per clock. The bandwidth figures are 533MBps, 800MBps, and 1GBps respectively.

The Pentium 4 uses a version of the GTL+ FSB interface except, as I mentioned in Chapter 1, it is quad-pumped. This means that data is transferred four times every clock. The bus is 64 bits wide and operates at 100MHz resulting in an effective transfer rate of 3.2GBps.

The Athlon (and the Duron) uses the EV6 FSB interface that is a DDR FSB, meaning that data is transferred twice per clock. The EV6 bus as implemented for the Athlon is 64 bits wide and operates at either 100MHz or 133MHz, resulting in peak transfer rates of 1.6GBps and 2.1GBps respectively.

Graphics Controller

The second function of the North Bridge/MCH is to provide an interface to your graphics card. Your graphics card, simply put, is what handles the display of the text and images you see on your screen. Obviously the card does much more than that but I will leave that explanation for Chapter 5. The most common interface for a graphics card today is using the Accelerated Graphics Port, or AGP.

The AGP bus connects the North Bridge/MCH to the AGP slot on your motherboard. This bus is what allows your CPU to communicate with your graphics card, and it is what allows your graphics card to interact with your system memory (it also has memory on the card itself, but when it runs out it looks no further than your system memory for storage). The AGP bus is 32 bits wide and operates at a frequency of 66MHz. This frequency is derived directly from the FSB meaning that it can vary with the FSB. The AGP operating frequency must remain at 66MHz, but if your FSB is at 100MHz, 133MHz or even higher, the only way to keep the AGP at 66MHz is by dividing the FSB by some number. This wouldn't be a problem if the AGP bus ran off of its own clock but that's not the easiest thing to implement. The fewer independent clocks you have in your board layout, the easier it is to implement. Chipset manufacturers thus implement certain divisors into the North Bridge/MCH of their chipsets that will look at the FSB frequency and apply the appropriate divider to keep the AGP bus running at or close to its 66MHz specification. This is true for a number of other buses in the system, such as the memory bus and the PCI bus (except the PCI bus divider is contained within the South Bridge). In the case of a 100MHz FSB, the AGP bus is set to run at FSB Clock * 2/3 and in the case of a 133MHz FSB the AGP bus is set to run at FSB Clock * 1/2.

There are various AGP operating modes that determine the bandwidth of the bus. The current modes are AGP 1X, AGP 2X, and AGP 4X. The multiplier listed at the end of the name (for example, 2X) indicates how many times data is transferred per clock across the AGP bus. This means that for AGP 2X the bus is capable of a peak transfer rate of 533MBps and for AGP 4X the bus offers ~1GBps of bandwidth. Again, do keep in mind that these figures are no more than theoretical and the real-world bandwidth usage statistics can be significantly different. So while AGP 4X seems to offer a noticeable amount of bandwidth to your graphics card when compared to AGP 2X, the performance difference might be next to nothing.

There is also a specification known as AGP Pro, which is nothing more than a higher powered version of AGP 4X (see Figure 2.4). By higher powered, I mean that it is capable of delivering more power to the graphics card. Its bandwidth and performance characteristics are identical to AGP 4X. There has been very little use of AGP Pro in the computer industry as a whole, and absolutely no use of it in the gaming industry as it is mainly intended for the professional graphics cards with significantly higher power demands than consumer/gaming graphics solutions. The higher power demands are met with two forms of AGP Pro called AGP Pro50 and AGP Pro110. AGP Pro50 delivers 50W of power to the graphics card, while AGP Pro110 can deliver up to 110W of power. For comparison, most 3D accelerators consume less than 10W of power because they're not burdened with having to drive multiple processors or those with unusually high power requirements. AGP Pro is backward compatible with all other AGP formats. This means that you can use AGP 1X, 2X, and 4X cards in an AGP Pro slot, but the contrary does not apply. Since even the most powerful gaming graphics cards don't need as much power as AGP Proffers, this might not matter much to you.

FIGURE 2.4
AGP 4X Slot versus AGP Pro Slot.

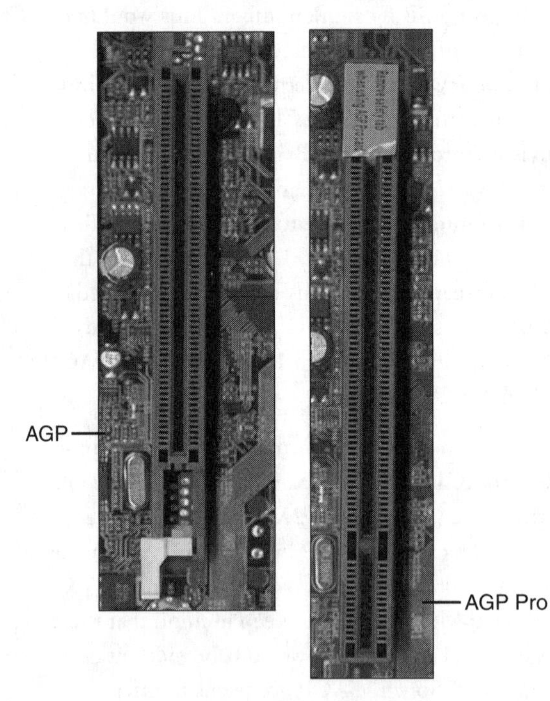

Integrated Versus External Graphics: What Gamers Want

I mentioned earlier that some North Bridges offer an actual graphics core integrated into the North Bridge. Although this would seem like a great idea, it wasn't meant for gamers at all. The idea of integrating a graphics core into the North Bridge (or MCH) is to provide an extremely low cost platform for the value PC markets (sub-$1,000 or sub-$600). Because the goal happens to be to keep costs low, chipsets with integrated graphics very rarely provide the best performing graphics cores in their designs.

Recently a number of graphics chip manufacturers have entered the PC chipset market with chipsets that do feature integrated graphics cores from their high performance gaming graphics cards. While this is a step up in terms of integrated graphics performance, your best option as a high performance gamer is to stick with your own external graphics card. By external I mean external to the North Bridge (but internal to your PC case, of course).

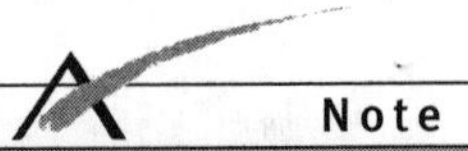

Note

In the case of NVIDIA's nForce, the rule of thumb to stay away from integrated graphics solutions doesn't apply nearly as well since the nForce's integrated graphics is quite powerful and the rest of the chipset is highly desirable.

It used to be the case that having integrated video meant there was no possibility for upgrading your video at a later date, but the i815 chipset changed all that. Now, if you are using the integrated video, the external AGP slot is disabled. However, if you would like to upgrade your video you can stick with the AGP slot on your motherboard, which disables the internal video. This only works on certain chipsets such as the i815 and NVIDIA's nForce. If this wasn't possible, the motherboard wouldn't have an AGP slot in the first place, so that's the easiest way to tell if it is upgradable.

In the case of IHA chipsets, one with integrated graphics does not feature an MCH; rather it features a GMCH or Graphics and Memory Controller Hub. There are some chipsets that offer both integrated graphics as well as an external AGP interface that disables the integrated graphics if used. If possible you'll want to avoid these solutions since you're essentially paying for an integrated graphics core that you're not going to be using.

Memory Controller

One of the most performance critical jobs the North Bridge/MCH has is to provide an interface to your system memory (refer to Figure 2.2 for an example of where these are located in relation to each other). It does so through the use of a memory controller that is located on the chip itself that provides an interface to the main memory in your system. Memory, as you should be able to guess by the name, is where data is temporarily stored on your PC. Your CPU uses it, your graphics card uses it, and all of the games you run on your PC use it as well. When you're running a game, the data that the CPU is crunching on is pulled to it from your memory.

Two systems having identically clocked CPUs and the same graphics cards and peripherals, but using different motherboards with different chipsets can exhibit widely different performance levels because of the superiority or inferiority of one memory controller to another. The performance differences caused by a memory controller and the type of memory interface it utilizes can be tremendous; I am talking about figures in the 20%–50% range.

One of the biggest examples of this was with the Pentium 4. As I mentioned in Chapter 1, the Pentium 4 is a memory bandwidth dependent processor and luckily its chipset's (i850) memory subsystem offers up to 3.2GBps of bandwidth when used with PC800 RDRAM (see Chapter 4 for more information on RAM types). However, Intel's entry level Pentium 4 chipset, the i845, only offers PC133 SDRAM support which instead of offering 3.2GBps of memory bandwidth can only provide 1.06GBps of memory bandwidth. This results in a 20%–30% performance delta between the two, although it's the same processor, with the same devices, the same clock speed, and running on chipsets made by the same manufacturer.

While I will get into the various pros and cons of the different memory types, on the most basic levels there are two types of memory controllers used on chipsets today—SDRAM and RDRAM memory controllers.

In terms of SDRAM memory controllers there are two major types as well—regular or Single Data Rate (SDR) SDRAM and Double Data Rate (DDR) SDRAM controllers. As you should be able to tell by now, DDR SDRAM basically transfers data twice per clock as opposed to once per clock in the case of regular SDRAM. SDRAM memory controllers in today's chipsets generally offer a 64-bit memory bus. However, more recently, chipsets from NVIDIA, for example, have offered a 128-bit memory bus. The difference is that the latter offers more memory bandwidth, but it also drives the cost up. Another interesting thing to consider is that a 64-bit DDR SDRAM memory bus operating at 100MHz offers the same theoretical memory bandwidth as a 128-bit SDR SDRAM memory bus operating at 100MHz. There is a slight loss of bandwidth due to inherent inefficiencies of DDR, but it is quite common to see manufacturers opting for a narrower bus and using DDR technology to increase bandwidth. Common operating frequencies for SDRAM and DDR SDRAM buses are 100MHz and 133MHz.

The basis behind RDRAM technology is geared much more towards serialized operation in that the RDRAM memory bus is only 16bits wide. However, it operates at up to 400MHz and transfers data twice every clock. The pros of this type of design are increased bandwidth and low implementation cost on a board level. Unfortunately, one of the major cons to the RDRAM architecture is that it generally features much higher latency than SDRAM. One benefit of RDRAM that helps counteract this problem is that multiple 16-bit channels of RDRAM can be connected in parallel to increase the bandwidth (and decrease latency) without resulting in too great of a cost. This is because the interfaces are each only 16bits wide. We will get into more SDRAM versus RDRAM discussions in Chapter 4.

There has also been talk about integrating memory into the North Bridge/MCH to provide a small amount of extremely fast memory (much like the CPU's cache). However, none of the major players have actually shown off an implementation of such a design.

Since it is a function of the North Bridge/MCH to determine the speed at which your memory bus runs, it is usually best to opt for a frequency (if given the option) that is synchronous with your FSB, allowing for lower latency operation.

Even though two North Bridges/MCHs might implement a similar memory controller, the performance of the two can be significantly different. Different chipset manufacturers have different memory controllers and some designs are simply more mature than others. I will provide the tools to investigate such differences in Chapter 14.

> **Note**
>
> Not only is the frequency/bandwidth of your memory subsystem controlled by the chipset, so is the amount of memory you can have as well as the type/size of memory modules that you can install.
>
> The configuration in which you install memory modules is also often governed by the chipset. For example, in a dual channel RDRAM setup, RDRAM modules must be installed in pairs because of the two separate RDRAM channels.

Putting the I/O in ICH

As I mentioned earlier, the South Bridge/ICH handles most of the peripheral functions in the system (refer to Figure 2.2). Intel refers to this part of the chipset as the I/O Controller Hub (ICH) for good reason—it handles a lot of the input/output in your system.

Integrated IDE Controller

One of the primary functions of the South Bridge/ICH is to provide an integrated IDE controller (see Figure 2.5). This IDE controller provides two IDE channels, each channel being able to support a maximum of two devices for a total of four devices supported by the integrated controller. By devices we mean anything that requires an IDE or ATAPI interface such as hard drives, CD-ROM drives, DVD-drives, and so on.

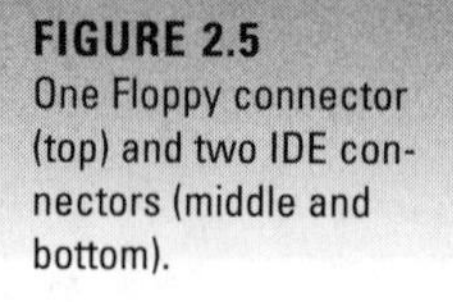

FIGURE 2.5
One Floppy connector (top) and two IDE connectors (middle and bottom).

Currently the most common integrated IDE controller in South Bridges/ICHs is one that complies with the Ultra ATA/100 specification. This specification governs the maximum transfer rate (or bandwidth) allocated to each device connected to the controller. For example, in the case of the ATA/100 spec the peak transfer rate is 100MBps. The previous standard was Ultra ATA/66 that, as you may guess, governed the max transfer rate at 66.6MBps.

These transfer rates aren't too much to be concerned with however, because no IDE devices transfer at rates even close to 100MBps. In fact, most IDE hard drives sustain transfers in the 40MBps–50MBps range and CD-ROM/DVD drives don't even come close to those levels. In the future, transfer rates of 100MBps and beyond will be commonplace, but at this point in time don't get too impressed by the high numbers.

Remember when we talked about the connection between the North Bridge and South Bridge being a potential limitation? Well that connection used to be made by the PCI bus, which offered 133MBps of bandwidth. Using the figures we just discussed, two relatively fast hard drives alone would eat up close to 75% of that bandwidth and we haven't even looked at the requirements of your other peripherals. If you weren't sure before, this should help illustrate for you the need for a higher bandwidth connection between the North and South Bridges. At 266MBps the interlink and V-Link buses that Intel and VIA use should be enough to last for some time to come.

What's After ATA/100?

The future of integrated IDE controllers is actually a very interesting one. After ATA/100, most manufacturers will be switching over to the Serial ATA spec. Serial ATA, as the name indicates, is yet another transition towards more serialized data transfers. A regular IDE channel features 26 signaling pins per channel because it is a parallel interface. However, a Serial ATA channel features no more than 4 signaling pins, because of its serial nature (see Figure 2.6).

Serial ATA will allow for much higher transfer rates; however it will definitely take some time for the market to become fully adapted to the Serial ATA standard. Once the transition is complete, manufacturers contributing to the standard expect that Serial ATA will last at least 10 years.

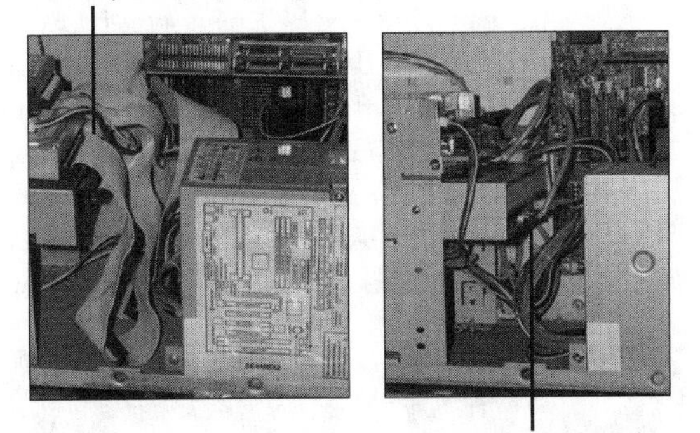

FIGURE 2.6
A system using parallel IDE ribbon cables (left) and one using Serial ATA cables (right).

To facilitate the transition from the standard parallel ATA spec to Serial ATA, there will be adapters that allow for the conversion from parallel ATA to Serial ATA. Unfortunately, the performance benefits Serial ATA offers will be negated by the use of such an adapter. Additional performance hits might be incurred by the translation process from serial to parallel ATA signaling.

Note

In mid-2001 Serial ATA 1X was made available and offered a transfer rate of 1.5Gbps or ~ 190MBps. Higher speed Serial ATA specs will be released as time goes on.

Peripheral Buses: PCI and Its Variants

Another very important duty of the South Bridge/ICH is to provide a connection to the various peripheral buses in your system. By far the most common peripheral bus used in desktop PCs is the Peripheral Component Interconnect bus or PCI bus. I introduced you to the PCI bus earlier when discussing the bus that used to connect the North and South Bridges. Indeed, this is the same PCI bus.

The PCI bus is a 32-bit wide bus that operates at 33MHz allowing for a peak transfer rate of 133MBps (see Figure 2.7). The types of devices that use the PCI bus are Sound Cards, Modems, Network cards, and high-speed storage adapters. Before the days of AGP graphics cards, the PCI bus was also used as a bus for graphics cards (and in some cases it still is). The graphics cards were the first to get their own dedicated bus after 3D applications and games really took off. The demands of these types of software made the graphics card very much a bandwidth hog on the PCI bus.

There is not much to the PCI bus; however, as is the case with many of the buses we have talked about, it eventually becomes a bottleneck. It has already become a bottleneck for most high-end servers and workstations, requiring the introduction of two new PCI extensions—PCI-64 and PCI-X.

As the name implies, PCI-64 is a 64-bit extension to the PCI specification (see Figure 2.8). The bus can operate at either 33MHz or 66MHz, and it does require a different slot. The specification is backwards compatible in that a 32-bit PCI card will work in a 64-bit PCI slot, however a PCI-64 card won't work in a 32-bit PCI slot if it specifically requires a PCI-64 bus. At 33MHz, the PCI-64 bus offers twice as much bandwidth as the PCI bus does and at 66MHz it offers four times the bandwidth.

FIGURE 2.7
32-bit PCI Slots.

More recently, PCI-X has become the higher bandwidth peripheral bus of choice for higher end systems. A trend you definitely notice is what is commonplace in higher end systems (for example, servers and professional workstations) eventually filters down, to the desktop platform. It will still be a while before we see PCI-X used in gaming PCs; however it is a technology that you will want to keep your eyes on. As more details on PCI-X become available (on the hardware enthusiast front), expect to see them at AnandTech.com.

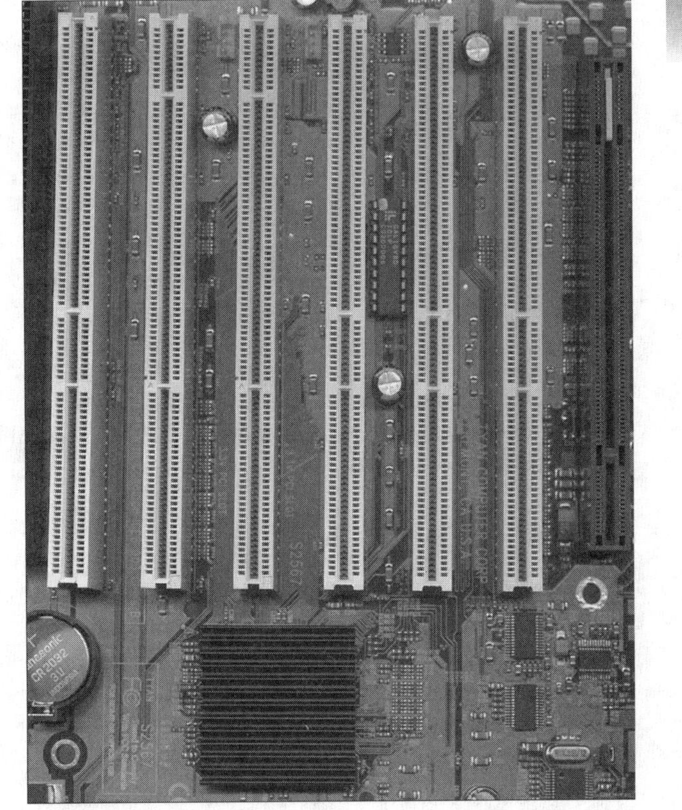

FIGURE 2.8
64-bit PCI Slots.

Today's High Performance Chipsets

Just as I showed you the architecture behind today's CPUs, and then introduced you to the CPUs themselves, I have equipped you with the ammunition to take apart a chipset's specifications. Now it's time to look at what's available and put that knowledge to use.

Unlike a CPU, dealing with chipsets can be a bit more difficult at times. For the most part, very little about the internal architecture of the chipset is made public. Any latency issues are very difficult to pick apart from a specification sheet. The only way to find out about performance differences between two virtually identical chipsets is to look at how the individual parts of the chipsets have faired in the past (for example, VIA reused its DDR memory controller from their Pro266 chipset in the KT266 chipset). You can also, of course, benchmark them yourself using the tools and knowledge supplied in Chapter 14.

Chipsets for the AMD Athlon

When the Athlon was released it was instantly the most powerful desktop x86 CPU on the market. Unfortunately its acceptance into the market was hampered by poor motherboard and chipset support. While the motherboard issues improved over time, chipsets have always been a problem for the Athlon. With AMD not interested in mass producing chipsets for the Athlon, only driving technology, they rely on third party manufacturers such as ALi, SiS, and VIA to produce solutions for their platform. Although SiS and VIA have recently improved, performance of these third party solutions is often sub par, unfortunately.

With the announcement of NVIDIA entering the chipset market things get very interesting for the Athlon, because of the potential for a high performing/solid chipset platform to push the Athlon to a new level.

NVIDIA's entry into the chipset market has raised the bar for entry level 3D performance, which is music to game developers' ears. This enables developers to be a bit more demanding with their games in terms of 3D hardware requirements. Although the nForce's integrated GeForce2 MX core isn't much more powerful than what game developers are aiming for in their minimum requirements, the future of the nForce and its acceptance into the market enables game developers to optimize for much higher minimum requirements as the integrated 3D core of the platform improves. Provided, of course, that the chipset does gain market share.

AMD 760

Historically AMD has taken the position of not wanting to be a mass producer of chipsets for their processors. They simply want to develop chipsets to drive technology and let the third party manufacturers like VIA deal with producing mainstream solutions that adopt the technology. Case in point would be the AMD 760 chipset, which was actually AMD's second chipset for the Athlon. The very first chipset for the Athlon was the AMD 750.

The AMD 760 was the first chipset for the Athlon with DDR memory support. The AMD 761 North Bridge it uses supports the 100MHz or 133MHz DDR FSB, for 1.6GBps–2.1GBps of bandwidth and that is paired up with the memory bus running at either 100MHz or 133MHz DDR for an identical bandwidth. The FSB and memory bus run synchronously for the best possible performance and their bandwidth is matched identically as well.

The North Bridge supports AGP 4X and was connected to the South Bridge via the PCI bus.

The AMD 766 South Bridge supports Ultra ATA/66. However, most manufacturers chose to use VIA's 686B South Bridge instead. AMD helped manufacturers by designing the chipset so that its South Bridge would be pin-compatible with the lower cost 686B, which is why most manufacturers opted to use the AMD 761 North Bridge and the VIA 686B South Bridge. While the AMD 760 was clearly one of the highest performing Athlon chipsets available, the unfortunate reality was that the chipset wasn't mass-produced by AMD and it eventually was replaced by cheaper solutions by ALi and VIA and higher performing solutions from NVIDIA.

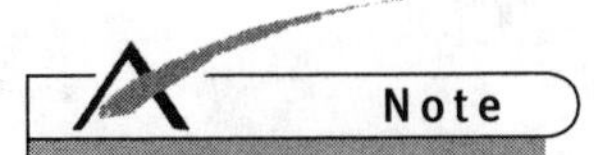

Note

AMD also released a dual processor version of the AMD 760 chipset, called the AMD 760MP. However, as I explained in Chapter 1, dual processors don't offer much of an advantage to you as a gamer, so let's just skip over this one.

VIA KT133/KT133A

The very first chipset for the Thunderbird core was the VIA KT133. In spite of the name, the only "133" came from the fact that the chipset supported a 133MHz SDRAM memory bus for use with memory that operated at 133MHz, otherwise known as PC133 SDRAM. The actual FSB ran at 100MHz DDR, for a peak bandwidth of 1.6GBps while the memory bus offered a 1GBps theoretical transfer rate. There are two problems you can see developing here:

- The FSB and memory clocks are running out of sync, which adds a slight latency penalty to FSB/memory transfers. (Reducing the memory clock to 100MHz could alleviate this. Unfortunately, the loss of bandwidth was not worth the drop in latency.)
- The potential for the system to become memory bandwidth limited as CPU clock speed increases and games become more demanding is quite significant since the FSB can accept more data than the memory bus can feed it.

The VIA KT133 North Bridge offered AGP 4X support as well and the North/South Bridges were connected using the PCI bus. The KT133 featured VIA's 686A South Bridge that offered Ultra ATA/66 compliance.

The issues with the KT133 were fixed with the KT133A that offered a 100MHz DDR FSB *or* a 133MHz DDR FSB for use with the Athlon-C processors (133MHz FSB Athlons). Although the FSB could still operate out of sync with the memory bus, users quickly discovered that the best combination was to run their systems at 133/133 in which the FSB ran at 133MHz DDR and the memory ran at 133MHz. Not only were the two in sync, but the combination offered the most bandwidth of any SDRAM platform at the time.

VIA KT266

The VIA KT266 is a heavily modified version of the KT133A with a DDR memory controller and a much more tweaked design for decreased latency and maximum bandwidth. The DDR memory controller is the same as the memory controller used in the VIA Apollo Pro266, and the North/South Bridges are connected using VIA's V-Link bus.

The KT266 also supports regular SDRAM in addition to DDR SDRAM for greater flexibility. Both memory types can operate at either 100MHz or 133MHz, either synchronously or asynchronously with the FSB. With DDR SDRAM, you are given a higher bandwidth solution.

The KT266 uses the 686B South Bridge that offers Ultra ATA/100 compliance.

Although the original KT266 performed horribly and wasn't implemented well at all in most motherboard designs, VIA worked closely with motherboard manufacturers to improve the situation allowing the KT266 to become a healthy alternative to the AMD 760.

ALi MAGiK1

ALi's first journey back into the performance chipset business since they took a much more subdued position in 1998 was with the MAGiK1 chipset, a DDR Athlon solution. The feature set was identical to the VIA KT266 and it supports regular SDRAM as well as DDR SDRAM.

The MAGiK1 was plagued by poor performance upon its release, and continued to lag behind competing solutions from AMD and VIA. The only reason motherboard manufacturers were interested in the chipset was because it was priced very aggressively from ALi, at approximately half of the cost of the AMD 760 and still 25% less than VIA's offerings.

Unfortunately, for ALi, a better price doesn't make much difference to hardware enthusiasts bent on killer game performance. One of the last things you should do in building a gaming PC is skimp on the chipset.

SiS 735

The SiS 735 was an interesting solution from SiS, seemingly out of nowhere. The performance of the chipset was instantly its biggest advantage as it was faster than the AMD 760, the previous owner of the performance crown.

The 735's biggest feature was that it was a single chip solution, with an integrated North and South Bridge. The two were connected by a high bandwidth internal bus that offered 1.2GBps of bandwidth between the two.

The chipset didn't catch on too much because past failures have left a bad taste in a lot of mouths in the market for the SiS brand. There were rumors that VIA was even pushing motherboard manufacturers to stick with their solutions instead of exploring options from SiS. You've got to love the politics of this industry.

NVIDIA nForce: A Chipset Unto Itself

Quite possibly the most important chipset release of all time has been NVIDIA's first entry into the chipset market with their nForce. The nForce is the same chipset (with a different 3D core) that's used in Microsoft's Xbox. However, because Microsoft and not NVIDIA has the license to use Intel's GTL FSB the desktop, nForce could only be used as an AMD platform solution. This obviously makes AMD quite happy, although it has given the folks at VIA quite a few sleepless nights. Why? Well, let's look at the architecture behind the nForce (see Figure 2.12).

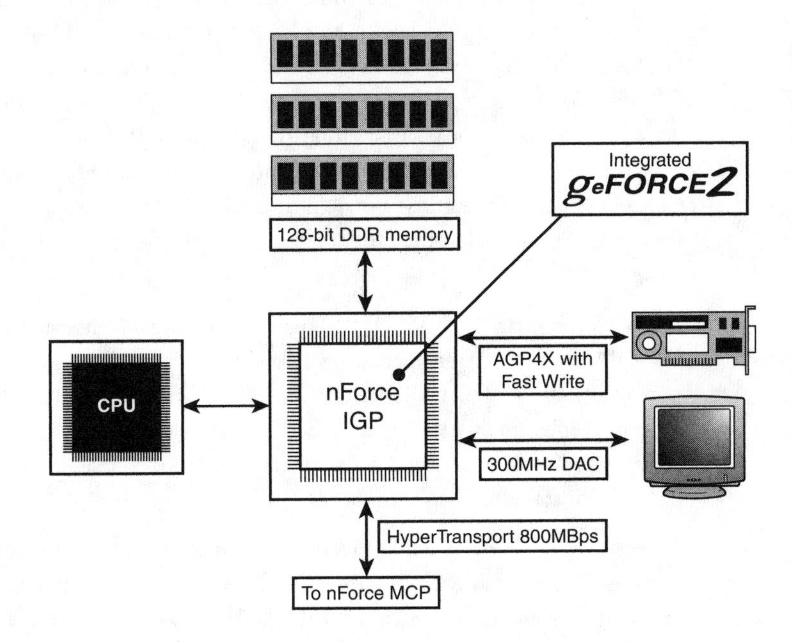

FIGURE 2.9
The nForce looks like a conventional chipset with the North and South Bridges renamed, but there's a lot more to this chipset than meets the eye.

The nForce is a two chip solution, but instead of referring to the chips as North/South Bridges, NVIDIA's excellent marketing team has come up with two new names: the Integrated Graphics Processor (IGP—North Bridge) and the Media and Communications Processor (MCP—South Bridge).

The Integrated Graphics Processor (IGP)

The IGP provides all of the normal North Bridge functions except it has some interesting features. First of all, it has an integrated GeForce2 MX graphics core that operates at 175MHz and has two rendering pipelines offering a theoretical fill rate of 350 megapixels per second (for more information on fill rates see Chapter 5). An external AGP 4X slot also exists for upgraded graphics. The nForce supports a unified memory architecture, meaning that the graphics memory is actually a part of main system memory instead of being a separate set of chips on the motherboard.

The second unique feature of the nForce IGP is its TwinBank Memory Architecture. The basic specifications of this memory controller enable it to provide a 128-bit, 133MHz (PC2100) DDR SDRAM memory bus which offers twice the bandwidth of any other DDR memory controller for the Athlon at 4.2GBps.

While this is quite impressive, TwinBank is actually much more complex than just a dual PC2100 memory interface. In fact, the 128-bit memory bus is actually somewhat misleading. Not because it's not really 128-bits wide, but because it doesn't tell the whole story. These 128-bits are actually divided into dual-independent 64-bit memory buses, each with its own memory controller. This means that either the CPU or GPU can access either or both memory controllers, enabling the most efficient use of memory bandwidth possible. This is made possible through NVIDIA's Crossbar memory technology, first used in the GeForce3 as I describe in great detail in Chapter 5.

Of course, standard 184-pin DDR DIMM's are only 64-bits wide and NVIDIA has no interest in creating a new memory standard. As such, you have to install two DIMM's in an nForce 420 board (explained in the following paragraphs) to take advantage of TwinBank Architecture. The IGP can fall back to 64-bit operation, at a performance hit of course, if only one DIMM is installed.

Because each memory bank has its own memory controller, the modules can be different sizes and even different speeds. A Single Intelligent Arbiter decides which memory controller will handle what data. Nevertheless, our assumption is that performance will be better if there is an equal amount of memory in each bank, because this enables the interleaving of data evenly between the two banks.

Interestingly enough, the IGP-128 supports 3 DIMM slots (an odd specification when there are two memory controllers). It turns out that the first slot is linked to the first memory controller and the other two slots are linked to the second memory controller.

Note that there will be two versions of the nForce IGP, one that supports the TwinBank 128-bit, 133 MHz DDR memory interface and one that only supports a standard 64-bit, 133 MHz DDR memory interface. The 128-bit model will be known as the IGP-128 and is included in the nForce 420 chipset, while the 64-bit model is the IGP-64 and is included in the nForce 220 chipset. Other than the memory interface, the two north bridges are identical.

Naturally, IGP-64 has a lower pin count, making the chipset and boards cheaper to produce, but at a pretty hefty performance penalty. Most motherboard manufacturers have shunned the IGP-64 and only produce nForce 420 solutions.

The nForce also features what NVIDIA calls a Dynamic Adaptive Speculative Pre-Processor (DASP). DASP acts as a hardware prefetch mechanism (see Chapter 1) that resides on the IGP. Based on data access patterns it prefetches data into a cache on the IGP and makes it ready for requests by the CPU before the CPU has even made such a request.

The Media and Communications Processor (MCP)

The nForce MCP (essentially its South Bridge) is also a very powerful entity. It provides all the standard South Bridge features, including support for Ultra ATA 100, 6 USB ports, 10/100 Ethernet, 1/10 HomePNA, 56k modem, and AC'97 sound (see Figure 2.10).

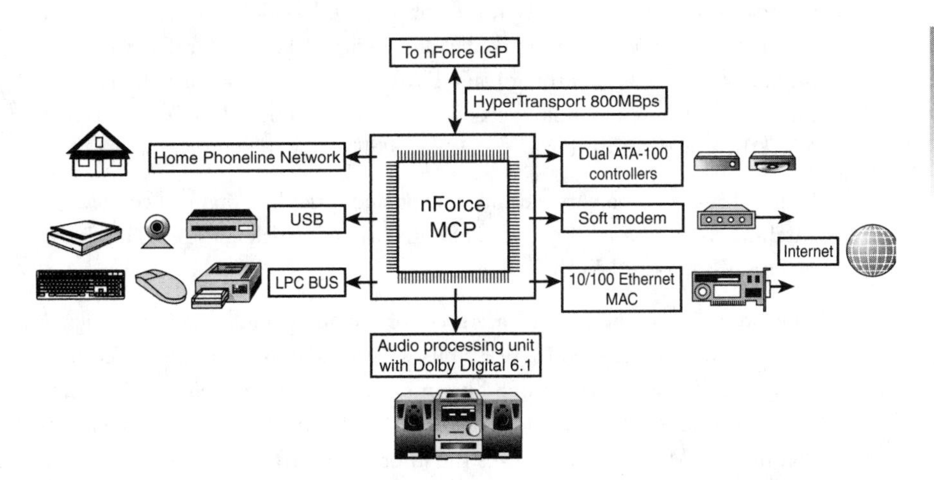

FIGURE 2.10
The nForce MCP is much more powerful than any other South Bridge, mainly because of its APU.

What differentiates the nForce MCP from other South Bridges is the Audio Processing Unit (APU) NVIDIA has integrated into the chip. This will be the first fully DirectX 8 compliant audio part when it hits the market. The APU supports 64 3D voices or 256 2D voices in hardware, 32 hardware sub-mixers, and is EAX 2 and I3DL2 compatible.

There are two versions of the MCP, with the difference being support for real time Dolby Digital AC-3 (5.1) encoding. This is by no means a trivial accomplishment and is the feature that distinguishes the MCP-D from the standard MCP. As such, the MCP-D is virtually identical to the MCPX found in the Xbox, but adds the PCI bus for which a console has no need. It seems that NVIDIA licensed the Parthus MediaStream DSP to integrate such a complex feature quickly enough to meet Microsoft's Xbox deadlines.

Dolby Digital AC-3 encoding means that you are able to digitally connect your computer to a home theater (or any other sound system) with a Dolby Digital Decoder and get sound quality that rivals a DVD movie if done properly. If you choose not to use an AC-3 out, the APU can work with 2, 4, or 6 speaker configurations using standard analog interfaces.

The 4 billion operations per second of the MCP's DSP aren't used just to encode Dolby Digital on the fly, but also to calculate occlusions, reflections, and HRTF functions, offloading these functions from the CPU. Thus, enabling 3D audio in games on an nForce-based system should not result in any slow down over standard stereo audio—at least in theory.

Hyper Transport Protocol on the nForce

nForce uses AMD's Hyper Transport protocol to connect the IGP and MCP components of the chipset (look ahead to Figure 2.11). Hyper Transport was originally known as Lightning Data Transport (LDT), but was renamed early in 2001. The technology has been disclosed to over 100 manufacturers, NVIDIA being one of the larger players with access to the technology.

Hyper Transport is a very elegant dual ported serial link that can connect anything from a North Bridge and South Bridge (which is the case here) to two multiprocessor North Bridges.

The two ports on the bus link are used for incoming and outgoing traffic. They can each be 2, 4, 8, 16, or 32 bits wide. The implementation used in the nForce has a link width of 8 bits and an operating frequency of 200MHz. The bus is double pumped meaning that the effective transfer rate is equal to that of a 400MHz bus. This gives the nForce 400MBps of bandwidth in any one direction or 800MBps total bandwidth between the IGP and the MCP.

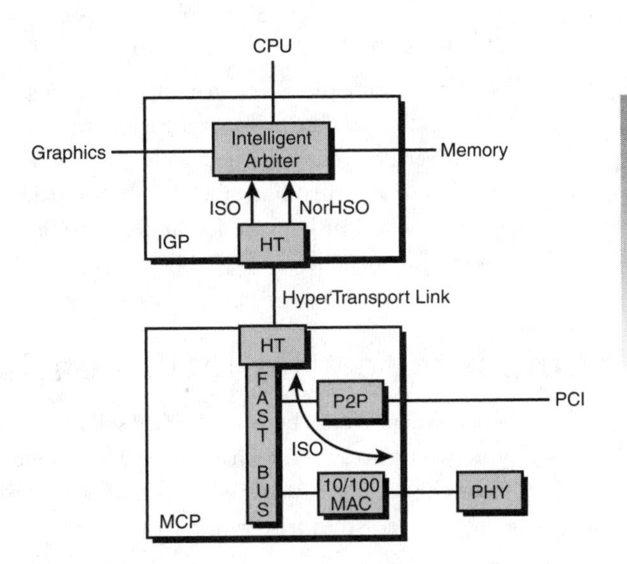

FIGURE 2.11
StreamThru uses the idea of isochronous devices to provide dedicated bandwidth to the integrated 10/100 network controller in the MCP. This keeps bandwidth usage efficient and latency low.

Should the need arise, NVIDIA can always increase the width of the Hyper Transport bus and/or increase the operating frequency, but for now 400MBps unidirectional bandwidth is enough.

One feature of AMD's Hyper Transport bus is the ability to support multiple virtual channels. A particular implementation of this is what NVIDIA is calling StreamThru as a part of their nForce technology (see Figure 2.14).

StreamThru guarantees that regardless of what other demands are placed on the chipset, the devices that are latency and bandwidth critical receive the ultra fast access and bandwidth to main memory that they need to operate properly.

Devices that are latency and bandwidth dependent are known as isochronous devices (ISO). The devices that aren't latency dependent (meaning they can be interrupted for a bit to let another device occupy some time) are known as non-isochronous devices.

An example of an isochronous device is the integrated 10/100 network controller in the MCP. NVIDIA's internal architecture, made possible courtesy of Hyper Transport's support for virtual channels, enables the 10/100 network controller to always get the bandwidth and low latency access to the graphics, CPU, and main memory that it needs to operate without any interruption.

This is what NVIDIA is calling StreamThru, but really the technology is made possible by Hyper Transport. It is useful nonetheless.

Unified Drivers

The final feature of nForce that happens to be the icing on the cake is that NVIDIA provides a single driver for nForce based motherboards that provide drivers for your Ethernet, Video, Audio, IDE, and regular chipset compatibility drivers in a single file. These drivers also work with an external NVIDIA video card, if you should decide to forgo the integrated graphics and upgrade to another.

Chipsets for the Intel Pentium III

The Pentium III has been a relatively solid platform in terms of chipset support, mainly because Intel has always been a solid chipset manufacturer. Their chipsets are always well supported by software and it is rare that any chipset driver issues arise with their chipsets.

Intel did make some poor decisions towards the end of 1999 with their first i8xx series of chipsets when attempting to push the Pentium III market towards RDRAM as a memory solution. The problem with RDRAM at the time was that the Pentium III couldn't use the additional bandwidth offered by RDRAM, and because RDRAM was no where near its peak production level, prices for the memory were easily 5 times greater than the conventional PC133 SDRAM used at the time.

VIA stepped in and provided chipset solutions during that time period that supported PC133 SDRAM, which helped them gain quite a bit of market share. Intel seems to have recovered from that incident and has been working quite hard to recoup the losses that were incurred during that period. However, for the most part, the Pentium III Chipset platform is dying because the processor itself is on its way out.

Intel 440BX

Quite possibly the most popular chipset Intel has made in recent history is the 440BX. The 440BX chipset was composed of the Intel 443BX North Bridge and the PIIX4e South Bridge. As you can guess by the nomenclature, the 440BX chipset did not use Intel's Hub Architecture and thus used the 33MHz PCI bus to connect the two bridges. The chipset only offered support for the 100MHz FSB, AGP 2X, regular SDRAM operating at 100MHz (otherwise known as PC100 SDRAM), and Ultra ATA/33 (33MBps max transfer rate).

The BX has since been phased out after its introduction in 1998; however it is a platform from which you might even be upgrading.

Intel 815/i815E/i815EP/B-Stepping

The reason the i440BX was phased out was because it was replaced by the i815 series of chipsets. These chipsets were based on the Intel Hub Architecture and thus featured the PCI bus as merely a peripheral bus extension of the ICH (I/O Controller Hub). The i815 MCH (Memory Controller Hub) supported the 100MHz/133MHz FSB, AGP 4X, a 133MHz SDRAM bus (supporting what was known as PC133 SDRAM) as well as backwards compatibility with PC100 SDRAM, and Ultra ATA/66 support. The i815 actually features a GMCH (Graphics & Memory Controller Hub), meaning it has an integrated graphics core. However, the chipset also supports an external AGP 4X slot, which disables the internal graphics if used. As I mentioned earlier, this was definitely not an ideal gaming solution, so most gamers simply opted to use the external AGP slot.

Intel later released a revision of the chipset known as the i815E that used the 801BA ICH or ICH2. This provided Ultra ATA/100 support. The regular i815 simply used the 801AA ICH or ICH1 that only supported ATA/66. The GMCH remained the same.

The i815EP is a lower cost version of the i815E without the integrated graphics core. That made it even more attractive for gamers since they weren't paying for a graphics core they didn't need. Unfortunately, by the time the i815EP was released, the Pentium III was on its way out and most gamers already had i815 boards so there was no compelling reason to upgrade.

The i815 B-Stepping is a newer revision of the chipset that supports Intel's Tualatin Pentium III processor. For more information on that processor, look back at Chapter 1.

Intel 820

The i820 carried the same feature set as the i815E, but without the integrated video. The only major difference between the two was that instead of a PC100/PC133 SDRAM memory controller, the i820 featured a RDRAM memory controller. Unfortunately the added bandwidth of RDRAM really had relatively no use on the Pentium III platform. If you'll remember, the Pentium III had a maximum FSB bandwidth of 1GBps and RDRAM can offer up to 1.6GBps of memory bandwidth. Couple that with the fact that the 1GBps of FSB bandwidth is never at 100% utilization and you'll see that a lot of the bandwidth advantage in the case of the Pentium III goes to waste. This lack of a performance increase, combined with increased RDRAM latencies over SDRAM, made the i820 the official "stay away from" chipset of 1999 and 2000. The chipset did poorly in the markets and ended up taking a backseat to the i815.

Intel 840

The i840 was an improvement over the i820, designed for more professional markets as it had two 16-bit RDRAM channels, which helped to significantly decrease the latency penalties of RDRAM. Unfortunately the chipset was rather expensive and the platform was, thus, inviable to adopt for most gamers. It was intended for use in professional environments, but even most of the professionals stayed away from it.

VIA Apollo Pro 133A

There was a period of time between the release of the i820 and the i815 where the only 133MHz FSB Pentium III chipset that was available was the i820. I have already shown you the downsides to the i820, so this unfortunately left the Pentium III B owners in a bit of a predicament. Rival chipset manufacturer VIA Technologies came to the rescue with their VIA Apollo Pro 133 and Apollo Pro 133A chipsets (the only difference between the two was that the 133A featured AGP 4X support). The 133A offered support for the 133MHz FSB, AGP 4X, PC133 SDRAM, and Ultra ATA/66. The 133A still used the conventional North/South Bridge design where the two were connected using the PCI bus.

Although it started off on a bad foot, the 133A eventually matured to be a solid chipset platform for the Pentium III. It was really the 133A's sales before the release of the i815 chipset that gave VIA the stepping stone to truly move on to bigger and better things with their Athlon projects later on. Much of the 133A design was reused in VIA's later Athlon designs.

VIA Apollo Pro266

With the market shifting focus to DDR memory, VIA jumped on the bandwagon with their first chipset that supported DDR memory: the Apollo Pro266 (see Figure 2.12). The Apollo Pro266 shared most of the same features of the 133A, with the exception that the Pro266's memory controller was VIA's DDR memory controller and the North/South Bridge are connected via a V-Link bus.

The DDR memory controller supports operation at either 100MHz or 133MHz DDR. Just as 100MHz SDR SDRAM was known as PC100,

> **Note**
>
> Because of the gargantuan price difference between SDRAM and RDRAM and the fact that RDRAM offered no performance benefit for the Pentium III on the i820, there was no point to using the i820 chipset. It was too expensive and offered no tangible performance benefit. Unfortunately, it was the only desktop platform that Intel offered that carried official support for the 133MHz FSB Pentium IIIs.
>
> Intel's solution to this was to use a Memory Translator Hub (MTH) to take the 16-bit, 400MHz RDRAM signal and "translate" it into a 64-bit, 100MHz SDRAM signal. Not only did this result in a 20% decrease in performance, but the MTH was quite hot during this translation process. Eventually a bug that was discovered regarding the MTH and system stability caused Intel to recall all MTH chips and instead provide the i815 as a solution for 133MHz FSB Pentium III processors.

FIGURE 2.12
An ASUS Motherboard using the Apollo Pro266 Chipset.

100MHz DDR SDRAM is known as DDR200 or PC1600 DDR SDRAM. At the same time, 133MHz DDR SDRAM is known as DDR266 or PC2100 DDR.

Just as was the case with the i820 chipset, the Pentium III didn't gain much benefit from the additional memory bandwidth offered by the Apollo Pro266's DDR SDRAM (1.6GBps or 2.1GBps for DDR200/PC1600 and DDR266/PC2100 respectively). Remember that the Pentium III can only be fed at most 1GBps of data, and the rest of the system is not going to consume the remaining 600MBps–1.1GBps of bandwidth. This is especially true when you consider that the V-Link bus at most is going to transfer 266MBps of data from memory.

The Apollo Pro266 did allow VIA to have the first DDR solution for the Pentium III platform, even though it offered no real performance improvement over the 133A or i815.

Chipsets for the Intel Pentium 4

The Pentium 4 kicked off with a very good chipset from Intel—the 850 platform. The chipset was very solid and its dual channel RDRAM memory controller offered the incredible bandwidth that the Pentium 4 needed.

Intel followed up with a much cheaper i845 solution that offered PC133 SDRAM support, and has plans to release a chipset with DDR SDRAM support, although that isn't due until 2002.

Competing solutions from VIA were able to bring DDR to the Pentium 4 much earlier, giving gamers and hardware enthusiasts playing in the Pentium 4 chipset market one of many choices just over a year into the processor's existence. ALi and SiS are also going to be providing Pentium 4 solutions, and although NVIDIA cannot bring the nForce to the Pentium 4 yet (because they lack the license for the Pentium 4's AGTL+ bus) they definitely have their eyes on it as the perfect candidate for their TwinBank Memory Architecture.

Intel 850

The i850 (or Intel 850) chipset was Intel's flagship launch chipset for the Pentium 4 (see Figure 2.13). It features dual channel RDRAM support for a total of 3.2GBps of memory bandwidth. This pairs up perfectly with the Pentium 4's quad-pumped 100MHz FSB that offers an identical 3.2GBps of bandwidth. The two buses thus operate not only synchronously, but they also offer perfectly identical bandwidth capabilities, which wasn't the case with many of the higher-bandwidth Pentium III solutions. Remember that the Pentium 4 depends on having an extremely high bandwidth setup, thus making regular SDRAM a non-option for the platform.

FIGURE 2.13
The i850 MCH (Memory Controller Hub).

The i850 features the ICH2, which offers Ultra ATA/100 support. The rest of the features such as AGP 4X are pretty much identical to what we've seen in previous Pentium III-based i8xx chipsets from Intel.

Intel 845

The 845 chipset, or Brookdale as it is known internally to Intel, was designed to bring the Pentium 4 to the mainstream population by supporting cheaper PC133 SDRAM. Unfortunately, with PC133 SDRAM only offering a bit more than 1GBps of memory bandwidth, it causes the Pentium 4 (and your games running on the Pentium 4) to start gasping for air as what bandwidth it has gets sorely tested. The i845 solution is about 20%–30% slower than the i850, meaning that the savings you gain in cheaper SDRAM is lost in the performance hit that is incurred.

Interestingly enough, the i845 chipset also supports DDR SDRAM. However, for political reasons (for example, not wanting to provide a better alternative to RDRAM immediately), Intel instructed manufacturers to only produce 845-based boards with SDRAM support promising DDR SDRAM support sometime in early 2002. Although the i845 with DDR SDRAM could prove to be a hard hitter, it seems as if Intel will only enable a 100MHz DDR memory bus on the i845 which means it could only offer 1.6GBps of memory bandwidth to the Pentium 4 which still isn't enough. A 133MHz DDR memory bus could close the gap between the 845 and the 850, but that's not necessarily what Intel wants.

Motherboard manufacturers are very happy with the 845 because it supports a memory type that they all like, and the chipset itself happens to be very stable. In fact, many are already proclaiming the i845 to be the next BX chipset.

VIA P4X266

VIA's P4X266 is their DDR solution for the Pentium 4. Consider it to be the KT266 except with support for Intel's AGTL+ FSB instead of AMD's EV6 bus.

VIA is claiming performance greater than the i850 with their P4X266. This is believable because the platform uses 133MHz DDR SDRAM instead of just 100MHz DDR SDRAM. Let's just hope for stability out of the platform. Look for more information on this chipset, as it becomes available, at the AnandTech.com Web site.

Chipset Feature Comparison

In Table 2.4 you'll find a feature comparison of the major chipsets available from this section.

Table 2.4 Chipset Features Comparison

	CPUs Supported	North Bridge	South Bridge	FSB Interface	Memory Type/Speed	Integrated Graphics	Architecture
Ali MAGiK1	AMD Athlon, Duron	ALi M1647	ALi M1535D/ M1535D_	100/133MHz DDR EV6	PC100/133 SDRAM DDR200/ DDR266 SDRAM	External AGP 4X	Conventional North/South Bridge—PCI bus link
AMD 750	AMD Athlon	AMD 751	AMD 756/ VIA 686A	100MHz DDR EV6	PC100 SDRAM	External AGP 2X	Conventional North/South Bridge—PCI bus link
AMD 760	AMD Athlon, Duron	AMD 761	AMD 766/ VIA 686A/ VIA686B	100/133MHz DDR EV6	DDR200/ DDR266 SDRAM	External AGP 4X	Conventional North/South Bridge—PCI bus link
Intel 810E	Intel Pentium III, Celeron	Intel 810GMCH	Intel ICH0/ ICH1	66/100/ 133MHz GTL/ GTL+/AGTL/ AGTL+	PC66/100/133 SDRAM	Internal i745	Intel Hub Architecture (IHA)
Intel 815E	Intel Pentium III, Celeron	Intel 815GMCH	Intel ICH1/ ICH2	66/100/ 133MHz GTL/GTL+/ AGTL/AGTL+	PC100/133 SDRAM	Internal i745/ External AGP 4X	Intel Hub Architecture (IHA)
Intel 820E	Intel Pentium III, Celeron	Intel 820MCH	Intel ICH1/ ICH2	100/133MHz GTL/GTL+/ AGTL/AGTL+	PC600/700/ 800 RDRAM	External AGP 4X	Intel Hub Architecture (IHA)
Intel 840	Intel Pentium III, Celeron, Pentium III Xeon	Intel 840MCH	Intel ICH1/ ICH2	100/133MHz GTL/GTL+/ AGTL/AGTL+	PC600/800 RDRAM	External AGP 4X	Intel Hub Architecture (IHA)
Intel 845	Intel Pentium 4	Intel 845MCH	Intel ICH2	100MHz Quad-Pumped AGTL/AGTL+	PC133 SDRAM	External AGP 4X	Intel Hub Architecture (IHA)
Intel 845D	Intel Pentium 4	Intel 845MCH	Intel ICH2	100MHz Quad-Pumped AGTL/ AGTL+	DDR200 SDRAM	External AGP 4X	Intel Hub Architecture (IHA)

Table 2.4 Continued

	CPUs Supported	North Bridge	South Bridge	FSB Interface	Memory Type/Speed	Integrated Graphics	Architecture
Intel 850	Intel Pentium 4	Intel 850MCH	Intel ICH2	100MHz Quad-Pumped AGTL/AGTL+	PC600/800 RDRAM	External AGP 4X	Intel Hub Architecture (IHA)
Intel 860	Intel Xeon	Intel 860MCH	Intel ICH2	100MHz Quad-Pumped AGTL/AGTL+	PC600/800 RDRAM	External AGP 4X	Intel Hub Architecture (IHA)
SiS 630	Intel Pentium III, Celeron	SiS 630 (Single Chip)		66/100/133MHz GTL/GTL+/AGTL/AGTL+	PC66/100/133 SDRAM	Internal SiS Graphics/External AGP 4X	SiS Single Chip Architecture
SiS 635	Intel Pentium III, Celeron	SiS 635 (Single Chip)		66/100/133MHz GTL/GTL+/AGTL/AGTL+	PC66/100/133 SDRAM	External AGP 4X	SiS Single Chip Architecture
SiS 730S	AMD Athlon, Duron	SiS 730 (Single Chip)		100/133MHz DDR EV6	PC100/133 SDRAM	Internal SiS Graphics/External AGP 4X	SiS Single Chip Architecture
SiS 735	AMD Athlon, Duron	SiS 735 (Single Chip)		100/133MHz DDR EV6	PC100/133 SDRAM DDR200/DDR266 SDRAM	External AGP 4X	SiS Single Chip Architecture
VIA Apollo Pro 133/133A	Intel Pentium III, Celeron	VIA VT82C693A/VT82C694X	VIA VT82C596B/686A	66/100/133MHz GTL/GTL+/AGTL/AGTL+	PC66/100/133 SDRAM	External AGP 2X/4X	Conventional North/South Bridge—PCI bus link
VIA Apollo Pro266	Intel Pentium III, Celeron	VIA VT8633	VIA VT8233	66/100/133MHz GTL/GTL+/AGTL/AGTL+	PC100/133 SDRAM DDR200/DDR266 SDRAM	External AGP 4X	VIA V-Link

Table 2.4 Continued

	CPUs Supported	North Bridge	South Bridge	FSB Interface	Memory Type/Speed	Integrated Graphics	Architecture
VIA Apollo KX133	AMD Athlon	VIA VT8371	VIA 686A	100MHz DDR EV6	PC100/133 SDRAM	External AGP 4X	Conventional North/South Bridge—PCI bus link
VIA Apollo KT133	AMD Athlon, Duron	VIA VT8363	VIA 686A	100MHz DDR EV6	PC100/133 SDRAM	External AGP 4X	Conventional North/South Bridge—PCI bus link
VIA Apollo KT133A	AMD Athlon, Duron	VIA VT8363A	VIA 686B	100/133MHz DDR EV6	PC100/133 SDRAM	External AGP 4X	Conventional North/South Bridge—PCI bus link
VIA KT266	AMD Athlon, Duron	VIA VT8366	VIA VT8233	100/133MHz DDR EV6	DDR200/DDR266 SDRAM	External AGP 4X	VIA V-Link
VIA P4X266	Intel Pentium 4	VIA P4X266	VIA VT8233	100MHz Quad-Pumped AGTL/AGTL+	DDR200/DDR266 SDRAM	External AGP 4X	VIA V-Link

Chapter 3

The Motherboard: Low Rent Housing for the CPU and Chipset

Blueprint for the Typical Motherboard

In the previous two chapters I introduced you to the most important chips (CPU and chipset) that lie directly on a board that is called the motherboard. However, the motherboard is actually much more critical to the proper operation and performance of your gaming system than you might think. Chapter 2, "The Chipset: The PC's Crossing Guard," covered how the CPU communicates with the rest of your system through the chipset using connections known as buses. It also discussed that unlike a CPU, you cannot buy a chipset or a bus individually. You're pretty much stuck with what you get in that respect. The motherboard is the part of your system that actually contains the very tiny wires that create these buses and connect the CPU to the North Bridge and the North Bridge to the South Bridge, and so on. Figure 3.1 shows an actual motherboard designed for use with a Pentium 4 CPU.

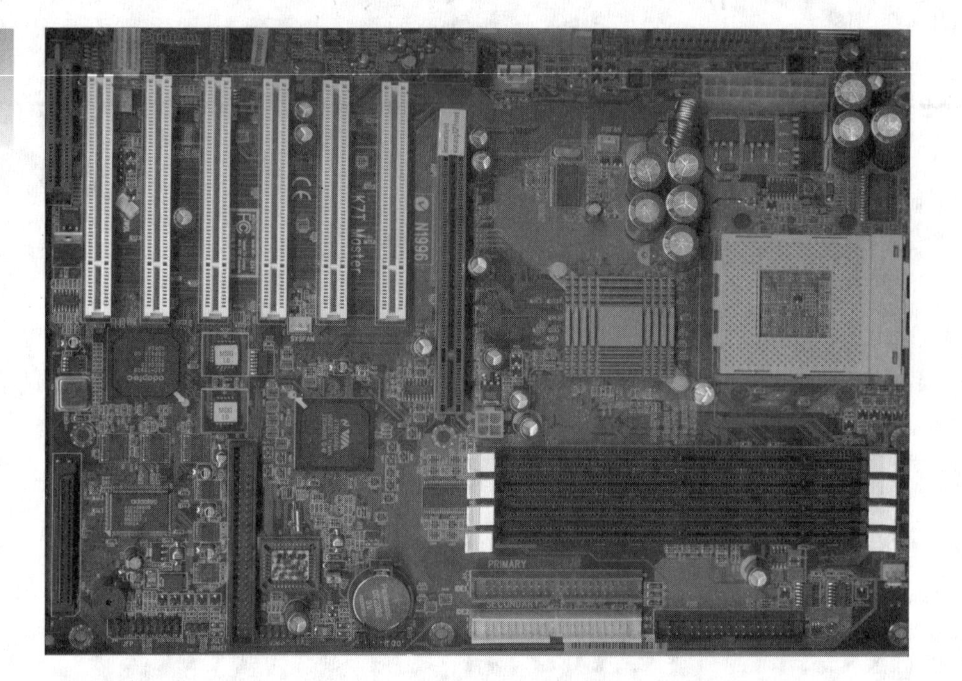

FIGURE 3.1
This Pentium 4 motherboard uses the Socket 423 interface.

Let's take a look at some of the basics on this board. As the name motherboard (also known as a main board or system board) implies, it is in fact a board with many components mounted on it. The name of the board itself, that all of the components are placed on, is called a Printed Circuit Board or PCB. It gets this name because the circuits that are present on it are essentially "printed" on.

The design of a motherboard is quite complex, as you can see in Figure 3.1. However, the magnitude of complexity is no where near what we saw with CPUs in Chapter 1, "The Central Processing Unit: The Heart and Soul of the PC." For example, you can easily see the resistors and other components on the PCB while you cannot see the millions of transistors that are present inside of a CPU. One of the reasons for this is that the CPU's transistors are much more sensitive to exposure to the outside world than the components on a motherboard.

Remember the AGP, front side, and memory buses we talked about in Chapter 2? These buses are much more than theoretical paths connecting two components. Rather, they are no more than collections of extremely tiny wires connecting various components on the board. For example, the 850 North Bridge and the Pentium 4's socket are connected via a set of these small wires as is the North Bridge and the AGP slot and memory slots. These very small wires are known as traces. While it is quite possible to see the traces on a motherboard, most of them are thinner than the width of a pencil lead (see Figure 3.2).

FIGURE 3.2
Traces between a North Bridge and memory slots.

The motherboard's PCB doesn't show and tell all of its secrets however, as there is much more to a PCB than meets the eye. Just as with any flat surface, there are two sides to a motherboard, the top and the bottom. However, the PCB is actually constructed of multiple layers in between the top and bottom layers. The most common motherboards feature four layers (including the visible top and bottom layers) while more complex designs require six or more layers.

There are pros and cons to a motherboard design requiring more layers. For starters, the more layers present in a design the better shielding can be done between the various traces that are on the board. There are traces on all board layers, and some traces actually run through multiple layers of the board. The more layers present in a PCB the more space for routing traces and the more space that can be kept between traces that would otherwise be very close together.

Many of the first revisions of chipsets with high speed FSBs and memory buses require six-layer board designs simply because data is being transferred over these tiny traces at extremely high speeds. As designs improve, boards are generally scaled down to four-layer PCBs. The reason for wanting to produce four-layer board designs is from a motherboard manufacturer's standpoint, it is much cheaper to use a four-layer design than it is to use a design with more layers.

Most of the time you will have to rely on manufacturer specifications to know of how many layers your board is constructed. You shouldn't base a buying decision on how many layers a board has; however, it is interesting information to know. Some motherboard manufacturers actually include a little indicator that lets you know how many layers your board happens to have. Gigabyte is one such manufacturer, and they use the indicator pictured in Figure 3.3.

FIGURE 3.3
A Gigabyte board, indicating its four-layer construction.

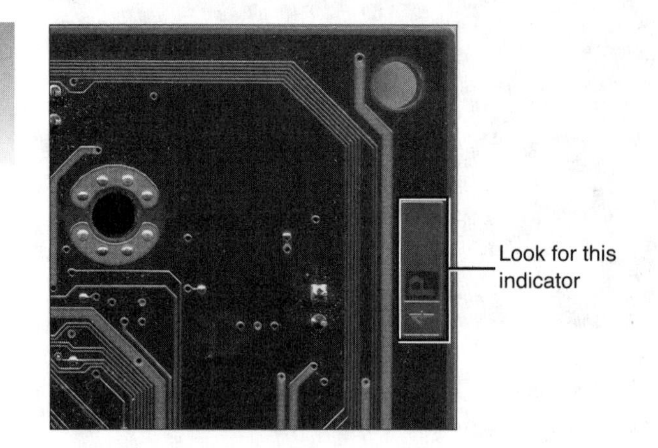

While a motherboard with more layers won't improve your gaming performance, it does attack the issue of stability in design which is very important regardless of whether you're using your system for gaming or just browsing the Web. Nothing is more frustrating than a computer that crashes every five minutes.

Motherboard manufacturers already make very little profit from a single board. With CPUs, the actual production cost of one CPU is usually 5%–20% of the retail price of the CPU. With motherboards however, this is definitely not true. The profit margins on motherboards are very low. The only reason motherboard manufacturers are able to stay afloat is by signing deals with major computer manufacturers and vendors to use their boards in massive volumes on the order of millions of boards per month. Although they do have considerably more overhead than the motherboard guys, a $20–$50 profit per motherboard is not much compared to the hundreds of dollars in profit CPU manufacturers make. Multiplied by the millions of units that are shipped, the profits can turn into some fairly impressive numbers.

This unfortunately means that many motherboard manufacturers tend to focus away from the gaming enthusiasts and focus on what their major contract OEMs (Original Equipment Manufacturers, for example, Compaq, Dell, IBM, and so on) desire. Recently, especially because of the increasing presence of enthusiasts in the online market, motherboard manufacturers have begun to pay attention to the DIY (Do-it-Yourself) market and have thus included features that we care about in their board designs. In general, OEMs are mostly concerned with the stability of such designs and could care less for other performance enhancing and expandability features. After all, instead of upgrading, these OEMs want their customers to come back to them for a new computer. You, as a gaming hardware enthusiast, should be concerned with stability just as much as the major OEMs are, but at the same time you will find use for a lot of the features that OEMs normally shun.

The goal of this chapter is to point out what to look for in purchasing a motherboard, as it can often be one of the most important decisions you make when building your new high- performance gaming system.

Not a Component to Skimp On: Choosing a Motherboard

In order to save money you can always buy a slower CPU, but one thing you should never do is opt for a no name motherboard. All the components in your system interface, from your Sound and Video cards to your CPU and memory, interface with your motherboard. The difference between a poorly designed motherboard from a company with a history of problems and one from a top tier manufacturer could be the difference between your system running for weeks on end without a reboot and having to reboot it every eight hours because of instability. While it is true that the motherboard isn't the cause of all of your stability problems, you definitely want to make sure that there is no reason to suspect your motherboard as the culprit behind instability.

> **Caution**
>
> The reality in today's gaming world is that game software, almost without fail, ships with bugs. Therefore, any failure or crash in the game (or Windows for that matter) is often attributable to buggy software. Many times, though, a lot of the instability you'll encounter might not be related to your OS or game at all. Most of my personal machines run Windows 2000 for 10–20 days without a crash or requiring a reboot. It's not always the software, but sometimes the hardware that causes these problems. The motherboard, among other components, can often be a culprit in some situations of system instability.

The Chipset

As we've already discussed, both here and in Chapter 2, the chipset wasn't a piece of hardware you could buy individually. Even if you could, you wouldn't have the tools necessary to mount the chips on a motherboard. The first step in deciding what motherboard is best for you is to decide what platform you're looking to run on, meaning what chipset you are interested in using. The prerequisite for knowing what chipset you want is knowing with what processor you want to use it.

Once you know what processor and what chipset your new system will be based on, then and only then should you start looking for a motherboard. You'll find that once you settle on these core features, it cuts through a lot of the legwork in narrowing down potential products.

Features

The features your motherboard supports are largely governed by the chipset it uses. You can't, for example, expect an i850-based motherboard, designed for the Pentium 4, to support the Athlon processor. It is important you realize that many of the basic features of your motherboard come directly from the chipset it uses. The basic FSB frequency supported, memory types and configurations as well as all of the other features we discussed in Chapter 2 are all controlled by the chipset. So what features does the motherboard manufacturer actually have control over?

Most of the features that the motherboard manufacturer has control over are in regards to overclocking and tweaking features. We will get into both of these topics in Chapter 14, "Tweaking and Overclocking: Turbo-Charging Your PC," but do remember that motherboard manufacturers are always constrained by the limitations of the chipset itself.

Other features motherboard manufacturers have control over are cooling, expansion, and layout. Most chipset manufacturers provide the motherboard manufacturers with what is known as a reference design, or a sample design that uses the chipset they are selling to the motherboard manufacturers. In the motherboard industry, it is rare that these reference designs get released without any modifications to them. The degree of the modifications usually depends on the board's target market. For the gaming enthusiast community, most motherboard manufacturers heavily modify the reference designs in order to tailor to the unique needs of the DIY audience.

Configuration

One of the biggest features motherboard manufacturers offer is a method for configuring and setting up your motherboard. A few years ago, motherboards were configured using large groups of pins. These pins were effectively the switches of the motherboard, the off position being an untouched set of pins and the on position being the status attained after placing a small cap across two or more of them. This cap featured a conductive interior that connected the pins electrically and allowed current to flow through them. These caps were known as "jumpers" and the process of placing a jumper across two or more pins was known as "capping" or "jumping" the pins (see Figure 3.4).

FIGURE 3.4
Two three-pin jumpers with two pins capped each.

Jumpers are still around. In fact, they are still used to perform relatively simple functions on motherboards such as resetting the data contained within the BIOS (more on that in Chapters 11 and 14) or enabling/disabling onboard sound. In terms of the sheer numbers of jumpers, that has decreased tremendously. Years ago the motherboard was used to configure the FSB frequency and clock multiplier fed to your CPU via combinations of tons of these little jumpers arranged in blocks of pins or jumper blocks as they were called. Now, CPUs come with locked multipliers from the factory and they generally have circuitry on them that tells the motherboard what FSB they want to use so the motherboard doesn't have as much to do anymore. This has led to a decrease in the number of jumpers present on motherboards.

Since it is human nature to at first be afraid of what you don't understand, jumpers have always been quite intimidating to the first time PC builders. However they're really simple little devices and you don't have much to fear. It is highly unlikely that you will do irreversible damage if you accidentally cap a jumper. If you happen to cap two pins that aren't a jumper pin set (for example, the power pins for a fan connector) then you might be in a bit of a situation, but in general the jumperable pins have a jumper cap across them already or on a single one. Covering a single jumper with a cap doesn't do any harm nor does it change the state of the switch. It's just a convenient resting place for a jumper.

In order to remove some of the intimidation and unnecessary complexity of dealing with jumpers, some manufacturers decided to go with dip switches instead (see Figure 3.5). These switches perform the same function as jumpers; however, they are organized in blocks of multiple physical switches that have an on and an off setting. They perform the same function as jumpers, but are more like the type of switches people are used to and thus they are less intimidating. The only problem with dip switches is that a single switch only has two positions, while a three pin jumper actually has three positions (pins 1–2 capped, pins 2–3 capped, or no pins capped). This isn't a huge issue however, since more combinations can come from simply adding more dip switches.

Even more recently (only a couple of years ago), pioneered by motherboard manufacturers ABIT and QDI, "jumperless" motherboard designs finally came about. These motherboards use software-based switches instead of physical ones present on the motherboard. You configure the motherboard through a utility stored in memory built onto the motherboard. This memory is known as the motherboard's BIOS and you will be introduced to it in Chapter 14. These jumperless designs have become much more popular in recent years and now it's relatively unheard of not to be able to perform the most common configuration options within this jumperless utility. Some OEMs don't like this idea because it allows end users to mess around with settings that they shouldn't be touching. In order to suit their needs, motherboard manufacturers sometimes outfit a board with a set of jumpers and dip switches and the ability to enable and disable a software jumperless setup or simply stick to jumpers and dip switches.

FIGURE 3.5
A set of six dip switches.

FIGURE 3.6
A motherboard with five PCI slots and one AGP expansion slot. The lack of ISA slots is common on most of today's motherboards since all peripherals that were once available only as ISA cards are now available in much more mature and advanced PCI versions.

Expansion Slots

While the chipset determines how many PCI and AGP slots your motherboard can have, and your case determines how many cards can be installed at once, it is up to the motherboard manufacturer to determine the expansion slot configuration. Figure 3.6 shows a motherboard configured with five PCI slots and an AGP slot.

Expansion slots are the physical interfaces between the cards you install and their respective buses. For example, a PCI bus sound card will install into a PCI expansion slot and will then be connected with the PCI bus on your motherboard stemming from the South Bridge/ICH (I/O Controller Hub).

You can have only one AGP slot in a system (since the AGP bus wasn't intended to be shared by other peripherals), so the rest of the slots on your motherboard are now primarily PCI expansion slots. Although there are a few motherboards currently available that offer a single ISA slot, this is quite rare and you shouldn't expect to find an ISA slot on any motherboard you'll purchase in the future. You are ultimately limited by the number of cards you can have installed at any given time, which for most cases happens to be seven. Reserving one slot for your AGP graphics card leaves a total of six more expansion slots. This means that motherboard manufacturers could theoretically outfit a motherboard with one AGP slot and six PCI slots. Unfortunately for us, motherboard manufacturers have to take into consideration the desires of their major customers, the OEMs. In doing that, they often outfit their motherboards with one or more of the following types of expansion slots: Audio Modem Riser (AMR), Audio and Communications Riser (ACR), or Communications and Networking Riser (CNR).

None of these three expansion types are conventional expansion slots because you can't plug any type of card into them. For example, although you can plug any type of card into a PCI slot as long as it is PCI compliant, only certain cards are manufactured for use with AMR, ACR, or CNR slots. The theory behind these interfaces goes back to the fact that modern CPUs are incredibly powerful, and very few users make full use of their potential. So Intel, VIA, and a number of other manufacturers decided that if they included commonly used functions in their South Bridges/ICHs (such as audio, networking, and modem functionality) they could rely on the fast CPUs to perform all of the calculations that would otherwise be performed on dedicated expansion cards (for example, PCI Sound Cards, Network Cards, and Modems).

So motherboard manufacturers provide their OEMs with one or more of these AMR, ACR, or CNR slots and extremely cheap little cards that do nothing more than provide an interface to the functions contained within the South Bridge/ICH that are processed by your CPU.

As a gaming hardware enthusiast you probably aren't too interested in building a cheap system without being concerned about quality and performance. You will most likely want to save every single CPU cycle that you can and go with a hardware-based sound, network, or modem card. It might be more expensive, but your frame rate will thank you.

There are three different slots because of the three competing standards. AMR, first introduced by Intel, only provided Audio/Modem functionality (see Figure 3.7). ACR was later introduced by Intel and offered networking support. Both ACR and AMR are very small slots compared to a PCI slot. A competing standard, partially driven by VIA, is CNR. It offers much of the same functionality of ACR. The slot design is different however, as the slot is simply a backward PCI slot offset slightly on the motherboard. For the most part you shouldn't be too concerned with filling up these slots. Chances are you won't be able to even find a card to put in one of them since they're not too common on the retail market.

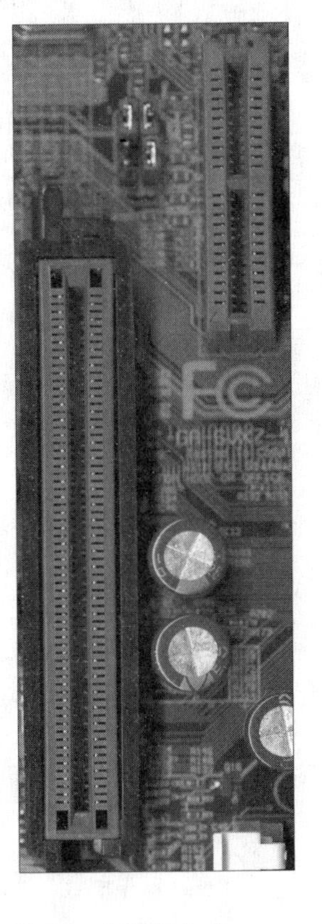

FIGURE 3.7
An AGP slot (left) and an AMR slot (right). Notice the difference in size because of the number of signaling pins and the sheer amount of data that must be sent to the AGP slot in comparison to the relatively small amount of data that must be sent to the AMR slot.

If you are strapped for cash, some motherboards do offer the AC'97 Audio Codec functionality (or software sound as we discussed earlier) without the use of one of these add-in cards. Instead they include the output ports for your speakers directly on the motherboard. The quality isn't the best and neither is the feature set, but in most cases this solution is better than nothing.

Support

As I mentioned earlier, there is absolutely no good reason to skimp on your motherboard purchase if system stability is even a minor concern for your PC. What good is an ultra fast system if it crashes all the time? It is of the utmost importance that you find a manufacturer with a solid track record and one that offers good support. Support for your motherboard is critical as it is very common for compatibility issues to creep up over time.

Remember that your motherboard is the one device that must make everything work together. It has a chipset that is hardwired to itself, a CPU that can be of a number of types and speeds, and as many as seven installed peripheral cards for starters. Chances are the time will come when you go to install a peripheral card and a compatibility issue with a chip on that card and your South Bridge causes your computer to freeze at five second intervals. While the situation might not be identical to that, there are infinite possibilities for weird problems like the aforementioned one to creep up. It is critical to find a motherboard manufacturer that provides timely support for their products, especially their older products (since the time will come that your brand new motherboard will be, amazingly enough, an older product). This support mainly comes in providing you with updated BIOS files for your motherboard.

The BIOS

Your motherboard's BIOS is its Basic Input Output System (see Figure 3.8). The BIOS is what provides the initial software so that your system can boot up and perform the necessary tests to prepare it for loading your operating system, such as Windows XP. The BIOS also allows you to configure various options on your motherboard, such as memory timings (that control memory latency), the size and types of storage drives you have plugged into the IDE channels, and other such options. Another major function of the BIOS is to complete what is known as a Power On Self Test or POST. The POST occurs immediately after a motherboard is given power. The only components necessary for a successful POST are a working CPU (with cooling device), memory, and a graphics adapter. The POST consists of a number of very basic tests to ensure that your system is able to complete the most simple of functions.

FIGURE 3.8
A BIOS chip.

The BIOS is located on a type of memory referred to colloquially as firmware or technically as EEPROM (Electronically Erasable Programmable Read Only Memory). As the name implies, this memory is generally "Read-Only" meaning you cannot copy and store your data in it. However, it is programmable in the sense that various bits contained within the memory can be set. These various bits correspond to the options and settings contained within the BIOS. The BIOS also handles some of the software communication between the rest of the motherboard and the chipset. Because the BIOS is electronically erasable, it can be overwritten or "flashed" with an updated BIOS file. These BIOS updates can often be quite useful in resolving conflicts with certain hardware, and the motherboard manufacturer generally accompanies each BIOS revision with release notes on what the particular BIOS fixes.

A manufacturer with a history of good support will have an extensive BIOS update section on their Web site, complete with updates for boards that are even a couple years old. The best way to find out about a manufacturer's recent history is to ask other users that have had experience with that particular manufacturer in online discussion groups such as the AnandTech Forums (`http://forums.anandtech.com`).

If all you're concerned with is getting a system up and running, then any basic BIOS will allow you to do that. However, as a gaming enthusiast interested in getting the most out of your system, you should only settle for those manufacturers that do give you the power to manipulate as many configuration options as possible. It is one thing if a manufacturer's default settings are optimized for performance and compatibility; unfortunately quite a few of the default settings are left unoptimized from the start. I will get into how to optimize your BIOS in Chapter 14, but be warned that a BIOS that doesn't give you the ability to change performance options isn't one that can be tweaked. When I refer to flexibility and tweaking options I am usually referring to features offered in the BIOS that pertain to either overclocking or other types of performance tweaking (see Chapter 14).

Certain BIOS manufacturers offer more flexibility than others. Personally, I've had the best experiences with AWARD BIOS setups and have generally favored AMI BIOS solutions much less because their implementations rarely rival AWARD's in terms of features. You might run into another type of BIOS manufactured by Phoenix BIOS, which is actually under the same roof as AWARD, so their newer BIOSes are quite similar.

Quality and Reliability

Manufacturing a motherboard is not a simple task by far. While it is much simpler than manufacturing a CPU, it is still just as much of a science. A company's manufacturing facilities and practices have a lot to do with the quality of the end product, which is the motherboard that you install in your system. Unfortunately, you rarely have the opportunity to travel to Taiwan or mainland China to inspect a manufacturing plant, so you must rely on the track record of various manufacturers to make a general assessment of the quality of their boards.

As is the case with most components, the quality and reliability of motherboards increases over the life of the production cycle. The first batches of motherboards generally have more faults than much later batches, so if possible you don't want to be one of the earliest adopters. However, it is understandable that you can't always avoid that.

Something you generally want to avoid is reworked boards. A reworked board is a board that had a manufacturing defect and was corrected through the use of an after production modification. The telltale sign of a reworked board is a wire connected to points on the PCB itself, as shown in Figure 3.9. Sometimes you don't have a choice when receiving these motherboards, but if you have the option, get one that is built properly, without the need for a rework in the first place.

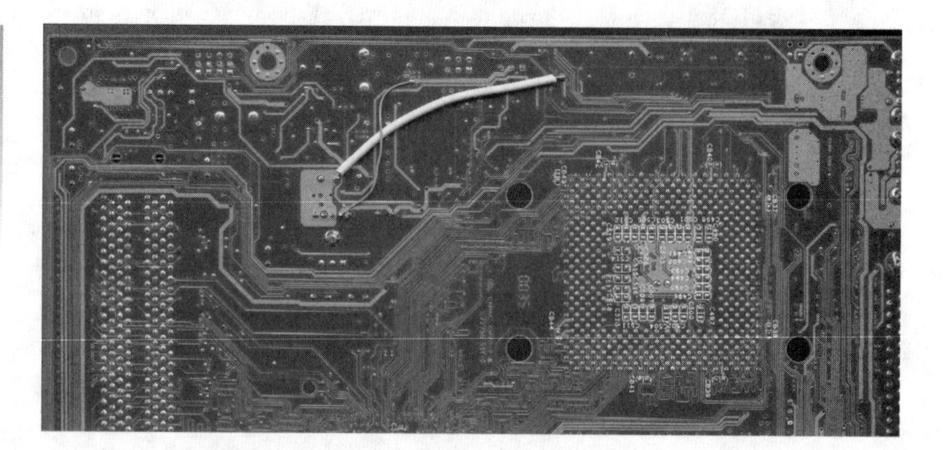

FIGURE 3.9
A reworked motherboard. The two wires you see here are correcting a manufacturing flaw and are a tell tale sign of a reworked motherboard.

The reliability of a motherboard is often determined by the quality characteristics just discussed, as well as the actual design and components used on a motherboard. Again, there is very little opportunity to do the proper research in order to find out if every little component used on a motherboard is of the best quality or not. This leaves the best way to judge the quality of a motherboard on the history of a company's product line as well as on other owners' opinions.

Form Factors and Ports

If motherboard manufacturers built their motherboards to whatever sizes they felt necessary we would be in quite a bit of trouble. Luckily there is a standard for motherboard size known as Form Factor.

The Form Factor of a motherboard governs the length and width of the board (not necessarily the exact numbers, but the ranges they can be in), as well as the positioning of connectors for I/O devices. The Form Factor also indicates what sort of case can be used with the motherboard (since the motherboard must be able to mount in the computer chassis) as well as what type of power supplies with which it will work.

Currently the most popular form factor is known as ATX, a replacement for the AT form factor that had been around for quite a few years. The move from AT to ATX occurred as there were a few shortcomings provided by the AT standard that needed to be taken care of. ATX brought the Soft Off capability, allowing an OS to shut down your computer completely as well as set more clearly defined standards for power supplies and cooling. The ATX form factor controls quite a few variables of motherboard design that are actually very useful.

For starters, most ATX motherboards measure approximately 8"×12". While the 12" width of the board is rarely deviated from, the length can range depending on the components that the manufacturer must make room for on the motherboard. If you have an ATX motherboard, you are able to purchase any case that meets the ATX specification and your motherboard will properly fit in the case. Not all cases are equal however, so some may fit your motherboard better than others, especially if you have a larger board. The Pentium 4 actually requires a different revision of an ATX case to support its unique cooling mechanis. However, most cases should be Pentium 4 compliant by now. For more information on ATX cases take a look at Chapter 9, "Cases and Cooling: Living in Style and Keeping Your Cool."

The ATX specification also dictates the layout of what is called the I/O Backpane of your motherboard (see Figure 3.10). This is where all of your on-board I/O ports are located for external access such as your printer port, some of your USB ports, your keyboard/mouse ports, and any ports for integrated devices such as on-board sound. The location of all these ports is set by the ATX specification so you usually don't have to worry about ports being placed in unusual locations. If you notice, I mentioned that this backpane only features *some* of your USB ports, not all. All of today's chipsets support more than the two USB ports you see on the back of your motherboard. Unfortunately, in order to make use of them you need to have extra ports. Motherboard manufacturers have been shipping their boards with a bracket for extra USB ports that mounts next to your expansion cards in your case. Unfortunately, not all motherboard manufacturers include these brackets. Still, there are those that do.

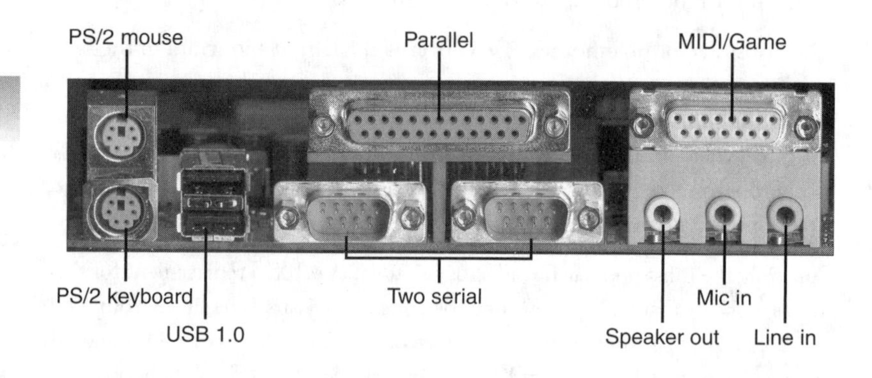

FIGURE 3.10
An ATX I/O backpane.

Power is another feature for which the ATX specification sets fairly strict guidelines for. The power switch in an ATX case isn't like a light switch; the switch doesn't actually turn anything off or on. Instead the switch simply connects two pins on your motherboard, which is constantly receiving a small amount of power (even when your computer is off). Once the connection is made, your motherboard gets the signal to turn itself on and then does so. Because the motherboard must constantly be supplied with power, the ATX specification calls for a special power supply, known as an ATX power supply (see Figure 3.11).

FIGURE 3.11
The 20-pin single block interface of the ATX power connector replaced the two connectors that the AT power supply specification used.

The ATX power supply is what allows the motherboard to turn on by itself and it is also what allows your operating system to automatically turn off your computer when you tell Windows to shut down. This power supply features a 20-pin connector that plugs into your motherboard. Many newer power supplies and motherboards actually feature up to two more connectors that plug into your motherboard. Figure 3.12 features each of these three connectors.

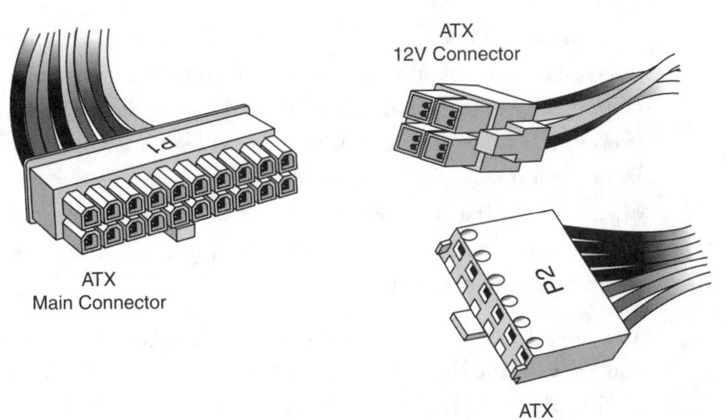

FIGURE 3.12
The three different power connectors that you might find wired to an ATX power supply.

Any ATX power supply has the main 20-pin connector. The two other power connectors are the ATX Aux, a seldom used auxiliary power connector, and the ATX12V. The Pentium 4, because of increased power requirements, was the first chip to require an ATX12V power supply with a special connector to supply power to the CPU (see Figure 3.13). If you have a Pentium 4 motherboard that needs power supplied through this connector, but don't have one with your power supply, you can buy special cable that converts a normal IDE power connector into an ATX12V connector.

FIGURE 3.13
A 2x2 ATX12V power connector is found in most Pentium 4 motherboards.

Performance

I'm starting this section with a warning: Before considering what motherboard you want, you should always choose what CPU and chipset you want before even beginning to look at the motherboards that are available. In doing that, you not only choose two of the major components in your system, but you also determine quite a bit of the performance of your system.

A motherboard's biggest selling point definitely is not the performance it offers. The performance offered should come mainly from the CPU and chipset. The motherboard merely connects the parts. For a mature platform (for example, one that has been out for at least a few months), motherboards from the top manufacturers should perform within a few percentage points of each other. If a motherboard happens to be performing unusually poorly against others that use the same chipset, it is usually due to a faulty implementation of the chipset or a BIOS issue.

You should be more concerned with the stability of your motherboard than you are with the slight 1–2% performance advantage it offers over a competing board. Remember that although we want to build the most powerful systems possible, a requirement is that they must be as stable as possible. Sacrificing stability for performance is not acceptable.

Popular Manufacturers and Their Boards

Among enthusiasts there are approximately 16 relatively well-known motherboard manufacturers. Here I will talk briefly about these 16. For those that I use and recommend, I will provide a bit more information on their history and where their strengths lie.

ABIT

ABIT has been a favorite of gamers ever since they released their Pentium Classic motherboards years ago. What made ABIT so famous so quickly was their offering of a truly jumperless BIOS configuration utility they named SoftMenu. ABIT brought us SoftMenu back in the days of mass crowds of jumpers spread all across the motherboard, and their technology was met with extreme enthusiasm and relief. There has always been much debate as to who was the first to bring a jumperless BIOS setup to the market. ABIT and QDI were talking about the technology around the same time, and one was the first to release it while the other was the first to announce it.

Regardless of who happened to be the first, ABIT has always been a name associated with the enthusiast and the performance tweaker.

ABIT showed their interest in the enthusiast market by being one of the first manufacturers to take an active role in the online enthusiast communities. Their initiative helped market the ABIT name quite well.

ABIT has always been one of the most perceptive to needs in the enthusiast community and thus their BIOSes are always up to date with the most configurable features you could imagine.

ABIT is not a major player in the OEM market, which unfortunately stunts their growth potential. This, at the same time, means that ABIT must depend quite a bit on the DIY market, which is a positive point as well.

AOpen

AOpen is a fairly large player in the OEM market and at the same time they have provided extremely reliable and stable solutions for us DIY folks as well (see Figure 3.14). AOpen has always impressed me with their build quality and board reliability. I haven't seen as much of them in the DIY market recently and unfortunately they have fallen behind in terms of the features we all tend to look for. Hopefully, in the future they will be able to turn this around.

FIGURE 3.14
Notice the clean layout of this Aopen motherboard, as well as the lever on the end of the AGP slot. This is an AGP retention mechanism designed to keep AGP cards in place during the shipping of a system.

ASUS

ASUS has been a favorite of mine simply because their philosophy is to be the best not only in quality and reliability, but in performance as well; and it shows. ASUS is one of the largest, if not the largest, motherboard manufacturer out of Taiwan and their products got them there.

What's impressive about ASUS is that they generally offer a reasonable set of features—maybe not equivalent to what a company like ABIT generally provides, but more than the average manufacturer would. However, their stability is generally unparalleled by any other motherboard.

It is very rare that you will go wrong with purchasing an ASUS motherboard unless there is a particular feature you must have that happens to be missing. ASUS is definitely one of my top picks.

The downside to their quality and efforts is that their boards are usually $10–$50 more expensive than the competition. Often the premium is worth it, although every now and then you can find an equivalent alternative that is cheaper.

Biostar

Biostar has kept a relatively low profile in the DIY market in spite of the fact that they used to be very popular motherboards to carry in most local computer hardware shops. Biostar boards are a bit cheaper than an ASUS for example, but remember what I said about trying to save a few bucks on your motherboard purchase. There isn't anything wrong with Biostar, although I don't put them on the same level as an ASUS.

Chaintech

I've always viewed Chaintech as an aspiring ABIT mainly because they used to rival each other quite a bit in the early days. See Figure 3.15 for a look at one of their boards. They are a good company, although they are much stronger in Europe than they are in the US. Their boards are solid, again not on the level of ASUS, but good nonetheless. The biggest problem you end up having with Chaintech is finding them in the United States.

FIGURE 3.15
This Chaintech motherboard has Year 2000 compliant printed on it because it was made when certain BIOSes only stored the year field in a two-digit variable rather than four. This Year 2000 compliancy label is mainly a marketing gimmick since most competing motherboards claimed similar compatibility.

DFI

DFI is another manufacturer that produces solid designs, though not particularly advanced in terms of the tweaking features I like to see, unfortunately. They are much like Chaintech in that their U.S. presence is relatively weak compared to some of the larger manufacturers, although you tend to find more DFI solutions than Chaintech solutions in the U.S. Also, like Chaintech, they are relatively strong in Europe.

ECS

ECS is more on par with DFI in terms of their U.S. presence; their boards are onpar with DFI's as well. They've historically included very few features that have the enthusiast in mind, so you'll probably want to look elsewhere for your needs. For other applications ECS would probably be an option but remember, our goal of building a PC geared to high-octane gaming involves building the most tweakable, feature-filled, and stable, yet high performing, gaming PC possible.

EPoX

Always an interesting company, EPoX made a name for themselves back in the days of jumpers-galore with a very interesting idea. While they didn't have a jumperless setup, they did have an extremely easy single jumper setup. One jumper would control the CPU clock multiplier and FSB for you. They later moved to two jumpers when users wanted to set their FSBs independently, but it was a very useful feature to say the least.

Of course those days are long gone but EPoX has still remained on our radars. They are more tweaking and enthusiast oriented than the DFIs and ECSs of the world, but they're not too big. Performing a quick search of stocked motherboards by brand name usually results in equal amounts of boards from EPoX, DFI, and ECS with Chaintech noticeably behind the two.

FIC

FIC has very close ties to VIA, the chipset manufacturer. This relationship usually means that FIC is one of the first to debut VIA-based designs (see Figure 3.16). Like most other manufacturers, FIC has concentrated on diversifying their product lines as much as possible, including exploring areas outside of simple motherboard sales.

FIGURE 3.16
The FIC AD-11 motherboard was actually FIC's first DDR solution for the AMD Athlon platform.

From a performance and features standpoint FIC usually offers the basic features that we, as enthusiasts need. However, they are no ABIT in terms of the flexibility of those features nor are they ASUS in terms of stability. One of FIC's attractive points happens to be that they are quite affordable, especially compared to the competition.

Gigabyte

Gigabyte has been another stability favorite of mine. They are one of the larger manufacturers and their boards have historically been very well made as well as high performing.

The only downside to a lot of Gigabyte motherboards is often they are not enthusiast oriented enough. Obviously the OEMs are the ones putting food on the table for these manufacturers and they could care less for a lot of the BIOS tweaking options we like to see. Regardless, it would be nice to get some more jumperless setups out of them. One thing I can always give ABIT credit for is having an extremely flexible jumperless BIOS setup. Unfortunately, that leaves Gigabyte (often times) at the other end of the spectrum.

To Gigabyte's credit, no company has been able to rival ABIT's SoftMenu (and its successors) in terms of ease of use and flexibility on such a consistent basis.

Iwill

If ASUS is considered to be the largest in Taiwan, then Iwill is generally considered to be the smallest; however Iwill is definitely an example of how being small doesn't mean that they cannot produce quality products.

Although Iwill doesn't push the same amount of volume that a lot of the other motherboard manufacturers do, their motherboards are generally very well featured and offer pretty solid operation. From an enthusiast's standpoint Iwill has definitely been very perceptive to the requests of the community and it shows in the overclocking/tweaking feature set included on many of their boards.

While this doesn't pertain directly to gamers, Iwill does have their hands in the high-end server and workstation motherboard market where only the best in quality is tolerated. Hopefully, some of that translates over to their desktop board production.

MSI

It is unfortunate for many manufacturers that the standard we hold to is ASUS, but that isn't the case for MSI. You can think of MSI as hot on ASUS' heels. They share a lot of the same strengths as ASUS: stability, reliability, quality, performance, and support. However, every now and then they run into some bumpy roads with their boards, but then, so do all manufacturers.

Like ASUS, and ABIT as well, it is quite easy to find MSI boards in the United States. As a gaming enthusiast you should keep your eye on MSI's product line; they often have a board that will catch your eye. Remember how I mentioned that every now and then you'll be able to find a board cheaper than an ASUS solution and equally or better featured? MSI is the type of company to provide those boards.

Shuttle

Unfortunately, another good company, Shuttle, cannot compete with the ABITs, ASUSs, and MSIs of the world in terms of the overall feature package they offer you as a gaming enthusiast.

Supermicro

Supermicro is quite popular, however not among gaming enthusiasts. The main reason behind this is they aren't an enthusiast manufacturer. Although very few are, Supermicro focuses primarily on the high-end server and workstation market. They have very stable motherboard designs, but you're probably not too interested in their quad processor solutions.

Transcend

I put Transcend on par with the DFIs and Shuttles of the world. They're a good manufacturer, but do very little to set them apart from the competition. Transcend is fairly unique in that they are also a memory manufacturer but that's about it.

Tyan

Tyan is much like Supermicro in that they are more concerned with the high-end server and workstation markets than they are with the DIY desktop motherboard market. Also like Supermicro, they do produce desktop motherboards as well but for the most part you will want to stick to manufacturers like ASUS and MSI for your needs.

Every now and then one of Tyan's high-end solutions does make a great base for your powerful computer, but generally they are just too high priced for a desktop PC.

Looking Forward

If you've built a computer in the past decade you will have had some experience with the motherboards of the past and the one thing I can say for sure is that the quality of the DIY solutions has definitely improved over time. Even motherboards from just a few years ago pale in comparison to what is currently available. I say this not only in terms of stability but in terms of features as well. Motherboards are shipping with multiple BIOS chips on board so that if one goes bad during the upgrading process (corrupted BIOS flashes do happen) the other can take over and recover the original. Motherboards do much more now than just beep if something is wrong. They are able to tell you what is wrong either via lights or actual numbers displayed.

With technology moving at the rate it has been, it wouldn't be too surprising to see motherboards offering even more features of this sort. The non-legacy motherboard is closer than you might think. This means the parallel, serial, PS2 ports, and IDE channels of yesterday are on their way out and will be replaced by USB, FireWire, and Serial ATA (see Figure 3.17).

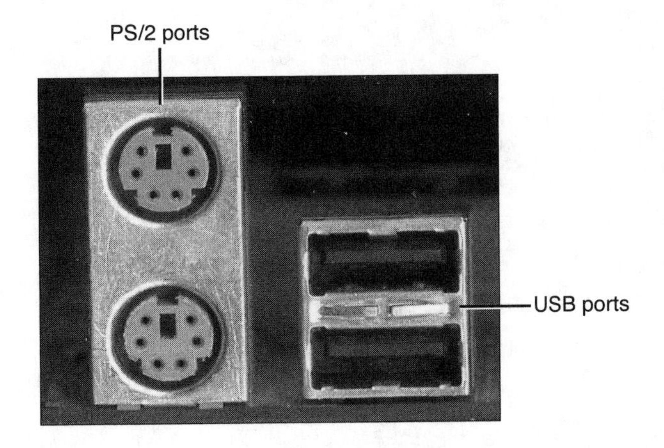

FIGURE 3.17
PS/2 ports versus USB ports. Not only do the connector shapes change, but the design of the physical USB connector avoids the possibility of bending any connector pins when inserting.

➤ ***For more information on IDE connectors, see Chapter 7, "Storage: The Slowest Part of Your PC."***

To find out more about input connectors like Serial, PS/2, USB and Firewire, refer to Chapter 10, "Monitors and Input Devices: Your Sense of Sight and Touch Restored."

Looking even further into the future, remember there is an obvious trend towards higher bandwidth solutions. You can eventually expect to see motherboard manufacturers phasing out PCI slots in favor of a higher bandwidth bus, but because of the number of PCI peripherals currently available, this transition will take time to complete. You can expect a couple of higher bandwidth slots to coexist with conventional PCI slots and eventually PCI slots will become legacy provisions and will go the same way as those long black ISA slots.

Remember in the end, the features that motherboard manufacturers have to play with are provisions made by the chipset. If you want to see where the motherboard market is headed, take a look at what the chipset manufacturers are promoting.

Chapter 4

Memory: Your PC's Scratchpad

The Role of System Memory

"I need more memory!" That statement has been made countless times by upgraders with slow game frame rates that very often didn't need more memory. Your memory subsystem just happens to be one of the easiest things to blame for poor performance. Saying "I need a new motherboard" is a bit more technical than saying "I need a new CPU" or "I need a new computer" for many. The result of this is that very little attention is paid to memory other than how much you happen to have in your system. And although memory size is indeed an important characteristic of your system, many more things need to be considered outside of memory size.

I have actually already introduced you to a type of memory, cache memory, back in Chapter 1, "The Central Processing Unit: The Heart and

Soul of the PC." I described cache memory as really fast memory because it is transistor-based much like the rest of your CPU. By being transistor-based, data is stored in the cache according to the state of the various switches or transistors that make up the cache. The state of the transistors does not change unless it is instructed to or unless the cache loses power (you turn off your computer).

The memory I am talking about now, however isn't as pleasant as cache, this is system memory. System memory is the stuff that lies on the other side of the North Bridge/MCH (Memory Controller Hub) and is connected to the North Bridge/MCH via the memory bus. System memory, unfortunately, isn't transistor-based; instead, it is capacitor-based. A capacitor, if you don't already know, is an electrical device whose sole function is to hold an electrical charge. The capacitor charges up by applying an electric current over it and is discharged when the electric current is removed. This is unlike a transistor in that the process does not occur instantaneously. When you hit a light switch, the connection is made and the circuit is complete. On the other hand, when you fill a glass with water, the process isn't complete until all the water has entered the glass. This is the difference between a transistor (the light bulb) and a capacitor (the glass of water).

So instead of making use of electrical switches, system memory uses capacitors with stored charge to indicate a 1 or a 0 value (remember, you're still in binary). This is similar to the cache I have been talking about in that when the power is removed from the memory, the data is lost. However, many more important differences exist between system memory and the L1/L2 caches explored in Chapter 1.

Comparing System Memory and Cache Memory

The major difference between your system memory and your cache memory is that because of the nature of a capacitor, which requires that it be charged as well as refreshed to maintain that charge, system memory is noticeably slower than the CPU caches I talked about earlier. The unfortunate part about this reality is that much more of your data is stored in system memory than it is in cache, so you get to deal with the higher latencies of capacitance-based memory.

It is often jokingly asked: "If the only thing that survives a plane crash is the black box, then why not make the entire plane out of the black box?" And in the computer world, it is often asked: "If system memory is so slow compared to cache, why not make everything out of cache memory?" Just as the case with the first question, things aren't as simple as that.

The major problem with the cache used in CPUs is that it is quite costly to produce when compared to system memory. Because it is capacitance-based, system memory is of a relatively simple construction. The switching nature of CPU cache requires many more components to create the same effect. With small sizes such as 256KB and 512KB, cache memory is relatively affordable, but if you realize that today's performance machines are using 256MB and 512MB of memory the cost associated with transistor-based memory is simply too great.

So now that you can tell the difference between cache and the system memory I'm going to be discussing, what makes it so important to you and the games you are playing? After all, aren't games only dependent on a strong FPU?

Although it is true that 3D games, such as NHL 2002 and Max Payne, do benefit from a CPU with a strong FPU, gaming is much more than just performing a lot of calculations. The calculations your CPU is doing only pertains to the position of the objects on your screen and what they're doing, but your CPU has to be getting this data from somewhere. The actual game you're running is loaded into memory from your hard disk or CD/DVD-ROM drive. From main memory, the CPU is sent data via the memory bus to the North Bridge/MCH then via the FSB to the CPU's caches.

Today's games can take up well more than 50MB in memory, which is just a *tad* too big to fit in the 384KB exclusive cache of the Athlon. Note that when I refer to memory here I am referring to system memory. Too often people mistake system memory, or memory as it is simply referred to, as being hard disk space. This type of "memory" is a completely different issue, which I discuss in Chapter 7, "Storage: The Slowest Part of Your PC."

As you can guess, it is much slower for your CPU to have to pull data from memory when compared to how long it takes to pull data from its caches. When your CPU needs a piece of information contained within its cache, even the L2 cache (assuming you've got a Pentium III Coppermine, Athlon Thunderbird, or better), all it has to do is pull from its on-die cache, which is operating at the CPU's clock speed. When your CPU can't find what it needs in its L2 cache, it must go to system memory that is significantly slower and much further away. You can analogize this to the following scenario in which you need to add more milk to your breakfast cereal. Getting "milk" from cache is the equivalent of having the carton sitting right next to you while you eat. However, if it's not right there, you end up going downstairs to your refrigerator for it, which takes a bit more time. The first way is by far the quickest and the most convenient, but if you have no milk you have no option but to make the treck downstairs, which is a necessary evil albeit much slower. However, it is taking it to the next step, which is having to get information off your hard drive. That would be more like discovering you had no milk left and had to get in your car, drive to the store and come back just so you can finish eating your cereal in the morning. If your CPU doesn't have the data it needs, it has to get it from somewhere, slow or not.

Bandwidth and Latency Still Apply

Chapters 1 and 2, "The Chipset: The PC's Crossing Guard," contained a great deal of talk about bandwidth and latency. That material applies here as well. Remember that your CPU is only as fast as the speed at which it is given data to process. If a 10GHz CPU is waiting around on a slow 10MHz memory bus to feed it data, much of that CPU power is going to waste and it shows up in a game's performance. The greater the bandwidth and latency difference your CPU sees between accessing data from its cache and getting data from system memory, the more likely your system is going to be performance limited. When this happens you notice that upgrading to a CPU that has a 33% higher clock speed might not provide you with nearly as much of a performance boost as you'd expect. The best case scenario is that such an upgrade would give you a 33% boost in performance, but if you're bottlenecked by your memory subsystem, that increase could be cut down to less than 10%. The ability for CPU performance to scale with clock speed is dependent on it being able to be fed by its FSB and memory subsystems.

System memory latency matters quite a bit because the higher the latency the longer it takes for the CPU to get the data it needs. Remember that the CPU always has a reasonably high latency when getting data from main memory because it must go to the North Bridge/MCH via the FSB, and then to system (or main as it is sometimes called) memory via the memory bus and back. The fact that the CPU has to go through the North Bridge/MCH adds a relatively significant memory latency penalty. Unfortunately, it is one that can't be avoided, which is not to say, however, that designers haven't made attempts. The most recent attempt to avoid that penalty, with an as yet unreleased Micron chipset called the Mamba, is to outfit the North Bridge/MCH with a sizeable amount of embedded memory (8–16MB). This type of a design could increase performance dramatically, especially with higher speed CPUs that are dependent on being fed by fast memory buses.

The only problem with having a North Bridge/MCH with embedded memory is that the data is still constrained by the bandwidth offered by the FSB, although latency is significantly improved.

Because system memory should be able to provide the CPU with similar volumes of data to what it's used to, bandwidth must never be overlooked. Keep in mind that the CPU is used to getting data, in some cases, at 50GB/s whereas one of the fastest memory buses is capable of delivering data at 3.2GB/s. The gap between the two is already large enough, making it even larger just holds your otherwise high performing CPU back even more. That's like buying a Ferrari and then driving it up and down 35-mph roads downtown.

So if this is why early motherboards using DDR SDRAM or RAMBUS technology did not provide much oomph to system performance, how is that DDR SDRAM became such an instant success story when used in graphics cards?

Remember that graphics processors perform very specific functions requiring gigabytes of memory bandwidth. Although opening and running MS Word doesn't really require all that much data to be transferred from your system memory to your CPU, in the case of 3D rendering, you're texturing, filtering, and antialiasing millions of pixels per second and dealing with polygons flying all over the place. It's definitely a much more bandwidth intensive endeavor.

Memory Types: It's Dynamic

The "capacitance-based system memory" I've been talking about thus far is actually known as Dynamic Random Access Memory or DRAM. You are probably more commonly familiar with the term RAM being used to refer to system memory. You should understand that many types of RAM exist and the DRAM system memory is just one of those types. It is okay to just call it RAM instead of saying system memory all the time.

Just as many types of RAM exist, so do many types of DRAM (a type of RAM). The three most common types of DRAM today are SDRAM, DDR SDRAM, and RDRAM. These three DRAM types are the ones I focus on the most here.

These types of RAM have a great impact on gaming performance because they all differ in latency and bandwidth offerings. Since 3D games have become much more popular in recent times than they were five years ago, the demand for higher bandwidth memory subsystems has increased tremendously. Those games that are still stuck in the world of 2D, although performance demanding, (case in point, Red Alert 2) they are not nearly as memory bandwidth intensive as most 3D first person shooters among other high quality, high speed 3D games.

SDRAM

SDRAM stands for Synchronous Dynamic Random Access Memory. Now you can see why enthusiasts love acronyms; try having to say that every time you explained to someone what kind of memory is in your system. SDRAM is packaged in modules called DIMMs, which you can see in Figure 4.1.

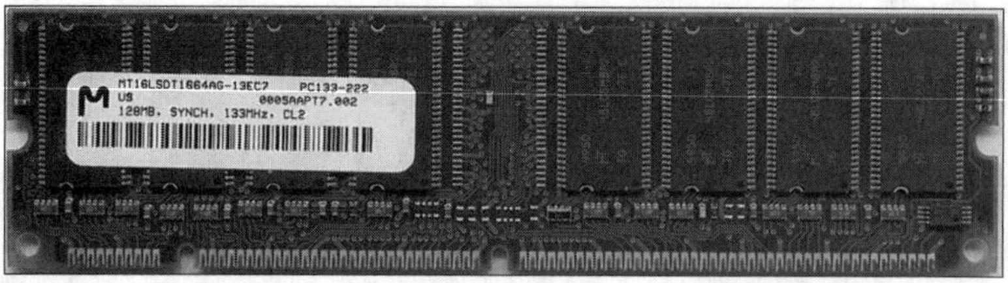

FIGURE 4.1
As you can see, an SDRAM module has two notches that prevent the 168-pin DIMM from being inserted backwards. If you do happen to try this, you are met with a system that doesn't boot and if you do it long enough, you are left with a smoking stick of memory. I kid you not.

The word synchronous comes from the fact that SDRAM is synchronized to the system clock. As I mentioned earlier, SDRAM has a 64-bit data bus to the North Bridge/MCH, however the frequency at which this bus operates is dependent on the type of SDRAM being used.

When SDRAM was first introduced it was rarely classified by its operating frequency like it is today. Instead, it was classified according to access time measured in nanoseconds (ns). This was the method in which previous asynchronous memory was rated because it was not synchronous to a system clock. Because SDRAM is, this caused a fair amount of confusion when comparing SDRAM with older standards. Because it boasts access times that were one-sixth of that of previous memory technologies such as EDO DRAM, yet offers performance that isn't proportional to the faster access time, SDRAM brought up the need for new nomenclature. It was because of this confusion that SDRAM started to be named according to its operating frequency, which is determined by the memory clock to which it was synchronous (which is a derivative of the FSB clock).

The first SDRAM modules were rated at 66MHz and then were later increased for compliance with 100MHz operating frequencies. These SDRAM modules were known as PC66 and PC100, respectively. Where the names came from is pretty clear. The 66 in PC66 refers to the operating frequency as does the 100 in PC100. As memory clocks reached 133MHz, PC133 SDRAM was born and it followed the same nomenclature as its predecessors.

SDRAM (sometimes referred to as Single Data Rate SDRAM because data is only transferred once every clock cycle) offers a bandwidth that is quite straightforward. Using the equations I discussed in Chapter 2, you are able to find out how much bandwidth the three types of SDRAM offer:

(Bus Width) × (Frequency) × (Data Transferred per Clock) / 8 = Bandwidth in MB/s

PC66 SDRAM:

(64-bit bus width) × (66MHz PC66 frequency) × (Data Transferred *Once* per Clock) / 8 = 533MB/s

PC100 SDRAM:

(64-bit bus width) × (100MHz PC100 frequency) × (Data Transferred *Once* per Clock) / 8 = 800MB/s

PC133 SDRAM:

(64-bit bus width) × (133MHz PC133 frequency) × (Data Transferred *Once* per Clock) / 8 = 1066MB/s

There have been no official SDRAM specs released after PC133 simply because any increase that could be offered would be minimal compared to what higher bandwidth technologies can offer. Although PC133 SDRAM only offers 1GB/s of bandwidth, it actually offers some of the lowest latency memory accesses possible with today's memory technology. You have to understand that this is partially dependent on a good memory controller in the North Bridge/MCH (because it contributes to the latency the CPU sees). However, generally speaking, SDRAM has a lower latency than either of the competing higher bandwidth memory technologies (DDR SDRAM and RDRAM).

For this reason, SDRAM seemed to be a better option than DDR SDRAM and RDRAM when they were both introduced. Remember how manufacturers like to plan ahead? The release of DDR SDRAM and RDRAM on their respective platforms was a precautionary release, in preparation for the time when CPUs and applications would need more memory bandwidth than regular SDRAM. Your gaming performance is dependent on memory latency, as well as bandwidth. If you have massive amounts of memory bandwidth that your game isn't taking advantage of, a lower bandwidth solution with a lower latency offers a performance advantage over your solution.

By looking at the earlier equations you realize that another way to increase SDRAM bandwidth is by increasing the width of the bus. Unfortunately, this is quite costly. SDRAM is already using a 64-bit interface, which occupies quite a few pins on the North Bridge/MCH and just as many traces on the motherboard. Adding the pins and traces for essentially another 64-bit interface would increase North Bridge/MCH size dramatically and would result in more expensive motherboards that are harder to make. It isn't impossible to do this, but most manufacturers would rather not.

When the PC100 SDRAM standard was introduced in 1998, quite a few changes took place over what had become known as PC66 SDRAM. Prior to the PC100 spec, there was very little standardization in the SDRAM market. This unfortunately resulted in quite a few poorly made modules being sold without anyone keeping these manufacturers in check. At the same time, it resulted in poor compatibility with the vast amount of motherboards out there. I mentioned 16 different motherboard manufacturers in Chapter 3, "The Motherboard: Low Rent Housing for the CPU and Chipset." Try combining that with the fact that more memory modules exist than motherboard manufacturers and that multiple motherboards implement a SDRAM controller. It is nearly impossible to guarantee compatibility with all motherboards. This was a problem since it gave SDRAM a bad rap from the start, and it already offered very little performance improvement over the standard it was replacing, EDO DRAM. The PC100 spec changed that.

One of the most important things the PC100 spec called for was a relatively tight manufacturing specification. Memory modules are actually built on little PCBs that are usually more than one inch high and a little longer than five inches. The PC100 spec demanded that all PCBs be six-layer designs to ensure greater signal integrity and thus system stability. Prior to this there were quite a few SDRAM modules built on four-layer PCBs and some of these designs contributed to the problems SDRAM encountered initially. Along with this demand for a six-layer Printed Circuit Board (PCB) came a number of very specific electrical requirements. These electrical requirements were made present because of the higher operating frequency of PC100 SDRAM (100MHz versus 66MHz) and to pave the way for even higher clocked SDRAM modules.

Another very important feature of the PC100 specification was the requirement for Serial Presence Detect (SPD) circuitry to be placed on every module. The idea behind SPD was that a module knows best how to configure itself, so it should tell the motherboard what settings to use in its BIOS. Through the use of its SPD circuitry, the module "tells" the motherboard everything it needs to know: operating frequency, memory timings, various latency values, and so on. The SPD is nothing more than a chip on the module that communicates with the North Bridge/MCH on the motherboard and tells it how it would like to be configured.

The PC100 specification also introduced a new labeling standard that stated that modules should be marked as PCxxx-abc-def where xxx corresponds to the operating frequency and the 'abc-def' string corresponds to memory timing values that the memory is able to work within.

Now I mentioned that the only types of SDRAM released were PC66, PC100, and PC133, yet if you do a search online you easily uncover PC150 and PC166 SDRAM. When a memory manufacturer produces the memory chips to go on the PCB they have to be rated at a certain speed. Let's take the 133MHz chips that PC133 SDRAM requires, for example. Each chip must be rated at 133MHz and the entire module must be able to operate at 133MHz. To guarantee that operation for every single PC133 SDRAM module they make, their ratings have to be a little more generous. This means that a PC133 SDRAM module can't just barely pass internal tests for 133MHz operation, it usually has to work within some tolerance range of operation to gain PC133 certification (for example, being able to work at 133MHz +/- 5%). When a manufacturer first starts making a particular type of memory, the yields on them are low. In other words, the percentage of usable chips out of all those that are manufactured isn't very high. As the manufacturing process matures and the kinks are worked out, not only does the yield improve, but the speeds at which these manufacturers are able to run their modules increases as well.

For PC133 SDRAM, manufacturers were able to run their modules at 150MHz and 166MHz and still pass all their compliance tests. Although they simply rated their modules at PC150 and PC166, no official PC150 or PC166 standards exist. However, a PC150 or PC166 module is of no use if your memory bus still runs at 133MHz (remember that your North Bridge/MCH controls at what frequency your memory bus runs, not your memory). Now you have to tell your chipset, through your motherboard, that you want to run your memory frequency at 150MHz or 166MHz. Running a certain component out of specification (in this case the North Bridge/MCH) is possible and it is known as overclocking. I get into greater specifics of overclocking in Chapter 14, "Tweaking and Overclocking: Turbo-Charging Your PC."

DDR SDRAM

Now, you learn a third way to increase the bandwidth that SDRAM offers. You already know that it can be done by changing the first two variables in the equation (bus width x frequency x data transferred per clock / 8).

Changing the third variable of the equation (how much data is transferred per clock) can also increase the bandwidth.

Take the SDRAM bandwidth equation for PC100 SDRAM and simply change the amount of data transferred per clock from once per clock to twice per clock. The bandwidth increases twice as much, making it greater than what PC133 can offer with a lower operating frequency and without increasing the bus width any. This type of SDRAM is referred to as Double-Data Rate (DDR) SDRAM (see Figure 4.2). The sending of two bits of data per clock gives DDR SDRAM the capability to be extremely close to SDRAM in terms of manufacturing costs, and is thus quite attractive to chipset and motherboard manufacturers.

FIGURE 4.2
When compared to a 168-pin SDRAM module, the 184-pin DDR SDRAM module (shown here) is the same length, but only has one notch in the connector. It can still only be inserted one way.

Upon its release, DDR SDRAM was released in two speed ratings: 100MHz and 133MHz. DDR SDRAM operating at 100MHz featured a peak theoretical bandwidth of 1.6GB/s and, at 133MHz, an incredible 3.2GB/s of data can be transferred. To maintain similarity between the PCxxx spec of SDRAM, a similar notation was used. Unfortunately, it is a bit misleading.

When running at 100MHz, and thus offering 1.6GB/s (or 1600MB/s) of bandwidth, this type of DDR SDRAM was labeled as PC1600. The name came from the amount of bandwidth offered and not from the operating frequency, which was misleading to someone that had just upgraded from PC133 or PC100 SDRAM and failed to see the improvement 12 or 16 times in performance that the memory implied.

As you can guess, 133MHz DDR SDRAM modules were thus labeled PC2100 because they delivered 2100MBps, or 2.1GBps, of memory bandwidth. Later, a competing nomenclature was introduced, referring to PC1600 DDR SDRAM as simply DDR200 and PC2100 DDR SDRAM as DDR266. This type of nomenclature is much less misleading, because 100MHz DDR SDRAM is effectively operating at 200MHz, hence the DDR200 and the same for 133MHz DDR SDRAM.

Another advantage of DDR SDRAM over regular SDRAM is that it features a lower operating voltage. While SDRAM requires an operating voltage of 3.3v, DDR SDRAM only requires a 2.5v source, making it much more attractive for situations in which low power is critical (such as when using laptops).

The biggest downside to DDR SDRAM happens to be its biggest selling point as well—its capability to sustain incredibly large data transfers. The downside to this is that the memory bus and its traces on the motherboard have to be able to handle transfer rates of up to 2.1GB/s up from the 1GB/s they had to handle with regular PC133 SDRAM. It's not impossible to do, it's just more taxing on the motherboard and thus helps expose poor designs with greater ease.

The foundation of DDR SDRAM is identical to that of regular SDRAM, meaning that it also gets the relatively low latency operation of SDRAM as well. Of course, DDR SDRAM pays a small latency premium over regular SDRAM, but it isn't much at all, especially compared to what is noticed with RDRAM.

The rest of the specs of DDR SDRAM are relatively similar to that of SDRAM. The modules also make use of SPD courtesy of the PC100 spec from years ago.

RDRAM

The first two memory types I have discussed are both types of SDRAM. They have a 64-bit data bus and have very similar characteristics. The SDRAM and DDR SDRAM specs were both open specs developed under the JEDEC (Joint Electron Device Engineering Council) Solid State Technology Association. However, in 1999, Intel brought a third competing specification into the eyes of the public. This one wasn't agreed upon at a JEDEC meeting, instead, a company known as Rambus developed the specification. The specification they developed was for Rambus DRAM or RDRAM (sometimes referred to as Direct RDRAM or DRDRAM) and is shown in Figure 4.3. Although DRDRAM had been used in applications prior to Intel's acceptance and promotion of it in 1999 (for example, in Nintendo's N64 console), it wasn't until Intel's support that it truly made its way into the desktop market.

FIGURE 4.3
The most notable difference between a RDRAM module (shown here) and SDRAM modules is the integrated heat spreader designed to remove concentrated heat from a single RDRAM device and spread it across the surface of the entire module.

On the most fundamental basis, RDRAM is no different from SDRAM, DDR SDRAM, or any of the other DRAM types out there. Capacitance-based memory technology still stores data according to the presence, or lack thereof, of a stored electrical charge in a capacitor. Where RDRAM truly differs from SDRAM is in its interface.

While both DDR SDRAM and regular SDRAM rely on a parallel 64-bit interface, RDRAM is yet another technology (including Serial ATA and Hyper Transport) that is based upon a smaller width serial interface. The RDRAM interface is only 16 bits wide but its serial operation allows for it to be clocked extremely high, the most common speed being 400MHz with data being transferred twice per clock. Let's plug these values into our equation and find out how much bandwidth RDRAM can offer:

(16-bit bus width) × (400MHz RDRAM frequency) × (Data Transferred Twice per Clock) / 8 = 1600MB/s = 1.6GB/s

Now that looks kind of disappointing, doesn't it? This brand new, supposedly revolutionary, memory standard can only rival DDR200 bandwidth levels; what's so revolutionary about that?

Remember that the wider the bus that you have, the more pins on your North Bridge/MCH that must be dedicated to the interface and the more traces that must be present on an already crowded motherboard PCB. The beauty of RDRAM is that the interface is only 16 bits wide, meaning that two RDRAM channels can be put together resulting in a 32-bit interface and still take up less pins/space than a SDRAM or DDR SDRAM setup. With two channels, RDRAM's bandwidth doubles to 3.2GBps. Just imagine what kind of bandwidth could be offered with a higher clocked RDRAM bus.

The key design points behind RDRAM mainly relate to a low pin count interface that operates at a very high frequency. Because of the incredibly high operating frequency, RDRAM modules generate *a lot* of heat. To help negate this problem, a heat spreader is present over the module to better distribute the heat RDRAM chips generate across the entire surface of the module.

Unfortunately, one of the greatest downsides to RDRAM is that it is noticeably more expensive to produce than SDRAM and DDR SDRAM. The die size of each RDRAM chip on a module is noticeably larger than the die size of SDRAM chips on a SDRAM module and unlike DDR SDRAM, RDRAM isn't a simple evolution of SDRAM. This means that setting up manufacturing plants for RDRAM production requires much more of a change than the DDR transition took. Another source of added cost comes from the fact that Rambus charges royalties on many parts of the RDRAM system, which contributes to the expensive nature of the memory. Luckily, the memory has decreased in cost over the years since its introduction as a PC platform memory solution, making it much more viable than it once was.

One of the quirks about the RDRAM memory design is that there cannot be any unpopulated RDRAM memory slots. Those memory slots that are unpopulated must be filled with a Continuity Module (see Figure 4.4). Manufacturers of motherboards designed to work with RDRAM modules supply these continuity modules along with the motherboard. In addition to having to worry about continuity modules, also remember that if a dual channel RDRAM solution is implemented, RDRAM modules must be installed in pairs. This is because each RDRAM module is only 16 bits wide, so for a 32-bit interface you need two modules and partial bus accesses are not possible.

FIGURE 4.4
A Continuity module is nothing more than a termination module. It's very simple in design, but is required for current RDRAM implementations. In the future, RDRAM implementations might not require a continuity module.

Although RDRAM is an extremely bandwidth friendly design, its latency is much higher than that of SDRAM. It is because of this high latency penalty that RDRAM did not look good on the first platforms it was debuted on, mainly the Pentium III. Not only did the Pentium III not have enough FSB bandwidth to take advantage of what RDRAM could offer, but also the CPU wasn't clocked nearly high enough to be that dependent on RDRAM. The performance of RDRAM (as is the case with any other high bandwidth memory subsystems) is quite dependent on the clock speed and pipeline depth of the host CPU to which it's feeding data.

For this reason RDRAM truly showed its muscle when paired up with the Pentium 4. In Chapter 1, I discussed that the Pentium 4 has a function known as hardware prefetch. This causes it to automatically fetch data it might need from memory into its caches. This is a heavy user of memory bandwidth in itself, and when you couple that with the Pentium 4's minimum operating frequency of 1.3GHz and with the Pentium 4 destined for 2GHz+ operation, you can see why the Pentium 4 is dependent on a high bandwidth memory bus.

Remember how I mentioned that the greater the gap between the bandwidth the CPU is used to having (to its cache) and the bandwidth its memory subsystem offers, the more limited the performance is by the memory bus? Well, the Pentium 4 has the highest bandwidth L2 cache of any processor in its class; at 2GHz the Pentium 4 has a 61GBps connection to its L2 cache. That makes even the 3.2GBps, that its dual channel RDRAM memory subsystem can offer, seem miniscule.

Just like SDRAM and DDR SDRAM, RDRAM has many different rated speeds. The one I've been telling you about operates at 400MHz and transfers data twice every clock. This type of RDRAM is known as PC800 RDRAM and offers 1.6GB/s of memory bandwidth. As you can see, as in PC2100 DDR SDRAM, this name is also misleading. In this case, however, not as much because the RDRAM is effectively clocked at 400MHz × 2 (because it is able to transfer data twice per clock).

RDRAM has two more speed grades: PC600 and PC700. PC600 RDRAM operates at 300MHz (× 2) while PC700 RDRAM operates at 356MHz (× 2). The PC700 spec was created in the early days of RDRAM on the desktop scene when it was discovered that not all manufacturers were able to get good yields on PC800 parts. However, since yields have improved, PC700 has been phased out and it is rare that you find PC700 RDRAM. In many retail systems, to cut costs, manufacturers have outfitted their Pentium 4 systems with PC600 RDRAM. This only offers 1.2GB/s of memory bandwidth, barely any more than PC133 SDRAM. For the Pentium 4, this is a performance killer as it truly depends on having a good deal of memory bandwidth at its fingertips. In fact, the overall performance of the Pentium 4 with PC600 RDRAM is approximately equivalent to the performance with PC133 SDRAM because PC133 SDRAM has a bit of a latency advantage over PC600 RDRAM.

With RDRAM, especially on the Pentium 4, PC800 is a minimum requirement. Luckily, yields have been improving on RDRAM that should make higher speed RDRAM a reality in the future.

Like all the other memory types I've talked about, RDRAM operates on a multiple of the FSB frequency. This is where the word synchronous in SDRAM comes from. The memory runs synced to the system bus, or as you know it, the FSB. The frequency at which the SDRAM runs is referred to as the memory bus frequency, but it is actually derived from the FSB.

In the case of SDRAM and DDR SDRAM, the memory bus generally operates at one times the FSB frequency. Some chipsets allow for a two-thirds multiplier, therefore enabling you to run PC100 or DDR200 SDRAM on a system with a 133MHz FSB. RDRAM actually operates at a much greater multiplier. In the case of the Pentium 4's 100MHz quad-pumped FSB, the RDRAM clock runs at four times the FSB frequency. Remember that although the Pentium 4's FSB is quad-pumped, it still only runs at 100MHz, it just offers a transfer rate identical to that of a 400MHz FSB. The RDRAM clock multiplier is flexible, and the best motherboards enable you to change that clock multiplier.

The high latencies associated with RDRAM have kept it off of video cards (which also have their own local memory), where DDR SDRAM has been welcomed quite a bit. In terms of mobile solutions, mobile are RDRAM modules designed. Unfortunately, they have little or no chipset support.

DRAM: RD Versus SD

Quite possibly one of the biggest controversies that has ever arisen from the memory market has been the RDRAM vs. SDRAM debate. RDRAM has truly been Intel's baby in that a few years ago Intel declared that the future of desktop memory subsystems would lie in Rambus DRAM. Their reasons behind it make sense, because it is a low pin-count, serial interface like many of the other initiatives they are behind (for example, Serial ATA). It makes even more sense when you look at Intel's vision of the future of computing. Without a doubt, applications and games get much more bandwidth intensive over time. However, by far the most bandwidth intensive applications are those that deal with streaming data, such as video editing, video conferencing, and general types of content creation applications. Intel sees this as the future of the applications people run on their home computers, which makes the argument for a high-bandwidth memory architecture quite solid.

Intel's goal for RDRAM is for the industry to use it in performance desktop machines, but not in the server markets. Intel does have hopes that eventually even the value PCs are able to use RDRAM. However, they do realize that RDRAM costs currently prevent this from being possible, leaving SDRAM, and possibly DDR SDRAM, for value systems. For the server markets, Intel sees the ideal memory technology as DDR SDRAM and not RDRAM. Indicating that they do understand the cost difference between the two platforms, as well as the latency differences.

The problem with RDRAM really stems from when it was introduced. When RDRAM was introduced it was priced at close to $1,000 for a 128MB module. Even if you're not familiar with memory prices, you know that $1,000 is *a lot* for 128MB of memory, especially if you're going to be putting more than 128MB in your system. When RDRAM was released, PC100 and PC133 SDRAM were the memory types of choice for most users, and a similar 128MB module was approximately $100–$200.

To make things worse, Intel introduced RDRAM on the Pentium III platform and it actually ended up performing worse than PC100 SDRAM on the old Intel 440BX chipset, a two-year-old platform at the time. You already know that PC800 RDRAM performed so poorly on the Pentium III because even though the Pentium III had a 1.6GBps memory bus, it only had a 1GB/s FSB. The 600MBps difference was not enough to make a performance difference because the ICH (I/O Controller Hub) never used its 266MBps peak transfer rate and neither did the AGP bus (see Chapter 5, "The Video Card: A Gamer's Heart and Soul," for more information). So all the added memory bandwidth was really going to waste. Combine that with the fact that RDRAM had a higher latency than SDRAM, and you had a much more expensive memory platform, with a much higher latency than SDRAM, yet offering approximately the same useable bandwidth to the CPU as PC133 SDRAM. Combine all this in a time when Intel was telling the world that RDRAM was the future of memory technology and it really sounded to many like Intel was trying to rip everyone off.

Unfortunately, Intel had very little choice than to debut RDRAM with the Pentium III. They knew very well that the RDRAM production ramp would take time to get up to speed, and if they had debuted it at thousand dollar prices with the Pentium 4 it would've killed the Pentium 4's initial sales. Instead, Intel made the release near the end of the life of the Pentium III, unfortunately the market didn't respond favorably at all. This was reflected in extremely poor sales of all Intel's RDRAM chipsets for the Pentium III.

There was also quite a bit of concern over the business practices of Rambus as a company, due to their attempts to use memory technology patents to obtain royalties from makers of both SDRAM and DDR SDRAM. Those concerns, however, have been left out of this book, as I'm here to talk about hardware.

The enthusiast community's extreme hatred towards RDRAM was reflected in the support the community threw behind DDR SDRAM. When DDR SDRAM arrived the performance improvement it offered was between 0%–20%, in most cases, when compared to PC133 SDRAM. The performance improvement in the negative percentages, however. At the same time, instead of charging an arm and a leg for DDR SDRAM, the memory modules were simply not present in most retail markets until months after the release of the AMD 760 chipset, the first desktop DDR platform. When DDR SDRAM was eventually released in decent quantities, its price was actually quite close to that of RDRAM, which at the time had dropped to $300–$400 per 128MB module. A few manufacturers then began promoting their DDR modules quite a bit and ended up dropping prices to very close to SDRAM levels, leaving RDRAM still at a premium that few were willing to pay.

The Pentium 4's release turned things around for Rambus because the processor actually showed the usefulness of the technology. The first Pentium 4 chipset to be released was the i850 with a dual channel RDRAM memory controller. The Pentium 4 and its 3.2GB/s of memory bandwidth, courtesy of dual channel PC800 RDRAM, offered considerably more real-world memory bandwidth than even the AMD Athlon with its 2.1GB/s DDR266 memory. To push RDRAM even more, Intel started bundling RDRAM modules with their Pentium 4 processors and heavily discounted the price of RDRAM on that front as well. When you're as large as Intel, you can do a lot to control elements of the market. Before the whole RDRAM fiasco, Intel invested significantly in various memory manufacturers, thus pushing them to produce and support RDRAM.

There was still a desire for a DDR SDRAM platform for the Pentium 4, and although competing manufacturers, ALi and VIA, were both working on one, Intel has been reluctant to release their own. Intel's roadmap does call for them to produce both a SDRAM and DDR SDRAM chipset for the Pentium 4; however, their hopes are to push RDRAM low enough in price that DDR SDRAM isn't necessary for the low end. This would leave SDRAM for the value PCs, RDRAM for the desktop PCs, and DDR SDRAM for the servers.

The Pentium 4 would most likely take a pretty big hit with only a 1.6GBps DDR SDRAM memory bus, and unfortunately it doesn't seem like Intel's chipset supports DDR266 SDRAM for use with the Pentium 4. Remember that the ideal setup is to have the FSB and memory buses running synchronously, and the Pentium 4 has a 100MHz FSB, meaning that the memory bus runs at 100MHz, as well. Competing solutions from ALi and VIA should allow for DDR266 SDRAM to be used with the Pentium 4, but history has shown that Intel's own chipsets usually perform better and have lower latencies than ALi/VIA solutions on Intel processors.

Will you see RDRAM on other platforms or will Intel fail to promote it as the next memory standard? AMD does hold a license for RDRAM memory controllers, meaning that they can implement an RDRAM design in an AMD chipset. It wouldn't be too surprising if AMD has had an RDRAM chipset up and running in their test labs at one point or another to see how it fares with their upcoming chips, but they publicly have no stance on whether they use RDRAM in the future.

Intel is truly left to do the dirty work in promoting RDRAM versus SDRAM, DDR SDRAM, and future technologies as well. If Intel succeeds in their plight, all AMD has to do is implement an RDRAM-based design in their chipsets. If Intel fails, however, AMD isn't at a loss because they've stuck to an SDRAM-based design. This is one of the unfortunate downsides to being the biggest CPU manufacturer and having the burden of driving the industry on your shoulders.

Future Memory Technologies

The picture I have painted thus far has been a black and white one, with SDRAM and RDRAM as the only two options. In fact, many more exist. A good amount of uncertainty is in the future of the desktop PC memory market. This uncertainty mainly stems from the directions the major players in the market, the AMDs and Intels of the world, take us in. Rest assured that you have alternatives to both DDR SDRAM and RDRAM if you are looking at higher bandwidth solutions.

Embedded DRAM

The first option is embedded DRAM, as has been proposed by Micron on numerous occasions. The idea behind embedded DRAM is to eliminate the latency that is inherent in any of today's memory designs. When the CPU has to go to main memory for a read, it has to cross the North Bridge/MCH twice. This introduces an inevitable latency that always holds back the performance of even the lowest latency DRAM technologies that are implemented for system memory. By embedding DRAM into the North Bridge/MCH, the latency issue is decreased significantly. In the ideal situation, the CPU would treat this embedded DRAM as a sort of L3 cache. Except to keep costs low, the embedded DRAM is capacitance-based and not transistor-based such as the CPU's cache.

> **Note**
>
> Because I'm talking about unreleased technologies, the details discussed here are obviously subject to change. To keep up with the most recent developments in RAM technologies, keep your sites set on my AnandTech Web site.

If properly implemented, the bandwidth of DRAM embedded into the North Bridge/MCH would be limited by the FSB of the setup, which should be identical to that offered by a conventional memory system. The efficiency of embedded DRAM should be much higher than that of a conventional memory system lying on the other side of the North Bridge because the data doesn't have to travel as far to get to the CPU.

The trick to making embedded DRAM work is to implement a large enough amount that the footprints of applications and games that can't fit within the CPU's cache can reside in the embedded DRAM while keeping it small enough that costs are relatively low. Realistically, an 8MB–16MB embedded DRAM could be implemented into a North Bridge/MCH and improve performance, especially in situations where latency is of the utmost importance.

DDR-II

Another technology to keep an eye on is DDR-II. Members of JEDEC's Solid State Technology Association are still working on the DDR-II specification. As it stands now, DDR-II is being positioned as an evolution of DDR SDRAM that offers higher bandwidth. The current estimates put DDR-II at PC4800 levels, which equals about 4.8GB/s of memory bandwidth.

This kind of bandwidth is perfect for the 3D games of tomorrow as they continue to require much more memory bandwidth than they do today. Remember that a fast CPU isn't necessarily the means to a fast gaming machine, but it's the interaction of the CPU with the graphics card and other parts of the system that lead to powerful gaming performance. A higher bandwidth memory subsystem is necessary.

The improvements DDR-II is geared to offer include improved bandwidth utilization (which is a strength RDRAM holds over DDR SDRAM), continued use of parallel architecture, meaning that latencies would continue to be kept low, and transferred data four times every clock. The operating voltage of DDR-II is supposed to be 1.8v compared to the 2.5v of current DDR SDRAM and 3.3v of regular SDRAM. This could make it even more attractive for mobile solutions as well.

The Near Future of System Memory

Without a doubt Intel is increasing the FSB and memory bus frequencies on the Pentium 4, resulting in even higher bandwidth RDRAM at the processor's disposal. It also seems like DDR-II would be able to rival RDRAM in terms of bandwidth.

More recently, NVIDIA has entered the chipset market with their dual channel DDR SDRAM interface, offering an effective 128-bit DDR SDRAM bus. This technology is from their experience in designing graphics card memory controllers. The amount of bandwidth offered by this solution is already close to what DDR-II is promising (2 × 2.1GB/s = 4.2GB/s). NVIDIA definitely is a key player to keep your eyes on for extremely high-bandwidth memory controllers, especially considering their extremely efficient graphics memory controllers.

How Does Memory Impact Game Performance?

I've really only focused on two aspects of memory: latency and bandwidth; while these do have an impact on how well your games run, the amount of memory you have also affects game performance.

If the data that your CPU and/or your video card needs is not present in main memory because of a lack of space (for example, you don't have enough memory) your game is going to come to a screeching halt. Your CPU/video card waits to get that data either from your hard drive or your CD/DVD-ROM drive. Being considerably slower than main memory, this is a situation you definitely don't want to find yourself in.

Games treat system memory in your computer, essentially, as a temporary storage area for calculations that they want the CPU to perform. The current level you're playing in a first person shooter is stored in system memory. The data on the enemies you're battling, the weapons you're using, and how much damage they inflict is all stored in memory. The faster the access is to this data, the less likely your CPU has to wait to find out what it needs to calculate next as you move throughout the level.

But let's first discuss how latency and bandwidth affect gaming performance.

Latency Versus Bandwidth

Two ends of the memory bandwidth spectrum are available when it comes to application needs. Office productivity applications, as they are often called, are things such as word processors, spreadsheet, presentation developers, and Web surfing applications. These applications, as you probably know, stress the integer calculation capabilities of your CPU and rarely have a large memory footprint. In fact, most of these applications fit their execution code quite nicely within the cache of a CPU. These applications are not memory bandwidth intensive, rather they are more influenced by lower latency memory solutions. Granted you need a decent amount of memory bandwidth, but in general PC133 SDRAM should be enough for today's applications.

On the other end of the spectrum you have the content creation applications that include functions such as video encoding, which are quite clearly memory bandwidth limited. These are floating point intensive applications that revolve around streaming data from memory to the CPU. These applications aren't hurt too much by a high latency memory subsystem because when the data transfers start, the latency takes a backseat to the amount of sheer bandwidth that is able to be transferred at once.

Unfortunately for gamers, most games don't clearly lie on one end of the spectrum or the other. Instead, they generally lie somewhere between the two. Although games are definitely more appreciative of memory bandwidth than office applications, they aren't nearly as intensive as video encoding applications. Latency is important in gaming performance as is bandwidth, but too many variables exist to make a clear generalization that states whether games would prefer lower latency or higher bandwidth solutions. One thing is clear, regular SDRAM just doesn't cut it anymore. As CPU speeds get even higher the need for higher bandwidth memory solutions are felt.

How Much Is Enough?

In terms of memory size, determining how much is right for your gaming system is actually pretty simple. When it comes to size you have to realize the progression of data storage in your system (see Figure 4.5). When you load up your game it is loaded from your hard drive (accessed in milliseconds, transferred in tens of MB per second) to your system memory (accessed in nanoseconds, transferred in hundreds to thousands of MB/s). From there it heads to your processor's cache, which the CPU can access in even shorter periods of time and transfer data to and from at speeds of tens of thousands of megabytes per second.

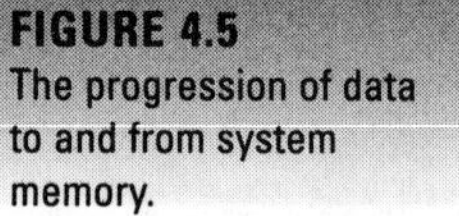
FIGURE 4.5
The progression of data to and from system memory.

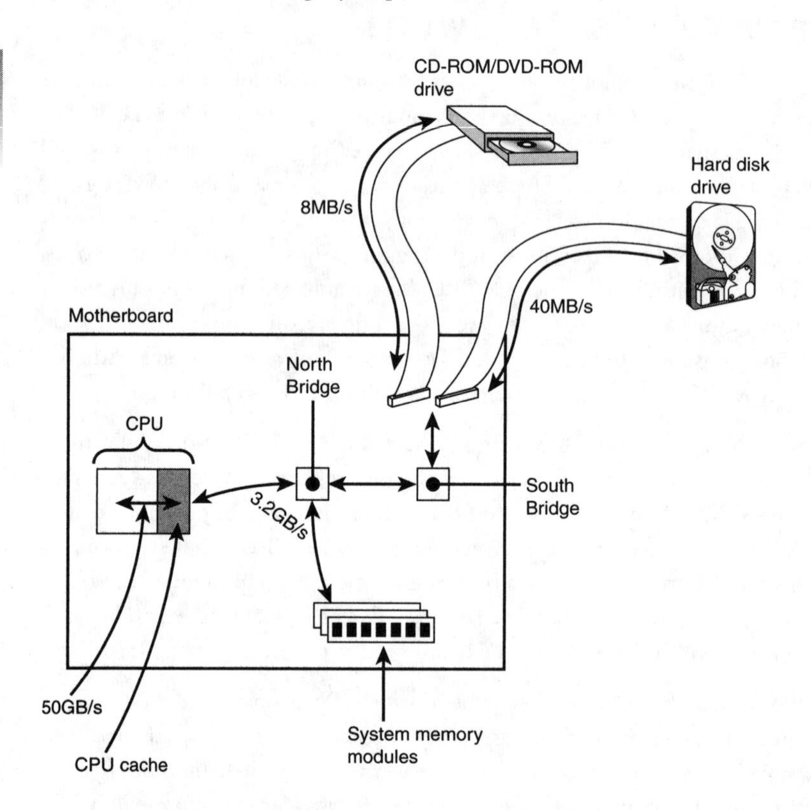

The performance decrease felt when your CPU must grab something it doesn't have in its cache out of main memory is significant, but at least you're still dealing with two mediums that have no moving parts and operate in nanoseconds (0.000000001 seconds). If the data isn't located in main memory, or if the amount of main memory to accommodate what the CPU or game needs is not enough, the next storage medium that is visited is the hard disk. The hard disk is one of the remaining devices in the PC that still has moving parts, and it is *considerably* slower than system memory. The accesses occur in milliseconds (0.001 seconds or 1 million times slower than system memory) and transfer rates are generally less than 100MB/s. Keep in mind that I have been talking about moving gigabytes per second in most of the discussion in these first four chapters.

If you are playing a game and your computer must "swap to disk" or use some of your hard disk space as memory (albeit very slow memory) your game slows down noticeably, almost to the point where it stops completely. The more memory you have in your system, the less often this happens. Don't forget about overkill. Memory isn't extremely cheap, so you don't want to buy more than you need.

How much memory you need depends greatly on the games that you run and the operating system you're running. It is safe to say that the bare minimum for a high performance gaming system should be 128MB. The sweet spot currently is 256MB with 384MB being more than enough for most gamers.

You shouldn't go nuts with adding memory, it isn't going to solve all your problems. Data has to come off the hard disk in one way or another because none of your high-speed memory in your PC keeps any data after you reboot or turn your system off. The more memory you have, however, the less frequently your system has to convert some of your extremely slow disk space to memory for storage. A common myth is that installing too much memory can actually slow down your PC. This is false. It used to be true in some cases where the L2 cache couldn't cache the entire memory area (take data from the entire area and store it), but for all means and purposes for you it is false.

Memory Modules

So far in this chapter we've been discussing memory in a very theoretical manner, but unlike a chipset, you can actually purchase and install memory yourself. As I mentioned earlier in the SDRAM section, the memory modules are built on PCBs that generally measure approximately 1" × 5".

The three main types of DRAM I've discussed, SDRAM, DDR SDRAM, and RDRAM all use different interfaces and modules. Their buses make them incompatible with one another (for example, you can't plug in four 16-bit RDRAM modules and expect to have a 64-bit SDRAM device). Their physical interface designs make them incompatible as well, partially to prevent users from inserting the wrong type of memory into the wrong slot (the consequences of this can be a pretty blue flame that you don't want to see).

Dual Inline Memory Modules (DIMMs)

Both SDRAM and DDR SDRAM are packaged onto modules known as Dual Inline Memory Modules or DIMMs. The name DIMM comes from the fact that the interface pins on the inline memory module are different on each side. Although a SDRAM has only 84 pins on it, each side is different, giving SDRAM a total of 168 unique pins.

DDR SDRAM uses a similar DIMM interface, except with 92 pins per side for a total of 184 pins. You can see a comparison of these two types of memory in Figure 4.6.

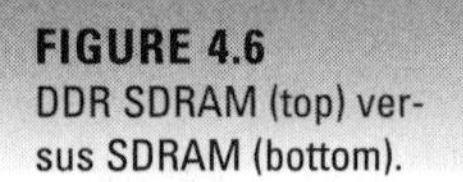

FIGURE 4.6
DDR SDRAM (top) versus SDRAM (bottom).

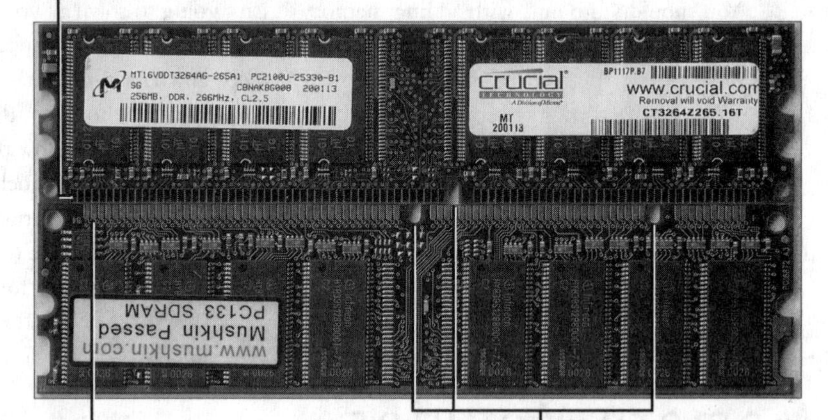

Rambus Inline Memory Modules (RIMMs)

Because the architecture is completely different, RDRAM is built on a different type of module than SDRAM. RDRAM chips are placed on 184-pin Rambus Inline Memory Modules, or RIMMs. As I mentioned in the RDRAM section, all RIMM slots on a motherboard must be populated. Unfilled RDRAM slots can be filled with a Continuity Rambus Inline Memory Module or CRIMM (see Figure 4.7).

Motherboard manufacturers provide enough CRIMMs with their motherboards to fill any empty memory slots after the initial amount of RDRAM is installed (which is always a minimum of two modules in dual-channel RDRAM motherboards).

FIGURE 4.7
Two RIMMs and two CRIMMs on a Pentium 4 motherboard.

Memory Sizes

In spite of the different physical specs, memory modules are made available in relatively standard sizes. The size rating on a memory module is determined by the sum of the sizes of the individual chips on the module. For example, a 128MB DDR SDRAM module with 16 chips uses 8MB chips. These individual chip sizes are usually referred to in Mbit sizes, meaning that the chips in the aforementioned example would be 64Mbit chips. The larger these individual chips are, the more memory can be put on a single module without increasing the chip count.

> **Note**
>
> Depending on the type of RIMM-based motherboard you're using, the arrangement of CRIMMs and RIMMs can vary. On most Pentium 4 motherboards, more specifically Intel's 850 board, your RIMMs go in one pair of sockets, with the CRIMMs in the other. Some boards, however, such as the ASUS P4T pictured in Figure 4.7, stagger the arrangement of CRIMM and RIMM modules.

Memory modules are commonly available in 64MB, 128MB, 256MB, and 512MB sticks. Your total system memory size is the sum of the memory sizes of all your installed modules. For example, if you have a 128MB module installed and a 256MB module installed, your total amount of system memory would be 384MB.

It doesn't hurt to mix and match memory sizes and speeds, unless you have to install the sticks in pairs. If you must install memory in pairs I suggest the modules you pair up are of the same size, speed, and manufacturer, if possible, although the third requirement isn't necessary. If you mix memory of different sizes across different banks you don't run into any problems. A bank, in this sense, is the collection of one or more memory slots that makes up the bus width of the memory bus. For example, a bank in a SDRAM system is one DIMM because it is 64 bits wide, while a bank in a dual channel RDRAM system is two RIMMs because it is 32 bits wide. However, if you have a DDR266 DIMM in one bank and a DDR200 DIMM in another bank, your motherboard (unless instructed otherwise) thinks you have two DDR200 DIMMs. Meaning that your memory is only as fast as the slowest module in your memory banks. Remember the talk about yields in reference to PC150 and PC166 SDRAM? The same applies to other technologies as well. Let's take the scenario where you have two DIMMs, a DDR266 DIMM, and a DDR200 DIMM. If the DDR200 DIMM, although rated at DDR200, happens to work at DDR266 speeds you can simply force your motherboard to accept the fact that you have two DDR266 DIMMs and all is good. If, however, your DDR200 DIMM doesn't work at DDR266 speeds, or if it barely works at that speed, your system fails its Power On Self Test (POST) or is unstable. If your system fails to POST, it is essentially inoperable.

A properly designed motherboard should perform just as reliably with all its memory slots full as it would with only one occupied. Unfortunately, it is rare that all motherboards are designed this well, so sometimes adding more memory can actually cause instability, especially if you're not using well made memory. The real trick is to find out how to avoid this by purchasing good memory and a good motherboard. Chapter 3 gives you some names to look for when shopping around for a motherboard, but what about for memory?

Why All Memory Isn't Created Equally

To understand the differences between different pieces of memory of the same type, you must understand how memory is produced. You all know the price difference between a Mercedes and a Ford, but would the added cost be worth it if the only difference between the two was a name change?

The two parts to the memory equation are the manufacturer of the actual chips themselves, of which is only a handful, include Nanya, Samsung, or Toshiba (see Figure 4.8) and the manufacturer of the PCB that these chips are put on. The PCB can be made by virtually anyone and any competent manufacturer can mount the chips.

FIGURE 4.8
A collection of 8 or 16 of Infineon SDRAM chips, such as the one pictured here, can make up a full memory module.

The chips themselves control, from a very broad perspective, how fast the memory module is going to be able to run. The yields on the chips also govern how far above their rating they are able to operate. If the first samples of a particular module overclock to incredible frequencies it is a sign that the yields on the chips themselves are quite high.

So why is it that two different modules with the same chips on them can reach drastically different operating frequencies? This is where the PCB manufacturer and the actual construction of the module come into play. A poorly constructed memory module paired with even the best in memory chips is no better than the PCB from which it is built. Building memory modules is very much a science. These manufacturers put their modules through extreme tests at very high and very cold temperatures for hours and even days on end.

The best manufacturers test their PCB suppliers and chips, as well as their own new designs, in stress chambers for up to a month straight before going to full production. The end result is a module with chips such as the one shown in Figure 4.9.

FIGURE 4.9
A Mushkin PC133 SDRAM module using Infineon SDRAM chips.

Obviously, quite a bit of money can be saved if a module manufacturer doesn't go to such great extents when testing their modules. Chances are you don't notice the difference between a module that has been rigorously tested and one that has been lightly tested, but assumed to be good because most of them are. The probability of you getting one bad module is quite low, but when you couple that with the fact that millions of modules are shipped out from these manufacturers, the ones with the better testing methodologies and more solid manufacturing practices have the lowest failure rate. The smaller that failure rate is, the better the odds are in favor of you not getting a poorly made module.

Luckily, one thing that doesn't vary between modules is performance. Two DDR266 modules perform within a very close margin of one another, so you shouldn't be turned on or off by performance comparisons of like modules. A DDR266 module is able to run (at its rated speed) at a higher frequency than a DDR200 module, but two DDR200 modules with the same timings specifications should perform identically. Another thing to keep in mind is that just because a manufacturer claims that their modules are DDR400 compatible (note, a DDR400 standard does not exist) that doesn't mean that you are actually able to run them at DDR400. Many obstacles are standing between you and the door marked "key to DDR400 operation" and unfortunately, those obstacles are generally too great to overcome. Such barriers include board and chipset limitations. Remember when you're running your memory out of spec, you're running your memory controller, and thus your chipset, out of spec as well. The discussion on this topic is limited, again, until Chapter 13, "Operating Systems and Device Drivers: Making Your Hardware Work," but it's always good to whet your appetite when appropriate.

Memory Timings

In addition to their bandwidth ratings, PC133 SDRAM, DDR266 SDRAM, and PC800 RDRAM all carry ratings that describe their internal latencies; basically how long it takes to complete certain functions. These timings, like bandwidth figures, are generally tolerant to a certain percentage variation. A well made module with high yield chips on it is more likely to be able to operate at more aggressive, or faster, memory timings than one that isn't well made or has very low yield chips from the manufacturer.

One commonly referred to timing parameter is the Column Access Strobe Latency, or CAS Latency. One thing you have to understand about the internal architecture of memory is that it is arranged in an array of capacitors. These capacitors, as you know, hold the charge that results in a value of a 1 or 0, and when the magnitude of the amount of capacitors is increased you end up with the capability to store quite a bit of data. Getting access to these capacitors could be potentially complex. Luckily, all you need to do to get to the data is find in what row and column in the array the data is stored. As you can probably tell by the name, the *Column* Access Strobe Latency is the amount of time it takes to find the right *column*.

The CAS Latency is just one of the many latency penalties that are added up during the process of memory reads and writes, but having a lower CAS

Latency does help improve performance. The quicker the data can get to where it needs to go, the less your CPU has to wait around for some slow memory, and the more data can be pushed through at once. This is how latency can actually affect bandwidth.

The most common memory timings to provide information on a module is the module's (really the chips') CAS Latency (see Figure 4.10). A lower CAS Latency rating is better, because the module works at more aggressive timings. This isn't to say that a higher CAS Latency rating on a module doesn't work at a lower rating, it just isn't guaranteed to work at a lower rating.

FIGURE 4.10
A label from a DDR SDRAM module indicating a CAS Latency (CL) of 2.5 cycles.

CAS Latency ratings are very small compared to the types of latency penalties that have been discussed thus far. They are generally on the magnitude of two cycles.

Chip and Module Manufacturers

To conclude this chapter, the following is a short list of some of the most trusted and reliable memory manufacturers and their Web sites (both chip and module manufacturers):

Corsair (modules)—`http://www.corsairmicro.com`

Infineon (chips)—`http://www.infineon.com`

Micron/Crucial (chips/modules)—`http://www.crucial.com`

Mushkin (modules)—`http://www.mushkin.com`

Toshiba (chips)—`http://www.toshiba.com`

Samsung (chips)—`http://www.samsung.com`

AnandTech

Chapter 5

The Video Card: A Gamer's Heart and Soul

The Graphics Card's Key Role in Game Performance

For years, the most important aspects of building the highest performing gaming PC were the CPU, the chipset, the motherboard, and the memory. However, somewhere along the line the market woke up and realized that playing pong for hours on end eventually got boring, and the demand grew for more realistic computer games.

In the earliest days of computers, using these massive machines that filled rooms for anything other than productive work was unheard of. It wasn't until the advent of the personal computer, the PC, that computer gaming truly came about. When PCs became affordable, they also took the first steps into the realm of an entertainment item. Although not on the level of the TV or VCR at that time, the PC was destined to become or even surpass the aforementioned forms of entertainment in the home. However, back then, no PC could provide the realism that real actors with real voices, faces, and personalities could provide over the airwaves.

The extent of PC gaming in the early days consisted of very little outside of blocks of text designed to appear to be anything from a pong paddle to a little yellow character known as Pac Man. There wasn't a demand for realism simply because no one expected that it could be accomplished on such a crude machine. You typed in garbled text using commands such as "dir" and "edlin" and the PC responded with more garbled text or if you were lucky, a beep or two. On the TV however, at the flick of channel you could have news from all over the world, action movies, explosions, and thrills—the works. It was all as lifelike as if you were really there. For some reason it was so much more realistic to see a man running from a murder than it was to see Mrs. Pac Man running from a ghost. That was all about to change, however.

The change came about not through the use of faster processors with wider and more bandwidth-friendly memory buses, although both of those factors definitely contributed. The change was the result of a revolution of another part of the PC, the graphics card.

The graphics card, as the name implies, is the card in your system that takes the 1s and 0s that are being crunched and converts them to the pictures you see on your monitor. The name comes from the fact that the graphics card is actually a card that interfaces, in today's systems, with an AGP slot, although in the not so distant past graphics cards used a PCI interface. As I discussed in Chapter 3, "The Motherboard: Low Rent Housing for the CPU and Chipset," the AGP slot on your motherboard is the physical connection to the Accelerated Graphics Port bus that connects directly to the North Bridge of your chipset.

Construction of a Graphics Card

The graphics card is built on a PCB, just like your motherboard, although it is much less complicated than a motherboard (see Figure 5.1). Instead of having to deal with the interaction of multiple components and buses, the graphics card only really has to deal with a handful of parts. You can actually think of the graphics card as being, on a physical level, much like an oversimplified motherboard without any hope for expansion. On a motherboard, if you're tired of your CPU or want a new sound card, you simply remove the old CPU or sound card and replace it with a new one. Provided that the new part is compatible, you don't have to throw away your motherboard just because you want a faster CPU or a better sound card. Unfortunately (and in some cases, fortunately), the same is not true for graphics cards.

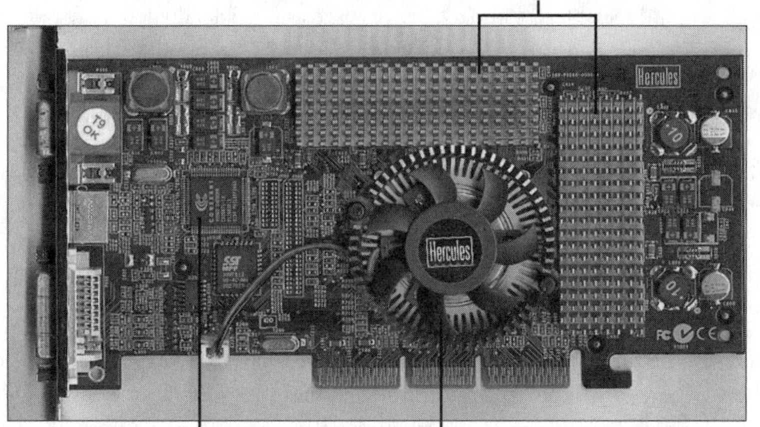

FIGURE 5.1
This Hercules GeForce3 graphics card (also known as a video card) has all the classic parts of a graphics card.

On your graphics card you have a few major components: the graphics processor, the graphics memory, the interface connector, and the input/outputs on the card itself. As you might be able to guess, the graphics processor is much like the CPU installed on your motherboard. The graphics processor is indeed a central processing unit, just a more specialized one than the CPUs I discussed in Chapter 1, "The Central Processing Unit: The Heart and Soul of the PC." The CPUs I discussed in the first chapter have to be able to play games just as well as they run your Internet browsers and office applications. Graphics processors, on the other hand, are only concerned with putting pictures on your screen and the calculations associated with doing just that.

The graphics processor has many of the same parts as the CPUs I discussed initially have, however quite a few of them are absent. Focusing on branch prediction with a graphics processor doesn't make sense, just as worrying about a desktop CPU's capability to apply textures to pixels is putting a powerful component in the wrong context. You can compare a graphics processor to a conventional desktop processor, but in doing so you're really setting yourself up for an apples-to-oranges comparison.

Desktop CPU manufacturers, such as AMD and Intel are concerned with running every single application imaginable at the highest levels of performance.

Their processor designs, including their efforts to squeeze as many transistors and metal layers into as small a space as possible, do definitely reflect that. Graphics processor manufacturers are only interested in dealing with displaying the items you see on your screen. Not to put down the importance of the graphics processor, but its duties are much less broad than that of your CPU.

Comparing a graphics processor to a desktop CPU is much like asking how well a broomstick works as a snow shovel. Granted the broomstick could accomplish the task, but it wasn't designed for it, just like a snow shovel wasn't designed to sweep dirt away. But enough analogies; let's dive into what this graphics processor does.

Because the graphics processor doesn't have to worry about interacting with any other components on the graphics card's PCB, an external chipset is not necessary. Many of the functions that a chipset would normally serve are actually taken care of on the graphics processor itself. As I mentioned earlier, the graphics card does feature a certain amount of memory. The memory on the graphics card abides by the same rules as the memory I discussed in Chapter 4, "Memory: Your PC's Scratchpad." In fact, in many cases the very same chips are used. In this case, however, they are generally rated at higher speeds and they aren't present on modules; they are physically mounted on the PCB.

This memory is often referred to as the graphics card's *local memory* or *frame buffer* because of the type of data it stores. The local memory on the graphics card is connected to the graphics processor via a memory bus. The memory controller resides on the graphics processor. Because an external memory controller to go through does not exist, the transfer latencies are very low and the available bandwidth is quite high.

Note

To give you an idea of just how fast a graphics card's memory bus is, compare it to today's system memory buses, which offer between 1GB and 4.2GB per second of memory bandwidth. Today's graphics cards can offer almost 9GB per second.

If the graphics processor runs out of local memory, it can always go through the AGP interface, over to the North Bridge on your motherboard, and store/retrieve data from your system memory. In most cases, your system memory size dwarfs the memory size of your graphics card's memory. The graphics processor absolutely *hates* to do this. The issue of latency plays a huge role in why the graphics processor hates having to leave the confines of the graphics card just to fetch or store some data. Think about the latency penalties your CPU incurs when it is reading data from main memory. Your graphics processor has to deal with even larger latency penalties because the AGP bus doesn't operate at the same frequency as the FSB does. Then you have the ever-present issue of bandwidth; the graphics processor gets an enormous amount of bandwidth added to its local memory. The amount of bandwidth it gets is much greater than the memory bandwidth that even your CPU gets. However, as soon as your graphics processor resorts to storing data in main memory, its memory bandwidth is limited by the bandwidth of the AGP bus. This is like having a car with an engine capable of outputting 400HP yet an exhaust that limits it to 110HP.

This is why graphics card manufacturers put quite a bit of memory on these graphics cards. In terms of solid performance oriented graphics cards, generally, a minimum of 32MB and realistically 64MB of memory is what you can expect for most cards today. Of course, the more memory that is present on the graphics card the higher the price of the board becomes because each individual memory chip takes up a certain amount of PCB space and the chips aren't exactly cheap. Just as is the case with main memory, having more on your graphics card doesn't hurt, it just means that it's even less likely that your graphics processor runs out of space on your graphics card and has to resort to storing data temporarily in main memory.

This isn't to say that the graphics card is completely independent. In fact, it requires quite a bit of communication with the CPU through the AGP bus. It simply performs better if it doesn't have to store any data off of its card.

How Graphics Cards Work

One key distinction must be made at this stage of the learning process as to avoid confusion later. A handful of manufacturers contribute to the production of a graphics card. The manufacturer of the graphics chip, the manufacturer of the memory on the graphics card, and the manufacturer of the graphics card all contribute to the production of a graphics card. Some chip manufacturers also make the cards such as ATI, while other chip manufacturers solely produce chips and sell them to third party manufacturers that use them to make actual cards. An example of the latter would be NVIDIA. They sell their chips to card manufacturers, such as Hercules, who make cards based on them.

Just as is the case with a chipset on a motherboard, you have no control over replacing the memory or the graphics processor on a graphics card. When you purchase a graphics card, you're stuck with what you get. If you want to upgrade, you have to get rid of your graphics card and buy a new one. The graphics card market changes too quickly to be feasible for the sort of plug and play upgrades you're used to when it comes to motherboards. Although it would be a nice feature, it's simply not realistic.

The technology in the graphics industry changes at a much greater pace than that in the CPU industry. Although either AMD or Intel releases a microprocessor architecture and expects it to scale well for the next 3–5 years, a graphics chip manufacturer cannot live off the same design for such a long period of time. The main reason is that today's CPUs are multifunction devices. They are extremely programmable and are only required to provide computational power for the programmers to use and take advantage of.

Graphics Card Development

Because of the discrepancy I just described in the previous section, graphics processors see a much different release schedule than the CPUs you're used to dealing with. The biggest difference is that you rarely see different speed grades released at various points during the life of a particular graphics processor. It isn't uncommon for a manufacturer to offer a higher speed version of a particular chip to diversify their product line a bit. However, it is almost unheard of to purchase a graphics card today only to find that a slightly higher clocked version is available 2 months later, and an even higher one made available two months after that.

Mostly lead by NVIDIA's gains in the market, graphics chips generally come out twice every year: once during the fall to make it in for the Christmas buying season, and once during the Spring. NVIDIA originally introduced this release schedule with the follow-up to their TNT graphics solution, the TNT2. The TNT2 made its way out six months after the TNT, and six months later was replaced with a GeForce, that was then replaced with a GeForce2, and so on.

Because NVIDIA introduced such an aggressive product cycle, the entire industry had to follow suit. This was a partial contributor to the demise of 3dfx, often considered to be one of the founders of the 3D gaming industry on the PC. Unable to keep up with the 6-month release cycles of NVIDIA, 3dfx found themselves releasing underperforming parts later than NVIDIA. Their products were simply too little, too late. These product cycles keep things very aggressive in the graphics chip manufacturing industry. Just like the high-cost of R&D and manufacturing keeps competitors from entering the x86 CPU manufacturing business, very short product cycles tend to steer many companies from the mainstream performance of the 3D gaming graphics chip industry.

In terms of manufacturing, the same rules that I discussed in Chapter 1 apply to manufacturing graphics chips as well. Die sizes, yields, clock speeds, and so on, are all important factors to consider when looking at the architecture behind a graphics processor. However, the graphics pipeline is considerably different from what you're used to in the x86 CPU world.

Inside the Graphics Processor

Just knowing the physical makings of the graphics processor is one thing, but knowing how it works is another. The majority of the graphics processor's die is going to be used up by what I refer to as its 3D core, or the part of the die that handles all the calculations for 3D rendering. Displaying 2D images doesn't take much effort these days, and any well-designed graphics core has solid 2D capabilities as well. I discuss the issue of 2D image quality later. The 2D unit in a graphics processor is what handles the display of your OS, your Internet browser, and just about any other application other than a 3D game. Even many games, like Baldur's Gate 2, are still heavily based in the 2D world, requiring the use of a graphics processor's 2D unit.

In the earlier days of 3D accelerators, because of the large die size of most 3D cores, they did not contain a 2D unit at all. These cards were essentially add-on boards that worked with your PC's main graphics card, switching between 2D and 3D environments as necessary. The most popular that used this design was the 3dfx Voodoo graphics accelerator, which used a passthrough cable to piggyback itself to your current 2D graphics card. There were obviously tradeoffs associated with this, such as a loss of 2D image quality, which resulted from the fact that before hitting your monitor your video signal would have to go through another cable/card.

These days the 2D unit, as I mentioned before, doesn't occupy much room on the die and it is rare that you see a modern 3D graphics accelerator with a poorly performing 2D unit. There have been some in the past, such as S3's Savage 2000 which was released when it was thought that all graphics cards offered equal 2D performance. It isn't surprising that the Savage 2000 met a quick death, but I discuss this later.

Although 2D acceleration is considered to be highly perfected, the same cannot be said about 3D acceleration of today's graphics processors. They are obviously improving as time goes on, but the day where you can say that 3D performance between various chips is negligible is far away.

3D Graphics APIs and Graphics Card Drivers

The first and foremost goal of the 3D unit of a graphics processor is to take the scene it is commanded to draw by the software, draw it, and output it to your screen. The first step in this process occurs when the game (or 3D application) that you are running sends a command to a software layer. This layer is known as the Application Programming Interface (API). The reason for using an API is to complement the ever-changing nature of graphics hardware.

Because graphics processors are being released at extremely fast paced intervals, if the manufacturers not only had to worry about releasing the chips, but also rewriting their drivers to work specifically with every single game out there, the process would take a significantly longer time. Instead they write API-compatible drivers that work with the major APIs used in the areas at which their chips are targeted; for gaming processors those APIs are Direct3D and OpenGL.

Game developers then simply need to make sure that their games work with a single API. The theory is that if both a particular game and a particular chip are compatible with an API such as Direct3D, they should work with each other. That theory has some holes in it, but it is for this reason that you have APIs.

After the API layer the device driver is used as a means of communicating with the graphics processor itself. This driver must maintain compatibility with the APIs that the manufacturer of the processor intends to support, as well as the OS that they intend to support as well. Good driver design is key to the success of a particular graphics processor. Poor driver implementation was one of the mistakes that S3 made with their entries into the 3D graphics arena. A powerful chip is useless if its drivers are holding back that potential or don't work with some of the more popular games out there.

Another example of drivers leading to the demise of a product would be the Matrox G200, which was released around the same time as S3's first true 3D solution, the Savage3D. The G200 lacked proper support for the OpenGL API that was used by games based on idSoftware's Quake and Quake 2 engines. The G200 ran virtually all Direct3D games just fine, but at the time some of the most popular games were OpenGL and that, unfortunately, disappointed many users. Matrox attempted to provide a temporary solution by bundling their G200 with a Direct3D wrapper that essentially took any OpenGL function calls, translated them into a Direct3D equivalent and processed that instead. The translation process resulted in a bit of a performance hit, and the wrapper itself wasn't perfect. This resulted in quite a few game incompatibilities.

From a driver standpoint, I have generally heard from developers at a lot of the major manufacturers that developing OpenGL drivers is considerably more difficult than doing so under Direct3D. From a gamer's perspective, you obviously want to play the best games available, and with 2002's release of Doom 3 destined to be another OpenGL title from id, you obviously want a card with good OpenGL support. Luckily, most of the major players have a solid OpenGL ICD (Installable Client Driver) in their drivers. Ever hear of a man named Darwin? Well, some of those other graphics chip manufacturers with poor OpenGL support aren't exactly on top of the market anymore for a reason.

Building a 3D Image

Let's say I managed to create an extremely entertaining game where a two dimensional triangle is placed in the middle of an empty world (you can see why I'm not a programmer already). Let's also assume that this game uses the Direct3D API, although this would work the same way if it were an OpenGL game as well. You start up my game and immediately the game makes a Direct3D call instructing the graphics hardware to draw a triangle. This request is sent through the graphics hardware's driver, and then transferred to the hardware itself. The hardware then draws the triangle, sends it to the frame buffer, and then outputs it to your monitor.

Staring at a single triangle isn't too entertaining, though. So you want to animate that triangle. Like most things in the world of 3D rendering, our desire for a better experience results in the creation of yet another problem: reducing flickering. For your animated triangle to be drawn, displayed, and animated without pauses between the animation you need to have a buffer to store the frame being displayed, and the one that is about to be displayed. This process of using two buffers is known as double buffering.

Double buffering requires that your frame buffer is large enough to not only store the frame data that is required for the frame that is about to be sent to the screen, but also large enough to contain the data for the next frame. The benefit of double buffering is that you always have two frames stored in memory, meaning that you don't have to wait on the graphics processor to finish rendering the next scene before you can view it because it's already stored in the frame buffer. If I was really feeling generous with my frame buffer I could opt to triple buffer the scene, which occupies three times as much memory; however, for the most part, double buffering is all that is necessary.

Constructing an Image from an Object

Animating this triangle is done by manipulating the vertices of the triangle (where two edges meet). The vertices can be translated to a different point in space to make the triangle move. They can also be moved in different directions to distort the triangle and so on.

That is great, but what if I tell you that this triangle is supposed to represent a human character? Not a very good art job on my part, but this can be fixed. Similar to your main CPU, a graphics processor doesn't know how to draw a face, but it can draw triangles. The more triangles, the more accurate the image is.

You have other options for creating images in 3D besides using triangles, such as using higher order surfaces. These surfaces use quadratic, third, fourth, or higher order curves to more accurately represent curved surfaces, such as archways. This is why higher order surfaces are often referred to as curved surfaces by manufacturers and developers. Surfaces that aren't curved are just as easily represented by a collection of triangles.

Regardless of whether a game is using triangles or higher order surfaces, the bottom line is that characters and objects in a 3D world are created by using a collection of polygons. A typical 3D scene can have tens of thousands of polygons, and calculating the current, and future position of the vertices of these polygons during an animation can be a very daunting task.

Transform and Lighting

One of the functions of the more recent graphics processors is to offload the process of converting or transforming these collections of polygons from their homes in the theoretical world space in which they originally are constructed to the screen where you can view them. If you've never heard the term *Hardware Transforming and Lighting* used before, what I am talking about is the Hardware Transforming part of that feature.

Now I've taken the time to create not only a realistic looking triangle, but I've put a few thousand of these together to produce a person. I've done the same, but with fewer polygons to produce walls, a floor and a ceiling as well as a few obstacles in the room. But if you look around, the room doesn't seem realistic at all. All I have done is put together what is known as a wireframe model of the environment (see Figure 5.2). In such an environment, these polygons have no color, no texture, and put simply, they have no appearance. I just mentioned Hardware Transforming and Lighting; this is where the lighting comes in.

FIGURE 5.2
A wireframe 3D scene. Notice how each shape is built on a compilation of various polygons.

The vertices of the polygons in my 3D scene are made visible by being lit. The characteristics of how they respond to various light sources is stored in the vertices themselves (actually in a database of values, but corresponding to each individual vertex). The lighting process is extremely compute intensive and since the release of NVIDIA's GeForce 256 GPU (Graphics Processing Unit) the graphics processor has been able to do these calculations in hardware instead of offloading the calculations to the host CPU. There have been some limitations to the success of this, however, I discuss that after you do a little painting.

Texturing

Although I have lit the polygons, they are still missing something; they have no texture to them. This brings me to the next job of the graphics processor, to texture the polygons.

A texture is nothing more than a coat of paint that can be applied to any surface. This paint is special in that it doesn't have to be a solid color, it can have a pattern that would give whatever the surface happens to be a painted or "textured" appearance, such as bricks or concrete blocks, which is perfect for walls (see Figure 5.3). Textures can also be things such as shirts or glasses on a polygonal character.

FIGURE 5.3
The wireframe 3D scene from Figure 5.2 with textures applied.

More than one texture can be applied to a surface. This is known as *multitexturing*. Although in the past multitexturing really only meant two textures, today's games are using many more than that. Why would you want to paint a wall with two different coats of paint? To have them complement each other, of course (see Figure 5.4).

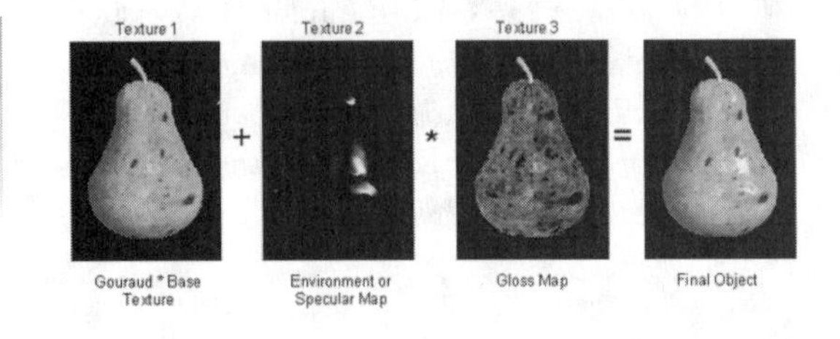

FIGURE 5.4
The combination of three textures in this case yields a very realistic looking pear.

One of the most common uses for a second texture was a light map, or a texture whose sole purpose was to cast the appearance of a light shining on a wall. Obviously this type of a lighting effect isn't exactly realistic. You all know that lights are produced by a source and aren't properties of the object on which the light happens to be shining.

The beauty of a light map is that it is relatively easy to implement. Among other shortcomings, using a light map creates problems for game developers in that they must create the light map (not a simple process). For our purposes, though, they are a good example of the use of a second texture.

Light maps were preferred to using a hardware lighting engine during the past years of game development simply because there was a lack of programmable hardware lighting engines. With the introduction of the GeForce3 and Microsoft's DirectX 8 this is changing. I save discussion on that for later. For now, the current widespread use of light maps has limited the functionality of the very first hardware T&L units to hit the market.

Another use for a second texture is to provide the appearance of depth or real texture to a surface. This type of texture is known as a bump map. Although one texture might be used to make a wall appear to be made out of bricks, a bump map gives the bricks the impression that they actually have some feeling to them.

Textures are also stored (preferably) in the local memory of the video card in an area known as texture memory. In reality, texture memory is no different from the memory used to store the frame buffer. The only thing that separates the two is that they occupy different areas of the local memory. In modern graphics accelerators they share the same local memory, however, and occupy different amounts depending on their needs.

Before I go any further it is important at this point to introduce the fundamental unit of constructing all these polygons and textures, the pixel.

The Pixel

You should definitely know how to draw a line, and even a triangle. If you're anything like me, drawing an entire person is a bit of a stretch. You pick up a pencil or pen, put it to a piece of paper and move your hand around. But how does a graphics processor do just that? Instead of outputting to a piece of paper, the graphics processor must output to your screen, but how?

The images displayed on your screen are constructed using a collection of very fine dots known as pixels. The number of pixels you can fit on your screen is variable if you have a regular CRT display; otherwise, it is fixed if you have an LCD display. Because most users still have CRT displays, I stick with them as the explanation for this.

➤ ***For more information on monitor technologies such as those found in CRT and LCD monitors, see Chapter 10, "Monitors and Input Devices: Your Sense of Sight and Touch Restored."***

Although your monitor is fixed at a certain size, the number of pixels you can fit on the screen at once can increase up to a certain level. That maximum level is determined by your monitor and your video card.

Because your monitor remains a fixed size, the more pixels that are displayed on your screen at once, the more detail can be seen. However, at the same time everything gets smaller. Imagine having a room with a bunch of balloons. The room can't get any larger and it can hold 100,000 balloons without distorting their form at all. You can cram 1,000,000 balloons into the room; however, each balloon compresses a bit and gets much smaller (I'm assuming they're not going to pop). This is the same phenomenon that occurs when you change the number of pixels displayed on your screen.

Another side effect of increasing the number of pixels on your screen is that the more you have, the more your graphics processor has to do. Remember that your graphics processor is what is outputting and displaying all these pixels, and they exist in 2D and 3D modes just as well. The only difference being that in the most commonly used configurations, increasing the number of pixels displayed on your screen at once does not result in any poorer 2D performance on today's video cards because of the power of most 2D graphics cores. Unfortunately, the same cannot be said about pixels in a 3D environment.

Resolution, Color Depth, and Refresh Rate

The number of pixels on your screen is known as your screen's resolution and it is expressed in the following form: Number of horizontal pixels × number of vertical pixels. Common resolutions are 640 × 480, 800 × 600, 1,024 × 768, 1,280 × 1,024, and 1,600 × 1,200 (see Figure 5.5). The larger your monitor, the easier it is to attain some of the higher resolutions; otherwise, things simply get too small to see clearly. In 3D games, you are generally limited by your video card from going to too high of a resolution because of memory bandwidth limitations. I explain why later.

Each pixel can take on a number of color values. The more values it can take on, the better the end result looks. In the past 16-bit color values (each pixel could take on any of 2^16 color values or 65,536 colors) were the norm. However, as game developers were given more powerful hardware, they began optimizing their games for use in 32-bit color modes. In most 32-bit color settings you are given 24-bits of color information (16,777,216 different colors) and 8-bits of transparency information known as the alpha channel. The problem with 32-bit color modes is that your frame buffer needs to be twice as large to store all the frame data. If you're using 32-bit textures as well, you have to have twice as much texture storage and bandwidth to get that data to your graphics processor.

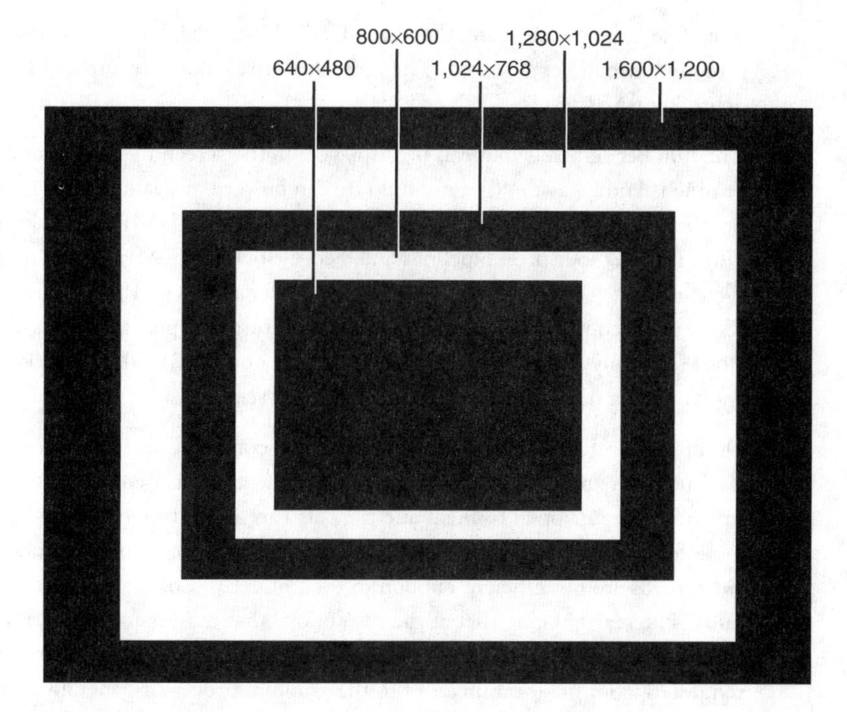

FIGURE 5.5
The rectangles from largest to smallest represent the relative resolutions, 1,600 × 1,200 down to 640 × 480 in the center.

Another value that must be taken into account is the Z-buffer precision. The Z-buffer is used to store how deep a pixel is located in the current screen, where depth is defined by how close or how far away the pixel is from the camera. Z-buffer precision is also measured in bits per pixel (bpp), and they are stored in 16-bit, 24-bit, or 32-bit values.

Just like any other video device, your monitor must refresh the screen every so often. This rate is the *refresh rate*. Common refresh rates are 60Hz, 72Hz, 75Hz, 85Hz, and 100Hz. The higher the refresh rate, the less strain on your eyes and generally the more comfortable you feel while looking at your screen. Attainable refresh rates are limitations of both your video card and your monitor. Keep this idea of a refresh rate in mind until later when I introduce the idea of frame rates, or how quickly your video card can draw a single frame versus how quickly your monitor can display it.

Texels and Fill Rate

Just like everything else in the display world, textures are measured in pixels. Just like screen resolution, they are measured in a horizontal × vertical fashion. For example, a 256 × 256 texture is a square with 256 pixels on each side. The larger the texture, the more detailed it can be, but the more space it requires when being stored. The individual pixels that a texture is made up of are known as texels.

The number of pixels that can be displayed on the screen in a given amount of time is known as the fill rate. Fill rate can be very misleading because the number is quoted under ideal conditions. For example, NVIDIA's GeForce2 Ultra features four pixel pipelines and a core clock of 250MHz. This means it can display 1,000,000,000 pixels (or 1,000 Megapixels (MP) or 1 Gigapixel (GP)) per second. The same chip is able to texture two pixels in a single clock. Multiply that by the four pixel pipelines and the 250MHz core clock and you get a texel fill rate of 2 Gigapixels per second.

Quoting fill rate numbers like this brings on a couple of problems. Pixel fill rate numbers are useless because pixels are almost never used without some sort of texture mapped to them and they also are put through various lighting effects. They are also useless because today's graphics processors and video cards are not efficient enough to even offer 50% of their advertised fill rates. The reason being that at the resolutions that most gamers play, the memory bandwidth requirements for the entire frame and texture data being requested from the local memory to the graphics processor generally saturates the local memory bus. This is known as a memory bandwidth limitation in the graphics world, just like it is in the system memory world.

The higher the resolution of the textures, the higher the memory bandwidth requirements. The higher the screen resolution, the more pixels have to be filled, and the greater the stress is on the graphics processor as well as the memory bus. Remember that at 640 × 480 only 307,200 pixels are displayed, at 1,024 × 768 786,432 pixels are displayed, and at 1,600 × 1,200 1,920,000 pixels are displayed. You can see why until recently 1,600 × 1,200 hasn't even been a reasonable resolution at which to run a 3D game. Even today, with all the effects you like to turn on in your games, 1,024 × 768 or 1,280 × 1,024 is the highest you can go to get smooth performance figures. More on performance later....

In Serious Sam, for example, the real world fill rate of a GeForce2 Ultra ended up being approximately 344 megapixels per second. This is just more than one third of the theoretical fill rate of the GeForce2 Ultra. Obviously chips with higher theoretical fill rates are going to have higher real world fill rates, but you can see how fill rate numbers can be misleading—much like a lot of numbers bandied about in this industry.

MIP Mapping

A very smart man once told me that perception is reality, and in many cases those words are the difference between success and failure. You know by now that textures are used to paint things in a 3D scene, but also realize that in a 3D scene some objects are closer to you (otherwise known as the camera) than others. The closer ones you want to see in the greatest detail possible, but do you really care about the quality of textures that are all the way on the other side of the room? Perception is reality right? So you shouldn't.

This is where MIP Mapping comes into play. MIP mapping enables the use of smaller textures, both in terms of storage in memory and the size of the object on the screen, the further you get from the camera (in this case the camera being your face looking at the 3D scene).

Texture Filtering

When applying textures to polygons you rarely have a situation where a single texture fits perfectly over the face of a polygon. Instead many little polygons are designed to represent quirks in the architecture of a building, or the body of a character. Unfortunately, this makes it very difficult to texture these types of objects.

What happens if you have a texel that lies between two pixels? Which pixel gets the color of that particular texel? The answer to this question is much more complicated than most would believe. It is solved using texture filtering. *Texture filtering* refers to the algorithms used to assign a texel when it lies between two pixels and not directly on one.

The easiest solution to the problem would be to assign the texel to the closest pixel. This is known as point sampling. A Serious Sam screenshot shown in Figure 5.6 speaks for itself, but obviously point sampling isn't the best texture filtering algorithm to choose. Point sampling is used because it's the fastest.

Bilinear filtering is the next step above point sampling. Here the filtering technique takes the four texels closest to the pixel being mapped to and averages them together to find the color used for the pixel that is being textured. As you can see from the Serious Sam screenshot in Figure 5.7, this improves things considerably.

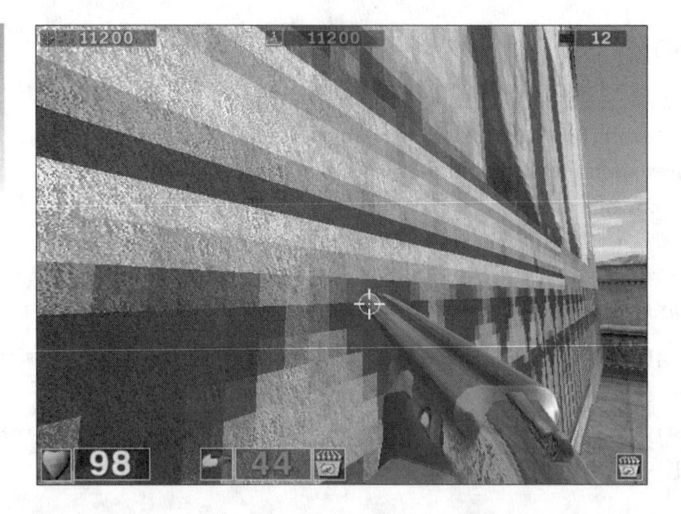

FIGURE 5.6
Point sampling is the highest performance texture filtering method, but it results in very poor image quality.

FIGURE 5.7
Bilinear filtering reduces the blockyness associated with point sampling yet reduces performance as well.

The downside to bilinear filtering is that because it takes more texel samples, more memory bandwidth is consumed. However, all of today's graphics processors are able to do this relatively effortlessly.

Trilinear filtering increases quality one notch above bilinear, although the areas that it improves is slightly different from bilinear filtering. Remember that idea of MIP mapping? Well as you move further away from the camera in a 3D scene, the MIP map levels change as the textures used get smaller and smaller. These divisions can become clearly visible and when combined with the effects of bilinear filtering, the end result is a very blurry progression of textures as they move further away from the camera.

The solution to this is trilinear filtering, which performs filtering between the various MIP map levels. Trilinear filtering eats up even more memory bandwidth than bilinear filtering. Although the visual impact of it isn't as stunning as the transition from point sampling to bilinear filtering, when you experience it you never want to go back.

The final type of texture filtering is anisotropic filtering. The beauty of anisotropic filtering is that it helps texture filtering when viewing objects at unusual angles (those other than 90-degree angles). The major issue with anisotropic filtering is that the performance hit you incur when it is enabled is pretty significant because of the added memory bandwidth consumption. As graphics accelerators become more powerful with more memory bandwidth (or more efficient ways of using memory bandwidth) anisotropic filtering becomes more commonplace. For now it's generally a luxury option that you turn on if you have the power.

Antialiasing

If you've ever played a 3D console game on your TV (especially on a Playstation or Nintendo 64 system) one of the most annoying things from a visual perspective is the jagged lines that seem to be everywhere. This is an occurrence that is generally referred to as aliasing. Realize, however, that many types of aliasing exist and this is only one of them.

The problem stems from the fact that your 3D hardware cannot draw a straight line. What it can do is plot pixels in the form of a straight line. However, because it can plot only whole pixels, the line is going to end up looking jagged unless it continually remains a completely horizontal or vertical line (not a frequent occurrence in games).

The obvious way to rid yourself of these jagged lines is to increase the resolution at which they are drawn. The more pixels that make up a line, the less jagged it appears. Unfortunately, this comes at a significant cost to fill rate and memory bandwidth, when running at 1,600 × 1,200, which isn't usually an option for most video cards. So there must be another way to get rid of the infamous jaggies.

This is where a function known as antialiasing comes in to play. Antialiasing has been around for years, however, it was first truly pushed by the late 3dfx in 1999–2000, not long before their demise. Antialiasing has two basic approaches, or as 3dfx branded it, Full Scene antialiasing (the antialiasing of all pixels on the screen). These two approaches are super sampling or multi sampling (see Figures 5.8 and 5.9).

FIGURE 5.8
A wireframe scene that is not antialiased.

FIGURE 5.9
A wireframe scene that is antialiased.

You can see that the lines in Figure 5.9, unlike those in Figure 5.8, have virtually no jagged edges and all appear to be quite smooth. A bit of blurriness is introduced because of the antialiasing filter.

Super Sampling Antialiasing

3dfx introduced super sampling as an antialiasing method in 2000. NVIDIA and ATI soon followed suit with their cards. The way super sampling works is by rendering a scene at a higher resolution, and decreasing the resolution to the value set by the user. For example, 2X FSAA (full scene antialiasing) would render at two times the resolution in one direction, either horizontally or vertically, and then decrease the resolution to whatever it was originally set. If I were running Quake III at 640 × 480 with a 2X FSAA mode enabled, one possibility would be that the card would render at 1,280 × 480 or 640 × 960, and use the added samples (twice as many if you calculate it out) to reduce aliasing. In a 4X FSAA mode, the resolution would be increased to 2X in both the x and y directions, and going with the 640 × 480 example from before the supersampled resolution would be 1,280 × 960. This results in four times the number of pixels being rendered and used to smooth out the jagged lines in the scene. This type of super sampling is known as ordered grid super sampling and was employed by ATI and NVIDIA with their first AA capable cards.

3dfx chose a slightly more elegant solution. Although it resulted in the same performance hit, it ended up offering a bit higher quality in certain situations. 3dfx's approach was still a super sampling one (although people often confused it with multi sampling), but instead of an ordered grid method 3dfx used a rotated grid super sampling algorithm.

Using what they called their T-Buffer, the VSA-100 (3dfx's first and only rotated grid super sampling capable chip) took two or four samples of the pixel. By shifting one pixel horizontally or vertically and combining (averaging) those two or four samples and outputting that value as the single pixel, that pixel has now been antialiased. Again, the performance hit was the same, but the image quality was improved.

The effects of this were dramatic. At most 2X FSAA settings games looked a lot sharper, and at 4X FSAA settings the image quality was unbelievable. However, there were some problems with the first wave of FSAA enabled cards.

First of all, you have to understand that FSAA does not require much hardware to implement, at least not in the form offered in the very first cards. Getting good performance out of one of these modes was another thing entirely. Performance with 4X FSAA enabled was unplayable on most cards in most settings, the reason being that now you had four times the memory bandwidth requirements because you were effectively quadrupling the amount of rendering work the graphics processor had to do. This made most 2X FSAA modes the only playable ones, and even then the decrease in "jaggies" (that was 3dfx's term, not mine) wasn't 100%. They were still noticeable, although much less so than without it enabled.

The second problem with FSAA is an inherent problem with the term "full scene" anything. Not only would the aliased lines get smoothed out, but also a lot of onscreen text became blurry. This increased the annoyance factor of enabling FSAA considerably. It performed slowly and made text look even worse.

The third and final problem with FSAA was that the usefulness in games was limited. In a first person shooter, although the benefits of FSAA were definitely visible, they were not desired as much as they were in a flight simulator, for example. Because relatively few flight or racing simulators have good benchmarks in them, it became commonplace to benchmark the FSAA performance hit in the very games that didn't demand FSAA—first person shooters. The inability for many gamers to understand the benefits of FSAA just by looking at a screenshot made it a feature that very few users could appreciate. Combined with the performance hit and the other side effects, one of which I have mentioned, FSAA wasn't too big of a win with many of the gamers. Because it was the backbone of 3dfx's marketing structure for their delayed Voodoo5 product, you can begin to see why the Voodoo5 was 3dfx's last graphics card to make it to the public's hands.

As far as my opinion on FSAA goes, after seeing 3dfx's demos and after actually using FSAA in the AnandTech lab for endless hours during benchmarks and screenshot comparisons, I can honestly say that it does improve the gaming experience for me, even in first person shooters. However, you need hardware capable of handling it. You also need a more mature form of antialiasing—multisampled AA.

Multisample Antialiasing

The biggest drawback of supersampled AA is the sheer fill rate and memory bandwidth requirements of the algorithms. Requiring up to four times the amount of fill rate power was simply unreasonable, even for the fastest graphics processors. This is exactly how multisampled AA differs from supersampled AA, in the memory bandwidth and fillrate requirements for the solution.

Instead of sampling different pixels, multisampling AA dictates that the samples that are taken should share the same color value as the original input pixel. This means that resending the texture data is not necessary because it is simply the same pixel sampled multiple times (see Figure 5.10). The difference being that the position of the pixel is shifted, resulting in the antialiased effect without as great of a performance hit.

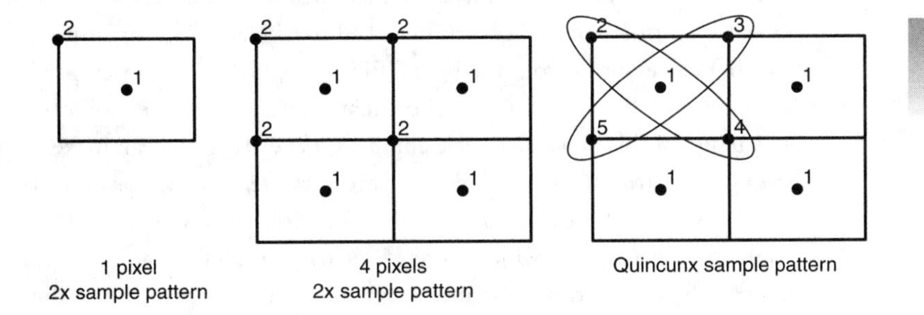

FIGURE 5.10 NVIDIA's Quincunx antialiasing pattern.

The success of multisampled AA algorithms such as NVIDIA's Quincunx and ATI's SMOOTHVISION depends on the combination of a high performance graphics processor, with effective use of texture filtering algorithms as well. Because you're reusing texture data on all these additional AA samples, filtering becomes even more important. A combination of a multisampled AA algorithm with anisotropic filtering turned on can prove to be a very attractive solution, however, the hit on memory bandwidth and fill rate can be tremendous.

Pixel and Vertex Shaders—The Graphics Processor Becomes a GPU

When the GeForce 256 was announced, NVIDIA was touting its achievement of bringing the worlds first Graphics Processing Unit (GPU) to the market. Back then, I hesitated in calling it a GPU simply because it drew a parallel between the GeForce 256 and a CPU that I was not willing to make. A CPU such as the AMD Athlon and Intel Pentium 4 was much more useful than NVIDIA's first GPU simply because they were truly programmable entities. They had an instruction set (x86) and programmers could write code to manipulate the CPU's power in whatever means they saw necessary.

The GPU, however, was not as advanced of a chip. Developers were stuck with a feature-set that NVIDIA's engineering team implemented and could not control the chip in the same manner with which x86 programmers can manipulate the Athlon or the Pentium 4. NVIDIA introduced a whole new list of features that were supported in hardware with the GeForce2 GTS and its shading rasterizer. However, if a developer did not implement a particular function as it was provided for in hardware, their function was useless in the eyes of the GPU. There was a severe lack of flexibility with this "revolutionary" GPU.

One of NVIDIA's most highly touted features was their hardware transforming and lighting engine that was designed to offload the transforming and lighting calculations from the host CPU to the GPU in an attempt to increase overall performance. Unfortunately, very few games still can take advantage of this powerful T&L engine. Quake III Arena can make use of the GPU's hardware accelerated transformation engine, however, its own lighting engine makes the GPU's other function useless. That is the least you could ask for. Games such as Unreal Tournament could not take advantage of even the GPU's transformation engine. With all due respect to the engineers at NVIDIA, they are not game developers and they do not know the best way to implement a lot of these features in hardware so that everyone is happy.

The solution to this ongoing problem was to take a page from the books of desktop CPU manufacturers. If developers are constantly asking for their features to be implemented in hardware, why not place the burden on them and make them write the code necessary to manipulate the hardware NVIDIA manufactures?

The GeForce3 did just that and because of its programmable capabilities I always refer to the GeForce3 as the first true GPU from NVIDIA. It still featured the same T&L engine from before, however, now it was fully programmable. The GeForce3 featured something NVIDIA calls the nfiniteFX engine that is made up of the hardware T&L unit from the original GeForce 256, plus an nfiniteFX Vertex processor and an nfiniteFX Pixel processor. This is where the bulk of the GeForce3's die came from.

The Vertex Shader Instruction Set

The instruction set the GeForce3 understands is what is known as the Vertex Shader Instruction Set. This is the equivalent of the x86 instruction set in the PC processor world albeit specifically tailored for the needs of the GeForce3.

The Vertex processor handles the initial geometry and setup math necessary for the production of the 3D scene that is being rendered. When you're dealing with polygons (and obviously their vertices, hence the name), the Vertex processor is your one-stop-shop for all your 3D calculation needs.

Operations such as vertex lighting, morphing, key frame animation, and vertex skinning are all functions that can be taken advantage of in programs that developers custom make. The Vertex processor runs these programs. These operations were around before the GeForce3's release, however, developers found themselves at the mercy of the graphics processor manufacturers in terms of how they could implement these features.

Examples of what the Vertex processor is able to produce are things such as facial expressions. Gone are the days when a developer uses a single blocky texture to represent a hand. Now things such as individual fingers moving across a keyboard can easily be represented. Using a combination of polygons and programmable lighting effects, some very realistic models and actions can be produced.

The next step in the process is the finalization of the lighting process and the actual rendering of the pixels present in the scene for final display. This is obviously handled by the Pixel processor. One of the basic concepts of 3D gaming is the idea of using textures that I introduced you to earlier in this chapter. In the early days of 3D gaming, a character could be represented by a few polygons covered with two-dimensional textures. The textures would store only a few bits of data, mainly pertaining to the color of the texture.

Applications of Pixel and Vertex Shaders

With the advent of the technology behind the GeForce3's GPU, the opportunity for the texture to become much more useful is limitless. Instead of just holding values for color, textures can now start to hold variables, direction vectors, and lighting vectors. All these values can actually be encoded into the texture.

What's the benefit of this? After the Vertex processor has setup the polygons in a scene and the Pixel processor comes in to apply textures, the textures not only tell the Pixel processor what color they are, but they also tell the processor how they react if certain events occur. Using the encoded direction and lighting vectors of a pixel, the pixels can now realistically reflect light through a dot product calculation. And the manner in which the pixel reflects light changes according to the direction vector of the light source.

Imagine a wrinkle on a character's face. That wrinkle now contains much more information than simply its color and general orientation. If a light source shines upon the wrinkle it now casts a realistic shadow through a series of vector multiplication operations. Through a series of pixel shader programs the developer can now make his game completely unique. *Doom 3* looks completely different from *Duke Nukem Forever* not because of the fact that idSoftware uses different textures than 3DRealms, but because their vertex and pixel programs are completely different.

Remember bump mapping from my discussion on the need for multiple texture layers? Instead of having another texture create the illusion of bumps on a surface, the GeForce3 can actually do real time calculation of the effects on ripples in water and how they interact with surrounding objects such as rocks.

The GeForce3 can take advantage of Dot3 bump mapping that again uses dot products of direction vectors to produce the resulting ripple effects in water. This isn't limited to water alone, as walls and other surfaces can receive the same treatment.

Dot3 has been around for a while, but is rarely used because of either poor implementations in hardware or a lack of flexibility for developers to use it. EMBM (Environmental Mapped Bump Mapping) was rarely used because the penalty of rendering another texture was often too great for the cards that supported it. With the GeForce3's extremely flexible GPU, developers can truly take the power into their own hands and you can finally expect more than just ugly looking 2D textures on walls and completely unrealistic water.

The GeForce3's Pixel and Vertex shaders weren't exclusive to NVIDIA. The technology was actually licensed from NVIDIA to Microsoft for use with their DirectX 8 API. ATI has similar functionality in their R200 chip, the successor to the Radeon.

For Pixel and Vertex shaders to be taken advantage of, there has to be specific game support for them. Upon the release of the GeForce3 there was almost no game support for these programmable units and even today support is still scarce. However, as time goes on developers most definitely jump on the programmable T&L bandwagon because of the endless possibilities provided by pixel and vertex shader programs.

Efficient Use of Memory Bandwidth—Making $1 Out of $0.15

Up to this point I've shown you some very interesting features, the quality they offer, and the potential they have to make your gaming experience even more exciting. However, every single time I've done that, I've complained about the real world feasibility of enabling those features due to memory bandwidth constraints.

In Chapters 1 and 2, I introduced you to the concept of memory bandwidth with regard to CPUs and chipsets, as well as in Chapter 4, which deals with memory in particular. The same rules discussed in those chapters also apply to memory bandwidth in the video sense, except the factors are magnified. Remember that today's graphics processors are given a minimum of 2–3 times the amount of memory bandwidth that today's CPUs receive. Although you're dealing with physically smaller amounts of memory, memory bandwidth is memory bandwidth regardless of how much memory lies on the other side of it.

Even though 7GBps–9GBps of memory bandwidth might seem like a lot, it's very easy for the graphics processor to become starved and demand more, or suffer the consequences (I explain those in the next section on performance). Unfortunately, higher speed memory isn't always easy to come by. In many cases higher speed memory simply isn't available, or if it is, the cost of putting it on a graphics card is entirely too high. Look at the GeForce3, for example. It was released with DDR SDRAM, the very same chips used in DDR SDRAM modules for desktop PCs, yet instead of running at 100MHz or 133MHz it ran at 230MHz. This is a DDR frequency, so the effective transfer rates were equal to that of a 460MHz memory solution. Finding memory that can run that fast is already quite an accomplishment. Pushing the envelope even further becomes increasingly difficult.

The graphics and memory industries are constantly looking for ways to increase the amount of memory bandwidth by using faster memory or by investing in newer memory technologies. However, with 6-month product cycles demanding newer, faster solutions there has to be another option because it takes years for a memory standard to become accepted by the industry, not months.

The option happens to lie in rendering efficiency. Instead of throwing more power at the problem, look at the source of it and try to fix that. Until recently this idea wasn't implemented too much. When a newer graphics processor was released companies simply cranked up the memory clock. With the release of the ATI Radeon graphics processor, things changed considerably.

ATI's Radeon and HyperZ

What was most elegant about ATI's Radeon was a particular part of its feature set known as *HyperZ*. The term was coined by ATI, but the functions were much more than the usual marketing gimmick.

The HyperZ technology is essentially composed of three features that work in conjunction with one another to provide for an "increase" in memory bandwidth. In reality, the increase is simply a more efficient use of the memory bandwidth that is already there.

The three features are: Hierarchical Z, Z-Compression, and Fast Z-Clear. Before I explain these features and how they impact performance, you have to first understand the basics of conventional 3D rendering.

More on the Z-Buffer

As I've briefly mentioned before, the Z-buffer is a portion of memory dedicated to holding the Z-values of rendered pixels. These Z-values dictate what pixels and eventually what polygons appear in front of one another when displayed on your screen. If you're thinking about it in a mathematical sense, the Z-values indicate position along the Z-axis.

A traditional 3D accelerator processes each polygon as it is sent to the hardware, without any knowledge of the rest of the scene. Because of this lack of knowledge, every forward facing polygon must be shaded and textured. The Z-buffer, as I explained earlier, is used to store the depth of each pixel in the current back buffer. Each pixel of each polygon rendered must be checked against the Z-buffer to determine if it is closer to the viewer than the pixel currently stored in the back buffer (remember you're dealing with double buffered scenes).

Checking against the Z-buffer must be performed *after* the pixel is already shaded and textured. If a pixel turns out to be in front of the current pixel, the new pixel replaces (or is blended with, in the case of transparency) the current pixel in the back buffer and the Z-buffer depth is updated. If the new pixel ends up behind the current pixel, the new pixel is thrown out and no changes are made to the back buffer (or blended, in the case of transparency). When pixels are drawn for no reason, this is known as overdraw. Drawing the same pixel three times is equivalent to an overdraw of 3, which in some cases is typical.

After the scene is complete, the back buffer is flipped to the front buffer to display on the monitor.

What I've just described is known as *immediate mode rendering* and has been used since the 1960's for still frame CAD rendering, architectural engineering, film special effects, and now in most 3D accelerators found inside your PC (see Figure 5.11). Unfortunately, this method of rendering results in quite a bit of overdraw, where objects that aren't visible are being rendered.

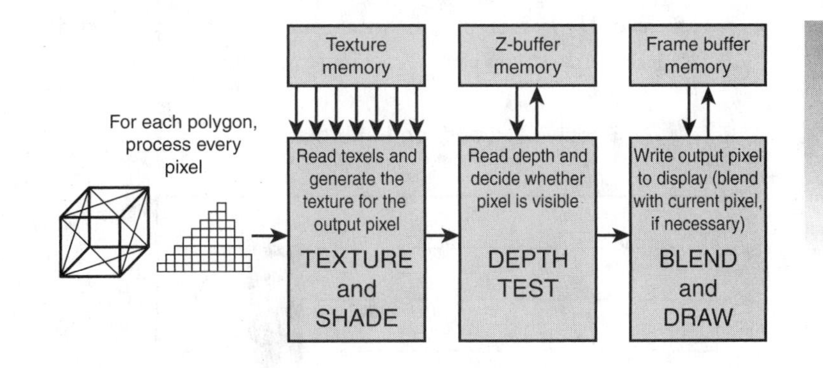

FIGURE 5.11
The Immediate Mode Rendering process (illustrated here), or something similar to it, is found in most of today's 3D graphics accelerators.

ATI's solution to this problem was to optimize the accesses to the Z-buffer. From the previous example of how conventional 3D rendering works, you can guess that quite a bit of memory bandwidth is spent on accesses to the Z-buffer to check to see if any pixels are in front of the one being currently rendered. ATI's HyperZ increases the efficiency of these accesses, so instead of attacking the root of the problem (overdraw), ATI went after the results of it (frequent Z-buffer accesses).

Features of HyperZ

The first part of the HyperZ technology is the Hierarchical Z feature. This feature basically enables the pixel being rendered to be checked against the Z-buffer *before* the pixel actually hits the rendering pipelines. This enables useless pixels to be thrown out early, before the Radeon has to render them.

Next you have *Z-Compression*. As the name implies, this is a lossless compression algorithm (no data is lost during the compression) that compresses the data in the Z-buffer thus allowing it to take up less space, which in turn conserves memory bandwidth during accesses to the Z-buffer.

The final piece of the HyperZ puzzle is the *Fast Z-Clear* feature. Fast Z-Clear is nothing more than a feature that enables the quick clearing of all data in the Z-buffer after a scene has been rendered. Apparently ATI's method of clearing the Z-buffer is dramatically faster than other conventional methods of doing so.

In terms of the performance offered by HyperZ, the increase in efficiency is definitely noticeable. The most noticeable example of HyperZ's efficiency is with the Radeon SDR from ATI. The Radeon SDR uses conventional single data rate SDRAM, offering no more than 2.7GBps of memory bandwidth. I did a test not too long ago using Unreal Tournament, which measured the effects of HyperZ on performance using this memory bandwidth castrated Radeon card. As you can see in Figure 5.12 the results speak for themselves.

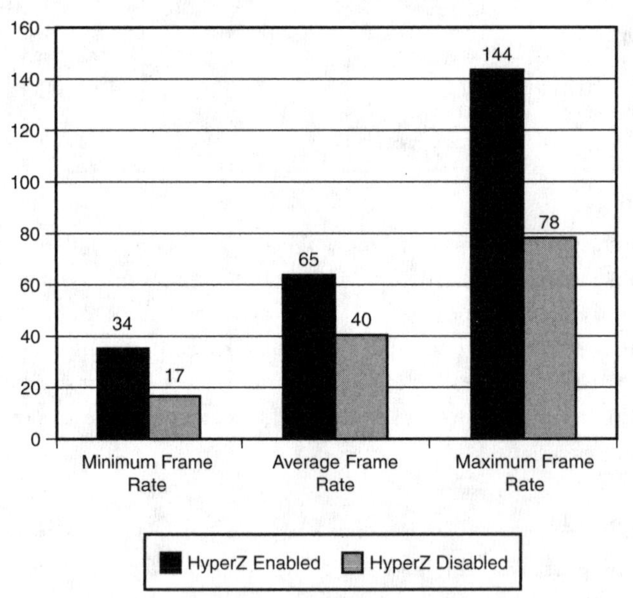

FIGURE 5.12
Under Unreal Tournament notice that HyperZ is really doing quite a bit for the Radeon SDR. Not only does it improve the minimum frame rate by around 50%, but it also increases the average frame rate by close to 40%.

The Radeon 8500 based on the R200 chip has an even more sophisticated HyperZ engine called HyperZ II that continues to improve efficiency.

NVIDIA's GeForce3 and Lightspeed Memory Architecture

With the GeForce3, NVIDIA introduced similar features to ATI's HyperZ in what they called their Lightspeed Memory Architecture.

The GeForce3's memory controller is actually drastically changed from the GeForce2 Ultra. Instead of having a 128-bit interface to memory, four fully independent memory controllers are present within the GPU in what NVIDIA likes to call their Crossbar based memory controller (see Figure 5.13).

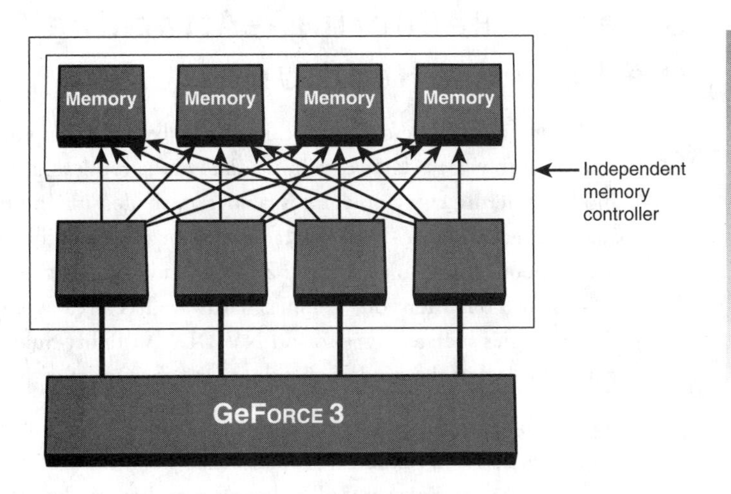

FIGURE 5.13
NVIDIA's Crossbar Memory Controller improves efficiency considerably. If a small memory access must be made, the amount of wasted memory bandwidth is minimized through the use of four independent, yet load balanced memory controllers.

These four memory controllers are 32-bits each in width that are essentially interleaved, meaning that they all add up to the 128-bit memory controller you're used to, and they all support DDR SDRAM. The crossbar memory architecture dictates that these four independent memory controllers are also load balancing in reference to the bandwidth they share with the rest of the GPU.

The point of having four independent, load balanced memory controllers is for increased parallelism in the graphics processor. The four narrower memory controllers come in quite handy when dealing with a lot of small datasets. If the GPU is requesting 64 bits of data, the GeForce2 Ultra uses a total of 256 bits of bandwidth (128-bit DDR) to fetch it from the local memory. This results in quite a bit of wasted bandwidth. However, in the case of the GeForce3, if the GPU requests 64 bits of data, that request can be handled in 32-bit chunks, leaving much less bandwidth unused. Didn't your mother ever tell you that it's bad to waste food?

The next part of this Lightspeed Memory Architecture is the Visibility Subsystem. This is the NVIDIA equivalent to ATI's Hierarchal Z feature. This technology isn't perfect, because in a number of cases the Visibility Subsystem fails to reject the appropriate z-values and some overdraw remains.

The remaining two features that make up ATI's HyperZ are also mirrored in the GeForce3. The GeForce3 features the same lossless Z-buffer compression as the Radeon. The compression savings can be as great as 4:1, which is identical to what ATI claims that the Radeon's Z-buffer compression can do.

Deferred Rendering—Attacking the Problem Head On

As I've mentioned before, everything I've talked about up to this point is in reference to what is known as immediate mode rendering. In immediate mode rendering every polygon is rendered, shaded/lit, and textured. After that, a check of the Z-buffer dictates what pixels are visible and which ones are hidden by other pixels. If the Z-buffer indicates that the pixel is hidden, it is thrown out after your graphics hardware has already done all that work. Technologies such as HyperZ and NVIDIA's Visibility Subsystem work to combat this, but the rendering style is kept the same for the most part.

The problem of 3D rendering can be approached in another way and that is known as deferred rendering, sometimes called tile-based rendering. Deferred rendering groups all polygons together and breaks down the entire scene into a series of blocks, or tiles (hence the name tile-based rendering).

These tiles are small enough to forgo the need for an external Z-buffer, which eliminates the use of memory bandwidth for Z-buffer checks. This is akin to what HyperZ and NVIDIA's Visibility subsystem accomplish, but by using a drastically different approach.

The benefits don't end there, however. The other major benefit of these tiles is that overdraw is completely eliminated. Because all the locations/visibility status of the polygons is already known, those that aren't visible are simply not rendered. This enables a considerable amount of performance to be unleashed with a very small amount of memory bandwidth (see Figure 5.14).

The downside to all of this is that it is very difficult to design an efficient tile-based renderer. Imagination Technology has been working on a deferred renderer for years now, and only very recently have they been able to get good quality or performance out of it. The technology has a lot of potential, but it is very difficult to master.

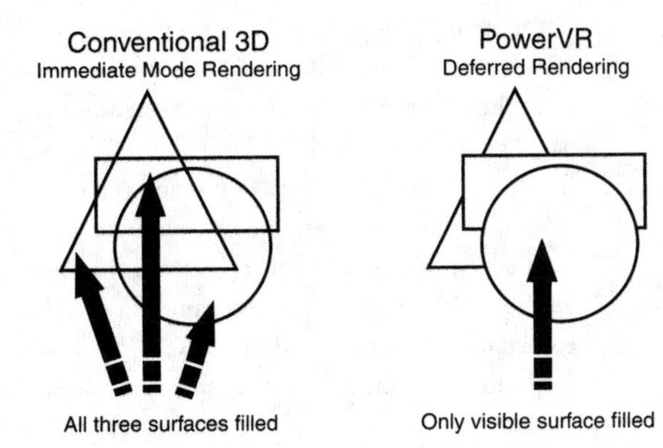

FIGURE 5.14 The PowerVR line of chips have implemented deferred rendering for a while now and currently are the most advanced deferred rendering graphics processors for desktop x86 systems. Their advantage comes from the fact that no overdraw exists in the rendering process.

Performance in 3D Graphics

The small discussion about fill rates aside, everything I've discussed up to this point has been about features in 3D graphics and actually rendering. But what about performance? That's what you're reading this book for in the first place, right? You want to know what is the fastest, what will be the fastest, and how to determine this.

Just as the fill rate is the rate at which pixels are drawn on the screen, the frame rate is the rate at which a single frame can be drawn on your screen. Think for a minute about how many frames you would need to see in a second to get a feeling of smooth/high performance?

Film is recorded at 24 frames per second (fps), NTSC TV is recorded at 30fps, and both of those look incredibly smooth. Does that mean 30fps is the target frame rate for a high-performance 3D card? If you've been told that before, forget it completely because in the world of high-performance gaming, 30fps is a joke. Maybe four or five years ago 30fps could be acceptable. I still remember running at more than 40fps with my Pentium II 266 and a 3dfx Voodoo-based Diamond Monster 3D in the original *GLQuake* at 640 × 480. However, today if I don't see at least 80fps in *Quake III* at 1,024 × 768 running at 32-bit color with 32-bit textures, I complain about performance.

What's in a Frame?

> **Note**
>
> Have you ever wondered why movies are called "motion pictures"? The reason is simple; a movie, TV show, or even a game is nothing more than a series of still pictures displayed one after another so quickly that it fools your eye into thinking that it's seeing an actual moving image. In terms of game performance, consider each one of these pictures to be a frame of video. Therefore, the number of these frames displayed in a second is directly related to the smoothness of the video playback. The higher the number, the smoother the playback looks. The lower the number, the more choppy it is.

The frame rate you're playing at varies depending on a few factors; for one the type of game you're playing. Frame rate is of the utmost importance in games that require fast responses from their users, such as first person shooters. The difference between your system waiting for you to input a command (such as strafing to avoid a rocket aimed at your upper torso) and you waiting for the system to register a command (take the same strafing example) can be like night and day when you compare the experience you get from the two. In the first case, you're tense, you're anticipating your enemy's next move, you're truly submerged in the game. In the second case, however, your entertainment is hindered by the fact that you've got to sit there and wait for polygons to be drawn on your screen that are supposed to startle and amaze you.

Want another example? When you're typing, you know you can press the letter 'a', and it almost immediately appears on your screen. If there was a delay between you pressing the letter 'a' and it appearing on your screen, you would most definitely notice it. This is similar to the delay that is perceivable when a frame takes longer to appear on your screen.

At 30fps a single frame is displayed every 33.3ms. When you consider that moving through a simple hallway can call for the displaying of hundreds of frames, taking 33.3ms to display each and every one can add up. Think about walking through a hall, and that sequence consisting of 1,000 frames that must be rendered. At 33.3ms per frame that's 33.3 seconds to display the entire 1,000 frames. Now if your character happens to be running and it's taking that long to get from one point to another, something is definitely wrong. When your system cannot keep up with things the potential to "drop" frames becomes reality. So instead of rendering all 1,000 frames it might drop a few here and there. This results in the jerky motion you might be used to if you've ever played on an extremely slow system. Thirty frames per second isn't too bad, but if it's at 640 × 480 and you crank up the resolution to 1,024 × 768 or 1,600 × 1,200, chances are your frame rate drops to single-digit levels very quickly. When you get into that zone, the game play experience is significantly deteriorated.

But the point of this book is to get you the hardware that enables you to only read about such awful things and not actually experience them. The unfortunate truth is that a hardware setup is rarely attainable. This gives you perfect performance across the board at all resolutions, in all games, and at the highest frame rates. But that's not what you're going for. You're going for something that is realistically obtainable and that provides you with an entertaining gaming experience. When you want more, hopefully there is an updated configuration for you to upgrade to.

That being said, what performance levels should you target? As I mentioned before, a lot of this depends on the types of games you're playing. When dealing with first person shooters such as *Quake III*, the upcoming *Doom 3*, *Duke Nukem Forever*, *Half Life* (*Counterstrike* included of course), and so on, the higher the frame rate the better. These are the games that can generally be helped by having faster graphics cards.

However, other games such as flight simulators, racing simulators, and real time strategy (RTS) games aren't much more fun when played at 100fps than when played at 60fps. In the case of RTS games it is often the case that the key to performance isn't how quickly frames can be drawn, but how responsive the system remains as more objects are drawn on the screen. If you've ever had a major firefight in a 2D game, such as *Red Alert 2*, you notice some pretty significant slowdown as more objects are placed on the screen. Having your screen drawing a new frame every 10 ms in a game like this is pointless, although the exact opposite is true in a fast paced, first person shooter.

Picking Adequate Hardware

So what type of hardware is required for this kind of performance? The first concept to fully grasp and understand is that memory bandwidth is key to the performance of your 3D graphics subsystem. Although your CPU can get by with only 3.2GBps of memory bandwidth, the same can't be said about your graphics processor. The main reason is that most of your everyday applications require no more than 100MBps–200MBps of memory bandwidth to your CPU. Although those numbers go up as applications get more complex (and bloated), even if they tripled you wouldn't be memory bandwidth limited. You find exceptions to this, but for the most part your everyday office and Internet applications are not memory bandwidth intensive. The same cannot be said about the role of memory bandwidth on your video card.

The data being requested from the local memory on your video card is quite large and very memory bandwidth intensive in design. Requesting tons of textures, constantly performing Z-buffer checks, and getting other types of frame data is extremely memory bandwidth intensive. The higher your video card's memory clock (memory bus width as well), the more memory bandwidth your graphics processor has.

Key things to look for when talking about memory bandwidth are obviously the raw bandwidth calculations, but also any other efficiencies that a particular memory controller or architecture might have, such as NVIDIA's Crossbar Memory Architecture or ATI's HyperZ Occlusion Culling (sometimes known as hidden surface removal). Obviously, tile-based renderers also gain points here and are able to do more with less memory bandwidth.

Second to memory bandwidth is core clock speed and thus fill rate of the graphics processor itself. Why on earth would core clock speed be less important than memory bandwidth? Case in point would be the NVIDIA GeForce2 Ultra and the GeForce3. They both have the same amount of raw memory bandwidth (7.36GBps) yet the GeForce2 Ultra is clocked at 250MHz versus the 200MHz core clock of the GeForce3. In non-DX8 games (to level the playing field because the GeForce2 Ultra doesn't have all the features needed to accelerate some DX8 games), the GeForce3 is faster than the GeForce2 Ultra—by a large amount at higher resolutions especially. The reason is NVIDIA's Crossbar Memory Architecture and their Visibility Subsystem, both of which the GeForce2 Ultra lacks.

Now that you understand that clock speed doesn't mean everything, don't forget that you can't just ignore it. A relatively high clock speed/theoretical fill rate is necessary to provide the horsepower to give you high performance 3D graphics. If you're not memory bandwidth limited, but have poor fill rate capabilities you're really out of luck. Don't get too dazzled by multiple parallel rendering pipelines. It has already been proven that even with four pixel pipelines the GeForce3 can barely reach even half of its fill rate potential. The more the better, but be very weary of improvements over a previous core if the only improvements are more rendering pipelines/higher core clock without any memory bandwidth enhancements.

Local memory size is something that generally is more of a marketing ploy than anything else. Because of the low cost of memory it only makes sense that video cards come with as much memory as possible so long as that "low cost" term still applies. Cards with 32MB of local memory are already a standard, 64MB is becoming quite common, and 128MB versions are sure to be on the horizon. The only benefit to having more local memory is the ability to store more textures and run at higher resolutions/color depths. However, it is very rare that you'd fill up 64MB of memory, much less 128MB. For most of today's games 32MB is enough. In the future, as textures get larger in size and games become more complex, 64MB becomes more of a requirement than a luxury feature. The same happens as the transition to 128MB local memory sizes takes place.

Performance and Quality in 2D Graphics

Although 3D performance and quality is key to your gaming enjoyment, you definitely don't want to skimp on 2D quality/performance. The reason is that every minute you're not in a 3D game, you're staring at the result of your graphics processor's 2D output capabilities. Believe me, some very poor 2D implementations are out there, even today.

To grasp the concept of 2D quality and image quality coming out of your video card, you have to understand how the digital bits of data that your CPU and graphics processor calculate translate into actual pictures on your screen.

Although I touch on this later in Chapter 10, the majority of monitors that accompany desktop PCs are known as analog CRTs. The acronym CRT stands for Cathode Ray Tube and it is the physical tube (usually three in a monitor) that operates as an electron gun, displaying the images you see on your monitor screen. The signal that is sent to your monitor (assuming it's an analog monitor) happens to be an analog signal. This means that somewhere along the line the digital information floating around on the inside of your PC has to be converted to an analog signal for output to your monitor.

The RAMDAC

Regardless of whether the data is for a 3D scene or a 2D image, binary data is binary data (sort of like food being all the same after it's in your stomach) and it needs to be converted. This process takes place on your video card, and in modern day video cards the graphics chip itself usually contains the device to perform this conversion. The conversion is done in a part of the graphics chip (or sometimes in an external chip) known as a Random Access Memory Digital to Analog Converter, or RAMDAC for short.

Many types of DACs exist in various electronic equipment (such as CD players), but the DAC on a video card is special. Otherwise known as a

RAMDAC, it takes data directly from your video card's memory (or RAM), performs a digital-to-analog conversion on it; then it sends it out through a video output connector on the video card itself.

RAMDACs vary in speed and quality. Although, generally speaking, the only metric that is made available for measuring differences between RAMDACs is how quickly it can take the data stored in your video card's memory and convert it to an analog signal for output. This measurement is the operating frequency of the RAMDAC and in most cases is in a range between 300MHz and 360MHz, although cards from a couple of years ago have slower RAMDACs, which limits their ability to convert the data quickly enough at higher refresh rates. Remember that higher refresh rates are often easier on the eyes and look a lot sharper, so a higher speed RAMDAC allows for support for the refresh rates that you want at the resolutions you want.

The RAMDAC issue isn't normally a concern for 3D gamers because you are rarely running your game at more than 1,024 × 768 or maybe 1,280 × 1,024 if you've got a really powerful video card, a less demanding game, or don't particularly care for high frame rates. Where a high quality and performance RAMDAC is really important is when you're dealing with higher resolutions, such as in most 2D applications. Although you normally run your games at 1,024 × 768, your desktop resolution (2D resolution) can be as high as 1,600 × 1,200 if you have a large enough monitor. This is where a higher-speed RAMDAC helps to enable higher refresh rates and better image quality at these settings.

Filters

The other part to the image quality equation is the filters on the video card itself. Between the RAMDAC and the output connector on your video card (usually referred to as a VGA connector, named after the standard it was originally used with) you have a set of traces. Interrupting those traces are filters (capacitors and so on) that are in place to meet the Federal Communications Commission's (FCC) regulations and for other reasons as well. Unfortunately, these filters have the potential to worsen the signal outputted by your video card, especially if cheaper filters are used. You have no way of knowing whether a card has higher quality filters or not, but the rule of thumb is that if a video card is made by a single manufacturer then the quality of the filters on that video card is identical to other cards made by the same manufacturer.

Before ATI enabled other parties to make boards based on their chips, they used to have some of the best image quality simply because they could control all manufacturing factors. On the flip side of things, NVIDIA cards have generally gotten a bad rap for having poor image quality mainly because not all manufacturers that make cards for NVIDIA use the same high quality filters between the RAMDAC and the output connector. Your best bet is to ask around about various manufacturers' image quality before purchasing a card.

Remember that image quality is often incorrectly referred to as "2D image quality" because that's where the quality degradation is noticed the most (you're rarely going to be running a current game at 1,600 × 1,200 × 32-bit color). However, the signal degradation is there for both 3D and 2D applications; you just happen to notice it more at higher resolutions.

In terms of 2D performance, for most of the applications/games you play all the major cards offer equivalent 2D performance. There have been some situations in the past where 2D performance has not been up to par, but those cards have since been discontinued or weren't even desirable in the first place so you shouldn't have much to worry about.

The Contenders

With the rapidly changing graphics world it's very difficult to stay on top of things. The fastest card today can become an overpriced hunk of silicon in 6 months. Unfortunately you, as a consumer, have little warning of what's on the horizon. I try to publish roadmaps as much as possible at AnandTech (`http://www.anandtech.com`) and in this section I give you an idea of whether the best out is really worth your money.

For this section I'm mainly going to deal with the chips and cards that are currently available, but for more information you definitely want to check out AnandTech.

ATI

It took ATI entirely too long to get back into the swing of things as the market shifted from a 2D dominated world to one governed by 3D gaming performance in the late 1990s. Product delays and parts that weren't performing up to par with increasing competition from NVIDIA resulted in ATI falling out of touch with a good portion of the market.

Hope came for ATI in the form of its Radeon. Not only did the name signify a departure from its previous failures at penetrating the 3D gaming market which all carried the name "Rage," but it also embodied the type of culture that the online gamer was raised in. Although the Radeon was a very solid performer, ATI lost a lot of ground to NVIDIA because of poorly made drivers, especially under Windows 2000. By the end of the Radeon's life, ATI had finally improved its drivers. However, by then it was ready to be replaced with a new core requiring new drivers. This new core can be found in the Radeon 8500 as well as the other 8xxx cards from ATI.

ATI has continued to focus on its driver development, but it still has a way to go before it can compete with NVIDIA on that front.

Previously, ATI had been the sole producer of graphics chips and cards based on them. Only very recently has ATI enabled third-party manufacturers to produce cards based on its chips, while ATI continues to produce its own cards as well. The differences between ATI made cards and third-party manufactured cards is in software bundles, clock speeds, cooling configurations, and so on while the chips themselves are the same.

Radeon (R100) GPU

The Radeon GPU was launched in July 2000, and as I mentioned in the earlier section on HyperZ, it contained a number of very elegant features that improved memory bandwidth efficiency. The 0.18-micron GPU itself featured two pixel rendering pipelines; it was somewhat inferior to the competing GeForce2 solutions from NVIDIA that had four pixel rendering pipelines. ATI hoped to make up the performance gap by being able to apply three textures to a pixel in every pipeline meaning that in a single clock cycle the GPU could output 6 texels per clock. On paper this would make the Radeon GPU still seem inferior to the competing GeForce GPU as the GeForce2 could output 8 texels per clock (4 pipelines × 2 textures per pipeline). What ATI was banking on was that game developers would begin using three or six textures per pixel on average where the Radeon would be able to outperform the GeForce2. Because the GeForce2 could only apply two textures per pixel pipeline in a single clock, if it had to apply three textures then it would take two clock cycles to complete the process while the Radeon could do the same in a single clock thus making up for the sheer lack of fill rate. Unfortunately, ATI didn't put its money in the right basket, and developers never really took advantage of this.

ATI's Hardware T&L engine was called the Charisma engine and was a fixed function T&L unit that comprised most of the GPU's 30 million transistors. The only interesting point of the Charisma engine was that it had some DirectX 8 features but no games supported them at the time so they went to waste. Because it wasn't a full DX8 feature implementation the Radeon GPU could not be considered a DX8 part.

The Radeon GPU was in the end saved by its very bandwidth efficient 128-bit memory controller courtesy of HyperZ. I've already described HyperZ in great detail. For more information, look at the section "Features of HyperZ," earlier in the chapter.

The Radeon GPU was referred to internally as the Rage6C and eventually the R100; it was the basis for a number of cards.

Radeon DDR

The Radeon DDR was the first Radeon card to be released based on the R100. Officially the card was just called the Radeon but most people ended up calling it the Radeon DDR because of the fact that DDR SDRAM had only just recently started being used on graphics cards and they wanted to indicate that the Radeon did use this Double Data Rate SDRAM. It also helped because later on ATI did release a version with regular Single Data Rate (SDR) SDRAM.

The retail version of the card featured 64MB of DDR SDRAM and later a 32MB configuration was made available. For the 64MB card its core was clocked at 183MHz and its memory was synchronized to the core clock thus also running at 183MHz DDR. For OEM versions of the 64MB card and for both retail and OEM versions of the 32MB card the clock speeds were 166/166MHz.

Radeon SDR

The Radeon SDR was a low-cost variant of the Radeon intended to hit the $100–$150 price point. The only change was that the memory ran at 166MHz and it used regular SDRAM. This meant that the card only offered half the memory bandwidth of its DDR counterparts, which severely crippled performance.

Radeon VE

The Radeon VE (Value Edition) was an even lower-performance card, which upset many users because ATI actually stripped out the Charisma engine to cut costs. The chip has only a single rendering pipeline and features a 64-bit wide memory controller instead of the normal 128-bit memory controller. Luckily, ATI gave it DDR SDRAM and a 183/183MHz clock speed, which helped performance a bit but not enough to make it faster than the Radeon SDR. Because of the vast differences from the original R100 core, ATI dubbed this core the RV100.

The real attraction to the Radeon VE was its HydraVision multimonitor technology. This technology allowed multiple displays to be driven off of a single Radeon VE, which isn't very difficult to do (all you need are two RAMDACs and two outputs) but the HydraVision software really completed the package. With solid management software and some pretty attractive features, the Radeon VE was a great multimonitor card but a horrible gaming card.

Radeon 7500

The Radeon 7500 actually uses a different GPU from the R100, although the feature set of the chip is still the same as the R100. The main differences are that the chip is manufactured using a 0.15-micron process, it has ATI's HydraVision multimonitor technology, and a slightly improved memory controller that fetches more data per clock than the original R100 memory controller. This chip is known internally to ATI as the RV200 in spite of the fact that it's not really a next-generation chip, just a 0.15-micron version of the R100 core.

The move to a 0.15-micron process enabled ATI to reach much higher clock speeds with the Radeon 7500. The retail card was launched at 250MHz core and 230MHz DDR memory.

Radeon (R200) GPU

The successor to the Radeon came in the form of the R200 GPU. This GPU was built on a 0.15-micron process and featured close to 60 million transistors; twice the amount found in the original R100 GPU that was released no more than a year earlier! The memory controller from the R200 is identical to the RV200 found in the Radeon 7500 in that it is still 128-bits wide and simply fetches more data per clock (256-bits versus 128-bits in the original R100 memory controller). The reason it can do this is because it's paired with DDR SDRAM allowing it to fetch 256-bits of data in every clock; the benefit of a larger fetch size with the R200 GPU is greater bandwidth efficiency. This isn't always the case but because of the way the R200 was designed it just worked out this way. The GeForce3, for example, fetches 64-bits of data at a time per memory controller (it has four memory controllers).

The R200 GPU was mainly targeted at NVIDIA's GeForce3 in that it featured a programmable T&L unit. The first card based on the R200 core is the Radeon 8500. The Radeon 8500 runs at a core clock speed of 250MHz with the DDR SDRAM running at 275MHz DDR (effectively 550MHz). The card is available only in a 64MB version, and some OEM cards might be clocked lower.

The R200 GPU had five main features, which I discuss in the following sections.

Charisma Engine II

ATI claimed that the Charisma Engine II was a "second-generation hardware accelerated, fixed function transform & lighting engine." The Charisma Engine II is really no more than the Charisma Engine from the R100 running at a higher clock speed (250MHz versus 183MHz). The Charisma Engine II works alongside ATI's programmable SMARTSHADER engine.

Pixel Tapestry II

I mentioned in the R100 GPU section that the original Radeon had some DirectX 8 features. These features were included in what ATI called their Pixel Tapestry architecture. The R200 GPU features support for pixel shader programs through their programmable pixel shader architecture known as Pixel Tapestry II. This architecture is comparable to NVIDIA's pixel shaders from the GeForce3.

HyperZ II

HyperZ was improved in two areas in the R200 GPU: Hierarchical Z and Z-Compression. Remember from my earlier discussion that Hierarchical Z works by dividing the screen into a bunch of blocks (or tiles) and discards overdrawn pixels one block at a time. The original Radeon used 8x8 blocks while the Radeon 8500 uses smaller blocks (4×4). The benefit here is mainly one of efficiency, provided by smaller blocks (much like how NVIDIA uses smaller memory accesses to increase memory bandwidth efficiency).

The next improvement is that the Radeon 8500 is capable of discarding 64 pixels per clock instead of 8 on the original Radeon. For comparison purposes, the GeForce3 can discard 16 pixels per clock.

ATI also implemented an improved Z-Compression algorithm that, according to their spec sheets, gives it a 20% increase in Z-Compression performance.

Video Immersion II

One of the most ignored but useful features of the original Radeon was its impressive video de-interlacing. To understand what de-interlacing is you have to understand how conventional, interlaced televisions works. Deeper coverage of these topics is found in Chapter 10, but for the purposes of this discussion I hit the basics here.

In your TV there is something called a CRT, or cathode ray tube, which is home to electron guns that essentially paint a picture on your screen by scanning from the left side of your screen to the right. A complete line from left to right of electrons shot from the gun(s) is known as a scanline (NTSC TV has a horizontal resolution of 480 scan lines). To keep manufacturing costs low, conventional interlaced TVs would only scan every other scanline. So if your scanlines were numbered 0–480, the electron gun(s) would scan the even ones first (0, 2, 4, 6, 8, and so on), and then they would go back and fill in the odd scanlines. This all happens so quickly that your eyes are tricked into thinking that the full picture is being presented in front of you when in all actuality only half of it (alternating scanlines) is present at any given time.

Computer monitors are non-interlaced, meaning that the electron guns in the CRT don't scan every other line, rather they scan every line of resolution. Newer HDTVs can also accept non-interlaced signals; these are often referred to as progressive scan signals and are called things like 480p, 720p, and so on, where the "p" indicates "progressive."

Some TVs can take an interlaced signal and convert it to a non-interlaced/progressive scan signal. These TVs implement what is known as de-interlacing, more commonly referred to as line doubling. De-interlacing is the process by which odd scanlines present in interlaced video are blended with their even counterparts and displayed at once, thus giving you a non-interlaced video output. If done properly, de-interlacing can make video look a lot better. However, if done poorly, it can also have some unfortunate side effects (like the presence of artifacts in the video).

ATI combated this type of problem with its Adaptive De-Interlacing on the Radeon. This technology dynamically chose between bob and weave algorithms to produce the best quality de-interlacing found in any 3D graphics cards. The R200 takes it one step further by introducing what ATI calls *temporal de-interlacing*. Although I didn't have enough time to thoroughly test it for this book, temporal de-interlacing supposedly offers superior blending between the odd and even lines to reduce de-interlacing artifacts (look to our coverage at AnandTech for the results of our full hands-on tests).

Also to further tailor to the home theater PC crowd, cards based on the R200 are compatible with a very cheap ($10–$40) DVI-I to Component output connector. This is very important for those who have Component (Y Pr Pb) but not VGA inputs on their TVs.

HydraVision

Finally, the R200 brings multimonitor support to a high-performance gaming card with HydraVision. The HydraVision implementation on the R200 is virtually identical to that which debuted on the Radeon VE but with higher speed RAMDACs.

NVIDIA

Earlier in the 1990s NVIDIA was on the verge of bankruptcy; the company was surely not going to last until the 3D revolution. Little did the world know that the company about to die would live on to become the king of the 3D graphics industry.

NVIDIA has prided itself on product execution and driver development. It is a little known fact that NVIDIA is actually more of a software company than a hardware company. NVIDIA's software/driver development team actually outnumbers its hardware engineers, which goes to show you exactly how important drivers are to the success of a graphics chip.

In spite of the heavy bias towards software, NVIDIA is a chip company. Unlike ATI, NVIDIA does not produce its own cards for sale. It does make reference designs for third-party manufacturers to follow but does not sell its own cards to consumers, just chips to manufacturers.

Although it gained a lot of popularity from its Riva 128 and TNT/TNT2 cards, NVIDIA's real power as a leader in the industry came with its GeForce line of GPUs. Not only did it introduce the world's first GPU (something I wasn't a fan of since it was fixed function), it also introduced the world's first programmable GPU (much more to my liking).

GeForce 256 GPU

The GeForce 256 GPU was built on a 0.22-micron process and features four pixel rendering pipelines. The GPU also featured a 128-bit memory bus that was the first to support not only SDR SDRAM but DDR SDRAM as well.

The term GPU (graphics processing unit) was appropriate for the GeForce 256 because of its Hardware T&L engine. But as a fixed function T&L engine very few games actually took any real advantage of it. Eventually, some games like Max Payne were written with fixed function hardware T&L in mind and performed much better because of this T&L engine, but most did not. Unreal Tournament did not use the T&L engine at all, while Quake III Arena could only use the Hardware Transform engine (not the Lighting).

Since NVIDIA isn't a card manufacturer there were no cards from NVIDIA based on the GeForce 256. NVIDIA's reference design was used heavily in retail GeForce 256 cards but their clock speeds did not vary. The core was running at 120MHz and the memory at 166MHz for SDR cards and 150MHz for DDR cards. Cards originally only came with 32MB of memory, then towards the end of the GPU's life you started seeing 64MB versions.

GeForce2 GPU

Six months after the release of the GeForce 256 GPU came NVIDIA's GeForce2 GPU. The GeForce2 was made on a 0.18-micron process and thus ran at higher clock speeds than its predecessor. The GPU still featured 4 pixel rendering pipelines, but it could now apply two textures per pipeline per clock, effectively doubling the GeForce 256's fill rate. To top things off the GPU now ran at 200MHz (up from 120MHz) and although it used the same memory controller as the GeForce 256, its memory now ran at 166MHz DDR (there were no SDR SDRAM GeForce2 cards).

NVIDIA also introduced the NVIDIA Shading Rasterizer (NSR) with the GeForce2, which proved to be a precursor to the GeForce3's pixel shaders. The T&L engine remained unchanged from the original GeForce 256; it simply ran at a higher clock speed.

The GeForce2 GPU found its way into a number of products from NVIDIA. The originally GPU was called the GeForce2 GTS (Giga Texel Shader) because it was able to attain a theoretical 1.6 gigatexels per second fill rate. The GeForce2 Ultra was then released at a higher clock speed (250MHz core and 230MHz DDR memory) followed by the GeForce2 Pro.

The GeForce2 Pro was cheaper to make than the Ultra and offered nearly the same performance by lowering the core clock down to 200MHz and a slightly lower memory clock (200MHz DDR). Finally the GeForce2 line concluded with the release of the GeForce2 Titanium 200 or GeForce2 Ti 200 for short. The Ti 200 increased clock speeds yet again.

NVIDIA also released a lower-cost version of the GeForce2 GPU known as the GeForce2 MX. This chip featured only two rendering pipelines (and thus half the fill rate of its older brother) and ran at 175MHz core. The 128-bit memory controller stuck around but was only used with regular SDRAM which unfortunately rid the GPU of its brother's performance.

GeForce3 GPU

The GeForce3 truly brought the acronym, "GPU" some justice, as it was the first programmable GPU, something developers have definitely demanded from the graphics companies. The chip obviously features the programmable GPU, but it also boasts a much more advanced memory controller, which is grouped into what NVIDIA calls its Lightspeed Memory Architecture. I've already diagrammed the details of this architecture earlier in the chapter in the section "NVIDIA's GeForce3 and Lightspeed Memory Architecture."

The GeForce3 GPU is already available in a couple of flavors. The original 0.15-micron GeForce3 ran at a 200MHz core clock and featured 230MHz DDR SDRAM, but because of its Lightspeed Memory Architecture the GeForce3 could outperform the similarly clocked GeForce2 Ultra.

Like the GeForce2, the GeForce3 was also refreshed with the Titanium branding. In this case it released a Ti 200 and Ti 500 model. The Ti 200 brought the price of the solution to below the $200 mark, whereas the Ti 500 was designed to outperform the Radeon 8500 by boasting a higher core/memory clock.

Chapter 6

Sound: Waking Up the Neighbors

Analog Versus Digital

An all too common misconception is that anything preceded by the word digital must be superior to the now archaic analog methods of data storage. In many cases, digital storage does have its advantages; it's easier to store a 1 or a 0 instead of having to deal with analog values that can be infinitely large or small, and millions of these 1 versus 0 comparisons can be performed in a single second without much effort. However, one area in which digital isn't clearly better than the analog technology it replaced is in audio storage.

The term digital audio sounds great as a marketing platform; however, to a true audiophile, saying that a CD sounds better than an old LP is almost sacrilege. If you happen to pull out one of your old records and play it, chances are that you are confused about all the fuss because today's CDs sound much better than what you bought for $2 years ago. The point is that it isn't necessarily the media that the audio is being stored on, but how it is being stored that determines the true quality of it. For example, if you put a piece of paper over a microphone and sing a song, recording it onto a CD versus doing the same without the piece of paper and recording it onto a record, you get better audio off of the record. So why do some think that storing audio on a CD is so bad?

Storing audio on a CD is not bad per se because CDs have considerably improved the way we listen to music. But the problem that exists is when you take data that was never intended to be one of two distinct values and force it to be either a one or a zero. This is like asking for a hamburger and being offered either a hot dog or pizza. Neither one is exactly the hamburger, but depending on your craving you can get close to what you want, although never exactly. Now let's apply this same theory to the way audio is recorded digitally.

Remember that when I'm talking about a digital recording of something, I'm basically talking about the storing of data in a binary number format, meaning that any data point can take only two possible values: either 0 or 1. You know very well that this isn't how sounds are generated. The 1 stands for the highest pitch sound you can possibly discern, and the 0 stands for the lowest. A number of gradual divisions are between the 0 and the 1 that your ears can pick up. However, in digital no such divisions exist; only 0s and 1s exist. Obviously, the way to make up for this is a combination of many 0s and 1s, increasing the interval at which a 0 is assigned and a 1 is assigned. So instead of 0 being lowest and 1 being highest, 000 can be the lowest and 001 can be a slightly higher pitch followed by 010, and then 011, and 100, and so on (I'm basically counting up in a binary number system).

The process I have just described is one known as *digital sampling*. You might be familiar with the math equivalent of this process, which is the approximation of a curve using a number of different geometric shapes, in this case rectangles. The curve you are approximating is an analog sound wave. In Figure 6.1 you see examples of both an analog sound wave and a digitally sampled analog song. The analog sound wave in Figure 6.1 is actually a sine wave; it has an infinite number of points that are connected to form a smooth curve. Whenever you approximate a curve made of an infinite number of points with a finite number of samples, you're going to lose precision. This is what happens with digital sampling.

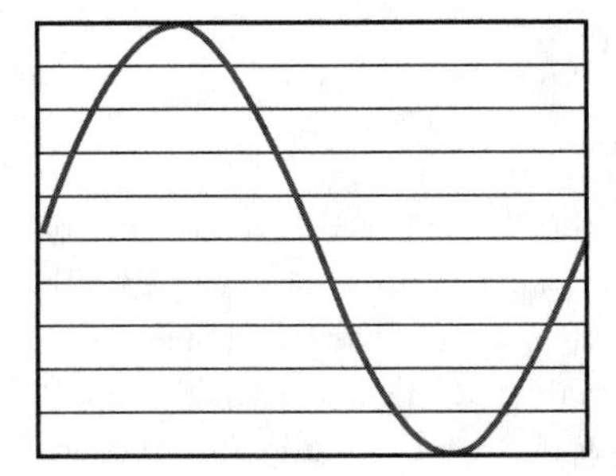

FIGURE 6.1
On the right is an example of an analog sound curve, as compared to the digitally sampled version of it on the left. Notice how the curve is no longer smooth; each point represents a digital sample.

When something is digitally sampled, the analog sound wave is effectively approximated by a certain number of digital (binary) samples (data points). As the number of samples you take increases, the quality of the digital reproduction of the sound increases as well. A general law states that to properly duplicate a sound generated, the sampling rate must be equal to twice the highest frequency attained during the playback. With human ears able to interpret sounds as high as 22KHz (kilohertz) in frequency, it makes sense that CD audio is recorded at a 44KHz sampling rate (44.1KHz to be exact). In spite of this, true audiophiles can still claim to hear a difference between digital CD audio and the original source of the sound.

One reason some are able to differentiate between analog sound quality and current standards in digital sound is that our ears don't interpret digital signals. Even with a digital source, audio is transmitted from our speakers to our ears in the form of analog waves, yet audio is handled internally by your PC in a digital format. So, to generate audio in an analog format when it is being produced in a digital setup, you need to use a digital-to-analog converter (DAC).

➤ ***Digital-to-analog converters are discussed in Chapter 5, "The Video Card: A Gamer's Heart and Soul."***

The function of a DAC in audio is the same as its function in the video world—to convert the internal digital signal used by your PC into an analog signal that can be outputted to your speakers. The DAC in your PC is present on your sound card, although your CD/DVD drives also have one (their internal DACs are used if you plug headphones into the headphone port on the front of the drive).

Sound Cards and Other PC Audio Solutions

As I just mentioned, the digital-to-analog conversion process occurs on a card known as the *sound card*. The sound card was originally introduced at a time when CPUs weren't powerful enough to handle all their tasks as well as audio processing. Back then, the only type of audio available on a PC came from the now obsolete PC speaker in the form of different frequency beeps—not very elegant at all (although it is still used today for system error codes).

Today, in spite of the fact that CPUs are powerful enough to handle audio processing while working on other tasks, the sound card still exists, although it is threatened. Integrated audio processors and other audio solutions that offload audio processing to the host CPU have climbed in quality and popularity, leaving the standalone audio card in a precarious position.

The very first mass-market sound cards, and the need for them, came about with the "multimedia" revolution of the late 1980s and early 1990s. The first generation of sound cards, such as the Ad-Lib, were mostly useful for gaming. Creative Labs began shipping its first "multimedia" bundles that packaged a CD-ROM drive as well as a Sound Blaster card. These packages were certainly interesting to play with and eventually caught on. However, in the early days, there simply weren't any games that took advantage of the mass storage capabilities of CD-ROMs, although a few started to use sound cards instead of the PC speaker for audio. It took a while for the CD-ROM to become necessary for game storage, but it didn't take nearly as long for game developers to come to love the advent of the sound card.

The sound cards of the early days were fairly simple; they started with 8-bit DACs and eventually moved on to feature 16-bit DACs. The concept of "3D sound" was one that had yet to be discovered, and the main way of differentiating cards was based on their MIDI capabilities. Game soundtracks were almost entirely MIDI based back then, and a card's MIDI capabilities would result in the quality of the music playback you'd hear during your gameplay.

These cards all used the ISA bus and actually ended up being one of the reasons the ISA bus took so long to die off toward the mid-1990s; people simply had never upgraded their old ISA sound cards because there was no reason to. Eventually, with the release of cards like the Sound Blaster Live! and other cards that promised buzzword features such as "3D sound," the transition to PCI-based sound cards took place. This improved the sound card installation process, as well as gave the sound card much more bandwidth courtesy of the PCI bus.

During the transition to PCI-based sound cards, a number of companies (Analog Devices, Creative Labs, Intel, National Semiconductor, and Yamaha) attempted to standardize on a specification that would define and enable various basic functions a sound card would have to offer. This specification became known as the Audio Codec '97 specification, or AC'97 for short.

The AC'97 Specification

The AC'97 specification calls for two parts to be present on any AC'97 sound card: an AC'97 Analog Codec and an AC'97 Digital Controller (see Figure 6.2).

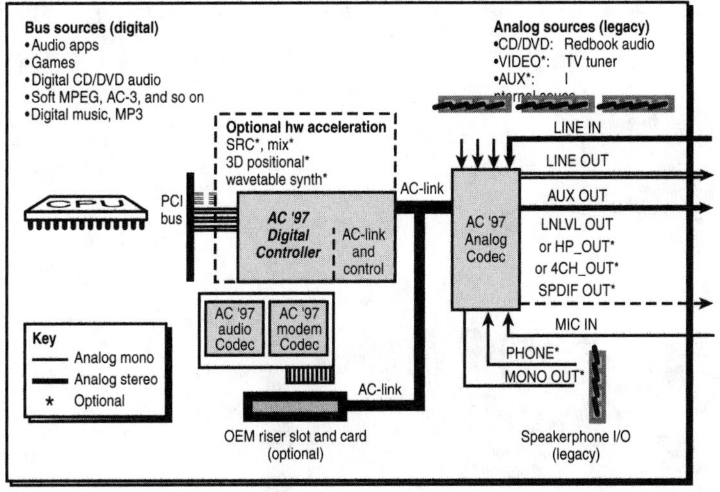

FIGURE 6.2
The AC'97 specification calls for an analog codec to handle all analog inputs/outputs as well as an "optional" digital controller for any additional sound processing.

The AC'97 Analog Codec handles all inputs and outputs on the sound card. These inputs/outputs are generally in the form of 1/8" stereo jacks and can be used for microphone/line inputs, outputs for 2/4 speaker configurations, and internal inputs for CD/DVD drives among other things. The reason this is referred to as the Analog Codec is because it handles legacy analog inputs (for example, CD/DVD drive inputs) and outputs analog signals (although sometimes it can output to a digital connector for external Dolby Digital

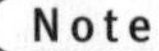

Note

Figure 6.2 refers to the digital controller as optional because, if it is not present, the processing is offloaded to the host CPU. Hence the term software sound (the CPU performs these calculations much like it would run a piece of software).

decoding). An Analog Codec, like the one shown in Figure 6.3, contains the DAC on the sound card.

The AC'97 Digital Controller is connected to the Analog Codec through a serial interface called the AC-Link. The Digital Controller can be as simple as something that takes the digital audio data that is transferred from the PCI bus to the sound card and sends it off to the Analog Codec. At the same time, the Digital Controller can be a much more complicated entity that offers hardware acceleration and support for various signal processing functions among other features.

The Digital Controller is what differs on various AC'97 compatible sound cards. For example, Creative Labs's Sound Blaster Live! series of cards uses the Sigmatel STAC9721T Analog Codec shown earlier in Figure 6.3; the same Analog Codec is used on many competing cards as well. However, what set Live! apart from the competition upon its release was the powerful EMU10K1 Digital Controller, shown in Figure 6.4. This was capable of processing 1 billion operations per second compared to the 10 million–50 million operations per second of competing digital controllers available at the time.

FIGURE 6.3
Sigmatel makes this Analog Codec that is found on the SoundBlaster Live! cards.

FIGURE 6.4
Creative Labs's EMU10K1 Digital Controller raised the bar on audio processor performance upon its introduction.

Of course things have changed quite a bit since then, as the nForce's Media and Communications Processor (MCP) is capable of processing 4 billion operations per second and isn't even on a sound card. It's a part of a chipset (see Figure 6.5).

FIGURE 6.5
NVIDIA's nForce Media and Communications Processor is capable of performing real-time Dolby Digital Encoding courtesy of its powerful DSP.

One of the reasons for such a powerful MCP was so that NVIDIA could offer features such as real-time Dolby Digital Encoding. The MCP was originally designed for the Microsoft X-Box, and only later was it made into a PC chipset South Bridge, hence the incredible power it possesses. Remember that with a console you've got to build as much power into it as possible since there is no upgrading after the hardware is out. The power of the nForce MCP is not too surprising.

Note

Parthus is an Intellectual Property company that specializes in the designing of integrated circuits. To reduce the design time of the nForce's MCP, NVIDIA licensed the MediaStream DSP from Parthus to provide the feature set it needed to be more than competitive in this sector. This is why you don't see competing solutions from other chipset manufacturers rivaling the nForce's MCP in features, especially when it comes to audio processing power.

Long ago there was a time when hard drive interfaces weren't integrated into chipsets and you had to purchase a controller card off which you would run your drives. For most users, with options available such as NVIDIA's nForce MCP, there won't be a reason for an add-in sound card anymore.

What do these powerful digital controllers actually do? One use is that they can be used to calculate how sounds reflect off different types of walls in games. For example, a gunshot in a long hallway makes a different sound than in an open air room. For an accurate re-creation, obviously a lot of physics calculations must be performed to differentiate between the two situations. These calculations can either be done by your host CPU or be offloaded to a powerful audio processor, such as the EMU10K1 or the integrated DSP (Digital Sound Processor) of NVIDIA's nForce MCP. If your DSP is powerful enough, offloading the calculations to it would make much more sense because your CPU is now free to work on other things, like game AI calculations, that are going on while these audio processes are occurring.

Another feature, which NVIDIA first introduced into the mainstream PC audio processing world, is real-time Dolby Digital Encoding. NVIDIA actually licensed the MediaStream DSP from Parthus to integrate into the nForce's MCP to enable real-time Dolby Digital Encoding (see Figure 6.6).

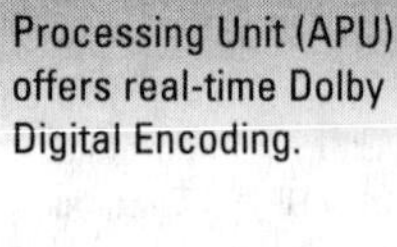
FIGURE 6.6
The nForce MCP's Audio Processing Unit (APU) offers real-time Dolby Digital Encoding.

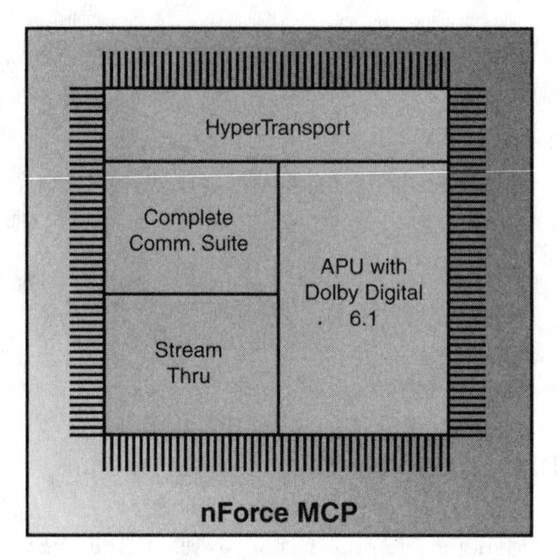

Dolby Digital 5.1 (AC-3) encoding enables you to output audio from your computer to a Dolby Digital decoder and get very high-quality digital sound output, much like what you would experience from a Dolby Digital AC-3 encoded DVD on a compatible DVD player.

On-Board Sound

The manufacturers of the various components inside your PC are always trying to incorporate more features into their products, but you can only do so much within a single realm. This often results in one manufacturer stepping into the realm of a previously non-competing manufacturer.

Case in point is the introduction of software-based sound solutions. Intel's main focus is still CPUs, in spite of its duty to drive the future of computing in general. Anything it can do to increase the consumer's demand for higher, more powerful CPUs helps pay the bills and put smiles on faces. With CPUs as powerful as they are today, Intel decided that it was time to take away these tasks from the dedicated audio processors on sound cards and make the CPUs do some of the work. This was the birth of the idea of having no digital controller on a sound card, but enabling the CPU to handle all the digital signal processing (DSP) tasks. You most commonly find this type of a solution known as *on-board* sound. The AC'97 codec is present on your motherboard itself, removing the need for an add-in sound card.

Other types of on-board sound include simply placing the AC'97 codec and the digital controller/DSP on the motherboard instead of on a sound card. Doing this has no benefit other than you saving a few bucks on manufacturing costs. This path is rarely taken because motherboard manufacturers are so concerned with keeping manufacturing costs of their boards as low as possible, and an expensive hardware sound solution isn't the best way to do that.

Most cheap implementations of the AC'97 specification on a motherboard include the AC'97 Analog Codec and a very simple digital controller. This unfortunately prevents many of these on-board solutions from implementing any 3D audio functions such as the reverb effects I discussed earlier, but it is enough to play music and regular sounds. Remember that although your CPU handles all the audio processing required for regular sound playback, the performance hit won't be too great because today's CPUs are more than powerful enough to handle those calculations.

If you care about 3D positional audio, you have to opt for either an external sound card or a motherboard with a more powerful digital controller capable of processing such instructions.

AMR/CNR/ACR Cards

You remember from Chapter 3, "The Motherboard: Low Rent Housing for the CPU and Chipset," that a feature on many motherboards is support for an Audio Modem Riser (AMR)/Communications and Networking Riser (CNR)/Advanced Communications Riser (ACR) card. One purpose of these cards is to provide a location for the AC'97 Codec—provided that it isn't on-board, or if it is, a manufacturer can choose to use one of these slots as a way of offering upgraded audio by simply using a more advanced codec or digital controller. The other purposes for these cards have to do with the communications part of the equation, such as providing a location for the physical layer of an Ethernet or HomePNA controller.

These cards are almost impossible to find in the retail market and have always been intended for OEMs only, so don't waste your time looking for one.

Sound in 3D

Just like 3D graphics, the idea behind 3D sound is to take the 2D plane of your monitor and extend it to three dimensions to make it seem as if you are truly a part of the game. The problem you run into with doing this is that to feel that you're a part of the game, you have to hear sounds all around you. When an enemy in *Red Faction* is yelling behind you, you want to hear his voice coming from behind you, not from in front of you. Part of this can be accomplished through the use of rear speakers, but it mostly involves sending certain sounds to certain speakers and using the properties of sound waves to simulate a 3D environment. As with graphics, this has required the use of an API (Application Programming Interface), of which for audio cards, a number of APIs offer support for 3D sound.

The most commonly used 3D sound API is Microsoft's DirectSound, which is a part of its DirectX package. DirectSound supports hardware acceleration of 3D sound streams as well as manufacturer-specific extensions to the API to provide for additional functionality. The most popular extension to the DirectSound API is Creative Labs' Environmental Audio eXtensions, or EAX for short.

The word Environmental in EAX is truly representative of where EAX excels, in that the API extension is commonly used for calculating reverberation effects off various types of surfaces. I mentioned earlier that a difference exists between a gunshot in a closed hallway and in an open area. Well, what about the difference between a footstep in a closed room with wooden floors and in a bathroom with tiled floors, as is encountered when playing *Thief*? And what about noises occurring underwater versus in an open air environment? EAX provides presets for these types of environments; provided that both your sound card and the game you're playing support EAX, you also can take advantage of these presets.

Another competing standard by a now defunct company is A3D by Aureal. A3D takes a different approach to sound manipulation. Instead of relying on presets of how certain sounds should reverberate off different surfaces, the A3D API actually uses the game's built-in geometry to calculate what happens to various sounds as they bounce around a room. This makes A3D superior in theory to EAX.

From my use of the word "defunct," you shouldn't expect to see much support for A3D in the future. The original A3D specs were actually viewed as being superior to EAX, but for a number of reasons (including the vast marketing reach of Creative Labs), the standard never took off. This is an example in which industry support (EAX in this case) triumphs over superior technology (A3D).

So far, all I have talked about is the manipulation of sound effects before they exit your sound card and are output to your speakers, but how can you truly be immersed in sound? Obviously, you can set up a speaker system with speakers surrounding you; however, even your 5.1 speaker setup (three fronts, two rears, and a sub woofer) aren't able to give you truly 3D positional audio. This is where Head-Related Transfer Functions (HRTFs) come into play. These manipulate the sound waves being output to your speakers to make the sounds appear to be coming from a particular location. Provided that your speakers are left unobstructed, this can be a relatively convincing feature that complements today's 3D games quite nicely.

Obviously, these features are rarely taken advantage of in games such as a *2D Real Time Strategy* game or *SimCity 3000*. However, in first-person shooters and other 3D games where you are supposed to be immersed in the 3D world, it isn't uncommon to see effects like these.

What Makes for Good Sound?

Now that you know the technology behind sound cards and processors, what makes one sound card any better or worse than another?

A number of things can control sound quality. Unfortunately, most of these aren't a part of the advertisements on the box, nor are they things that you can change once you do pick your sound card.

Obviously, if the AC'97 Analog Codec is what handles the digital to analog conversion, any loss of audio quality that occurs in that phase results in poorer quality sound. Which Analog Codecs are the best? Unfortunately, it's difficult to tell, and there honestly isn't a good way of comparing Analog Codecs using the currently available cards. Why is that? Well, after the digital signal gets through the DAC, it has to make its way to an output. In most cases it is an 1/8" plug (or more than one) on the back of your card, which is where your speakers plug into. Between the DAC and this connector is another small distance where quality loss can occur. Again, with equipment you have laying around the house you cannot measure the quality loss that occurs here.

So, how do you find out which sound card provides the best audio reproduction? The most you can do is ask around and see what other people's experiences have been. The problem with this is that very few people have experienced all the sound cards available on a single set of speakers in a controlled listening condition, and even then, the conclusions to be drawn are highly subjective and vary wildly from listener to listener. You can always try the "buy all of the available cards and keep the one you want" tactic, but not everyone has the credit line to take that route.

The main thing to remember is that although companies can dazzle you with the specifications of their sound cards, when playing music, most sound cards (if properly designed) do sound the same. Where you start getting into differences is when you're dealing with which cards support which 3D Sound APIs or other audio technologies like those based on 5.1 surround sound. However, even those concerns have pretty much died down in terms of their popularity in games. The visual experience has by far become much more of an issue for game developers than sound effects in recent times. Maybe things will change in the future, but for now you should be fine with just about any brand-name sound card that provides the features you're interested in for gaming.

Another thing to look at when purchasing a sound card is driver support. Visit the manufacturer's Web site, and see how often drivers are updated. Check the discussion forums online and see whether you can find any compatibility issues with any of your current hardware. Buying a new sound card is pointless if it doesn't have drivers for your particular OS, for example.

Sound Card Recommendations

As long as the codec is implemented properly on the motherboard, sticking to an on-board sound solution doesn't hurt. The SoundMAX codecs are some of the best available; unfortunately, they're not too common on motherboards other than those from Intel. Analog Devices' codecs aren't bad, either.

Those are the minimum requirements, but you probably want a bit more if you're going to be taking advantage of any of the more advanced audio functions—especially if you want to enable things such as EAX in games. If you have a nForce motherboard then you already have a very impressive audio setup and don't really need to consider anything additional. However, if you don't fall into either of these initial categories, you have one more option.

The card to really look out for is the Creative Labs Audigy, which was released in the fall of 2001 in various flavors (Player, Platinum, Platinum EX, and so on). The overall quality of the Audigy cards is solid, and they all feature a 24-bit/96KHz DAC compared to the 16-bit/48KHz DAC on most other sound cards. The Audigy cards also feature a built-in IEEE-1394 controller, which is an added plus (see Chapter 7, "Storage: The Slowest Part of Your PC"). The Audigy line also has a more powerful DSP capable of performing more advanced EAX functions; however, game support for these functions is still lacking. The main benefits are quality improvements with the card, making it the clear choice for a third-party add-in sound card.

Speakers

Unlike sound cards, choosing the right set of speakers is much more complicated than saying that all well-designed speakers sound alike, because they don't. Designing a good set of speakers at the price point most computer enthusiasts are willing to pay is quite difficult. If you walk into any high-end home theater store (for example, Best Buy or Circuit City), you'll see speakers priced at more than $500 each, receivers that run you a minimum of $800, and multi-thousand dollar setups that truly amaze you.

I had always been skeptical about the need for truly high-end computer speakers since I got my first set of speakers as a part of a 2X CD-ROM drive + Sound Blaster package. The speakers were okay, but back then the only music coming out of a home PC was rudimentary game music and audio effects (mostly just MIDI recordings of a few instruments) and any Windows sounds you happened to configure. Today's PC is obviously used in a much more multimedia-oriented fashion. With the advent of the MP3 standard for compressed audio, it's common for users to not even have a stereo in their computer rooms and simply use their PCs to handle all music playback.

Today's CPUs are fast enough to handle MP3 playback without any noticeable slowdowns. They are even fast enough to create MP3s in a matter of seconds from an original CD-Audio source file. However, for your music to actually sound good and have accurate reproduction (or as accurate as possible for the price you're paying) of the audio you're listening to, you really need a nice set of speakers. Granted, if you have a poorly manufactured sound card, you won't get good audio out of your PC. However, assuming that you do have a decent sound card, what kind of speakers should you get?

The biggest mistake I ever made was that I never grew out of the $20 PC speakers phase. Whenever I built or upgraded a system, I never factored the cost of a decent set of speakers, so I always found myself purchasing the cheap, generic speakers that always had the 500W power rating in big letters across the front of the box. This all changed when I listened to my first set of real PC speakers, which happened to be a solution from a company known as Klipsch (see Figure 6.7).

FIGURE 6.7
Notorious for providing a lot of power, Klipsch has not always been a fan of audiophiles looking for the cleanest sound, but in a game, the more power you can, get the better.

The Klipsch Promedia line of speakers truly raised the bar in terms of bringing true audio quality to the PC. They have been a favorite among gamers, and their higher-end solutions are widely used by Home Theater Enthusiasts. My experience with the Klipsch brand has changed my opinion on PC sound forever, and from the reviews I've had experiences with on AnandTech.com, a world beyond the realm of $20 no-name PC speakers definitely exists.

The World of Fidelity and the Decibel

The first thing you must make certain not to do is to under budget your speakers. If you're going to use your PC for any sort of music, and if you're actually going to be using your PC as a gaming machine, then you're going to have to put aside between $100–$300 for a good set of speakers. That is a lot of money, but when you realize that you spend that much on your graphics card just so things *look* better, it's worth it to spend a comparable amount so that things *sound* better as well.

Before jumping directly into the technical nitty-gritty, some explanation of the measurement standards used in audio is necessary. For everyone who knows the difference between dBm and dB SPL, and especially how they relate to the audio industry, feel free to skip directly to the specification breakdown. Audio specifications are not exactly transfer rates or IP addresses, so some background can be helpful.

The key unit in audio is the decibel (dB). Technically one tenth of a Bell (yes, it is named after Alexander Graham Bell and carries the capitalization when abbreviated), it is a logarithmic scale that compares two power quantities. Logarithmic, besides being a hard word to spell, is a technique used when relatively large quantities, such as 10 and 1000 for example, are compared to each other. A logarithmic scale compares the difference based on the ratio of the second quantity to the first instead of the difference between the two as in a linear scale. Figure 6.8 demonstrates the logarithmic curve of the decibel scale. Note that it does not follow a straight line. In the dB scale, a change from 1W to 100W would be measured the same as a change from 10W to 1000W because it compares the first value to the second. Both changes would be measured as 20 dB.

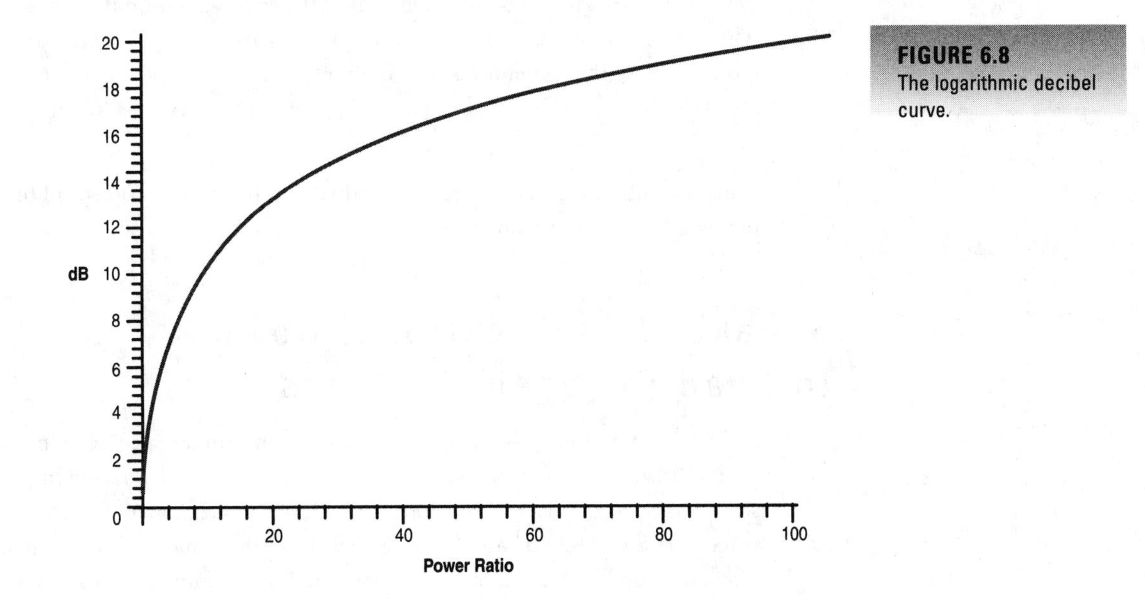

FIGURE 6.8
The logarithmic decibel curve.

Because the dB is a measurement based in comparison, it can be used in various applications. In audio, the two primary comparisons are made with power and force. The electric power in a system is typically measured against a reference level of 1 milliwatt (.001W). Although it might seem arbitrary, this level comes out of standards for interconnections and the corresponding powers dating back to the early era of radio, first set forward in 1940. The equation that dictates decibels measuring power is $dB=10 \times \log (P_1/P_2)$. If you work the math, this means that twice the power results in a 3 dB difference, so specifications dealing with audio signal power are dictated by this rule of three: 3 dBm=2 × the power.

The electrical analogy of a speaker's air movement (what makes the sound), is voltage in a circuit. As the human senses are logarithmic, it is convenient to continue to use the decibel scale when describing speaker volume. However, because the analogy is to voltage and not power, the Bell equation must be slightly modified. Power is related to voltage by the equation $P=E^2/R$ (where E is for voltage and R is for resistance). Substituting this into the earlier equation, and moving the exponent to outside the log results in the equation for comparing Sound Pressure Levels (SPL): dB SPL=20 log (E_1/E_2). The reference level (0 dB SPL) used for the scale is the threshold of hearing for a youngster (before listening to the heavy metal music that starts to kill his or her ears). The threshold of pain is about 120 dB. As this equation has been slightly modified, twice the SPL equals a 6 dB difference. Therefore, the sound pressure levels in speakers are dictated by a rule of six: 6 dB SPL=2 × the sound pressure. As a note, the human body perceives about 10 dB SPL to be twice as loud—again, the body acts as a logarithmic scale.

Well, enough of the math review. Let's dive into the specifications and find out what's really going on in the speakers.

Speaker Specifications: How to Read Between the Lines

Before listening to any speaker system, the manufacturer's specifications provide a basis for comparison. Through a variety of tests to determine the sonic quality and electrical characteristics of the speakers, manufacturers determine the numbers intended to reveal the performance of their systems. However, results can, and often are, presented in an ambiguous manner that appears to enhance the specs of a system. To reveal these possibilities, careful examination of each specification is necessary.

Drivers

Drivers are the actual speakers used in the cabinet (see Figure 6.9). The physical components of a speaker are fairly simple. The cabinet, or enclosure, is the wood or plastic box that contains the drivers, or speakers, and the electronics involved in making the sound, such as an amplifier and crossover networks. This specification indicates the size and type of transducers (speakers) used.

FIGURE 6.9
This is a speaker from a VideoLogic DigiTheater DTS 5.1 setup. This driver is exposed, but they are usually hidden behind a protective cover.

The number of drivers is very revealing as to the nature of the speaker system. With more speakers, they can be tailored to fit particular sound spectrums as each component handles just part of the frequency range. In a two-way system, low and mid frequencies are reproduced by the woofer, whereas a tweeter reproduces the highs. A three-way system is one in which a sub woofer reproduces the lowest frequncies, a mid-range woofer powers the intermediate frequencies, and the tweeter provides the high frequencies. When a transducer handles a smaller frequency band, it can handle higher levels of power. Sound is energy, and if they are reproducing a more limited range of energy, they can handle higher levels.

In these multispeaker units, a crossover network is used to split the sound spectrum and route the parts to the appropriate speaker. The crossover can also control the relative output levels for the speakers, actually balancing the sound across the frequency spectrum. Most importantly, they are set so as not to overwork the speakers and shorten their life spans by sending high-energy frequencies to speakers that are not designed to handle them.

The following is a breakdown on the components often used in speaker systems. Through a combination of these components, a speaker is able to reproduce the full (or almost full) spectrum of sound.

Tweeters and Woofers

Tweeters are used for high frequency sound, usually sounds over 1.5KHz.

Woofers, on the other hand, are used for low-frequency sound reproduction up to around 1.5KHz. Because low frequencies have a longer wavelength, woofers must be larger to move the air volume necessary to reproduce these lower frequencies. As a result, the larger a woofer, the more power it can carry, and the louder the bass is. In addition, for all the rumbling low-frequency noise, the body senses the energy as much as feels it. When used for both low- and mid-frequency sound, woofers produce sounds up to around 1.5KHz.

Sub Woofers

Sub woofers reproduce the lowest frequencies, usually up to 500Hz. These provide the rumble element to the sound system as they move the most air and shake the body as much as the eardrums. The larger the sub woofer driver, the more energy it can handle, and the more impressive it can be.

Frequency Response

Frequency Response deals with how much and how accurately the speakers can reproduce the sound spectrum. The response is measured using an analyzer that reads the speaker's reproduction of a standard audio test signal.

Human hearing spans the frequency response of 20Hz–20KHz, and in an ideal world, a speaker would reproduce all these frequencies. Unfortunately, when indicating the frequency response of speakers, manufacturers often fail to tell the whole truth. If they do not indicate how accurate the speaker response is, specs can often look far better than the speaker actually sounds.

The simple description of frequency response of 20Hz–20KHz would seem ideal; however, this is a true statement even if the sound at 20Hz is 40 dB SPL lower than the sound at 1.2KHz. This means that the lowest bass frequency is 100 times less powerful than an average midrange frequency. In other words, the speaker might reproduce all those frequencies, but nowhere near at the same level.

A much clearer method of specifying frequency response involves giving a tolerance, the range within which the speaker produces all the frequencies within its frequency response range (see Figure 6.10). For example, a frequency response of 20Hz–20KHz +/– 3 dB indicates a much superior speaker to the one mentioned earlier with a bass roll off of 40 dB. Basically, the latter speaker maintains its level all the way into its lowest frequency, whereas the former just goes away (rolls off) in its lower frequencies. The lowest bass frequency is at most only half of what a typical mid-range frequency is reproduced at. Without indicating the tolerance on the specifications, companies can create extremely misleading specifications.

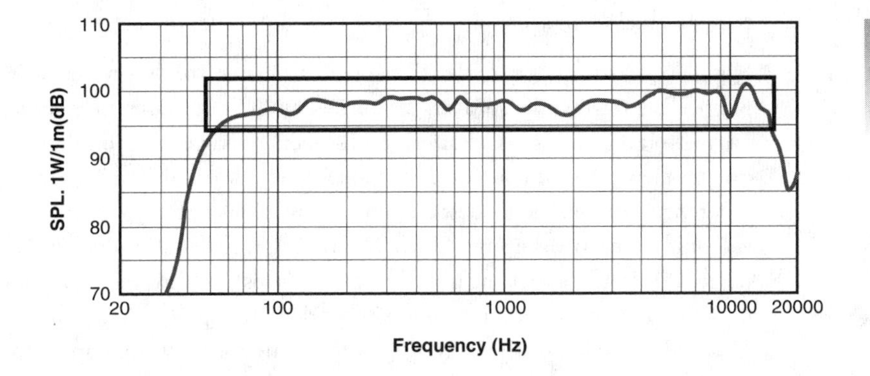

FIGURE 6.10
The frequency response chart for an anonymous speaker.

Specifications given in Figure 6.11 could indicate that this speaker responded from 35Hz to 20KHz—it reads on the diagram across that entire spectrum. However, the box indicates what frequency range would be offered with a tolerance of roughly +/– 5 dB, or a range of roughly 50Hz to about 17KHz. Both specifications would be true, but only the second one would be honest.

If a speaker company does not indicate a tolerance in its specifications, it raises the question of what it is trying to hide. In addition to indicating how the ends of the frequency spectrum differ, the tolerance indicates the accuracy of the spectrum. The tolerance indicates that at no point in the spectrum are there extreme spikes or discrepancies that would not show up in a spec without a tolerance reading. Each speaker has its own frequency response that gives it "color," a speaker's individual tonal qualities or sound. This characteristic determines how the frequency response shapes the sound to make it better by emphasizing certain frequencies.

Impedance

Technically, *impedance* is the opposition to current flow in an alternating current circuit. Its significance in audio is a way to ensure that components work together correctly. The audio input needs to use up the current from an output circuit.

Typically, input impedances are higher than the output impedance of the circuit to which they are connected. So, a powered speaker system is taking in a line level input and should have high impedance.

Signal to Noise Ratio

The Signal to Noise (S/N) ratio is the difference between the nominal program level, or speaker volume, and the noise floor, or underlying hiss and static in an electronic circuit. The larger the S/N ratio, the better.

Higher S/N is very noticeable. The sound is cleaner with less noise during playback, and when the speakers are turned on but not in use, they are quieter with less residual hiss. For critical listeners, this specification should carry some weight. If your music or games have a broad dynamic range (the difference between the loudest and quietest portions of the program), it is very important to ensure that the S/N ratio is larger than this dynamic range. If it is not, either the quietest portion is lost beneath the hiss of the noise floor or the loudest portions will overload the speakers and cause clipping and distortion. Either way, the listening environment is unsatisfactory and deducts from your overall computing experience.

Output Power

Output power measures how much power the amplifier provides to the speaker system. The amplifier is often integrated into one or all of the speakers in a configuration known as "powered speakers," as opposed to having an independent amplifier like in a home stereo system. A larger output power leads directly to a louder speaker system. In a multichannel system, the principal stereo speakers should be more powerful than the surround speakers that are just used for spatial effects. Finally, in a sub woofer, higher powers lead to a punchier system with more presence.

When examining a speaker's handling of power, sometimes the speaker's efficiency is presented. As a speaker is a transducer, its job is to convert forms of energy, from electrical to physical movement of the air. The efficiency measures how much energy is actually transformed instead of lost to heat. Given two equal speakers, one with a higher efficiency attains higher volume levels at lower power and performs better than the less efficient speaker.

The trick with output power is how it is measured. When not indicating the standard used in measuring, any specification talking about output power can be deceitful. The most common, and fairly honest, standard is to use the RMS (root mean square) testing method. This technique takes the average of an alternating current signal, such as the power sent to speakers, and gives a specification that would be equivalent to the power dissipated in a comparable direct current circuit. If a company chooses to instead list peak power, this doesn't always reveal the full truth of the speaker.

Sound is produced by alternating current with ever-changing levels, and the RMS value gives a much better idea of what the system can really do, instead of the instantaneous peaks in power. Some other methods, such as describing "music power" or "program power" varies based on the signal used to create the specification and can prove to be more deceptive, yielding higher ratings than the actual performance in normal listening conditions.

Another specification bundled into output power is the total harmonic distortion, or THD. This is a measurement of the purity of the audio signal. Like digital artifacts in imaging, electronic equipment can introduce distortion in the form of harmonics, or frequencies not present in the source, but reproduced as integer multiples of the source frequency (for example, a 100Hz source produces an output with 100, 200, 200 Hz, and so on). Besides the loss of quality, the human ear is bothered by these imperfections.

The distortion can be presented in two ways: in signal between source and harmonics in dB or by giving a percentage to indicate the ratio between the harmonics and the original source. Therefore, the lower either of the two numbers are, the higher quality of the audio. Given a typical reading of so and so watts at 0.1% THD, this means that the artifacts are going to be 1/1000 of the program level, or 30 dB lower. Translated into speaker pressure, that's 1/64 of the program source in perceived loudness. What does this all mean?

If the program's dynamic range is greater than 30 dB, the harmonics are going to be evident in the program as they fall within the dynamic range. However, the dynamics would be present within the range only under the loudest portions, which would drown them out. This makes 0.1% THD reasonable, but a lower value would mean a better speaker.

These specifications can be tested in a quick way or a thorough way; the two don't go together. When checking distortion, it is possible to examine just one frequency and how the system reacts to it, or to look at the full spectrum and present the system's overall distortion. THD across the entire spectrum indicates a more accurate picture of the speaker's quality. And seeing as sound is much more than just a test tone. This gives a more accurate picture of how well the speakers actually sound. Also, computer manufacturers aren't subjected to the requirement to present all their specifications from stereo mode, like on home receivers. So their measuring environments might not resemble an actual listening environment. Instead they might be optimized for good specs.

Speaker Formats: From Simple to Surround Sound

The expansion of speaker technology for home theater has trickled down to the computer industry, bringing a variety of new choices for gamers and audiophiles alike. The advent of surround sound has opened new options for experiencing sound. Even the concept of adding remote sub woofers has had computer desks shaking for some time, and new virtual positioning technologies have even empowered the older concept of stereo speakers. When considering what speaker format to buy, it is important to consider how you use your computer. Each format has its own benefits that must be weighed against its cost. The fancier the technology, the larger the price tag.

When determining which format to purchase, it is important to examine what your needs in a speakers system are. By generalizing your needs into one of four categories, it can be easier to classify what speakers are right for you. Four convenient categories are

- Basic computer sound
- Music playback
- Gaming
- Computer-based home theater

Basic computer sound includes only the alert noises or simple sounds that the computer uses to interact with you, as well as vocal reproduction from Webcasts. A simple sound system is sufficient. Music playback is the next level of speakers. At a minimum, stereo should be required. Adding a sub woofer extends the frequency response and improves the tonal quality of the sound. Higher-quality speakers also more accurately reproduce the sound.

Gaming systems and computer-based home theater are moving into the surround sound environments. Gaming manufacturers have begun to integrate positional audio into their systems, and when combined with a surround sound system, they create an immersive gaming experience. Computer-based home theater, especially as new DVD drives enable movie playback at the computing station, offers the opportunity to get a cinema-like experience from your computer. These systems are able to decode the surround signals embedded in the audio tracks of movies and reproduce these at the desktop.

Stereo

Your standard stereo speakers do an excellent job of reproducing music and basic audio at a very affordable price. Setup is easy—just two speakers to plug in, and then you sit between them. The stereo image lends a sense of direction to the sound and allows for basic effects. For music playback or basic computing, stereo speakers are efficient and well priced. They are sufficient for many games, although they do not provide the most immersive listening experience. Although, it is competent for basic gaming, it is not well suited to those seeking an in-depth experience.

2.1 Speaker System

2.1 is a cute way to say stereo plus a sub woofer. This is a format that expands on the concept of stereo speakers. It adds a third speaker, usually a remote-powered sub woofer that reproduces only the lowest frequencies. The sub widens the frequency response of the system by providing the lows small computer speakers can't provide. Well suited to music playback, the added frequency response ensures more accurate reproductions of everything from rock to techno to classical. Also, a 2.1 system provides an entry-level game system that shakes the table top with added bass.

4.1 Speaker System

A logical extension to the 2.1 setup, a 4.1 system adds two rear speakers to literally surround you with sound (surround sound standards are discussed in the following section). This is generally the best overall setup you can get for a gaming machine, provided that you have enough room in your computer area to deal with four speakers. A 4.1 system is useless if your two rear speakers are not placed somewhere behind you; it's all too often that users group the four speakers in front of them, completely defeating the purpose of a 4.1 system.

5.1 Speaker System

As the name implies, a 5.1 system builds off the 4.1 base by adding a fifth speaker. In this case, the fifth speaker does nothing for you in most games but is for watching movies with 5.1-encoded audio. The fifth speaker is your center channel, and with properly encoded audio, all speech comes out of that speaker. A good center channel is key to a solid-sounding home theater system, but if all you're interested in are games, you don't need to bother with a 5.1 system because no games truly take advantage of it now.

Surround Sound Standards

Multiple companies have developed methods to create surround sound, or the conceptive of creating an immersive environment of sound that lends both direction and positioning to the audio image. Dolby Laboratories has developed many of the various surround technologies used in home theater that are now making their way into the computer realm. In addition, Creative Labs has offered its own technology, called EAX.

Surround sound technology heightens the gaming environment as designers have grasped this new creative freedom to prey on another of our senses with positional audio. The introduction of surround sound technology to computers has also continued to merge our home theater systems with our home computers. Keep in mind that surround sound can be produced only off encoded signals. However, any stereo source plays through the front stereo speakers without any problems. Even for those who don't choose a surround sound system, any Dolby-encoded audio source always plays back over the most basic stereo system without problems, even without a decoder.

Dolby Surround

Dolby Surround is the first surround technology developed based on a commercial theater system. It consists of the playback of three channels—stereo left, stereo right, and a mono surround channel with a limited frequency response that would feed speakers behind the listener. This was the first Dolby format available to the consumer that enabled the playback of Dolby encoding used for cinematic playback years before. It offers access to three of the four cinematic channels encoded in the stereo signal and it does not produce the center channel for vocal reproduction that is localized to the source.

Dolby Surround Prologic

The next step in the Dolby evolution was to access the center channel in cinematic surround sound. The consumer gained this access with Dolby Prologic, which provided the stereo left and right, mono surrounds, and mono center channel. The advantage of the center channel is that vocal frequencies are reproduced in a speaker ideally placed at the visual source, localizing the vocals in a movie to the actual faces on the screen. The Prologic design is based on processing that "steers" the sound to the center channel if it falls within the vocal frequency range and is present in both the left and right front channels. However, most computing speaker systems are set up around a near field listening system. That is, the speakers are already close to the listener as well as the visual source. So, the directivity issues that Prologic addresses in larger systems with separated speakers is not an issue at the computing station. However, if the computer was going to be used by multiple people at once, the center channel could be useful as the sweet spot between the speakers that can't be shared by all viewers or listeners.

Dolby Digital

This technology is centered around the 5.1 Surround standard. It consists of six discrete channels—stereo left and right front, stereo left and right surrounds, center channel, and the low frequency channel. The low frequency channel is the ".1" channel—it requires one-tenth of the bandwidth of the other channels because it is only reproducing one-tenth of the frequencies of a full range channel. The other 5 channels are all full-range channels that enable extensive creative use. They combine to place the sound in a three-dimensional environment around the listener. The low frequency channel feeds a sub woofer that provides the rumble to complete the viewing experience.

Dolby Virtual Surround or Dolby Multimedia Surround

This approach to surround sound is based on psychoacoustical processing. Basically, the theory is that if an individual with two ears (sound sources) can accurately place where a sound is coming from, there should be an algorithm that enables two speakers (again, sound sources) to create a three-dimensional sound image. Loading a speaker with directional drivers and shooting sound in more than one direction combined with electronic processing creates the surround image from only two speakers sitting on the desktop. However, the sweet spot, or ideal listening zone, is smaller due to the nature of the processing.

A3D

Aureal's role in the computer surround sound market comes under their product name A3D. Based in the processing concepts used in virtual surround sound, A3D serves as a 3D sound solution based in either a two speaker setup, or with A3D 2.0, a four speaker setup. However, A3D recommends using headphones to take full advantage of the spatial effects. This makes sense under the theory of virtual surround sound—two point sources close to the ears should be just like reproducing what the ears would hear in a 3D environment. Processing algorithms gives the audio a position within a three-dimensional listening field by computing how the sound would react to its surroundings. A3D 1.0 established these hardware-based algorithms. The newer 2.0 standard added on some features such as environmental audio, occlusions, and reflections. Occlusions are how a sound is perceived when passed through a surface (closed window or brick wall) while reflections calculate how the sound is perceived as bouncing off of such surfaces. The 2.0 standard also includes wavetracing. The graphics data describing the environment (the picture of the walls) is used to realistically calculate how that room would sound. This data is taken directly from the data sent to the graphics card. The A3D processing technique is based in the sound card, and requires some processing time, which may result in a performance hit. However, this internal processing sends out the audio signal to any speakers connected to them, creating the 3D audio environment. Unfortunately, the demise of Aureal and the lack of support for A3D have pretty much sealed the fate on this standard. A lot of the technology behind A3D will live on in other products, however.

Creative Labs EAX

EAX, or Environmental Audio Extensions, is based on algorithms developed by Creative Labs that have been implemented in their sound cards, speakers systems, and Personal Digital Entertainment (PDE) products. EAX is based in a 4.1 surround sound concept, absent the center channel for vocal range directivity. It also is based on the concept of environmental audio, or standard processing algorithm designed to make sound characteristic of an environment. Gaming manufacturers use the capabilities to add environmental audio to their games, such as an underwater or arena effect, through programming control over processing done by the sound card. The user can also customize and apply these environments. As a standard designed more for the PC gaming industry, it is geared towards computer multimedia in a near field listening situation. The speaker format that supports this standard is based in stereo front and rear channels, as well as an added sub woofer.

Let Your Ears Be Your Guide

When finally sitting down to purchase a speaker system, the previous information can only serve as tools. The final decision is personal—it is all about what sounds good to you. However, making these decisions is a process that requires careful development. Some basic guidelines can be extremely useful in deciding which units to buy.

What Do You Need?

Decide carefully what your needs are as a user. Is listening to MP3s, Webcasts, or CDs your most common activity? Or are you the ambitious gamer that rides the leading edge of technology in search of the most immersive gaming experience possible? Or finally, is your computer becoming your home theater system, and you want it to sound like one? Surround sound carries a price, and stereo can sound great for much less.

Also, examine the possibility of adding a sub woofer. The smaller speakers used for short range listening often do not carry the frequency response of larger speakers that would be overkill. However, the frequency range can be extended with the sub woofer that puts some punch back into music and basic games. Also, the lows can be run at a higher volume without raising the high-pitched frequencies that are more likely to damage hearing.

How Do the Specifications Look?

Carefully examine what the manufacturers say about their own speakers. Also, look at what they don't say. Frequency response can be one of the most deceptive specifications when presented without a tolerance. Power ratings are often misrepresented. All too often do you find 400W speakers for $19 and I can tell you now that they're not the best ones ever made. Also, the signal to noise (S/N) ratio can prove to be important as it describes how clean the sound is. Make informed decisions as to which speakers are worth listening to, but don't necessarily eliminate all of the others. Keep an open mind, and open ears. Remember to get speakers that are magnetically shielded if they are near the monitor because otherwise they distort the screen.

Listen, Listen, Listen

Try to find a store where you can actually get your hands on the speakers. Try to stand (or even better, sit) with the speakers in a position similar to the one they would be in when at your computer. Play your favorite song—one whose sound you're familar with. Then, just listen. Make sure that everything is there that you want to be—the highs are warm and crisp, the lows are present, and everything seems balanced. Then, listen to another set of speakers and decide whether it is better or worse. Taking some time is worth it because the speakers are with you for a while.

Chapter 7

Storage: The Slowest Part of Your PC

Why You Need Mass Storage Mediums

The millions of calculations that your CPU is performing are completely useless if you can never store the data anywhere. Luckily, as you found out in Chapter 4, "Memory: Your PC's Scratchpad," your CPU has a place to store the results of its calculations in main memory. A consequence of the extremely fast DRAM-based memory is that as soon as power is removed from the capacitors in the memory modules, all your data is lost. Although many users leave their computers on for days on end, it's useful to have a more permanent place to store things.

So why not just keep a special section of memory powered at all times using a battery? The problem with using DRAM technology as the basis for mass storage is that it is expensive when used in large quantities. Although I mentioned in Chapter 4 that the sweet spot for the amount of memory to have in your gaming PC is between 256MB and 512MB, that isn't nearly enough memory to store your Windows installation directory. Windows XP alone can eat up to 1GB of space not to mention that it would have to be constantly recopied to memory every time your system was powered down. This makes the requirements for a mass storage device in your PC something that can accommodate large amounts of data, on the order of tens and hundreds of gigabytes, and the data must be permanently stored on this device. For example, removing power from the device shouldn't cause all data to be lost.

When you look at these two requirements they eliminate DRAM-based mass storage devices because by definition, a DRAM cell must be constantly refreshed with power to retain its data. The next problem is that most of today's applications and games require quite a bit of storage space. For example, a full install of Red Alert 2 can take up 500MB of space. That is definitely more than even the most robust gaming systems have in memory. Even if you could provide DRAM cells with enough power to retain data, the cost of putting together an array of 100GB of a DRAM-based storage device would be incredible. By removing DRAM and other such memory technologies from the running, you pretty much limit yourself to noticeably slower alternatives. You are often willing to sacrifice performance when the cost is factored in. This is the birth of mass storage in the PC—the hard disk drive (HDD), a mass storage device with plenty of space at a very affordable cost per GB.

Hard Disk Storage

Just as memory is stored using the idea of capacitance to hold a charge, hard drives store data by using magnetism. Although they aren't used much today, there was a time when music was primarily stored using a similar principle on cassettes. The music was stored on the actual "tape" that was in these cassettes using magnetic patterns that were read by a player. This same principle, writing data in a series of magnetic patterns on a surface that can later be read back, is the basis for storage on hard drives. The first part of this chapter focuses on hard disk storage.

How a Hard Disk Works

All the technology I've talked about up to this point has been on the magnitude of thousands to millions of times faster than hard disks. The reason being that the hard disk still relies on a lot of mechanical operation to store data while technology, such as memory performs its functions entirely electronically through the movement and storing of charges.

To understand how a hard disk works you have to look at the name "hard disk." This name comes from the actual surfaces that the data is stored on, which are literally hard disks, also known as platters (see Figure 7.1).

FIGURE 7.1
The internal platters of an IDE hard drive.

A single hard drive can have one or more platters that control the maximum amount of storage space that the drive can offer because data is actually stored on these platters. The platters in a hard drive are usually made up of some sort of combination of glass, aluminum and/or ceramic materials and are coated so that magnetic data can be written to them.

The characteristics of an individual platter determine how much data can be stored on it. A platter, circular in shape, is divided into concentric storage areas known as tracks. These tracks are so densely packed on modern hard drives that you can't even see them without some sort of magnification equipment. These tracks are then subdivided into sectors. Using this data you can come up with an equation for the amount of data stored on a platter:

Amount of data stored in a sector × Number of sectors per track × Number of tracks per platter × 2 = Amount of storage per platter

If you notice in the previous equation you multiply the result of all these factors by two. That's because each platter has two surfaces to which data can be written (top and bottom). In some situations only one surface of a platter can be used for data storage, but generally that's not the case.

It is common for a hard drive to have multiple platters. After all, the more platters the greater the storage capacity of the drive and you can do so without incurring a performance penalty. The only downsides to having more platters are increased cost, weight, and cooling requirements.

The platters are mounted on a rod known as a spindle. The spindle is what enables the platters to move and it rotates them at very high speeds. Most common hard drives rotate at 5,400–15,000 rotations per minute or 90–166 rotations per second. Obviously this generates quite a bit of heat, which can make cooling a major concern when it comes to hard drive construction and operation.

Luckily, the drive itself is designed to deal with the incredible heat by including technology to cool itself during operation. Because of the high rotational speed of the platters, quite a bit of inherent cooling is built into the drive courtesy of the air that is brought into the drive. This eliminates the need for a heatsink/fan type of cooling solution that most other components in your system use. Combined with the fact that hard drives also use the metal chassis they are installed in to dissipate heat, the need for additional cooling is little. When dealing with multiple drives spinning at 10,000RPM+, it is common to implement drive coolers that are essentially fans that blow air over the surface of the drive, but for most systems these types of coolers.

The reason the platters must spin is because the data stored on them is written to and read from by a little device on the edge of a fixed position arm. This device is known as a head and the arm is known as the actuator arm. The actuator arm can only move the head in two directions: backwards and forwards. In other words, to gain access to data not in its immediate path, the platters must spin.

On most modern hard drives each surface of a platter has a head that handles the reading and writing for that surface. So for a drive with two platters, it wouldn't be uncommon to have four heads (four platter drives have eight heads). Some more complex drives have even more platters/heads, but for the most part the two heads per platter relationship applies to the drives you encounter.

The actuator arm is moved forward and backward using a motor that receives signals from the controller logic asking it to find a particular bit of data. When your computer reads a file off the hard disk the circuitry on the disk sends a signal to the actuator controller to move the arm to the correct track on the correct platter. It also sends a signal to read the data as soon as the sector(s) it is contained in spin(s) below the head. As you can guess, this is a very delicate process and requires the utmost precision from the components in the hard disk themselves.

The hard disk gets even more interesting when you realize that during the read/write process, the heads never actually come in contact with the surface of the platters. Instead, the heads operate on the same principle as the wing of an airplane. With the platters spinning below at very high speeds, the heads glide above the platters at an extremely low altitude and read/write data using the shape of the heads and the velocity of the platters to create lift, enabling the heads to essentially float.

By enabling the heads to float over the surface of the platters reliability is increased dramatically because no physical contact occurs during the reading processes. There can be situations in which the heads come in contact with the platters. This process is generally met with a highly unpleasant crashing sound as the head collides with the platter. These head crashes can often result in data loss or even permanent damage to the disk, creating bad sectors.

When the platters aren't spinning at a high enough velocity or at all, the heads do rest on the platters in a special area known as the landing zone. If you've ever had to "park" your heads on an older hard drive, you were just instructing them to move to the landing zone so that when power is removed they can fall down to a place on the disk where no data is stored. During the shutdown process, and even when power is removed from the drive unexpectedly, modern hard drives automatically align the heads with the landing zone. This might occur if your computer loses power all of a sudden or you have to shut down your computer manually because of a crash. Most newer drives do their best to make sure that the heads don't come in contact with the data areas on the platters.

The writing process is pretty simple. The controller logic on the drive receives a command from the disk controller in your system to write data. This causes the actuator motor to move the actuator arm to the track where the data is located. Finally, the head begins writing as soon as the sector(s) to which it can write the data spin(s) beneath it. The reading process is virtually identical, but it occurs in reverse order.

When a read command is issued, the drive's controller logic receives word that it must read data off one of the platters. The actuator motor moves the arm with the correct head mounted on it to the track where the data is located and the head waits for the data to align itself directly underneath the head before beginning to read. But what happens to the data after it is "read" by the head?

The data is sent through an internal bus to a small amount of memory located on the drive itself known as the drive buffer. Modern day hard disks can have buffers between 2MB and 16MB in size. Manufacturers generally match the buffer size and speed on a hard disk with the characteristics of the disk so that the performance or capacity of your drive's buffer almost never limits you.

Transfer rates to and from the buffer are often either noticeably higher than what the hard drive controller in your system is capable of sustaining or higher than what the physical disk is able to deliver.

The buffer's primary purpose is to cache reads from the disk. As is the case with your CPU's cache, if the data being read can be found in cache, performance is improved significantly. In this case, the read doesn't have to take place using the slow mechanics of the hard disk. The buffer is also used in caching writes to the disk. Caching can help write speed tremendously because data is written to the cache and then later written to the platters. However, the rest of the system doesn't have to wait until data is physically written to the disk; it continues working just as soon as the data has finished writing to the cache. This saves quite a bit of time because writing to the platters themselves takes a significantly greater amount of time than just writing data to a cache.

The buffer does have another purpose and that is to cache prefetch data. Remember from Chapter 1, "The Central Processing Unit: The Heart and Soul of the PC," that some of the latest processors from AMD and Intel have a hardware prefetch mechanism that looks at data access patterns requested by the CPU and prefetches data into the CPU's cache before it is requested. In the event that the data is later requested, it is already available in the CPU's cache and performance is improved tremendously. In the event that the data was mistakenly prefetched into the cache and it is never requested, no performance hit occurs at all. The controller logic on a hard disk also looks at data access patterns and prefetches data it thinks is requested next into the cache.

The Importance of Disk Performance

A main theme in the hardware world is the location and hopeful elimination of bottlenecks within your PC. By now you know that a Pentium 4 2GHz combined with an ATI Rage 128 is no faster in Duke Nukem Forever than a Celeron 566 with a NVIDIA GeForce3. The reason is the Pentium 4's gaming performance is held back by the poor performance of the system's video card, in that often the CPU is waiting around for the graphics card to complete its tasks before it can move on. This same concept of finding and eliminating bottlenecks is present in the storage world, and although having a faster hard disk rarely improves your in-game performance, it can definitely speed up your overall computer usage.

Think for a moment about what happens when you click an icon to start up your game (see Figure 7.2).

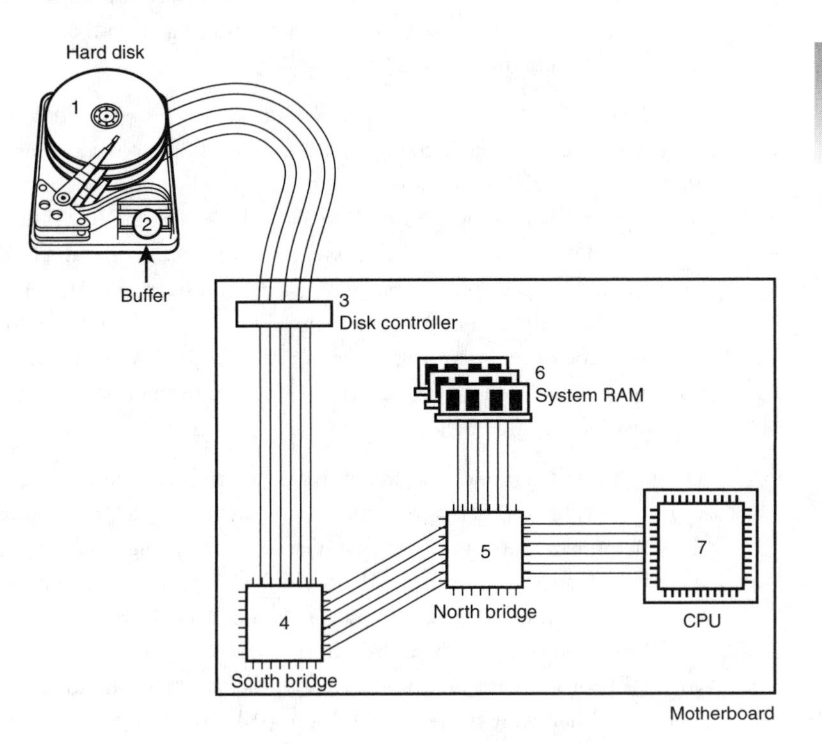

FIGURE 7.2
The flow of data from the hard drive to the CPU.

The following is what happens:

1. The game's execution and data files are all contained on the hard disk and are effectively read off the drive into the buffer on the drive.
2. The drive's buffer then sends the data through the interface to your disk controller, which is either a part of your chipset (for example, in the South Bridge) or elsewhere on your motherboard (for example, in a PCI expansion slot).

3. The data is then sent over to the North Bridge, which takes the necessary data and puts it in main memory.

   From there your CPU has direct access to it (via the North Bridge) and can then begin crunching away whenever it needs the data.

From the previous example you can see that one of the first benefits of a fast hard disk is that you get faster load times for your applications. Remember that a hard disk can find data in milliseconds (10^-3 seconds) while memory accesses can happen in nanoseconds (10^-9 seconds) so it is almost always the case that your CPU and memory are just waiting around on your hard disk to send them information.

Now let's say you're playing a game of *No One Lives Forever* and you complete a level and are ready to move on to the next one. Now assuming that all the level data is stored on your hard disk as well (sometimes it might be stored on another storage device such as a CD in your CDROM drive that is even *slower*) the same reading process must take place so that the level data can be loaded into memory. During this time you hear a lot of noise coming from your disk drive. The amount of noise depends on how quiet your hard drive is (some of the newest drives are very difficult to hear over the roar of the fans in your case). This gives us an extension to the first benefit of a fast hard disk: faster in-game load times.

Despite faster load time, one area in which a faster hard disk *doesn't* help you is in improving your game performance. The reason being that almost all the data that must be processed while you're actively playing your game should already be loaded into memory. If you don't have enough memory for all the necessary data for the current level or situation to be stored, the data that can't fit remains on your hard disk. In this scenario, everything is fine until your CPU or graphics card needs some of the data that isn't loaded into memory. When your system does have to pull something off the hard disk, provided that the data is critical to whatever you are currently seeing and doing in the game at that point, your performance comes to a halt. These pauses can be bearable in a slow paced quiz game or they can cause Joe Creeper to take your virtual head off with a large cannon while playing a first person shooter, such as Unreal Tournament (bummer). The only real way to avoid this is to make sure you have enough system memory, as I mentioned in Chapter 4.

Having a faster hard disk also almost always guarantees you faster out-of-game performance as well. When you're browsing the Net, loading word processing applications and loading up any other applications you are mainly going to be bottlenecked by your I/O (input/output), in other words, your hard disk performance.

Although a faster hard disk does not necessarily improve boot times (the amount of time it takes to start and fully load Windows) too much because your boot process can be slowed considerably by things such as device driver initialization, it can help in some situations. Improving boot time isn't a reason to upgrade your hard disk. Chances are that if you're happy with your disk performance except for the time it takes to boot up your PC, your hard disk isn't a bottleneck.

The beauty of having a storage device that is composed of moving parts is that it can give you quite a bit of feedback about what's going on. The main piece of knowledge it offers is that if you hear the disk "crunching" then data is either being read from or written to the platters. This is a huge help in diagnosing when your hard disk is your bottleneck. If your system gets really slow and all you hear is your hard drive crunching, there is a very good chance of a faster hard disk speeding things up. Then again, if your hard disk is crunching away in the middle of running through a room in *Tomb Raider*, it is more likely that increasing the amount of memory you have in your system helps more than a faster hard disk.

There has been a lot of talk about not having enough memory to store all the data needed by your particular application or game. Your operating system actually has a way of using more memory than is physically present in your system by using virtual memory. Virtual memory isn't memory at all, but nothing more than a section of your hard disk that is used to store data that isn't able to fit in main memory. This section is normally a single file that is called your swap file or page file. When you run out of memory and the data in memory must be exchanged or copied to your swap file, the process is known as swapping to disk. The basic goal is to keep from swapping to disk as much as possible. Making sure that you have enough memory for your applications can prevent this. Having a faster hard drive helps improve the performance when you are swapping to disk, but that still doesn't save your butt when running from a guard in *Thief II*.

Keys to Disk Performance

Knowing that having a fast hard disk is necessary is one thing, but it's another thing to know what makes a hard disk fast. You know that a CPU's clock speed isn't indicative of its performance; it's the amount it can do per clock multiplied by the clock speed that gives you the overall power of the CPU. But what's the equivalent relationship in the hard disk world?

A number of factors can influence hard disk performance. The first and most obvious performance factor is the rotational speed of the platters. The rotational speed of the disk is measured in the number of rotations per minute (RPM). Some of the most common rotational speeds are 5,400RPM, 7,200RPM, 10,000RPM, and 15,000RPM, although the latter two are usually reserved for the highest performance drives and thus carry quite a price premium.

The faster the rotational speed, the quicker the heads can get to the data. So rotational speed is directly related to latency when it comes to hard drives. Remember from my initial discussion about latency in Chapter 4, it is the amount of time it takes to get to the data. Latency is a particularly important factor to take into account for most gaming systems because very rarely are you transferring hundreds of megabytes per second worth of data; instead you are usually moving relatively small files and searching for them all over the platters.

In reference to hard drive performance, latency is actually only one part of how long before you can actually read/write data. When a manufacturer refers to latency of a hard disk they mean the rotational latency, the amount of time required to complete a single spin of a platter. The actual amount of time it takes to get to the data on your hard disk is the sum of the amount of time it takes to find the right platter, the right track and the right starting sector where the data is or will be located. Hard drive manufacturers generally provide various portions of this data in the specification listings of drives.

Deciphering the manufacturer's specifications is often a useful way to find out what truly matters when it comes to performance. To make this section easier I've pulled the specifications for the IBM 60GXP Hard Drive off IBM's Storage Web site and placed them in Table 7.1. Following the table, I go through each specification explaining what it means to you.

Table 7.1 Specifications for the IBM 60GXP Hard Disk Drive

Performance	
Data buffer	2MB
Rotational speed (RPM)	7200

Table 7.1 Continued

Performance	
Latency (average ms)	4.17
Media transfer rate (max Mbits/sec)	494
Interface transfer rate (max MBps)	100
Sustained data rate (MBps)	20.9–40.8
Seek Time (Read Typical)	
Average (ms)	8.5
Track-to-track (ms)	1.2
Full-track (ms)	15.0

Data buffer—The size of the buffer on the hard disk, fairly self-explanatory. A larger buffer helps performance a bit, but it is rare that you find two identical drives with two vastly different buffer sizes so you have very little choice when it comes to buffer size. Most IDE drives today have a 2MB buffer. You're not likely going to see anything less than that.

Rotational speed—The rotational speed of a drive is the speed at which the platters are spinning, the higher the better. Currently the best overall choice would be a 7200RPM drive (in terms of price versus performance). This value actually determines the next specification, which is latency.

Latency—Directly related to the rotational speed of a hard disk, the latency is the amount of time to complete a half or a full rotation of a platter. This figure is really the rotational latency, but is also referred to as just latency for simplicity's sake. The number in Table 7.1, quoted as the average latency, is the amount of time to complete half a rotation of a platter. All 7,200RPM drives have a virtually identical average latency figure. It is rare for a manufacturer to quote the amount of time required for a full rotation as the drive's latency. but if they do, the number is usually referred to as a maximum latency and is also measured in milliseconds.

Media transfer rate—This spec tells you the maximum speed at which data can be read off the platters. For whatever reason this spec has almost always been reported in Mbits per second as a peak figure. The average media transfer rate isn't too far off the maximum value. As you can see here, the media is capable of transferring at no more than 61.75MBps (494Mbps / 8 = 61.75MBps).

Interface transfer rate—The interface transfer rate is the maximum transfer rate supported by the drive's interface. The 60GXP drive from which these specs were taken uses an Ultra ATA/100 interface making the maximum transfer rate it can sustain (on an Ultra ATA/100 controller) 100MBps. In most cases, this figure means nothing because it doesn't reflect the actual performance of the drive, just the maximum at which the interface can transfer. In the example used previously in which the drive could transfer only 40.8MBps, you really only use less than half the available bandwidth. This is like saying your speedometer can go up to 200mph, yet your car can go only 174.

Sustained data rate—In the best case scenario, the data you are reading is located physically in the same general area on the tracks of a single platter. The sustained data rate is sometimes referred to as the sequential transfer rate and gives you an indication of what the best case scenario transfer rate of the hard disk is. For this particular drive, if you notice, the maximum value here is 40.8MBps, which is less than half of what the Interface transfer rate offered. Now can you see the uselessness of that number? The sustained data rate (also called sustained transfer rate) is an important value to take into account.

Seek time—The sustained data rate tells you how much data can be read off the disk, but what about how quickly you can get to the data? That's where the seek time comes in.

Average—This figure tells you how long it takes to get from one track to another random track. This number is quite useful.

Track-to-track—As the name implies, this figure gives you the amount of time required for the heads to get from one track to an adjacent one.

Full-track—Finally you have the amount of time required to get from the innermost track to the furthest track from the center of the platter.

Another specification that used to be thrown around a lot, but has since died down is *access time*. The access time of a hard disk is primarily the sum of seek time and rotational latency. It gives you a real-world value for how long it takes between the time a read request is received and when the head is ready to start reading. Access times can be quite misleading depending on what values for seek time and rotational latency the manufacturer chooses to include, partially why most drive manufacturers have stopped using it as a performance metric.

Size Versus Performance

The theme of this chapter thus far has been to limit the amount of time your computer spends waiting around for the disk to provide it with data. This is generally accomplished by having enough memory so that very little or no disk swapping occurs during any of your normal tasks. However, you can't get around the fact that data must be stored on your disk drive, so you eventually have to decide whether you want an extremely large, but slow hard drive or an extremely small, but fast hard drive.

Even for just a gaming system, a 5,400RPM hard drive can cause some headaches during periods of intensive disk activity. A 7,200RPM drive is generally nice to have, and anything faster would be overkill for a system primarily used for gaming.

In terms of size, remember that most game installs take up more than 500MB of space on your hard disk. Most recently there have been titles such as Diablo II that can occupy more than 1GB of space on your hard disk. When you have five or six of these installed at once, you can easily find yourself running low on space on some of the smaller hard drives. Don't forget to take into account the ever increasing OS install size; my Windows XP installation directory was over 900MB in size at the time of writing this.

My recommendation is to stick with a minimum of a 20GB drive. Anything smaller than that does not save you much money and ends up limiting you as time goes on. The sweet spot right now is around 60GB, considering how cheap storage has become. With 100GB+ drives hitting the market, they definitely drive storage prices even lower, making a lot of the more reasonably sized drives easier to obtain.

Keep in mind that buying a lot of storage today with hopes of not having to upgrade for years to come isn't always the best way to approach things. The disk technology available two years ago is completely outshined by what is available today, so buying for the future isn't much of an option if you intend to ride with the performance wave.

Something that a lot of users happen to do is purchase a slightly smaller, but fast hard drive and another noticeably larger and potentially slower hard drive. The smaller hard drive holds all their OS, application, and important game files (for example, frequently played games) and the larger one holds all MP3s, movies, and things that take up quite a bit of space, but are less performance dependent (for example, less frequently used games). For example, most MP3s are recorded in 128Kbps–256Kbps mode, meaning that the hard drive on which they are stored must be capable of reading at most 32KBps. With drives capable of sustaining transfers of beyond 40MBps, being able to play MP3s doesn't require that robust of a disk subsystem.

If you have the budget for it, this two drive solution is a good way to get the best of both worlds. If you don't, however, I'd suggest sticking with a single 7,200RPM drive that is around 40GB–80GB in size.

Interface Influences on Performance

Up to this point I've only talked about how the physical construction and specifications of a hard drive correlate to the performance of the drive. However, the question remains: How does the data get to your CPU and main memory after it is read off the hard drive?

A hard drive controller usually sits on the PCI bus and receives all the read/write requests to the drives, but the interface that connects the controller to the drive does hold a good deal of importance.

IDE/ATA

By far the most popular interface is the Integrated Drive Electronics (IDE) interface, which is also sometimes called the AT Attachment (ATA). In all modern chipsets, an IDE controller is integrated into the South Bridge/ICH (I/O Controller Hub), which is discussed in Chapter 2, "The Chipset: The PC's Crossing Guard," thus you can see why it is the most popular interface. This means that you can usually go out and buy an IDE/ATA drive and have it work perfectly with your system without having to purchase any external controller cards.

The IDE/ATA standard has been around for a very long time, and since its introduction the specifications being used have evolved tremendously. Today IDE drives are rarely referred to as just IDE, rather they are referred to by unofficial names such as Ultra ATA/100. Although it's not the correct name for the interface or a drive using it, this is one of those times where marketing manages to gain so much ground that it just makes sense to become a sheep and follow the flock.

The IDE/ATA interface is a parallel interface such as SDRAM, in that it transfers multiple bits of data in parallel. This is in contrast to serial interfaces such as Serial ATA and RDRAM that transfer data in a single bit stream, but at a much higher frequency. I get into the tradeoffs of the parallel nature of the interface later, but for now all that's important is an understanding that IDE/ATA is a parallel storage interface.

Many flavors of the IDE/ATA specification exist. The most common and most recent are Ultra ATA/66, Ultra ATA/100, and the very new Ultra ATA/133 specification. While changes always occur from one spec to the next, the major changes that were present between the three aforementioned specs was the maximum transfer rate supported by the interface on a single channel. The Ultra ATA/66 specification has up to 66MBps of bandwidth transferred over a single channel, Ultra ATA/100 has 100MBps, and Ultra ATA/133 has up to 133MBps. It doesn't take much thought to realize that the older Ultra ATA/33 specification offered 33MBps of bandwidth to storage devices that implemented the spec.

The thing to take away from this is that although each of these specifications can have transfer rates as high as 133MBps, this has absolutely no bearing on the performance of a drive itself. Remember the "interface transfer rate" spec from the "Keys to Disk Performance" section? That comes directly from the type of interface supported by the drive and controller.

All current implementations of the IDE/ATA specification (for example, Ultra ATA/100) also include support for devices other than hard drives (for example, CD/DVDROM, CDRW, and so on). This support is provided using an additional interface that has been integrated into the Ultra ATA specification, which is known as the AT Attachment Packet Interface (ATAPI). This enables not only hard drives to work with IDE/ATA controllers, but other types of storage devices as well using the same controller and the same cabling.

By far the most common IDE/ATA controllers feature two independent channels, each supporting up to two IDE/ATA or ATAPI devices per channel (see Figure 7.3).

FIGURE 7.3
Finding two of these 40-pin IDE channels on a motherboard is not uncommon. The integrated IDE controller drives these ports in the South Bridge/ICH of the chipset.

The physical IDE/ATA interface is made via a 40-pin connector present on the controller board (usually on the motherboard) and on the drive itself. The connection is made via a 40-pin ribbon cable. For Ultra ATA/66/100/133+ devices a special 40-pin cable must be used with two times the amount of conducting wires in the cable than conventional IDE cables. In the past, IDE cables only had 40 conducting wires that carried data from one end of the cable to the other. With ever increasing transfer rates, the need for greater insulation between these 40 individual wires increased. The newer 80-conductor cables offer another 40 grounding paths between the 40 signal carrying wires that help to decrease the amount of interference picked up by the signal carrying wires when operating at very high data transfer rates. Luckily most newer cables are 80-conductor cables. You can tell them apart from older 40-conductor cables by the thickness of the wires on the ribbon (see Figure 7.4).

FIGURE 7.4
On the left you can see the thin wires in the 80-conductor cable compared to the thicker wires in an older 40-conductor IDE/ATA cable on the right.

The great majority of gamers do not need anything more than an IDE/ATA hard drive. The types of applications and games you run are in no way disk intensive enough to require anything more than what the IDE/ATA specification can offer you. The fact that your motherboard (courtesy of your chipset) already has a built in IDE/ATA controller makes this an even easier choice. If however, you find yourself with a craving for even higher performance disk solutions, you have another option.

SCSI

For the longest time I didn't know the proper pronunciation of the acronym for the Small Computer Systems Interface (SCSI), so the first thing I do here is to mention that the acronym SCSI is pronounced "skuzzy."

The SCSI interface is yet another parallel interface standard such as the IDE/ATA interface with one major difference: A SCSI controller handles all the processing required when reading or writing to or from SCSI devices, whereas an IDE/ATA controller offloads all such processing to your host CPU.

The reason I say that SCSI isn't a necessity for a gaming machine is because when you're only dealing with moderate disk usage over a couple of storage devices, the CPU utilization of IDE/ATA devices is very low. With the ever increasing speed of today's processors, you are rarely using 100% of your CPU power, so losing a few percent to I/O operations usually doesn't hinder your performance too much if at all.

When I refer to the SCSI interface I am actually talking about a very specific standard known as the SCSI-3 standard. Entirely too many SCSI standards exist to be discussed in this section and they would honestly confuse things much more than they need to be. The main thing to remember here is that the newer SCSI drives implement a version of the SCSI specification known as SCSI-3.

SCSI offers some other advantages over IDE/ATA, including support for external devices. An external IDE/ATA device does not have a set interface standard, but SCSI does. In fact, just about any SCSI peripheral you can have installed inside your system can be made to work outside of your system without any loss of performance because the interface is the same. Because the IDE/ATA spec only offers support for internal devices, most external storage devices used to use a Parallel Port interface that allowed for data transfers often lower than 1MBps. The advent of the Universal Serial Bus (USB) has enabled higher transfer rates for external devices (12Mbps or 1.5MBps) and other technologies such as USB 2.0 and IEEE-1394 have raised the bar even further beyond 400Mbps (50MBps). In spite of all these advancements, nothing can compete with the type of performance SCSI offers external devices. Having an interface that enables transfer rates much higher than 50MBps doesn't make much sense with a single drive. However, with multiple drive RAID configurations (I explain this later in the section "RAID: Tool for Professionals Only or Useful Gaming Hardware

Technology Too?") transfer rates easily can exceed even 160MBps. This is where SCSI really comes in handy, both on the inside of your PC and on the outside. Normally such high performance storage configurations are reserved for high-end workstations and servers. I guarantee you that your gaming experience isn't improved too much by having a multi-thousand dollar SCSI disk setup, so you shouldn't worry about this too much.

Another feature that SCSI offers over IDE/ATA is the capability to support up to 15 devices (internal and external) on a single channel. Remember that IDE/ATA enables only up to two devices per channel, and with only two channels on most motherboards, four devices might not be enough. A single SCSI channel provides much more room for growth than you have drive bays for in your case, however.

In terms of transfer rates, a few current SCSI-3 implementations are the most popular right now. The following are the names for these standards. Just like Ultra ATA, they are very unofficial yet pretty easy to remember.

Ultra2 SCSI—When running in 16-bit transfer mode (sometimes called "Wide" mode), the Ultra2 interface can offer up to 80MBps of bandwidth to the devices located on a single Ultra2 channel (see Figure 7.5).

FIGURE 7.5
An Ultra2 SCSI cable. These cables often carry a very high markup in retail stores in spite of the fact that they are relatively cheap to make.

Ultra160 SCSI—Ultra160 SCSI only runs in "wide" mode, meaning that the data bus is 16-bits wide. The Ultra160 spec actually runs at the same clock frequency as the Ultra2 spec, yet data is transferred twice every clock (sort of like DDR memory) yielding a peak transfer rate of 160MBps. If you notice, 160MBps is more than the 32-bit/33MHz PCI bus can offer, so for a single Ultra160 channel to be truly saturated, it must run on a 64-bit PCI bus.

Ultra320 SCSI—The only difference between Ultra320 and Ultra160 is the clock speed of the interface. Ultra320 operates at 80MHz resulting in a 320MBps peak transfer rate (hence the name Ultra320). Notice that 320MBps is more than the 64-bit/33MHz PCI bus can offer. So to fully saturate a single Ultra320 channel you have to first have a drive array capable of transferring close to 320MBps and second you must run the controller card on a 64-bit/66MHz PCI bus (or another high bandwidth bus).

Because of the target market for SCSI drives, they normally feature the highest performing components and are often available in configurations that an IDE/ATA drive would never be offered in at the same time (for example, 15,000RPM, 16MB buffer). This also means that they carry a hefty premium over an equivalent size IDE/ATA drive (now do you see why I recommend you stick with IDE/ATA for a purely gaming box?). Couple that with the fact that you also need to purchase a SCSI controller card (some motherboards have on-board SCSI controllers, but those boards are often expensive as well) and your storage subsystem just became a few hundred dollars more expensive. You're better off saving the money and spending it on more memory, a better graphics card, or even a faster CPU.

USB 1.0 for Storage

The Universal Serial Bus (USB) was only brought into mass use a few years ago (see Figure 7.6). This is in contrast to the IDE/ATA and SCSI standards that have been used for close to two decades. Unlike the aforementioned standards, USB is much more than just a storage interface medium. It can be used to connect peripherals, which is actually its most common use. Don't get me wrong; the USB interface does work well as a storage interface, but its performance limits its usefulness as one.

FIGURE 7.6
A USB cable. The fact that USB is a serial interface enables the cable to be very thin. The end on the left connects to the USB ports on your computer. The end on the right connects to a USB 1.0 device.

In contrast to the parallel IDE/ATA and SCSI interfaces, USB is a serial interface. Because serial interfaces use fewer pins, a USB cable can be very small (width wise) in comparison to the wide IDE and SCSI ribbon cables. The purpose of using a serialized interface is to decrease the amount of signaling pins (and thus the amount of interference generated) and increase the transfer rate of the interface to the point where it not only makes up for, but exceeds the loss associated with transferring only single bits of data at a time versus a parallel interface.

The trend toward serial interfaces has been one that the industry has seen quite a bit of lately. USB was a contributor to the trend; and RDRAM is another. The architecture of the Pentium 4 (NetBurst) is also very much a serial design in that it is optimized for streaming data calculations rather than expecting a great deal of parallelism in the execution code. In the storage industry, standards such as USB 2.0, IEEE-1394, and Serial ATA are all continuing the trend toward higher-speed serial interfaces.

In terms of performance, USB doesn't offer too much bandwidth to its devices. Each channel can have up to 127 devices, but they all must share the theoretical maximum of 12Mbps of bandwidth in "high" mode (1.5MBps). A "low" operation mode also exists that allows for 1.5Mbps of bandwidth (0.1875MBps) for devices that don't demand that much bandwidth, such as mice. These are peak bandwidth numbers, so real-world figures are a bit lower, usually on the magnitude of 80% of what is advertised because of driver/OS overheads. The first thing that is easily noticeable is that the interface supports an enormous amount of devices on a single channel. While a single channel usually only has one port, you can purchase USB hubs to enable more devices to connect to a single port. Some devices even have built in hubs that can be used to daisy chain other peripherals up to that 127 device limit.

Because of its relatively low bandwidth nature, the USB interface has never been big with high speed storage devices (remember that most hard drives can transfer in the tens of megabytes per second). What the USB interface is quite useful for are things such as keyboards, mice, joysticks, and PDAs (see Figure 7.7). It isn't surprising that those areas are where USB has gained the most support.

It costs next to nothing for a motherboard manufacturer to implement multiple USB channels on a motherboard, so many have taken advantage of chipset support for up to 6 channels and provided more than just two ports on the motherboard.

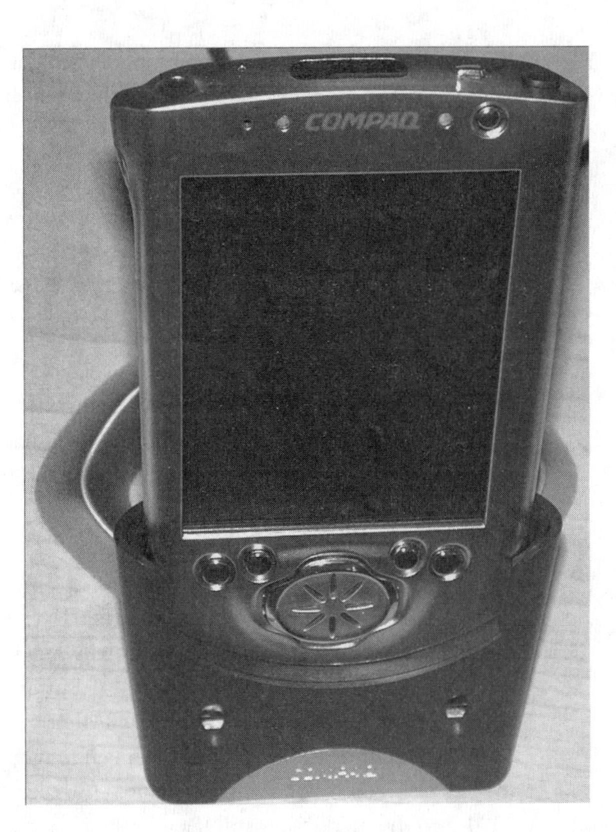

FIGURE 7.7
The Compaq iPAQ Pocket PC can sync to your desktop computer using a USB 1.0 interface. It doesn't need much more than the 1.5MBps of bandwidth that USB 1.0 offers because it only has 32MB of storage space.

USB 2.0

The biggest shortcoming of the original USB interface is the 12Mbps bandwidth limitation, which is exactly what its successor USB 2.0 is designed to fix. Although backwards compatible with USB 1.0, the 2.0 specification calls for much higher transfer rates of up to 480Mbps (60MBps). This would make USB 2.0 a suitable interface for transferring massive amounts of data as would be needed by hard drives or digital video cameras.

As I just mentioned, the interface is backward compatible with USB 1.0. The connectors and ports are all the same. In other words, you can use a USB 1.0 device on a USB 2.0 channel. However, doing so doesn't make the USB 1.0 device any faster; it's still limited to the 12Mbps transfer rate of USB 1.0.

Although USB 1.0 costs next to nothing to implement on a motherboard, the controller is integrated into almost all chipsets. The same cannot be said about USB 2.0. Currently, manufacturers have to go to third party manufacturers to provide USB 2.0 controllers to put on motherboards. Intel plans on integrating a USB 2.0 controller into a future version of their ICH (either ICH3 or ICH4) but until then, the only way to get USB 2.0 support is by having a separate controller on your motherboard or by purchasing an add-on card.

With the lack of present day peripheral support for the standard you'd be better off not getting too excited on picking up a USB 2.0 controller or opting for a motherboard with one on-board. Chances are that when the peripherals are available, the controller is integrated into the chipsets available at the time.

Intel has quite a bit of interest in promoting USB 2.0 as the high bandwidth peripheral interface standard because the only real competition to the interface is a standard introduced by Apple, not a big friend of Intel's.

IEEE-1394

The competing standard to USB 2.0 is IEEE-1394 (pronounced "I-triple-E thirteen ninety-four"), which was originally introduced by Apple as FireWire (see Figure 7.8). IEEE-1394, another serial interface, offers similar bandwidth capabilities to USB 2.0 (up to 400Mbps or 50MBps) and has actually been around in implementations for much longer, whereas USB 2.0 controllers only recently became available. However, the penetration of IEEE-1394 into the market has still been limited.

FIGURE 7.8
An IEEE-1394 cable. While the controller interface end of the cable (right) looks much like a USB interface; the device end of the cable is noticeably smaller (left).

The IEEE-1394 specification calls for three different operating modes: 100Mbps, 200Mbps and 400Mbps. Transfers over the IEEE-1394 bus can occur in one of two ways: a conventional asynchronous transfer or an isochronous transfer. Asynchronous transfers occur the same way transfers over any bus occur; data is sent to its destination and a confirmation of reception is produced. Isochronous transfers actually take place at a specified rate that is never dropped below. Similar transfers are enabled through Hyper Transport's Isochronous Virtual Channels as I described in Chapter 2.

Like USB 2.0, it is still expensive for motherboard manufacturers to implement IEEE-1394 on their boards because the controller is not integrated into any of today's chipsets (see Figure 7.9). Intel definitely doesn't integrate into their ICH something for which they have to pay royalties to Apple. Until a competing chipset manufacturer manages to do the same, it won't become as prevalent as USB 1.0.

FIGURE 7.9
On the left are three ports off an IEEE-1394 controller, and on the right are two ports off of a USB 1.0 controller.

The pitch that many key players in the industry are making about IEEE-1394 is that it should be the high bandwidth companion to USB 1.0. That would leave USB 1.0 for things such as keyboards and mice while IEEE-1394 would be used for external storage devices and digital video cameras.

Although IEEE-1394 has gotten a head start over USB 2.0, over the years Intel has had a way of putting their weight behind standards that usually triumph over the competition. That's not to say that history always repeats itself, but it's something to keep in mind.

RAID: Tool for Professionals Only or Useful Gaming Hardware Technology, Too?

In the microprocessor industry, one way to get around the limitations of technology that prevent faster CPUs from being released every day is by pairing up multiple CPUs into something such as a symmetric multiprocessor (SMP) system. While this doesn't give you a complete doubling of performance, it does manage to offer a way of getting higher levels of performance than the highest speed CPU can offer you. It turns out that a similar technology exists in the hard drive world.

I'm a pretty big RTS (Real-Time Strategy) fan. Westwood, is one of the developers that manages to capture way too much of my time. In *Red Alert 2* your source of resources is the ore that is deposited around the map. Assuming you're playing on a map with an abundance of resources, the amount of income you can rake in is determined by how quickly your harvesters can get you the ore. If you have enough harvesters working, you eventually become limited by the fact that only one harvester can deposit ore at any given time. So how do you increase your rate of cash flow in the game if you're in this situation? You build another refinery. Now you can mine twice as much, but the ore mined is still deposited into the same resource pool. A similar technique is used in the storage world, except instead of building two refineries to double cash flow you create an array of two or more hard drives to increase your I/O performance. This is known as a *Redundant Array of Inexpensive Disks (RAID)*.

Note

Although the term originally meant Redundant Array of Inexpensive Disks, RAID has since been renamed to mean Redundant Array of Independent Disks which holds much more meaning today.

RAID comes in many flavors. Because it's rarely useful for a gaming system I only talk about three of the most common incarnations: RAID 0, RAID 1, and RAID 5.

RAID 0

This is the simplest form of RAID. RAID 0 requires two or more disks and creates one large array equal to the sum of the sizes of all the drives included in the array. For example, if you have two 12GB drives in RAID 0, your total array size is 24GB. Although it is highly recommended, for RAID 0 you don't have to use identical drive sizes or types. To your OS a RAID array, regardless of how many drives it is composed of, appears to be one physical drive.

The way RAID 0 improves performance is by splitting all the data that is sent to the array into multiple parts, known as stripes. These stripes can be as small as 4KB or as large as 4MB and even higher. Let's take a two drive RAID 0 array with a 128KB stripe size and say you want to write a 512KB file to the array. The first 128KB of the 512KB file is written to drive 0, the second 128KB is written to drive 1, the third stripe is written to drive 0, and the final stripe is written to drive 1. Because you're writing to two drives at once the first and second stripes are written simultaneously as are the third and fourth stripes, thus doubling write performance. The same sort of parallelism is present when reading the file back, so read performance is effectively doubled as well (see Figure 7.10).

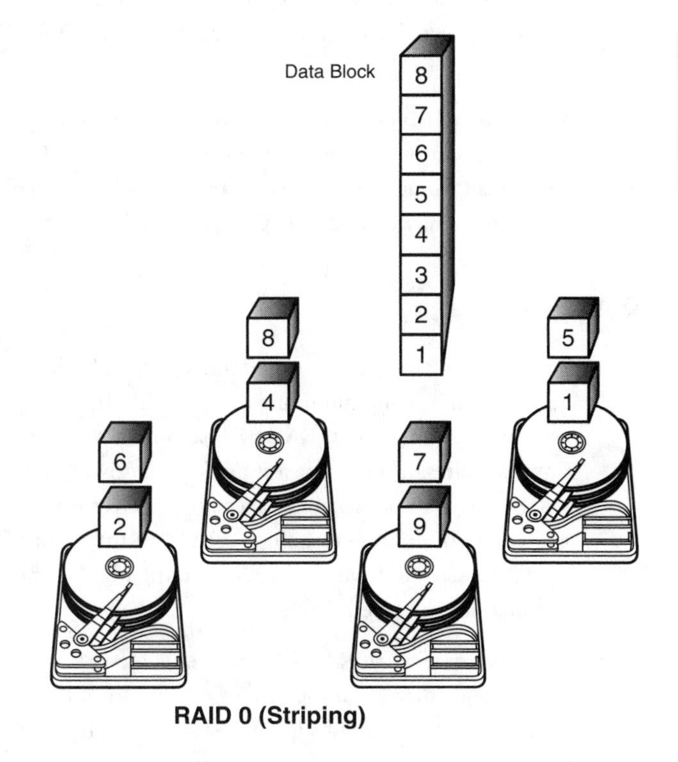

FIGURE 7.10
RAID 0 works by breaking up the data into equivalent sized stripes and sends one stripe to each drive in the array.

Does this mean that your disk performance gets twice as fast with RAID 0? Not necessarily. All RAID 0 (sometimes referred to as striping) does is increase the bandwidth your disk subsystem offers, so two drives in RAID 0 that are each capable of sustaining transfer rates of 40MBps create an array that is capable of sustaining transfer rates of 80MBps. Four of those drives in RAID 0 again double the sequential transfer rate to 160MBps. Now do you see why a need exists for higher bandwidth buses other than 32-bit/ 33MHz PCI?

If you think about it, you are rarely transferring such large volumes of sequential data in your system. When you first run a game, or when loading a level off your drive, performance is improved by RAID 0. For the most part, however, the types of disk accesses you are doing are random seeks, and much smaller random writes and reads. When doing random writes and reads you are generally limited by the seek performance of your drives because the heads have to search all over the platters to find what they need.

During normal gameplay there should be no noticeable disk accesses, otherwise your frame rate surely suffers, so RAID can't help you there. Although improving level load times is great, it's not worth the investment that RAID 0 offers.

While the reliability of drives improves as technology improves, it is worthwhile to mention that one of the drawbacks of RAID 0 is that the chances of your array failing are twice as great as a single drive failing. The reason being that if any drive in a RAID 0 array fails, the entire array is lost.

RAID 1

The next type of RAID is called mirroring and is known as RAID 1. RAID 1 again requires a minimum of two drives, but instead of offering performance as its main selling point, RAID 1 boasts fault tolerance—the ability to continue working normally even if one of the drives in your array fails. The way RAID 1 works is by writing data to both drives in the array so that you have two copies of the data (see Figure 7.11). In the event of a failure of a single drive, the second drive can take over until a replacement is found and installed for the failed drive.

The only time when RAID 1 can offer somewhat of a performance increase over a single drive is in the case of reading from the array. In this case the RAID controller should support reading from both the source drive and the mirrored drive to improve performance.

Generally if your hard drive fails, your gaming machine you might lose a few hours reinstalling all your applications and games, but that's all. The most common applications for RAID 1 arrays are situations in which down time equates to money lost such as in a database or Web server.

RAID 1 is sometimes combined with RAID 0 to form RAID 0+1 or RAID 10, both requiring a minimum of four drives and enjoying the benefits of both striping and fault tolerance.

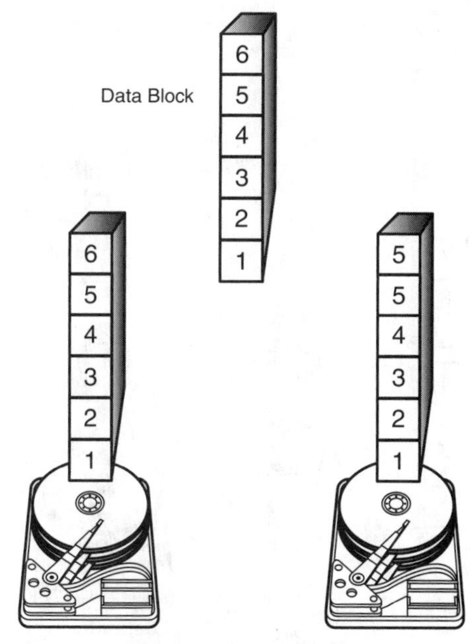

FIGURE 7.11
By sending a copy of each bit of data sent to one drive in the array, a perfect duplicate is kept of all data in a redundant array (RAID 1).

RAID 5

By far the slowest RAID implementation of the bunch, RAID 5 offers the benefits of striping as well as parity so that if one drive dies, the data can be reconstructed. The minimum requirements for a RAID 5 array are three drives. Similar to RAID 0, data is broken up into stripes. In the case of a three drive RAID 5 array, data is broken into two stripes and written to drives 0 and 1. The third drive receives a parity bit that is created by performing a logical function on the data that is being written to the other drives. The beauty of RAID 5 is that the parity bit isn't just written to one drive, but it's cycled through all the drives in the array. As shown in Figure 7.12, on the first write the parity bit is written to drive 2, drive 0, drive 1, and so on. This prevents any one drive from being a limiting factor (this type of an array is known as a RAID 3 array).

The reason RAID 5 is so slow is because whenever data is written to the array the controller must perform a logical operation on the data (known as an XOR) to get the parity bit. That's the best case scenario. So for every write that is performed, a second write must complete before the array can proceed. Although read performance of RAID 5 arrays is generally decent, this slows down write performance tremendously. In some situations with RAID 5 the setup could be even slower than a single drive.

FIGURE 7.12
By using a parity bit, the data can be reconstructed if a single drive fails in a RAID 5 array.

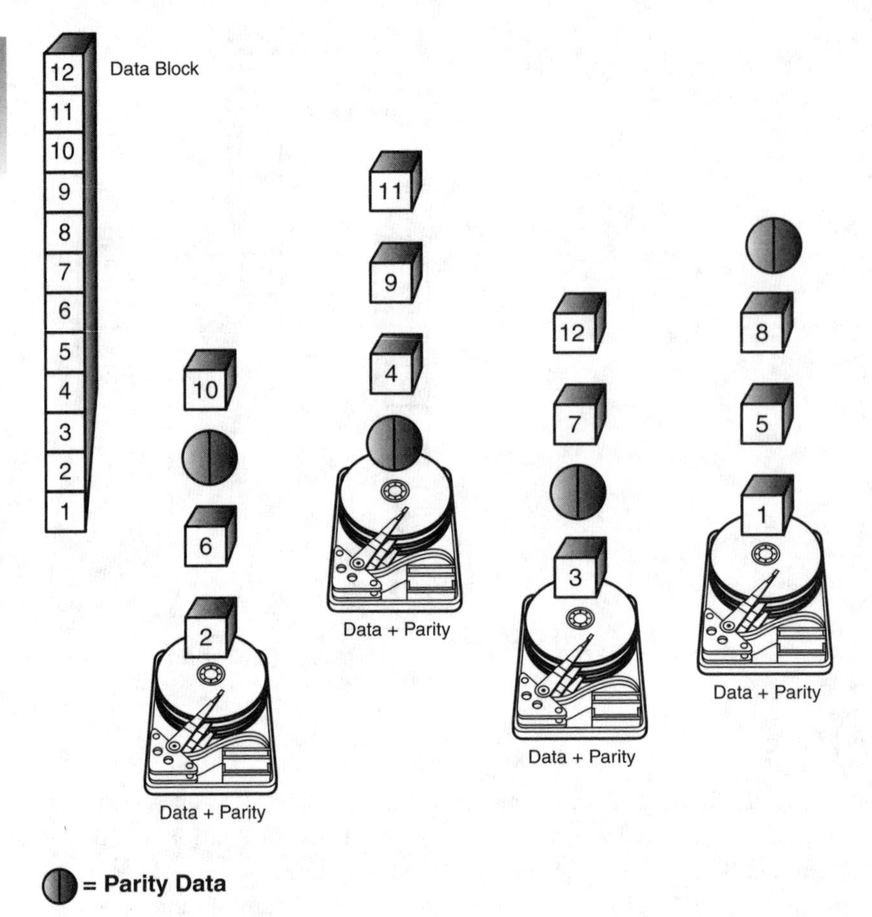

If any of the drives in the array fail, the data isn't lost because it can be reconstructed using one data stripe and one parity bit. If two or more drives in a three drive RAID 5 array fail, the entire array and all the data on it is lost.

If you are even considering RAID for your gaming system, RAID 0, RAID 1, or RAID 0+1/10 are the only options you should consider.

Software Versus Hardware RAID

Although it used to be the case that RAID could only be implemented using a special controller card, it is now possible to RAID drives together using your OS and no special hardware. For RAID 0 and RAID 1 this is fine because very little computational power is needed to split up data into stripes or duplicate blocks. However, for RAID 5, significantly more computational power is necessary to generate and write the parity bit.

Today's CPUs are fast enough to handle even RAID 5 without offloading the calculations to a separate controller. However, because RAID 5 is usually implemented in systems that need every single CPU cycle free, it is rare that you see a card offer RAID 5 support without a special CPU on the card to handle the generation of parity bits. One such CPU is the Intel 960 processor that is commonly found on many RAID 5 cards.

Most of the RAID controllers found on desktop motherboards are actually "software" RAID controllers meaning that they don't offload any of the calculations from the host CPU; your CPU handles all the processing for the array. This is in spite of the fact that these solutions are often called "hardware" RAID. The only benefit they offer is that you can boot off a RAID array controlled by one of these chips, whereas you cannot boot off a RAID array created using Windows 2000's built-in RAID functionality.

IDE RAID

Originally very high-end workstations and servers only used RAID, so it was reserved for SCSI drives only. Most recently, with prices on IDE hard drives dropping to very low levels, and the motherboard industry becoming increasingly competitive, many motherboard manufacturers have implemented IDE RAID controllers on their motherboards.

The benefits of RAID extend to IDE drives just as they did to SCSI drives. The only difference is that the majority of these on-board RAID controllers are still software-based controllers (meaning your host CPU handles all calculations) and only really enable you to boot off the RAID array (see Figure 7.13). There's nothing wrong with that—you just have to learn to not believe the marketing when many of these solutions are marketed as "hardware" RAID.

Some manufacturers have even produced true hardware IDE RAID add-in cards such as Promise and AMI (see Figure 7.14). These cards are generally much more expensive and offer much more flexibility than the on-board solutions. Their price point keeps them from being reasonable solutions for a gaming system where disk performance isn't too important, and it also somewhat defeats the purpose of opting to use IDE hard drives in the first place.

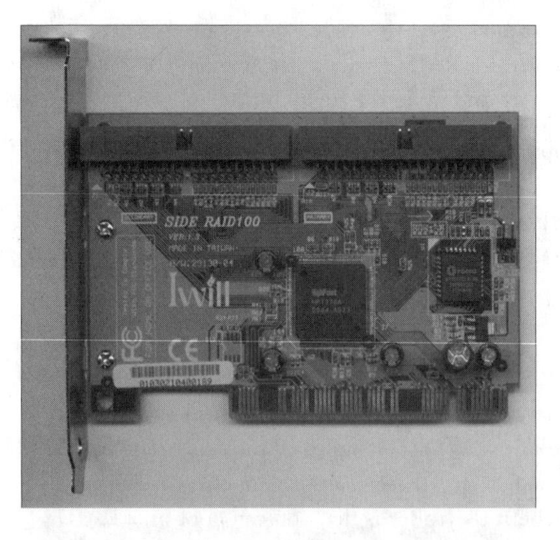

FIGURE 7.13
Iwill's SIDE RAID100 is an IDE RAID controller that relies on your CPU to handle all the RAID calculations.

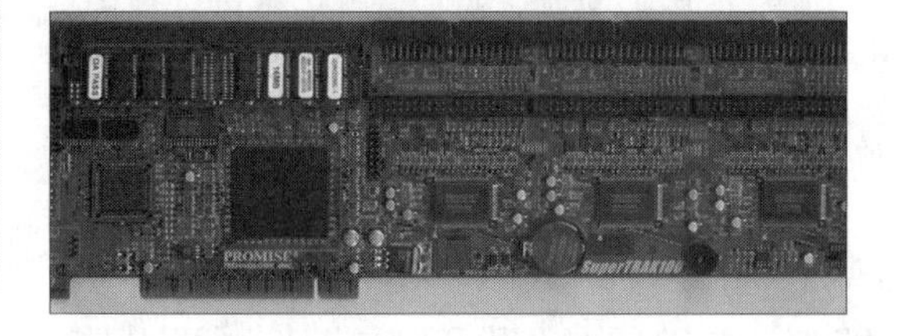

FIGURE 7.14
The Promise SuperTRAK100 is a hardware-based IDE RAID card and uses the i960 processor to handle all array calculations.

RAID Controller Cards

RAID controller cards are fairly easy to find and it is not much of an art to pick which one is right for you. The main things to look at are which RAID levels are supported, which features are supported in the controller's on-board BIOS, as well as any other unique features that the card has.

Some RAID controllers (usually the higher end ones) are sold as "caching" RAID controllers and usually contain a bit of memory or the potential to add memory on the actual RAID controller itself. What this does is give you another "level" of cache between the rest of the system and the drive array. This cache acts much like the cache/buffer on the drives except it buffers reads/writes to the RAID array itself, thus helping to improve performance.

Recommendations for RAID

As I mentioned in the performance section, as a gaming system your computer has no reason to implement an overly elaborate RAID setup. The only time RAID would make sense is if your motherboard happened to have an on-board RAID controller that you wanted to take advantage of. In that case, RAID 0 is fine, as is RAID 1. Some on-board controllers even support RAID 0+1/10, so if you really want to go overboard you can setup a four drive RAID array in that case.

A two drive IDE RAID array with some relatively fast IDE drives can speed up performance in most disk intensive Windows applications such as MS Office, general usage, and so on by 10%–20% easily. Just don't expect them to make a world of difference while playing *Arcanum*.

Optical Storage

Up to this point the type of storage I've been talking about has been entirely magnetic based storage. The next major type of storage that I discuss is optical storage, where data is stored and read back using lasers instead of magnetic pulses and electromagnetic fields. A few drives are built around the principles of optical storage. The main ones I talk about here are CD-ROM, CD-R/RW, and DVD-ROM drives.

In optical storage, although the performance characteristics are measured similarly to the magnetic hard drives I just finished explaining (for example, latency is still latency, seek time is still seek time), the internal mechanics of an optical drive are obviously different from those of a magnetic hard drive. However, the similarities extend much further than you would expect.

For example, in a hard drive you have multiple platters spinning courtesy of a spindle motor. In an optical drive the media (whether it be a CD-ROM disc, or a DVD disc) is spinning courtesy of a spindle motor as well. The reason for spinning the media is the same as it was when dealing with magnetic hard disk storage; data is stored on the platter (or in this case the CD or DVD) in concentric circles called tracks. To read all the data on a single track either the media must spin or the device reading the data must rotate along the track. It turns out that it is not only cheaper, but also easier to make a mechanism that limits the movement of the device that reads/writes to the media (called a head) and simply make the media spin.

The head in an optical storage device isn't anything like the head in a hard drive, in that it doesn't fly over the surface of the media. Instead the device that actually reads the data is completely stationary. The way optical storage works is by a laser reflecting off of a mirror and into a lens that focuses it on the part of the media being read. Depending on whether or not data is actually stored there, the laser light reflects back in a certain way. This reflected light is then captured by a device that converts the optical signal into an electrical one, at which point the value of the data stored at that point on the track of the media is translated from an optical signal to an electrical signal representing binary digits.

The tracking mechanism on the optical drive moves the focusing lens (also known as the pickup lens) from the inside of the media to the very outer edges of it. If you haven't already noticed the parallel, this is much like the actuator arm in a hard drive, except instead of moving the whole "head" it is only moving the part that focuses the light on the media.

After the optical "head" has read the data, the process is identical to what happens when data is read off a platter on a hard drive. The data is sent to an on-board buffer and from there it is sent out to the controller to which it is attached, and then to main memory or the CPU or whatever part of the system happened to request the data that was read off the drive.

So the fundamentals of optical storage are pretty much identical to that of hard drives with a few quirks. Now let's get into some of the details behind the major types of optical storage drives you run into when building your gaming machine.

CD-ROM Drives

By now you know the acronym for ROM is Read Only Memory, and if you've listened to music in the past decade you know that the acronym CD stands for compact disc. Putting those two acronyms together gives you a hint at what the biggest shortcoming of CD-ROM drives happens to be: After data is written to them, it cannot be erased.

The way data is placed on a CD is by actually etching a pit into one of the layers on the CD media that are in the recording device. After this pit is etched into the media, it cannot be "un-etched," it is there for the life of the media. Now you can purchase drives that actually do the recording for you (they don't etch the media, but I explain how they record in the CD-R/RW section later in this chapter), but when you're dealing with a plain vanilla CD-ROM drive all it can do is read data off a CD.

The main performance measurement characteristic when it comes to CD-ROM drives is the peak transfer rate the drive is capable of attaining when reading data off a CD. Remember that CDs became popular in the music world before they were used as application/data storage on PCs. So when reading the audio off a CD there was no benefit to reading it any faster because it would always play back at the same speed. The standard set for CD audio dictated that the transfer rate that an audio CD player must sustain to properly play back the music is 150KBps. This became unofficially known as a 1X CD-ROM drive. Compared to the 40,000KBps that some hard drives transfer at, you can see that you're dealing with some very low transfer rates.

In the early days of CD-ROM drives, the motor that spun the CDs inside the drive operated at a variable speed. To understand the reasoning behind this you have to look at how a CD's tracks are laid out (see Figure 7.15). If you lay out the inner most track on a CD in a straight line, it would be around 5.7 inches long. If you do the same with the outer most track on a CD it would be around 14.4 inches long. So more data can be stored on the outermost track than on the inner most track. However, if you spin a CD once so that it makes a full revolution, it takes the same amount of time to get from start to finish on the innermost track as it does to get from start to finish on the outermost track of a CD. This means that the CD-ROM drive would read much more data in a single revolution the further away it got from the center of the CD it was reading.

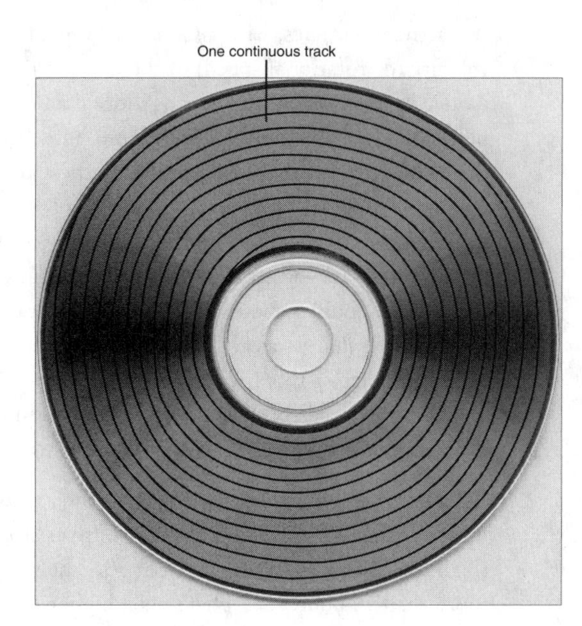

FIGURE 7.15
As you can see, the innermost track on a CD is much smaller than the outermost track. Tracks on a CD are not actually laid out in individual circles like they are on a hard disk platter. CDs really have just one continuous track.

The earliest CD-ROM drives had trouble dealing with variable amounts of data being read per revolution, especially when the amount being read increased so much over the span of a few tracks. So these early drives simply slowed down their motors when reading further from the center of the CD and sped them back up when reading back towards the center again. This type of a CD-ROM drive is known as a *Constant Linear Velocity (CLV)* drive. With this drive the velocity of a line of track over the pickup lens never changes regardless of where you are reading from on the disk.

Obviously, this became an issue as CD-ROM drives increased in speed. Although it didn't make sense to make an audio CD player that transferred data at greater than 150KBps, it definitely made sense to make a CD-ROM drive that did so. This was the birth of 2X, 4X, and 8X CD-ROM drives. Most of these drives were CLV drives, but as the speed of the drive increased, so did the range of speeds the motor would have to maintain as the read mechanism moved back and forth along the CD. Around the time of 12X CD-ROM drives (that transferred at 12 times the original 1X standard: 12 × 150KBps = 1,800KBps) it became necessary to stop switching motor speeds and find a way to deal with the fact that more data would be read at the outermost tracks of a CD than on the innermost tracks. Hence the transition from Constant Linear Velocity (CLV) drives to *Constant Angular Velocity (CAV)* drives.

As the name implies, with a Constant Angular Velocity drive the angular velocity (or rotational speed) of the drive remains constant. As I mentioned earlier in this section, this means more data is read per second off the outermost tracks of the CD than in the innermost tracks. To properly describe this to the market that was purchasing these drives it became common to name a CD-ROM drive according to its maximum transfer rate along the outer edges. At this point in the history of CD-ROM drives it became common to see drives advertised at 18X MAX transfer rates, however an 18X MAX drive could sometimes have an inner transfer rate of 6X–8X. Considering that data on CDs is written from the innermost tracks to the outermost tracks, this became the reason for a lack of faith in advertised CD-ROM drive speeds because they would seemingly not improve performance much over previous CLV drives.

Today, CD-ROM speeds have pretty much reached their peak, with CLV drives virtually nonexistent and CAV drives stopping at around 50X (7,500KBps). Keep in mind that at 50X the rotational speed of the CD is at more than 10,000RPM! That's even higher than a hard drive in most cases.

Getting more performance by increasing the rotational speed of your CD-ROM drive is going to become more difficult, raising the need for another method of improving transfer performance.

SMP CPUs, RAID Hard Disks, and Multibeam CD-ROM Drives

One method of improving transfer rate is an approach taken by Zen Research in their Multibeam and Broad Beam Illumination designs. With these designs the goal is to simultaneously read from as many tracks as possible, thus increasing the overall transfer rate of the drive (see Figure 7.16).

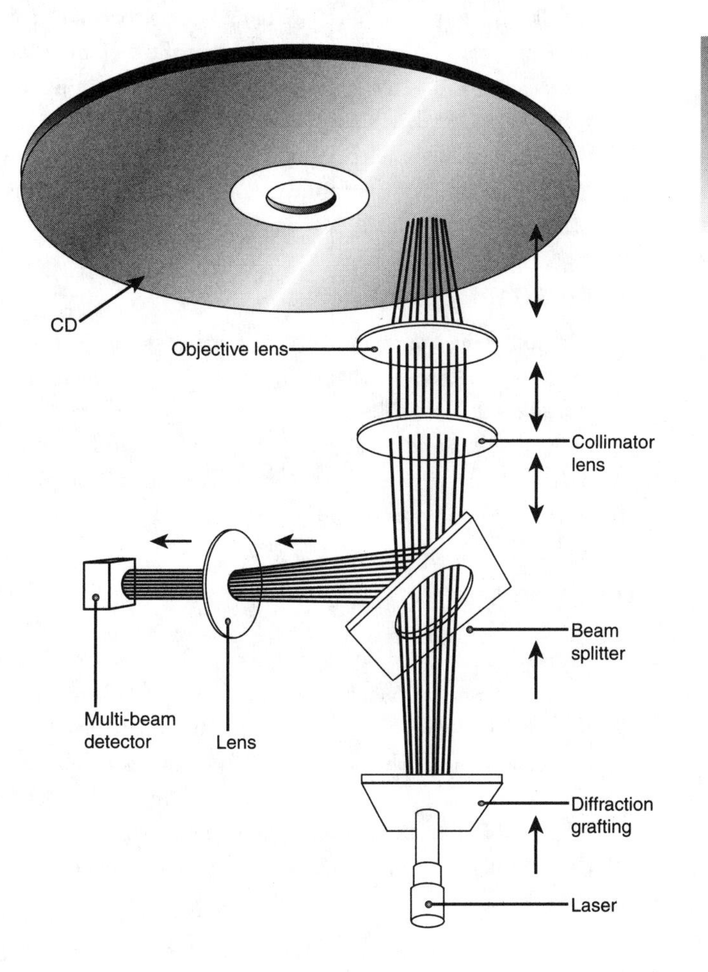

FIGURE 7.16
Zen Research's Multibeam Illumination technology increases transfer rates by illuminating more data at once.

This technology has been implemented in a few Kenwood drives, namely the Kenwood TrueX family of Multibeam CD-ROM drives. Unfortunately, reliability problems plagued most of the drives in that series.

For now, the relatively cheap price of CD-ROM drives and the transition towards writable CD drives, as well as DVD-ROM drives, has limited the attention that obtaining faster conventional CD-ROM drives had been receiving up to this point. If you are buying a regular CAV CD-ROM drive, ask around Internet message boards about reliability, noise generation (these things can get quite loud at 10,000+RPM), as well as overall comments about the drives before you purchase one. The performance parameters are the same as a hard disk. You want to look at the seek time specifications, transfer rates (inner and outer), and any other performance figures that are thrown at you. CD-ROM drives are also available in IDE and SCSI variants just as their hard disk counterparts. For more detail as to what all those terms mean, look back earlier in the chapter at the "Keys to Disk Performance" section.

CD-ROM Media

The following are two ways of measuring storage capacity on a CD: in minutes of CD-audio that can be stored or in megabytes of data that can be stored on the CD. Most CDs can store 74 minutes of CD-audio or 650MB of data, with some capable of holding 80 minutes of CD-audio or 700MB of data. Although these are much more rare, an even higher capacity CD can store 90–99 minutes of audio.

DVD-ROM Drives

Just as it was once thought that you would never need more than 640KB of memory, it was once thought that the 650MB of storage space on a 74 minute CD would be enough for all multimedia needs. As history has shown us so many times, this was eventually challenged and the need for a higher capacity optical storage medium was present. Although 80- and 90-minute CDs could offer more storage, it wasn't nearly enough for the type of quality that was planned on being stored on this new medium. This was the birth of the DVD.

The first debate that surrounded DVD, or Digital Video Disc or Digital Versatile Disc, was what the acronym stood for. Most of today's DVD supporters side with the latter because it is being used for more than Digital

Video, most just refer to it as DVD. You've already probably been bombarded with enough acronyms in this book to not have to worry about yet another one.

The way data is read off a DVD disk is identical to that of a CD so I don't go into detail there, but the way data is stored is slightly different enabling for its increased capacity.

The amount of data stored per track on a DVD has increased tremendously over the amount of data stored per track on a CD. The pits that are etched into the DVD are much closer together and thus require a much more precise laser to read them. The result of this is that DVD players reflect light with a shorter wavelength than CD players (650nm versus 780nm). This unfortunately means that DVDs cannot be read in CD drives. Most DVD drives, like the one shown in Figure 7.17, have a second laser that is used for reading CDs so it is rare that you find a DVD drive that cannot read a CD.

FIGURE 7.17
A PC DVD-ROM drive looks almost identical to a PC CD-ROM drive except for the lettering present on the drive indicating that it reads DVDs.

One of the biggest problems with media such as CDs and DVDs is a greater potential for damage to the data stored on the media. With a hard drive, you're never handling the platters, so the only damage that can be caused to them is dust accumulation or a head crash. However, with a CD or DVD you're constantly touching the surface of the disk. So, if some of the grease from your hands gets on it or if you happen to scratch the disk, it becomes more difficult for the laser to get an accurate reflection from the surface of the disk. To work around this problem, a lot of redundant data is written to CDs so that if a data read error does occur, usually some type of error correction mechanism is there to fix things and continue reading as normal. However, the error-correction scheme used on CDs is quite old and inefficient. The error-correction implementation on DVDs has been improved to the point where it is not only better than what is on CDs, but also occupies less space, offering more room for data storage.

The final increase in storage capacity comes from the capability of a DVD to be multilayered. In other words, the pits can be written to more than one layer on the disk itself. It is possible to have a single sided DVD with a single layer for data storage that is capable of storing approximately 4.5GB of data. A single sided DVD with two layers for data storage can hold approximately 8GB of data. A double-sided DVD with one layer for data storage can hold around 8.75GB of data, and a double sided/double layer DVD can store almost 16GB of data.

Unless a DVD drive has two lasers (one at the top and one at the bottom of the media tray), you have to flip a double sided disk to gain access to the other side where information is stored (see Figure 7.18). Access to data in another layer of one side of a disk is made possible by focusing the light differently on the disk.

Because a DVD is the same size as a CD, yet contains much more information, the transfer rate sustained when spinning a DVD at the same speed as a CD is much higher. A DVD spinning at 1X transfers 1,250KBps of data. That is a little more than what an 8X CD-ROM can deliver. It is common to have 4X, 6X, and 10X DVD drives, but they have not reached the spindle speeds of the 50X CD-ROM drives quite yet.

When looking at the performance specs of a DVD drive the same characteristics that apply to a hard drive and CD-ROM drive apply here as well. The only difference is that transfer rates are listed separately for DVDs and CDs because they vary in data density.

As the name implies, a DVD-ROM drive is a read-only drive just like a CD-ROM drive. The disks that are normally played in these drives can only be written to once and that's it.

FIGURE 7.18
A double-sided DVD disc. Both sides have data written on them, which leaves no room for a label on either side. Instead, the labeling is done on the center ring of the DVD.

Writable Optical Drives

All this time I have been talking about reading from CDs and DVDs, but it is very useful to be able to write to them as well. Writable and Rewritable CD drives have become very popular in recent times, and in the next year or so Writable and Rewritable DVDs will begin picking up speed as well. Whether it's for storing backups of audio CDs and DVD movies or for off-site data backup (a properly stored CD/DVD can have a very long lifetime), writable optical drives can be quite useful.

The way writable optical media works isn't by etching pits into a blank CD or DVD but by using a special intensity of light it changes the chemical composition of the data layer to either reflect or not reflect light (actually reflect less light). By doing this you actually simulate the process of light being reflected off the edges of a pit in a regular CD or DVD.

This works for write-once media, meaning that you can never delete the information off the disk. Rewritable media performs a similar function except by shining a different type of light on the disk the layer is restored to almost its original state. Obviously you have a limitation to the number of times this works before the disk is ruined.

CD-R

CD-R is the basic type of write once recordable CDs. These CDs are extremely cheap and can usually be purchased in bundles for a few cents per CD, making them almost disposable.

The media is usually sold according to capacity (74 minutes versus 80 minutes versus 90 minutes and so on) and speed rating (for example, capable of burning at 4X, 6X, 8X, 12X, and so on). The burn speed rating is usually ignored because most of the media that are available for purchase work fine at the most common burning speeds that are available.

In terms of burning speeds, they work the same way reading speeds work in terms of nomenclature. A 1X CD-R burns a full CD in 74 minutes, a 2X CD-R does so in 37 minutes, a 4X does it in 18.5 minutes, and so on. If you're not burning a full CD, the amount of time it takes decreases (a 1X CD-R can write 150KBps of data, 2X can write 300KBps, 4X can do 600KBps, and so on).

Around the time of 20X CD-Rs, companies started using *Partial Constant Angular Velocity (P-CAV)* technology to improve the burn speed towards the outer edges of the CD. Some 20X CD-Rs burn at 16X up to the first 32 minutes of the CD, and then gradually increase to 20X as you get further away from the 32-minute mark. Be sure you know if you're purchasing a regular CD-R or if the speed you're being quoted is a P-CAV speed.

Because data is burnt from the innermost tracks to the outermost tracks, you want to opt for a drive that has the highest speed on the innermost tracks.

One of the biggest problems with CD-R drives is what is known as a buffer under-run. In order for a CD to be properly burned the laser must never stop working until it is done burning the data. The data, of course, is coming from the drive's internal buffer. If the flow of data to the drive's internal buffer is interrupted long enough for the laser to be without data to write, even temporarily, the burn fails and you have a partially burned disk that is useless.

To get around this problem many drive manufacturers have implemented technology (the most common referred to as BurnProof) that enables the laser to effectively stop in mid burn until the buffer is full again and continue burning. This eliminates much of the dreaded buffer underrun.

CD-R disks can be read in almost all CD-ROM drives and audio CD players although some older ones have problems with the disks.

CD-RW

The CD-RW standard is the Rewritable CD standard that enables data to be rewritten to a CD-RW disk over and over again. However, eventually the disk loses reflectivity and you aren't be able to erase and start again.

Most of today's CD-R drives actually support RW as well, although their RW speed is usually lower than their regular recordable speed. When a CD-R/RW drive is advertised it is usually listed as a X/Y/Z drive. The X stands for the write speed, the Y stands for the rewrite speed, and the Z stands for the read speed. For example, a 16/12/40 CD-R/RW drive would have a 16X write speed, a 12X rewrite speed, and a 40X read speed.

CD-RW disks are a bit more expensive than CD-Rs, but have come down in price tremendously. However, because CD-Rs are so cheap they are almost disposable. That leaves little reason to use CD-RW.

Because of the nature of CD-RW disks, many drives don't read them because they don't reflect light well enough, although some newer CD-ROM drives read from CD-RW disks just fine.

Recordable DVD Formats

A number of competing recordable/rewritable DVD standards exist. I briefly go over them here as well as the potential candidates for future standards:

- **DVD-R**—Similar to CD-R disks, DVD-R disks are write once. Although, they cannot yet be full capacity double sided/double layered disks, they can be read in conventional DVD players.
- **DVD-RAM**—This standard doesn't work with current DVD players and provides 2.6GB of storage per side of a disk.
- **DVD-RW**—Don't let the name mislead you. This isn't the DVD counterpart of CD-RW. Instead DVD-RW is a rewritable standard that isn't physically compatible with normal DVD drives. This causes it to lose a good deal of industry support.
- **DVD+RW**—Currently DVD+RW appears to be the standard with the most promise as its single sided 4.7GB format is backwards compatible with current drives. The cost of drives and media is currently too high but, as time goes on that will change.

The Future of Storage

It is very clear that the type of storage present in today's PCs is quite crude at best. Every other internal of the computer that once had moving parts has been replaced by a faster, more efficient electronic counterpart. The future of the storage industry is almost inevitably headed in this direction as well. However, predicting when, where, and how is well beyond the scope of this book.

For now, any PC you build with gaming in mind should contain

- **7200RPM IDE hard drive**—Although you can get more storage at a lower price with a slower 5400RPM drive, those drives are slowly being phased out. By far the most popular drives out today have a rotational speed of 7200RPM and give you the best bang (in terms of size and performance) for your buck. Remember that while a fast hard drive might not give you higher frame rates, it definitely makes your system feel a lot faster. When you're loading a level or just playing around in your OS, you're mostly bound by your hard drive. Unfortunately, 10,000RPM+ drives are currently limited for more expensive SCSI solutions, otherwise they'd be a solid performance recommendation.
- **CD-R/RW/DVD+RW drive**—In the early to mid 1990s the quest for the floppy replacement was in full force. Companies like Iomega and SyQuest thrived on this idea that everyone was looking for the faster, cheaper and larger replacement for the 3.5"/1.44MB floppy drive. Although not officially dubbed as such, the writable CD ended up assuming the role. Today blank CD-Rs are so cheap that you don't mind burning a few for your friends and throwing one or two away doesn't do an ounce of harm. Looking towards the future, even the 650MB–800MB you can store on a blank CD-R or CD-RW isn't enough; with technologies such as DVD+RW set to take off over the coming months, make sure you have a drive that can write to one or more of these formats. If you really do a lot of copying, it doesn't hurt to have a DVD reader in addition to your recorder.
- **USB 1.0/2.0 controller**—USB 1.0 controllers are essentially free on every motherboard as they are integrated into virtually every South Bridge. This is very important as USB peripherals are so very dominant in the market that you shouldn't be caught dead without support for them. Looking towards the future, USB 2.0 support becomes the standard and if you're big on digital video (DV) today, having an IEEE-1394 controller wouldn't hurt either as it is the high-bandwidth DV interface of choice today.

Chapter 8

Networking: Gamers Unite

Networking and Multiplayer Gaming

So far I've introduced you to the internals of your next gaming PC, but one of the best parts of PC gaming is the multiplayer aspect. With a console system your only options for multiplayer (although this is changing somewhat with the most recent generation of gaming consoles) were to have a bunch of friends over and maybe play two or four player cooperative matches. The idea of each individual player being able to have his own screen, sound, and game settings has been unheard of in the console industry. However, with each player in a multiplayer game on the PC being able to have their own computers, they can configure their screens the way they want, they can have their sound as loud or as quiet as they want, and they can have their game set to be extremely high quality or extremely high performing on their systems. These are the beauties of multiplayer gaming. The biggest downside of course is with a console you simply plug in another controller and all is well. With a PC, however, you have to enter and understand the wide world of networking, something that can be more intimidating than it actually is if you understand all the concepts behind it.

Put simply, a network in the technological sense is a collection of devices that are able to communicate with each other using dedicated pathways. Think of a network of roads that connect individual buildings in your city. Now replace the buildings with computers and you can understand what a PC network is like. You can even consider the components on the inside of your PC to be "networked" with one another using a series of pathways known as buses (such as the PCI bus, the Front Side Bus, and the memory bus). At the same time, one of the biggest shortcomings of the internal network that all PCs have is that these networks aren't necessarily compatible with one another. You can't put an Athlon CPU in a Pentium 4 motherboard (even if you could get the CPU to fit) because the AGTL+ Front Side Bus would not be able to communicate with the Athlon, which requires an EV6 FSB interface.

Using the road analogy, you can consider a small town to be composed of a local network of roads, the computing parallel being a Local Area Network (LAN). A large collection of these local road networks connected together can form a much larger network of roads with a wider spread, again the computing parallel being a Wide Area Network (WAN). For now, think of the Internet as a Wide Area Network, while the network of your PC and your friends' PCs is a LAN.

In the first part of this chapter I focus on a type of Local Area Network, small networks of a few PCs connected to a single device such as a router or a hub (if you don't know what those two terms mean, don't worry, I explain). In the latter half of the chapter I explain in greater detail what a Wide Area Network is.

For a network of PCs to work, it would have to be designed around the fact that many types of PCs are connecting to this network, running various operating systems, and potentially running different types of microprocessor architectures as well. In order for a Network protocol to succeed, it would have to be widely supported and accepted; it would have to be a standard. Luckily, such a specification exists—Ethernet. Ethernet is a specification for a type of Local Area Network. If you can imagine how difficult it would be for people if not all roads worked with all cars, you begin to appreciate exactly what Ethernet can offer.

Introducing Ethernet

By far the most common type of computer network today is an Ethernet network. The Ethernet standard boils down to a specification that governs the connection of two or more devices (not necessarily computers) using cables known as Ethernet cables. Ethernet has many flavors and for simplicity's sake let's only focus on the most popular two: 10BASE-T and 100BASE-T Ethernet. Unless you've got an exorbitant budget, any network you build at home makes use of one of these standards.

When it comes to Networking, the Ethernet spec is the layout for the roads that are connecting the networked computers together. What happens to the data that is traversing these roads is governed by another protocol, but for all intents and purposes you can think of Ethernet as being the roadway system for our network.

When you have the roads in place you have to be able to know what can travel over these roads. Outside your house or apartment, obviously, you see a bunch of cars and trucks. In the Ethernet world traffic travels in the form of packets. An oversimplified explanation (the full architecture is beyond the scope of this book), this is one of the few times that the name assigned to a computer term isn't misleading. A packet is exactly what you think it is: a bundle of information.

This bundle of information contains the following:

- The data being sent
- Where the data is being sent
- Where the data is coming from
- Some error checking code

Among other things, the purpose of the error checking code is to make sure that the data being sent does reach its destination in an unchanged state. After all, sending a 1 if it's going to end up looking like a 0 at the other end of the line is pointless.

In terms of size, packets are generally no bigger than 1KB. When data is sent from one computer to another via an Ethernet network the data is broken up into packets and sent down the Ethernet cabling to the other computer at which point the packets are reassembled. When reassembled, the packets are checked for consistency with what was originally sent (error checking and correction). If all is okay the data is reconstructed.

A few issues are worth mentioning and discussing here. First of all, keep in mind that the transfer rate (bandwidth) and latency (how long it takes to get from Computer A to Computer B) determine the usefulness of an Ethernet network. This is where the two flavors of Ethernet, 10BASE-T and 100BASE-T, come into play.

The length data that has to travel inside your PC is generally pretty controlled. Although some traces can be quite long, you usually don't have to worry about your data having to travel miles to get from your memory to your CPU. That isn't necessarily the case with an Ethernet network; therefore, the speed that data transfers through the network is quite important and is dependent on the type of cabling used in the network. The type of cabling commonly used by both 10BASE-T and 100BASE-T Ethernet is what is known as Category 5 (CAT 5) twisted pair copper wire. Data can propagate through the network at close to 180,000kmps over CAT 5 cabling. That's almost 396 million mph. This governs the length of the cabling in a 10BASE-T or 100BASE-T Ethernet network, which is, theoretically, 100 meters. Generally, for a private LAN you shouldn't have to worry about cabling being too long unless you're trying to connect two rooms that are far apart in a very large house.

Now that I've established the ground rules, let's get into what the terms 10BASE-T and 100BASE-T actually mean. I've already informed you about the latencies associated with an Ethernet network. The longer the data has to travel across a cable the higher the latency is getting from point A to point B. Also, any other traffic it encounters along the way or any bumps in the road (for example, a poorly made cable, or one that has been repeatedly gnawed on by your dog) increases latency.

The next specification is the maximum transfer rate (cable length permitting), which is what I am talking about when I say 10BASE-T or 100BASE-T. The first number in the xxxBASE-T nomenclature indicates the transfer rate of the Ethernet network. In the case of a 10BASE-T network you'd be talking about a 10Mbps (10Mbps/8 = 1.25MBps) peak transfer rate with a 100BASE-T network you're talking about a 100Mbps (100Mbps/8 = 12.5MBps) peak transfer rate. The second entity in the term is the common word BASE, which refers to these two networks being baseband networks. A baseband network is one that transfers data only over a single channel between devices. The opposite is a broadband network where data is transferred across multiple channels on a single cable. This is accomplished by varying frequencies, but I save that discussion for the section "Getting Online," later in the chapter. The final part of the xxxBASE-T nomenclature is the -T, which signifies the type of cabling that the standard calls for. In this case the -T stands for twisted pair cabling (it is sometimes referred to as T4 because it uses four pairs of twisted wires). In the same sense, -TX stands for a different cabling requirement The main difference is that it calls for two pairs of twisted-pair wiring. More uncommon to home networks is -F which calls for fiber optic cabling.

The maximum transfer rate directly relates to gaming performance across a LAN. The higher the transfer rate, the more data that can be sent across the network, meaning the smoother the gameplay. In spite of this, 10Mbps is enough for most simple gaming LAN setups although a 100Mbps LAN can be helpful with larger multiplayer networks. There is much more to gaming performance over a network than simply peak transfer rates, but for that flip forward to the Setting up a Gaming LAN section.

Again you're blessed with a term that actually means what the name implies. Twisted pair cabling is used to reduce electromagnetic interference between wires; insulated wires are physically twisted around each other. Both members of a twisted pair are required to properly transmit a signal, but by using two wires to transmit the signal you can cut down on the interference that is picked up by the signal and interference with adjacent twisted pairs as well. Getting into the physics of why this happens is beyond the scope of this book, so just trust in the science.

From this point on I refer to 10BASE-T networks as 10Mb Ethernet and 100BASE-T (and -TX) as 100Mb Ethernet to keep things simpler. Notice that these are the more common names for both of the network types.

Obviously a higher bandwidth network enables more data to get through, but how much data do you really need to send between computers when playing a multiplayer game? Before I answer that question, you and I have to go a little further into the realm of networking to understand the various networking protocols.

Communicating Over the Network

The basis for communicating over an Ethernet network is a protocol known as *Carrier Sense Multiple Access with Collision Detection (CSMA/CD)*. This basic protocol states that all devices on the network listen for transmissions. If nothing is transmitting, a transmission can begin. In the event of two simultaneous transmissions, a collision occurs and the transmission pauses, after which it resumes with hopes that no more collisions occur. An excess amount of collisions over a network reduces network performance. Reducing traffic on the network or using more intelligent switching hardware are ways to limit the number of collisions.

The most popular protocol for transferring data across a CSMA/CD Ethernet network is TCP/IP. The reason for the slash in the name is because TCP and IP are actually two separate protocols, but by working together they can produce a very useful single protocol.

The Transmission Control Protocol

When you meet someone one of the first things you normally do is you stick your hand out and greet the person. The same is true when two computers want to communicate over TCP/IP. The Transmission Control Protocol (TCP) can be thought of as the handshake maker.

When one computer wants to send data to another, TCP establishes a handshake between the two computers. Technically this handshake is obtained by sending a command from the first computer to the second, sending a command received back to the first, and a handshake established notification to the second computer.

TCP plays a very important role in communication over TCP/IP as it guarantees reception of data. Imagine landing at an airport that you've never been to, in a city you know nothing about. Somewhere in the airport there is a driver waiting for you; the driver knows nothing about you and as far as he is concerned, there are hundreds of other people that could very well be you. Now instead of thinking of an airport full of people to understand the fundamentals of network data transmission, imagine an area full of packets. Dedicated links through which only a specific type of data is sent do not exist; packets are broadcast over the network with a bit of information about where they are going and are sent on their way. Packets are continuously sent over networks meaning that whatever organizational structure (protocol) they follow to ensure they get to their destinations is critical to proper operation of the network. Without getting into the specifics of it just yet, the "IP" part of the TCP/IP protocol is the packets' travel agent. It finds out where to send the packets and ensures that the packets get sent. But what about guaranteeing reception? Although sometimes it seems as if travel agents don't care if you get to your destination, making sure that these packets arrive at their destinations is again, very important. If a large percentage of your packets don't make it through when you're in the middle of a fire fight in *Unreal Tournament*, your movements seem choppy. You might even get stuck while the person you were shooting is now staring at your character's motionless body stuck in mid air and decides that it's time for the rabbit to attack the wolf. This (not the process of you getting killed in *Unreal Tournament*) is known as *packet loss* and is generally measured in the percentage of packets that make their way through to their destinations. Any significant amount of packet loss is negative and can lead to serious network performance issues. I discuss packet loss and how to avoid it later in the section "Network Performance."

This is where the other half of the TCP/IP protocol comes in—the Transmission Control Protocol (TCP). If IP is the travel agent, TCP is the guide to make sure that the packets actually reach their destination and that they are unchanged from their original state.

Other network communication protocols, such as UDP and IPX, are used less frequently than TCP/IP, but they all accomplish the same basic task. Certain games do require protocols other than TCP/IP to properly work with multiplayer setups such as Westwood's *Red Alert 2* that requires IPX (Internetwork Packet Exchange) to work on a private LAN. The reason for this in Westwood's case was because they wanted all online multiplayer capabilities to have to go through their own Westwood servers where they could monitor who was playing and make sure that they had a valid CD serial number. If Westwood had enabled users to play via TCP/IP it would enable direct connections between players on the Internet, which is definitely not what Westwood wanted in that case.

The Internet Protocol

The Internet Protocol (IP) can be thought of as a traffic director. It takes a packet, prepares, it and sends it on its merry way. However, it does not guarantee that it reaches its destination. As soon as the packet leaves, the Internet

Protocol could care less; its job is done. This is why the Internet Protocol must work together with another protocol (for example, Transmission Control Protocol) to ensure reliable data transfer. As I mentioned before, sending a 1 is pointless if the receiving end gets a 0 or nothing at all. How does the IP know where a particular packet must end up? To answer this question you have to look at how devices are identified on a network. As shown in Figure 8.1, a piece of hardware is in each device that acts as a communications controller for the network. These controllers are commonly referred to as Ethernet controllers, or when installed in PCs they are usually called Network Interface Cards (NICs).

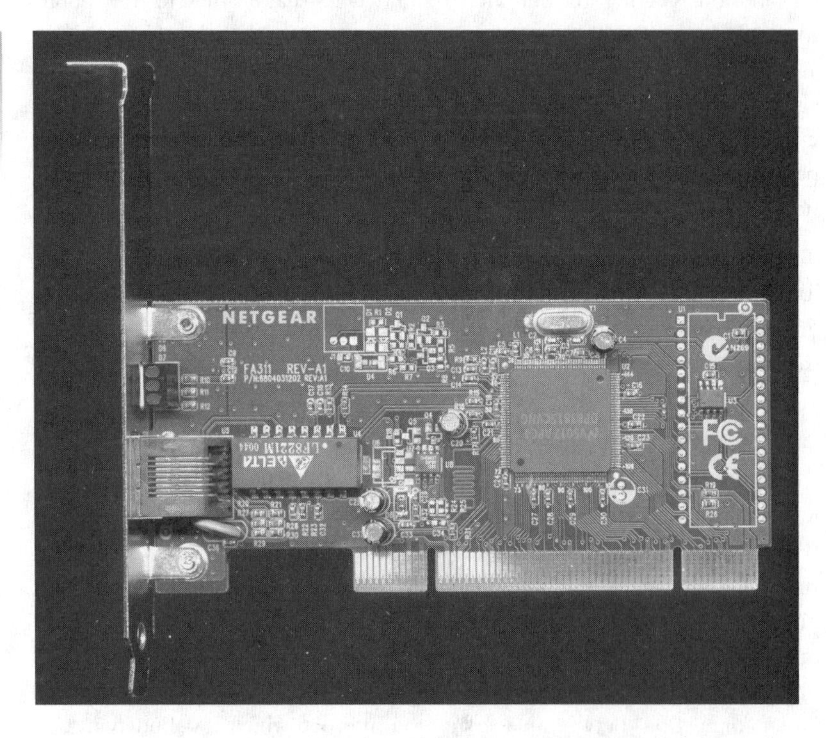

FIGURE 8.1
Network Interface Cards provide a PC with a connection to the rest of a local area network.

Each Ethernet controller or NIC (to keep things simple I only use the term NIC from now on) has a special code placed on it during manufacturing known as the *Media Access Control (MAC) address*. This address is unique to that piece of hardware and is generally left unchanged unless you consciously do it via some software configuration options. This MAC address is what can identify a single device on a network. It ensures that when you're on a network, you don't receive someone else's data.

Now IP doesn't understand a MAC address, but it understands an IP address. So when dealing with an IP network, all the devices on the network are assigned IP addresses. The only stipulation here is that no two MAC addresses can share the same IP addresses. For example, the MAC address of a NIC in a computer on a LAN could be 00-20-78-C5-0D-BF while the IP address corresponding to that MAC address could be 192.168.1.100. In the aforementioned case, another computer with a NIC whose MAC address was 00-20-78-C5-0D-BE could not share the same IP address, although it can have more than one IP address that references that MAC address. This is just like having a telephone number. You can have multiple phones forward calls to one telephone number, but you cannot have two individuals in two different places with the same exact telephone number (hence the creation and use of area codes to separate the two).

This also means that to communicate over an IP network, you need to have an IP address assigned to the device/computer you are using to communicate. This IP address can either be manually allocated to you or you can use another protocol known as Dynamic Host Configuration Protocol (DHCP) to assign you an available IP as necessary (provided that the network is setup for DHCP). Most of the time, using DHCP makes the most sense if the network you are on supports it.

In terms of valid IP numbers, the range from 0.0.0.0 to 255.255.255.255 is valid, but just like a mailing address no two devices can be assigned the same IP address. So for private networks (such as your personal gaming LAN) the ranges 10.0.0.0 to 10.255.255.255, 172.16.0.0 to 172.31.255.255, and 192.168.0.0 to 192.168.255.255 can be used.

Let's take a step back and look at the nature of IP addressing. The protocol used today to determine valid IP addresses is the Internet Protocol Version 4 or IPv4. This protocol enables unique identifiers, known as IP addresses, to be assigned to all computers on the network. IPv4 uses 32-bit IP addresses meaning that it can theoretically support up to 4,294,967,296 IP addresses. These IP addresses are divided into four 8-bit, three-digit numbers separated by periods. An example of such an address is: 192.168.1.1. To get around the limited number of IP addresses available in IPv4, the ranges that I mentioned before were specified as off-limits for public networks. This means that no Internet site has the IP: 192.168.0.10, only private LANs can use those IPs.

Connecting It All Together

As I mentioned before with the 10Mb and 100Mb Ethernet networks, the most common type of cabling is CAT 5 twisted pair. The most common type of connector used on these cables is known as an RJ-45 connector. The prefix RJ comes from the word Registered Jack and the -45 indicates the type of connector. An RJ-45 connector looks a lot like the connector off a telephone cable, which is also a registered jack connector (RJ-11), except that it's wider (see Figure 8.2).

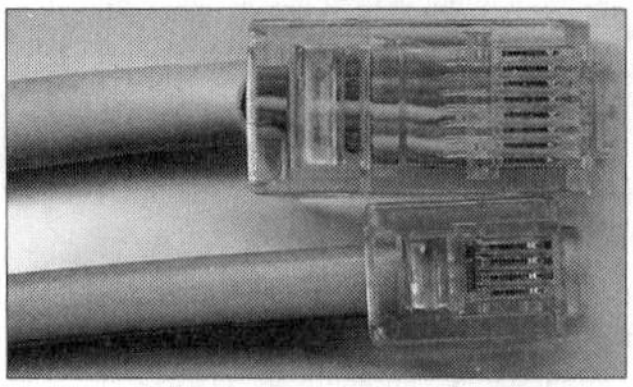

FIGURE 8.2
A RJ-45 connector (top) is much like a wider RJ-11 connector (bottom), except the cabling has considerably more shielding because data is being transferred at a much higher rate through it.

The RJ-45 connector has an 8-pin interface that contains the signaling pins for transmitting and receiving data across the cable. In the most basic type of network configuration, you can connect two computers via a single CAT 5 cable. The only requirement for this to work is that the send/receive pins have to be switched on one end of the cable. This type of a cable is known as a crossover cable because the send pins on one end of the cable are flipped to the receive pins on the other end and vice versa.

What's the point of a network if all you're going to do is connect two computers together? A true multiplayer LAN is one where you can connect more than two computers. But how do you do that if each NIC in a computer only has a single port? Obviously adding more ports to your NICs isn't the way to solve the problem because a network of five computers would require that each NIC have four ports on it. Luckily, another way to tackle this very problem is through the use of another networking device known as a hub.

A hub is a device that enables computers (or any kind of network enabled device) to connect to it and from there each individual device attached to the hub can gain access to everything else on the hub. This is much simpler than having a single port on a NIC for every computer you plan on connecting to your system in your network.

From an architecture standpoint, a hub is a very simple device. If the data comes in on Port 1 and needs to go out to Port 5 a hub ensures that it does.

The intelligent way to ensure that data coming in on Port 1 goes out on Port 5 is to have some sort of a processor in the hub that examines the packets coming in and directly forwards them to the appropriate port. A hub lacks this intelligent architecture, so it works by broadcasting the packets to all the ports. When the appropriate port is found the data is received by it. Because of the simplicity of the device, the more simultaneous accesses you have to a hub the lower performance you get out of it as a hub does not have any intelligent routing capabilities to help manage the load and direct traffic. At AnandTech an article was published that compared how a hub faired under load to the same setup under no load. When transferring 500MB of data over a hub from one computer to another on a 100Mb network, the hub realized a sustained transfer rate of fewer than 80Mbps. After you figure that about 20% of the performance is lost to I/O bottlenecks as well as driver/OS overheads, that figure sounds about right. However, with five machines transferring an even larger amount of data all at the same time the transfer rate decreased down to around 23Mbps.

In highly loaded situations a different type of hub (also referred to as a switched hub or a switch) is usually necessary to maintain high data throughput (see Figure 8.3). A switch actually looks at the packets being sent and makes sure that they get to where they are going in the most optimal way possible.

FIGURE 8.3
A switch such as the Netgear 10/100 switch pictured here is capable of more intelligently managing traffic across a network.

A switch has the hardware to determine for which port the packets were intended and will send them directly to that port rather than broadcasting them to all ports. Thus traffic is managed much more effectively on a switch. For example, in the loading test I just discussed, when a switch was used instead of a hub the performance did not drop at all when moving data from one transfer between two computers to five transfers between five computers. The reason behind this being that if you have five computers all broadcasting packets to all the computers connected to the hub, you will have a significant amount of collisions and it takes a lot longer for the data to get where it needs to go. Because a switch intelligently establishes direct links between ports for sending packets, each port is guaranteed the full bandwidth available from the switch. For example, on a 100Mbps switch, each port is capable of transferring at 100Mbps while on a 100Mbps hub the 100Mbps of bandwidth is shared among all computers connected to it.

Some switches have router functionality built in that aids them in their connection between multiple networks. Routers are generally present at the point where a connection to a WAN is served into a LAN (see Figure 8.4).

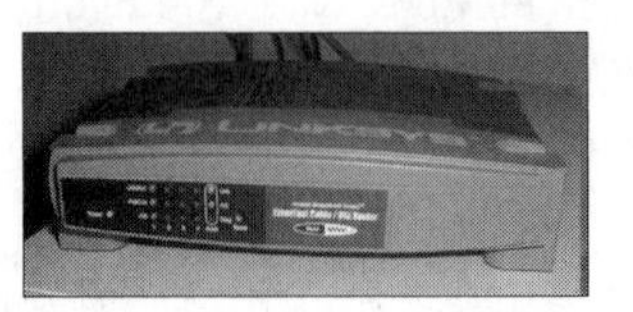

FIGURE 8.4
The Linksys Cable/DSL router pictured has an integrated 4-port 10/100 switch.

The router shown here takes an incoming Internet connection and distributes it to all the computers connected to its integrated switch. This function is known as Network Address Translation (NAT). Routers can generally be thought of as more intelligent switches. They can perform analysis on what is the best route to get packets from one place to another as well. They also keep track of poor routes to avoid using them.

Hubs, switches, and routers are platform independent. As long as you have an Ethernet controller in your system you can connect it to any of these devices and they handle your traffic.

In terms of bandwidth, you deal with three basic types of hubs/switches/routers if you are looking to setup a 10Mb or 100Mb network. The first type is a 10Mb hub/switch/router that is only capable of accepting and delivering traffic at 10Mbps. Because most 100Mb NICs can be set to work in 10Mb mode, compatibility shouldn't be a problem. However, the performance is limited and you can never upgrade to 100Mb later without throwing away the device. The next type is a 10/100 device that is either autosensing (it detects whether transfers are occurring in 10BASE-T or 100BASE-T mode) or manually configurable to work with either 10Mb or 100Mb networks. These are the most common. One very deceiving thing that a lot of manufacturers of 10/100 hubs do is call the device a 10/100 hub with switch. However, they are referring only to the capability of the hub to "switch" between 10Mb and 100Mb modes (make sure to look for the word autosensing). The final type of hub/switch/router is a full 100Mb device, meaning it doesn't work with any 10Mb devices on the network.

Finally, another specification to look for in one of these devices is the capability of transferring in full-duplex or half-duplex mode. Full-duplex means that data transfers can occur simultaneously and use the full 10/100Mbps of bandwidth. Half-duplex does not have that simultaneous 10/100Mbps transfer. Full-duplex is especially useful in situations where you're pulling data off a computer while simultaneously writing data to the computer. A half-duplex hub would face quite a few collisions in this type of a situation.

Choosing the right one depends on your needs. For a basic gaming LAN even a 10Mb hub is sufficient. However, as soon as you want to start doing some large file transfers over the network, a 100Mb hub would make a lot more sense. A switch is nice to have although they are usually too expensive for the types of tasks for which you use them in a home environment. For the most part you can run a nice multiplayer LAN over a 100Mb hub and get some pretty good transfer rates out of it.

In terms of manufacturers, most switches and hubs perform within one or two percentage points of one another. You'd be better off worrying about which looks the coolest than worrying about one hub outperforming another. Be sure to understand how the hub or switch you're buying handles full-duplex traffic and 10Mb connections, and also what sort of warranties come from the manufacturer. A hub should at least come with a multiyear warranty—no reason why it shouldn't because they are relatively simple devices and have been perfected for quite some time now.

Specialty Networks

Obviously building a 100Mb LAN isn't the only way to get multiplayer functionality. One of the reasons why it isn't too appealing is because it can be expensive. With a good hub running at least $30–$50, a pair of NIC cards at about $20 each, plus the purchase of adequate cabling (which varies, but is potentially the most expensive part of the equation), it's not exactly a cheap way of getting connectivity between multiple computers. In addition, everyone does not have a room for a bunch of computers. Instead they are scattered all over the place. Running CAT 5 cables all over the floors and along the walls can be a bit unsightly. If you're in an apartment, you can't really drill holes in the walls to run your cables through to keep them out of sight, so what other options exist?

HomePNA

One of the most popular methods of low-cost LAN construction is using a standard set forth by the Home Phoneline Networking Alliance, or the HomePNA standard. The beauty behind HomePNA is that it can have transfer rates as high as 10Mbps (equivalent to 10BASE-T Ethernet) to be sustained over the wiring that's currently in your house, over conventional phone lines (for a cost of about $50–$100 for everything you'd need).

The way HomePNA works is by transmitting data over telephone lines at a higher frequency than regular voice and data (for example, DSL, dial-up modem, and so on). Remember when I mentioned that the BASE in 10/100BASE-T Ethernet stood for baseband? Well HomePNA is a form of broadband networking because multiple channels of data are transmitted over a single cable by varying frequencies of transmission. This way you can still use the regular phone lines for voice and data communication without interfering with network traffic across the lines.

Originally, HomePNA was only offered in a 1Mbps version. However, since then 10Mbps HomePNA has become much more popular. The benefit is no costs for any cabling or hubs because the ports and cabling have already been wired to your location. You simply plug in up to 25 devices to any telephone (RJ-11) outlets and connect to your computer using either an internal or external HomePNA adapter. The only costs associated with implementation here are those for the actual interface cards/devices themselves. HomePNA adapters are usually made available in USB or PCI card forms (see Figure 8.5). Remember, though, that with USB 1.0 or 1.1 you are limited by the bandwidth that it can offer, so don't daisy chain a USB HomePNA adapter off a chain with many other devices. It should be on its own channel, so it can get a full 12Mbps of bandwidth.

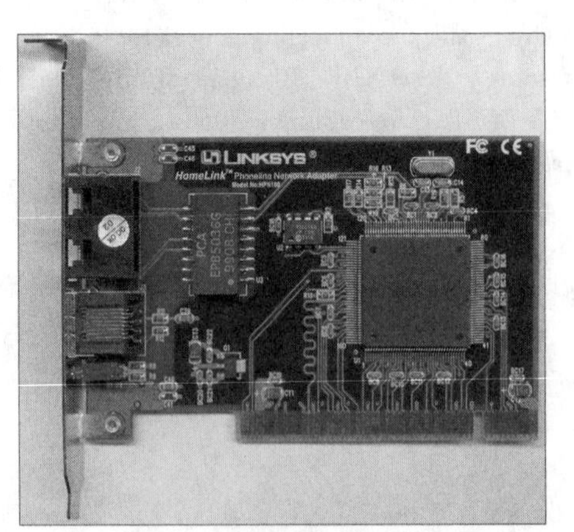

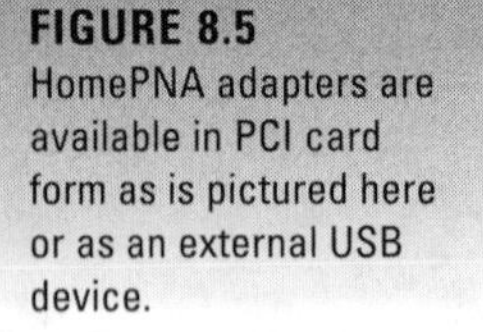

FIGURE 8.5
HomePNA adapters are available in PCI card form as is pictured here or as an external USB device.

The shortcomings of HomePNA are that if the quality of your phone line wiring is unusually poor you might not be able to sustain very high transfer rates, or you might not be able to connect at all. Also, it is very easy to eat up a lot of bandwidth on a HomePNA network as more and more devices are connected. An intelligent switching mechanism is not present in a HomePNA network, so if multiple computers are simultaneously transferring data then performance suffers tremendously. With a maximum of 10Mbps of bandwidth, it's easy to become bottlenecked by your network. Then you have the issue of compatibility. If your friends bring their computers over to your place for some multiplayer gaming, for example, and they don't have HomePNA adapters, they are out of luck. The same argument can be made for regular 10/100 Ethernet adapters though, although they are far more prevalent in the market than HomePNA adapters.

Wireless Technologies

The most elegant solution for a network would be one without any cabling at all, and in the past couple of years wireless networking has become more and more popular with the advent of technologies such as Bluetooth, HomeRF, and 802.11b (WiFi).

Bluetooth

The Bluetooth specification was finalized in July 1999 and has become a widely accepted standard for short distance wireless communication. Bluetooth operates at a 2.4GHz frequency and has been engineered to cause as little interference as possible with other devices that operate at that frequency (for example, cordless phones and microwave ovens).

Currently, Bluetooth offers data transmission rates of up to only 1Mbps; however, it is engineered for operation between 2Mbps and 12Mbps. With only 1Mbps of peak available bandwidth it is unlikely that Bluetooth becomes the gaming network connection of choice in its current state, especially for large multiplayer LANs with more than two computers.

With the current classes of Bluetooth devices, such as the USB Bluetooth receiver shown in Figure 8.6, transmission can occur up to 30 feet of unrestricted airspace (for example, no walls). A specification for higher class devices can also transmit up to 300 feet through walls; however, the more interference provided, the shorter the range is.

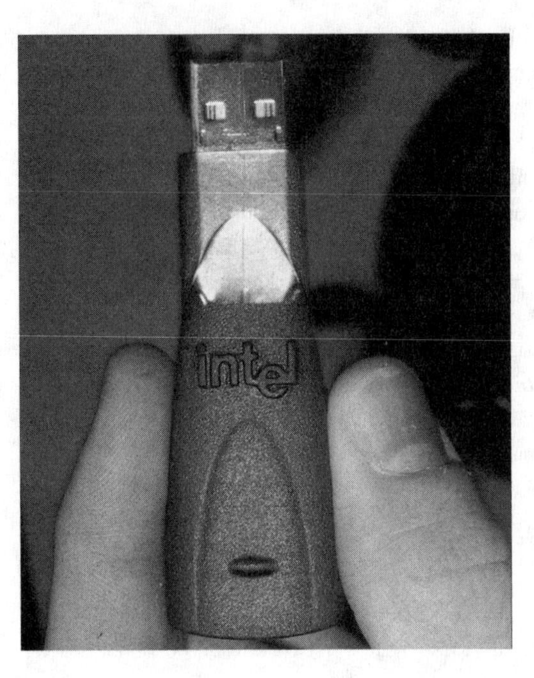

FIGURE 8.6
Its small size enables a Bluetooth receiver to be quite useful in applications such as mobile telephones. Imagine a phone that when placed near your computer would download any new contacts that were stored in your computer.

Bluetooth is great for synching portable devices to networks such as laptops and PDAs, but it will be a while before it is feasible for use as the basis for an entire network. Even over 100Mbps Ethernet, large file transfers (for example, transferring a game image across the network to another computer for installation—650MB) can take a bit of time. Imagine how slow it would be across a 1Mbps connection. Transferring just a 100MB file would take at least 13 minutes, but more realistically (factoring in driver/OS overheads) you can expect a transfer like that to take 20 minutes.

One function in which Bluetooth could be useful would be streaming music from the hard drive of a PC to a receiver in another room where it can playback and browse through your entire music collection. Sort of like a CD changer except a lot of our music ends up being stored on our hard drives and not on CDs.

HomeRF

Also operating at 2.4GHz, Home Radio Frequency, or HomeRF offers up to 1.6Mbps of bandwidth and is geared at the same market as Bluetooth, except it has a shorter range.

The receiver shown here can replace the conventional CD player in your home entertainment center. You would just store your music in a compressed digital format on your PC (for example, as MP3 files) and this receiver then streams the files from your computer's hard drive to its buffer where they would play through your stereo receiver speakers (see Figure 8.7). The display will show information about the file you are playing that is provided through its ID3 tag for example. Such information (if provided in the MP3 file itself) would include artist, track name and album name. HomeRF would be used as the transmission method to stream the audio from your PC to this device.

FIGURE 8.7
An example of an audio receiver that is made possible using HomeRF wireless networking.

As the name implies, HomeRF is really geared towards the home user market and isn't made for the intensive data transfers that a gaming network would require.

802.11b

By far the most popular wireless standard in large networks right now is 802.11b (see Figure 8.8). The reason is that 802.11b offers much higher transfer rates (up to 11Mbps, although theoretically up to 20Mbps if properly implemented). The standard operates in the same 2.4GHz frequency range as Bluetooth and HomeRF, but its bandwidth offerings make it the most attractive.

Currently the cost of 802.11b adapters (for example, PCI cards) are much more than a 100Mbps PCI Ethernet adapter. Even more expensive are the wireless access points (WAPs, shown in Figure 8.9) that play the role of a switch in an 802.11b environment. As demand for these products increases, the costs go down. We have already seen 802.11b setups decrease in price from close to $1,000 to a more reasonable $200–$300 range.

FIGURE 8.8
802.11b is quite popular with notebooks. Pictured is an 802.11b PC Card (a notebook peripheral interface standard) that enables notebook using authors to write outside of the house on a nice day while still remaining connected to the internal network.

FIGURE 8.9
The SMC unit on top of the Linksys switch is an 802.11b Wireless Access Point (WAP). It plugs into the Linksys switch below and acts as a device on the LAN; it gives all wireless devices access to all devices on the LAN.

From a performance standpoint, the 11Mbps potential of 802.11b is not often realized. Rarely do you see much more than 25% of that figure, and as you travel away from the broadcasting station, the transfer rates can drop even further. This leaves low expectations for competing wireless solutions, but as the technology improves, so do transfer rates.

The successor to 802.11b is 802.11a and it operates in the 5GHz–6GHz frequency range. This, combined with other enhancements, enables much higher transfer rates although it limits the range of the technology. For the most part 802.11b devices can span around 300 feet. 802.11a is promising transfer rates as high as 54Mbps, but has yet to be formally introduced in any products.

One of the largest drawbacks of 802.11b (and eventually 802.11a) is the cost of implementation which is currently too high for most home users (albeit perfect for corporate use). Again, as the technology improves, so does the price, but it is still in its infancy.

At this point wireless isn't really an alternative for gamers looking for a multiplayer LAN. In the future that surely will change, but for now I'd stick to conventional Ethernet networks or maybe HomePNA.

Setting Up a Gaming LAN

Now that you know about the technology, it's time to get into setting up your own LAN for multiplayer gaming. The first choice you have to make is what type of network you want this to be.

If you are going with a 10/100 Ethernet network you're going to need to have a hub, switch or router, NICs for all the PCs you have on the network, and the proper amount and type of cabling.

If you are going to implement a HomePNA network, all you need are HomePNA adapters and RJ-11 cables to go from the HomePNA adapters to your RJ-11 jacks. If you're going to be implementing any wireless elements you have to have a Wireless Access Point (WAP) and wireless access cards for all the PCs on your network.

Of course you can mix and match various parts of these network types in your network configuration. For example, you can have two NICs in your system, one connected to a 10/100 hub and another connected to a telephone jack for connectivity to a system in another room. Some HomePNA bridges can plug into 10/100 hubs/routers/switches as well.

I'm assuming that at this point you have all the hardware necessary to proceed.

Hardware Setup

Setting up the central part of your network isn't too big of a deal. For the most part all you have to do is supply power to your hub, switch or router (wireless or wired) and it should start working immediately.

The next step is to begin cable connection and wiring of your area. Keep in mind that usually one port on your hub (the same on a switch or a router) is shared with the uplink port. This port is used for connecting multiple hubs (switches, routers…from now on I'm only saying hub), and by using this port you disable the port with which it is shared. If you aren't using the uplink port for anything, you don't have to worry about this; just keep it in mind for future reference.

Plugging in the CAT 5 cables into your hub isn't much of a task either; they should click into place. You want to keep all CAT 5 cables away from areas with a high traffic of people. Just like your toes, CAT 5 cables don't like to be stepped on. They like to be kept straight and away from anything that might step or gnaw on them (pets included, unless you have friends that gnaw on cables too). Keeping them straight and out of harms way ensures that you get the maximum performance out of your cables.

After all your wiring is done the next step is to install NICs in all your computers. Installing a NIC is usually not too problematic and you're in even better shape if your NIC happens to have drivers built into the OS. This is the case with a lot of the NICs you encounter with the exception of most USB Ethernet adapters. Keep in mind that if you happen to have a USB Ethernet adapter connected to a 100Mb Ethernet network, you will never be able to transfer more than 12Mbps off that adapter because of the inherent limitations of USB 1.0. This doesn't apply, however, if you have a USB 2.0 adapter.

At this point all that is left is to plug your CAT 5 cables into your NICs (or plug your RJ-11s into the wall) and you should be good to go.

Note

To open Network Properties in Windows 9x look for a Network Neighborhood icon, right-click it and choose Properties from the shortcut menu. In Windows 2000, click Start, Control Panel, Network and Dial-up Connections, right-click Local Area Connection and then choose Properties.

Software Setup

The software portion of setting up a home LAN used to be a problem. To be honest, Windows networking was quite poor in the past; however, with the release of Windows 2000 things have gotten much better. Networking under XP has definitely improved as well.

But let's deal with the part that generally requires real help—setting up a network under Windows 98/Me. After installing your NIC, Windows most likely detects and installs drivers for you or it prompts you for a driver location (usually a floppy disc of CD-ROM provided with the NIC). After getting these drivers squared away, Windows installs the necessary networking components. Using the Network Properties dialog box shown in Figure 8.10, you can install protocols such as TCP/IP as well as IPX. You want to install these as your needs demand.

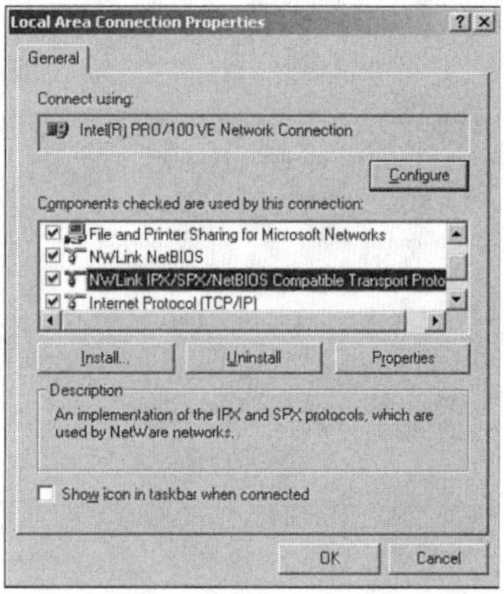

FIGURE 8.10
The Network Properites dialog box in Windows gives you control over all devices and protocols associated with your LAN.

Under the properties of any of the installed protocols you are able to set your IP address, subnet mask, gateway, and DNS addresses for the NIC that is installed in that machine. For a private network with no access to the outside Internet, you don't have to worry about the gateway or DNS addresses for that particular NIC (you can leave them blank) and your subnet mask can be calculated using a number of calculators available online. A subnet mask is one method to group together members of a network. The actual calculation process is beyond the scope of this book, but the easiest thing to do is assign your IP addresses in the 192.168.0.0–192.168.255.255 range where the subnet mask is 255.255.255.0 (see Figure 8.11). For example, one computer in your network can be assigned the IP address 192.168.0.1, the second one is 192.168.0.2, and so on. The subnet mask for all these IPs is 255.255.255.0.

Entry of these IP addresses and subnet masks is done in the network protocol properties sheet for the protocol you're modifying. The most common place is the TCP/IP properties sheet (in the Network Properties dialog box, click the TCP/IP listing for the device you wish to view/modify, and then click the Properties button).

You can pick your own network workgroup name, although it isn't necessary that all computers on the network be members of the same workgroup. Under Windows 2000/XP this is selected in the Network Identification tab of your System Properties sheet. To access System Properties, right-click the My Computer icon on your desktop (or Start menu in the case of Windows XP) and choose Properties (see Figure 8.12).

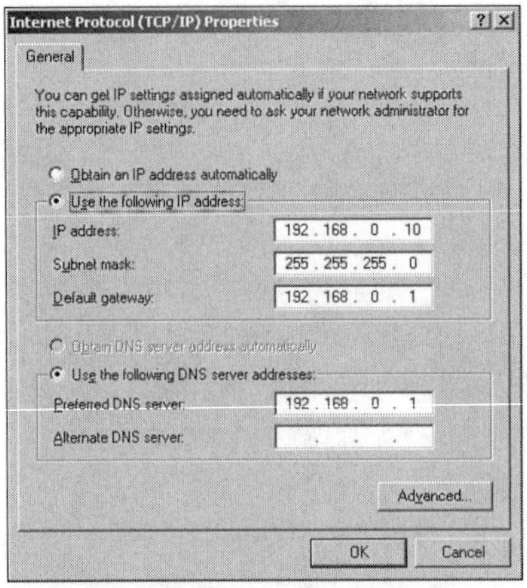

FIGURE 8.11
Use the TCP/IP Properties dialog box to configure Internet Protocol, DNS and subnet mask information for your network device.

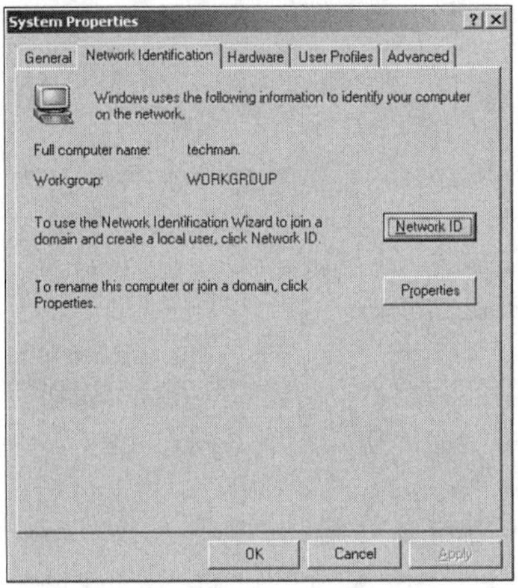

FIGURE 8.12
The PC shown in here is known as "techman" to the rest of the network and is a part of the "WORKGROUP" workgroup.

Tip

A quicker way to access System Properties in Windows is by hitting the Windows Key, and then Pause/Break, but don't tell anyone else about that.

This setup is identical under Windows 2000/XP except much less rebooting is involved and it is easier to connect to other computers, especially when dealing with file sharing.

If your PCs are all on the same network, have the proper protocols and all have IP addresses you should be able to play any multiplayer game that works over a private LAN.

Network Performance Issues

Just as with any part of your system, if your network isn't running properly your performance can suffer. In this case, a network performance issue can result in slow file transfers or choppy gameplay over your LAN. Poor network performance has many causes, but they all result in the same effect: packets not being able to get to their destinations in a speedy and reliable manner. As I mentioned before, when packets don't reach their destinations, it is referred to as packet loss.

Packet loss can occur because of poor cabling, and it is often one of the causes of degraded networking performance. If you ever get a chance to visit a datacenter where Web servers are hosted, notice that all the CAT 5 cables are neatly organized into bundles. You don't see any crimps in the cables themselves and they have enough slack that the cable is never being stretched to fit into a RJ-45 jack. These cables are *always* out of harms way; no one steps on them or accidentally tugs on them because they are tied up and run underneath the floor and along the corners of the racks that house the servers. Although you don't have to go to such extreme measures in setting up your own LAN at home, I can't stress enough how important it is to keep these cables away from any high foot traffic areas.

Although a much more rare case, performance can vary greatly from one NIC to another. Anything you can buy at the store, as long as it has proper driver support under your chosen OS, should perform fine. The real problems you run into are with NICs that are older and don't have proper driver support under your OS. I once had a NIC that would work fine under Windows 98, but the default drivers Windows 2000 would install caused the 100Mbps NIC to transfer at speeds below 0.5Mbps. This is by no means a recommendation to buy a major brand name such as Intel when looking for a NIC, but it's something to keep in mind when purchasing a NIC.

A saturated hub/switch is another cause of poor network performance. This generally happens when more than four or five computers are connected to the same hub (switches have much greater scalability) and are all transferring simultaneously. As I described in the earlier example from a test that was published at AnandTech, when five computers simultaneously executed transfers across the 100Mbps hub the network performance dropped to about 23Mbps.

The easiest way to diagnose this problem is to stop a few of the computers from accessing the network and see if performance improves. Note that your game running slowly over the LAN doesn't necessarily mean that you have a network performance issue; the server hosting the game or the game's network code itself could be the cause.

At the same time, it could be a combination of all three. No games require a 100Mbps network to work properly over a LAN. If a two-person network slows down on a 100Mbps LAN, even only on a hub, then it's more likely that either the server hosting the game or the game's network code is at fault. If slowdown doesn't occur with only two or three people playing, but with eight simultaneously, chances are that the bottleneck is either on your server or your network. If at that point moving to a faster computer for your server doesn't improve performance, the bottleneck is almost definitely in your network. You either have to upgrade to a faster network (from 10Mbps to 100Mbps) or move to a switch from a hub to rectify this situation.

Benchmarking your network performance can be done in many ways. You often come to the realization that your network will never perform at 100% of its potential. Seeing driver/OS overhead knock off about 20% of the theoretical maximum is common. This means that a 100Mbps LAN might end up running at a real-world peak of 80Mbps which is 10MBps. That's for a perfect setup LAN. With poor cables, a saturated hub/switch, or any of the other performance issues I've discussed here, you can expect performance to drop below that mark.

If you want to measure the performance of your network, utilities such as NetCPS are very useful. NetCPS runs on two computers on the network. This is a command line executable file that is run on one computer with a server switch and on the other computer with an ipaddress switch ("ipaddress" is the IP address of the server). The test measures how long it takes to send 100MB from the server to the client and gives you a performance reading according to that. Remember that tests like these do not take disk performance and other such bottlenecks into account, but if you have a bottleneck in your system that doesn't let you transfer at 80Mbps, you have some seriously slow hardware.

Getting Online

Up to this point all the discussions have been about the technology behind and the creation of a private LAN for multiplayer gaming, but what about actually connecting to the Internet for your multiplaying gaming fix? This is where baseband gets shoved aside and broadband networks become the popular solution.

The Internet is nothing more than a large WAN, meaning that it is nothing more than a large collection of computers that all happen to be communicating via the TCP/IP protocol. Although sometimes a direct route is between two computers connected to the Internet, for the most part getting from one point on the Internet to another requires multiple hops across various networks and computers. This is what gives the Internet its flexibility and its ability to exist on a global basis.

Have you ever wondered how someone in the United States can download a file from a server in Belgium? Or how your friend in Russia can transfer files with you when a direct line connecting your two computers is not available? Although there might not be a direct connection between Computer A and Computer B, they can communicate by sending data through a third computer, Computer C that is connected to both.

For example, by using a command called a Trace Route (tracert under Windows 2000/XP) I can see how many hops it takes to get from my computer in Raleigh, North Carolina to one of the servers of `www.quepublishing.com` (see Figure 8.13). The more hops (or networks) I have to bounce off before I get to the Web site I'm looking for, the longer it takes to get there. Luckily, each one of these hops happens to take between 10ms and 30ms, so it isn't that long of a wait for me.

```
C:\WINNT\System32\cmd.exe
Tracing route to quepublishing.com [63.69.110.193]
over a maximum of 30 hops:

  1    16 ms    16 ms   <10 ms  10.233.64.1
  2   <10 ms    15 ms    16 ms  24.25.1.125
  3    15 ms   <10 ms    16 ms  rdu26-33-161.nc.rr.com [66.26.33.161]
  4    15 ms    16 ms   <10 ms  24.93.64.93
  5    31 ms   <10 ms    15 ms  acr2-serial2-1-0-0.Raleigh.cw.net [208.174.17.12
9]
  6    15 ms    32 ms    15 ms  acr1-loopback.Atlantaald.cw.net [208.172.66.61]

  7    31 ms    16 ms    31 ms  ATM1-0.BR1.ATL5.ALTER.NET [204.255.168.73]
  8    15 ms    32 ms    15 ms  146.at-6-0-0.XR1.ATL5.ALTER.NET [152.63.80.118]

  9    31 ms    31 ms    16 ms  0.so-0-0-0.TR1.ATL5.ALTER.NET [152.63.9.225]
 10    31 ms    32 ms    31 ms  129.at-6-0-0.TR1.NYC9.ALTER.NET [152.63.0.114]
 11    31 ms    32 ms    31 ms  287.ATM7-0.XR1.EWR1.ALTER.NET [152.63.21.5]
 12    31 ms    31 ms    31 ms  193.ATM7-0.GW7.EWR1.ALTER.NET [152.63.24.197]
 13    31 ms    32 ms    31 ms  headland-media-gw.customer.ALTER.NET [157.130.19
.94]
 14    32 ms    31 ms    31 ms  63.69.110.193

Trace complete.

C:\>_
```

FIGURE 8.13
A Trace Route gives you an idea of how many hops it takes to get from one point on the Internet to another.

This introduces the issue of network latency, which is much more of a problem when playing games online than it happens to be in your private LAN. On your private LAN you don't have to worry about the connection being poor because if you set everything up properly, you should get a very high bandwidth and low latency connection between all the computers on your LAN. However, when online, you have to depend on the LANs all over the world and if any one of them is having any sort of performance issues your performance might suffer. Luckily, the routers that run the backbones of the Internet are intelligent and usually route traffic around problems if a problem router is down or overly congested.

Another issue that is present when dealing with Internet connections is bandwidth. Count on it being a while before you get the bandwidth of a 100Mb connection directly to your home as your Internet access connection. If you're really in the mood for extremely fast Internet access you can get something quite high in bandwidth such as a DS3 (same as a T3 line) that is capable of up to 45Mbps of bandwidth, but runs you a few thousand dollars per month at a minimum. The problem is that with limited bandwidth, a lot of network congestion, and unknown reliability and capacity of servers, playing games online can become a very frustrating ordeal when compared to playing over a private LAN.

Have you ever noticed lag while playing a game online? This could be caused by a number of things, all of which I have mentioned, including:

- Poor network latency
- Network congestion
- Insufficient bandwidth
- Servers that are simply bogged down with too many people trying to play at the same time

Do keep in mind, though, that the faster your Internet connection is (dial-up modem versus DSL or Cable), the less likely your Internet connection is going to be the cause of any of those problems. It also can make any serious lag when playing online less likely (assuming that your Internet service provider [ISP] has good connectivity to the location of the server on which you're playing).

So what kind of Internet connection should you pair up with your new blazingly fast system? You have a couple of options in theory, but in actuality you're lucky if you have all these options at your disposal.

Dailup Versus Broadband

In the past the most common form of accessing the Internet was through a dialup connection. The reason it was called this is because a device in your computer known as a Modem (modulator demodulator) would dial up a server using your phone lines and establish a connection with a server that would give your computer access to the Internet via your modem/phone lines.

There were a number of problems with dialup Internet access, including the fact that when connected, the phone line your computer was attached to would be busy; no phone calls could be made or received. A dialup Internet connection is essentially a baseband Internet connection because a single channel is being used to transmit data.

Performance was virtually nonexistent on dialup because of the bandwidth limitations of conventional phone lines at the frequency which voice was being transmitted. The fastest dialup modems ever got was 53Kbps, which was a peak transfer rate (you might have heard of this standard as 56K dialup, although it was limited by the government to 53Kbps). If you do the math on a peak connection speed of 53Kbps you realize that the greatest transfer rate you could ever attain would be 6.625Kbps, definitely not impressive.

Note

Also keep in mind that the numbers presented here are only for downloads. Uploads are limited to 33.6K, which is fine for Web browsing where you don't need to send out much information. However, uploads are critical to network gaming performance because you're constantly sending positioning data to the server.

As if the bandwidth offered by dialup connections wasn't already poor enough, network latency was often poor at best. This caused quite a bit of lag when playing multiplayer games. You've probably heard the term "ping" used before. That is the time required to send and get a reply from a particular host on a network (see Figure 8.14).

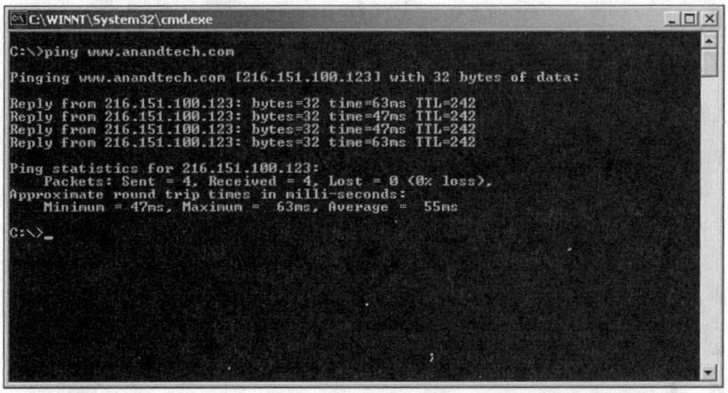

```
C:\WINNT\System32\cmd.exe

C:\>ping www.anandtech.com

Pinging www.anandtech.com [216.151.100.123] with 32 bytes of data:

Reply from 216.151.100.123: bytes=32 time=63ms TTL=242
Reply from 216.151.100.123: bytes=32 time=47ms TTL=242
Reply from 216.151.100.123: bytes=32 time=47ms TTL=242
Reply from 216.151.100.123: bytes=32 time=63ms TTL=242

Ping statistics for 216.151.100.123:
    Packets: Sent = 4, Received = 4, Lost = 0 (0% loss),
Approximate round trip times in milli-seconds:
    Minimum = 47ms, Maximum =  63ms, Average =  55ms

C:\>_
```

FIGURE 8.14
A ping is a quick way to test a connection to a server.

You can ping your own computer from another terminal (the command in most OSes is ping *ipaddress*, where *ipaddress* is the IP address of the host you want to ping). Ping is normally used in multiplayer games to refer to the network latency seen by your computer connecting to the server hosting the game. The higher this number, the longer it takes to get data back from the server. If a 500ms ping is between your computer and the server, it takes half a second (at least) to register a keystroke you sent to the server. In a first person shooter game this can be a problem where movements must be precise and instantaneous.

The solution to the performance issues involved with dialup Internet connections happens to be broadband Internet connections. I've already defined the term broadband, but what kind of broadband Internet connections are currently available? The two competing standards that currently exist are Cable and xDSL. Luckily more than one exists, because neither are available in all locations.

Cable

When you turn on your TV, multiple channels are available that can be sent to your TV over a single medium. This medium is the coaxial cable that connects to your TV or cable box (see Figure 8.15). It turns out that the same coaxial cable is capable of transferring bidirectional data at up to 30Mbps over a single channel. Welcome to the beauty of broadband Internet.

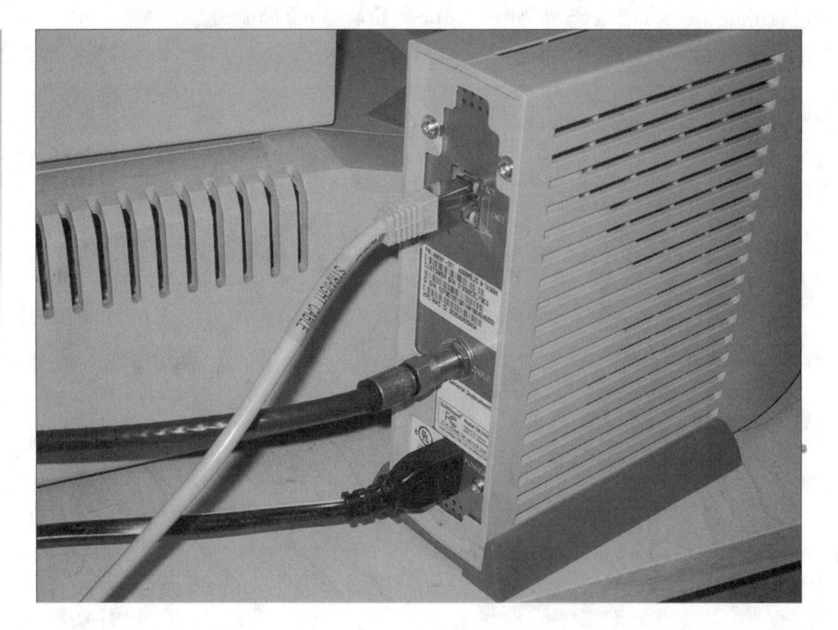

FIGURE 8.15
This should be a familiar sight; coaxial cable such as the cable pictured is conventionally used to bring a cable TV signal to your television or cable box. In this case, it's bringing Internet access to a cable modem.

Seeing visions of dollar signs dancing in their heads, many cable companies decided to take a step into the ISP ring and make use of this Internet capability of the existing wiring and technology that they already have in millions of homes. This is the birth of Cable-based Internet, usually just called Cable modem access because a special access box is necessary for connection to this broadband network that is conventionally called a cable modem (see Figure 8.16).

FIGURE 8.16
A cable modem enables you to access the Internet through the same lines that your cable TV runs over (with provider support of course).

The benefits of cable are usually low monthly fees (compared to DSL) and more importantly that it is usually available wherever you can get cable TV. Widespread availability makes cable one of the most attractive broadband solutions especially because it is difficult to get other forms of broadband in some areas.

The major downside to cable is that it uses shared node access principle to deliver bandwidth to communities. Cable doesn't offer a dedicated connection from the server you connect to up to your computer. However, a dedicated connection exists between the cable company's servers and an area of town (cable companies usually refer to the shared area as your "neighborhood." However, it usually spans a much larger distance than just your immediate neighborhood). For example, TimeWarner cable might bring their Road Runner cable modem access to a particular section of a city. They bring a pipe to the area capable of transferring say 50Mbps of bandwidth. They then sell the service to 1,000 homes in the area, and they cap each of the cable modems at a 2Mbps download speed (upload speeds are conventionally much lower than download speeds with cable service). If you work out the math, you realize that if every one of the homes in the "neighborhood" has a connection, each computer gets only 0.05Mbps of bandwidth, or about 50Kbps. The basis of cable service, however, is that not everyone in a neighborhood uses their Internet connections 100% of the time (and certainly not everyone has a connection to begin with), meaning that if only half of the neighborhood is using their connections, performance can improve considerably. And if very few are downloading files and are simply surfing the Net, performance becomes much closer to that 2Mbps download cap that is placed on the modems.

The real problems with cable can occur in overcrowded areas, but only if the cable companies serving those areas refuse to upgrade their service. It must be tempting for them to simply lower the download cap and sell more services on a single node, thus decreasing performance across the board while increasing their own profits. Remember, though, that there have been quite a few good cable implementations deployed across the United States alone, and most offer excellent download and upload speeds. Your best bet is to consult with other people in your area and have them share their experiences with their services.

DSL

The other major broadband option is known as a Digital Subscriber Line (DSL). The beauty of DSL is the weakpoint of cable, in that the connection is a dedicated one that isn't shared by anyone. So if your DSL provider guarantees a 2Mbps downstream connection, you generally get a guarantee of very close to that download speed (always be sure to read the fine print).

DSL runs over conventional telephone lines, but at a higher frequency so that you can use a single line to run voice communication and DSL data transmission without any interference of the two. This is a double-edged sword because DSL is quite picky about the type of lines connecting your house to the telephone company's equipment.

Most conventional forms of DSL require 100% copper wiring between the telephone company's equipment and your home. The problem with this is that brand new homes/subdivisions often have a bit of fiber-optic wiring in place over which conventional DSL cannot work. Very old homes, on the other hand, might not have clear enough lines over which to run high-speed data. This leaves a relatively few number of houses that are old enough to have 100% copper wiring to their location yet new enough to have relatively good quality lines. This brings us to the shortcomings of DSL, which are numerous.

First of all, it is very difficult to get in many areas. The fact that DSL is quite picky can leave the majority of users unable to get DSL, or if they can get it, only at a very low speed. Some users are lucky and can get high-speed DSL at a cheap price, but it is very easy to be just a little too far away to get DSL. The distance between the telephone company's equipment and your house isn't measured in the shortest path, rather whatever path the cabling takes. This means that you could theoretically move to a closer driving distance from your telephone company's equipment yet actually be farther away in terms of the distance that the telephone lines have to travel. The wiring in your house can also prevent you from getting DSL. However, if that is the problem, it's usually fixable, but you might have to spend a bit more to get it done.

If you can get DSL, other issues such as cost arise. Most of the time cable ends up being cheaper than DSL, which raises the question of "DSL or cable?" for the lucky users who can get both. This is pretty much the "Tastes Great, Less Filling," debate of the new millennium.

Cable Versus DSL

Provided that your cable provider is reliable and constantly upgrades their capacity, you almost always get more bandwidth out of a cable connection at a cheaper price. However, in rare cases you get a similar deal from a DSL provider. Assuming that the reliability of your DSL and cable providers are similar, you want to look at what kind of downstream (downloading) speeds they offer. A 2Mbps cable connection versus a 384Kbps DSL connection is an easy choice in the favor of the cable connection, but that same cable offering versus a guaranteed 1.5Mbps DSL connection might be a tougher decision.

Then you have the issue of upload speeds. Remember that when you're playing online games you're not only receiving data, but also sending (uploading) to the servers you're playing on. So the higher the upload speed the better, although you generally appreciate a faster download speed more because you're usually downloading (for example, surfing, ftping, and so on) more than you are uploading.

In terms of latency, generally speaking, DSL connections usually offer lower latency because you are not sharing your connection with any users, although a well-maintained cable service shouldn't be too far off. Also, remember that latency is a function of the servers to which you are connected and the path you take to get to those servers.

DSL has many flavors. For this reason I usually refer to DSL as just xDSL, the x representing the many prefixes DSL can take. The two most common forms of DSL are Asynchronous DSL (ADSL) and Synchronous DSL (SDSL having a synchronous upload/download speed although ADSL doesn't). A form of DSL known as IDSL also exists. It is a very low speed DSL 144Kbps upstream/downstream. Although it is better than a dial-up modem, it's still pretty slow by today's standards.

Setting Up Your Game for Network Play

Ten years ago, network gaming was around, but was not nearly as advanced as it is today. Setting up your game for network play used to involve typing in your friend's phone number and using that to connect your two modems together. Today, network play involves much more behind the scenes, but is just as easy to setup.

Most games have a Network options setting where you can either make your computer a host for the game (other users connect to your computer) or you can select to be a client (you connect to another host). Being a host has its pros and cons. On the upside, you control who gets on the server, what maps/levels you run, what rules, if any, apply to the game, and because you're the server network lag is minimal. At the same time, your system takes a small performance hit (if you've built a system according to what I've diagramed in this book, you shouldn't have a problem). Also, if you're hosting an online game, your Internet connection constantly uploads data to all clients who connect to you.

You normally want to host a game if you've got the fastest (particularly with upload speed) and most reliable internet connection of those that are playing; having a high powered computer doesn't hurt either. One option as a host (in some games) is to make your computer a "dedicated server." This means you cannot play the game on that computer while it's a server; instead its sole purpose is to serve the game. This prevents the server from being as much of a bottleneck as it doesn't have to deal with all of the calculations associated with you playing the game as well as the number crunching associated with everyone else connecting to it. Unfortunately it also means that you need another computer on which to play.

As a host you are able to make any settings for the game (for example, levels, rules, maps, and so on). All you have to do is either make sure your server is broadcast on some gaming network (this is usually built into the games that support this type of a feature) or hand out your IP address to those you want playing on your server. As a client, most games have an integrated browser to find other online games. In the event that you're playing over a LAN, you should be able to see any hosts broadcasting over your LAN. If you don't see any games on your LAN or on the Internet, or if you have trouble connecting, do two things. Make sure that your Internet connection is working, and also make sure that your computer has the proper protocols installed such as IPX or TCP/IP (the latter is installed by default with any network card in a Windows OS, whereas IPX must be manually installed).

The Future

The future of private networks is going towards even higher bandwidth solutions such as Gigabit Ethernet (1,000Mbps transfer rates). Wireless technology continues to improve as well with the introduction of standards such as 802.11a and the improvement of currently available wireless technologies.

In terms of Internet access, the trend is towards higher bandwidth and lower latency solutions. Just two years ago, a 2Mbps Internet connection was still out of reach for many. It won't take much longer for 5Mbps and 10Mbps connections to become popular as well. Eventually, 100Mbps connections to the Internet will be possible.

What this means for you, the gamer, is that today's games will play online much more like they play over a private LAN. Even more importantly is that tomorrow's games, which will be capable of sending even more data across the network as the result of increased bandwidth, will play better as well.

Chapter 9

Cases and Cooling: Living in Style and Keeping Your Cool

The Importance of Cases

Wanting to have something that is aesthetically pleasing is human nature, so it makes perfect sense that a big part of your gaming PC is its appearance. By looking at a computer you cannot tell whether you're running a high-performance 2GHz Pentium 4 or nothing more than an old Pentium 75. So, many users like their powerful gaming machines to have an equally powerful presence that they focus a great deal of their attention on their system cases.

The system case or chassis is about much more than just looks. Although you do want a case that looks good, you also want it to provide you with adequate room for your needs. It should also be easy to work in, and you shouldn't have to worry about losing a limb whenever you're reaching around in there (given that the metal edges on some cases are as sharp as razor blades). This brings me to the first major rule about purchasing a case for your system: You always want to pick functionality over form. Otherwise, you end up spending entirely too much money on a case that does nothing but frustrate you. The fact that it looks cool quickly loses its appeal when you're frustrated.

Case Form Factors

Remember from Chapter 3, "The Motherboard: Low Rent Housing for the CPU and Chipset," that various motherboard form factors are available, the most common being ATX and slight variants of that standard (for example, extended ATX, microATX, and so on). The first requirement for your case is that it should be compatible with the motherboard you are using. For example, if you have an ATX motherboard, you should purchase an ATX case. Because the ATX standard has become very widespread, you usually don't have to worry about a case not being ATX compliant, but every now and then you might run into an older AT case. Note that these AT cases do not work with current ATX motherboards; they do not have the proper cutouts on the back of the case or the right type of power switch for an ATX motherboard.

In terms of compatibility, an ATX case generally accepts microATX, regular ATX, and extended ATX motherboards. The only trouble you run into is with extended ATX boards putting components in areas obstructed by drive bays. The most common situation is an extended ATX motherboard being placed into a regular ATX case; however, the memory—when installed—is in the way of the drives installed in the case.

Even though an "extended ATX" case does not exist, some ATX-compliant cases easily can fit even the largest extended ATX motherboards.

The only other situation you have to worry about in case/motherboard compatibility when dealing with ATX boards is with a microATX case. A microATX case works only with microATX motherboards, although you could put a microATX motherboard in a standard ATX case. These cases cannot accept a regular ATX motherboard because they are physically too large to fit in a microATX case.

Cases also have form factors of their own. I'm not talking about ATX versus microATX, but rather the different sizes and styles of cases available. These sizes and styles have lost a lot of their distinction because almost all cases are now upright standing (otherwise known as *towers*). During the days when most cases layed flat on a desk (known as *desktop* cases), it was common to hunt for either a desktop or a tower case. Today, almost everything is a tower case, and although you can classify different-sized towers, a standard system of doing so does not exist. Nevertheless, the following sections still attempt to make some size classifications and then get into the various things to look for in a case.

Drive Bays

The biggest difference between cases other than the motherboard form factor is the number of drive bays the case offers. The more drive bays, the more drives you can install in the case—pretty simple, huh? The three types of drive bays are 5.25", internal 3.5", and external 3.5" (see Figure 9.1).

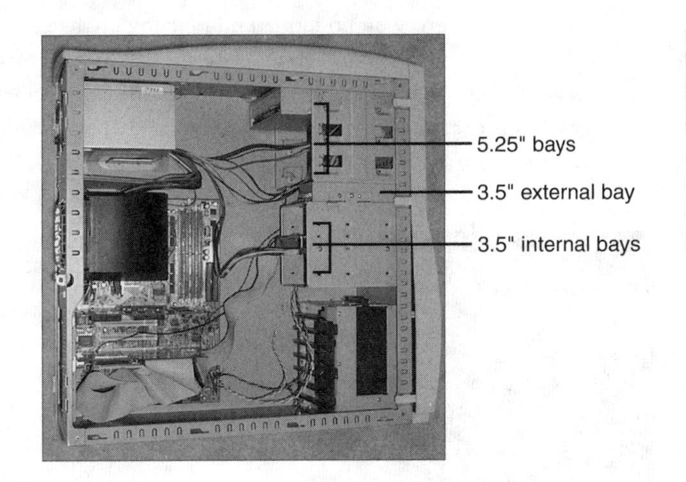

FIGURE 9.1
The drive bays in any case are located at the front of the case. This Fong Kai case is large enough to accommodate a regular ATX motherboard and still have space for the drives.

The size differences indicate the type of drive these bays can accept. A 5.25" bay can accept a 5.25" device such as a CD or DVD-ROM drive, whereas a 3.5" bay can accept a 3.5" drive such as a floppy drive or a hard drive. The internal versus external distinction governs whether the drive bay is accessible from the outside of the case. The only time you need an external drive bay is for a floppy drive or any other type of drive that requires you to insert or remove media. Hard drives work fine in both internal and external drive bays; in the latter situation a face plate is placed on the case's bezel to cover up the opening.

The use of the word *external* to refer to the bay is often a misnomer because the bay is still internal to the case. An external drive enclosure does actually sit outside of your case. However, when you're looking at case specifications, that's what an internal/external drive bay is. Sometimes internal drive bays are referred to as *hidden bays*. Having an internal/hidden 5.25" bay is very uncommon.

Even though most cases these days are of the tower variety, you can still find some ATX desktop cases. These cases generally have one or two 5.25" bays and usually up to four 3.25" bays. The desktop design is really useful if you want to hide a case away somewhere, but because it occupies a lot of desk/floor space and has a limited number of drive bays, towers are generally more desirable.

The next type of ATX case is a mini-tower. These cases have slowly evolved into microATX cases because a mini-tower ATX case is not necessary given the relatively large size of most ATX motherboards (see Figure 9.2). These towers often give you no more, and in many cases less, expansion options than a well-made desktop case. They are perfect for small file servers you want to keep in addition to your main computer, possibly for archive storage, MP3 storage, and so on. However, you rarely find a high-performance PC that you can put together in such a cramped area.

FIGURE 9.2
This Enlight microATX tower is too small to accommodate anything bigger than a microATX motherboard.

The most common type of ATX case is a mid-tower. A mid-tower is generally outfitted with around three 5.25" drive bays, one or two external 3.5" bays, and even more internal 3.5" drive bays. These towers can accommodate virtually any type of ATX motherboard, although some of the larger extended ATX motherboards might find themselves a bit cramped inside of the case itself.

Finally, you have full tower ATX cases, also referred to as *server/workstation* cases (see Figure 9.3). These labels are often also misnomers because, although powerful workstations commonly come in large cases, servers commonly are placed in a rackmount case for storage inside a rack. The server/workstation name normally comes from the fact that the only reason for a case this big is because you have a lot of drives and only have that many drives when you're running a very powerful machine, such as a server or workstation, not a gaming box.

FIGURE 9.3
The Supermicro SC750-A is one of the most popular full tower/workstation cases among enthusiasts. The case offers support for up to nine cooling fans.

Other types of cases exist, such as the FlexATX case shown in Figure 9.4. These are even smaller than microATX cases and are designed to support FlexATX-compatible motherboards. Next are WTX cases, which can accommodate WTX motherboards. These motherboards are slightly wider than regular ATX motherboards. These cases and form factors are beyond the scope of this book, and you generally do not have much reason to consider either of these options, but a little extra knowledge never hurts.

FIGURE 9.4
Peering into a FlexATX case you can see that it has enough room for only three PCI slots.

If you've noticed, the biggest differentiating factor between the various case sizes is the number of drive bays the case offers. A physically larger case gives you more room to work on the inside and comes with more cooling options (more space for mounting fans), but for the most part, a larger case is a good option because it accommodates more drives. Don't let the sheer size of a case reel you in. Larger cases are obviously much more expensive because they are constructed of more metal. Look at the number of drives you have now, take into consideration the types of drives you would upgrade to in the future, and plan for at least a couple of bays for future growth. Although you can't always predict what ends up in your system, looking for a case that offers seven 5.25" drive bays is pointless when you currently have only one drive that requires such a bay.

Note

Because of the small power supply in a FlexATX case, AMD had to work very closely with power supply manufacturers to make sure that its Athlon and Duron processors would work with such a low-powered unit.

Expansion Slot Cutouts

The physical number of cutouts on the back of your case that enable expansion cards to be screwed or somehow attached to the case is also an expansion limitation. However, unlike the number of drive bays, this number is pretty standard across all cases (see Figure 9.5). Whether you're looking at a large full tower or a regular mid-tower ATX case, seven expansion slot cutouts are always on the back of your case.

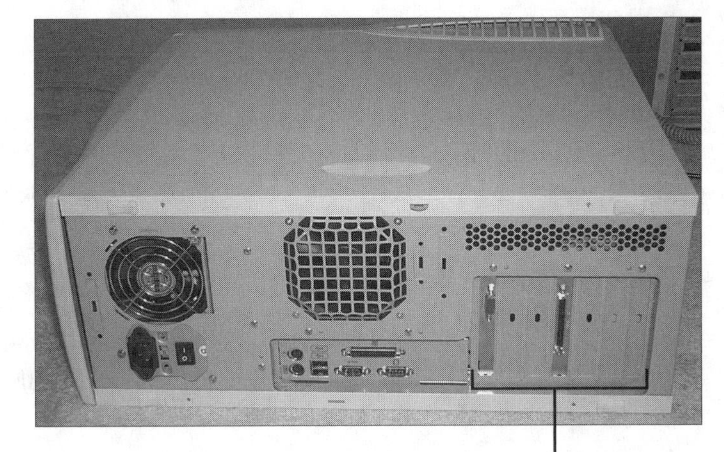

FIGURE 9.5
Only two of the seven expansion slot cutouts are in use on this case. You can see how they limit the installation of more than seven cards easily in this picture. No more cards can fit.

The exceptions to the number of expansion slot cutouts come when you move to different form factors. MicroATX motherboards have only four cutouts because the boards are physically smaller and the specification calls for a maximum of four expansion cards to be installed. The specifications also differ for FlexATX and certain other server case form factor specifications.

Riser Cards

Quite possibly one of the most popular designs that the major manufacturers implemented back in the days of desktop cases was the use of a riser card to provide room for expansion cards. Instead of having four PCI slots directly on the motherboard, there would be only one interface slot that a special card, a riser card, plugged into. This riser card would then be perpendicular to the plane of the motherboard and usually between 2 and 3 PCI slots (or other types of slots, depending on the particular platform) would stem from it.

In building your own system, you don't have to worry about riser cards because you rarely find a case built around that principle. If you are upgrading an older system, however, this is a limitation you must keep in mind because very few motherboards—especially present day ones—work in such a situation. Usually in this situation, your only course of action is to purchase a new case to go with the rest of your upgraded components.

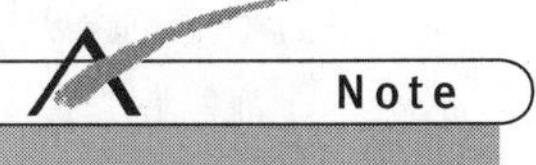

Note

A motherboard with a shared slot means that the particular slot is placed so close to another one that only one card can be physically installed at any given time. Both slots are operational and if you have two cards plugged in at the same time they both work. Installing two cards in two adjacently shared slots without somehow modifying one of them is physically impossible.

Rails Versus Screws

Just a few years ago virtually all available DIY cases were poorly made and very difficult to install or remove components from. Over the past couple of years, a trend has developed toward making cases more user friendly (as has been the trend with most other areas of the PC world), thus making the insertion and removal of components easier.

In an effort to make drive installation even easier, many case manufacturers have started offering screwless drive installation as a feature. These cases offer screwless drive installation by using rails that clip into the screw holes on 5.25" and 3.5" drives, enabling them to then slide into the case and click into place (see Figure 9.6).

FIGURE 9.6
A drive rail is easily mounted onto a drive. In this case, Enlight chose to mount the rail to the drives with screws. Although you can easily move the drive from one Enlight case to another, this somewhat defeats the purpose of drive rails in the first place. Most drive rails simply clip onto the drives.

The use of these rails greatly reduces the installation time for things such as DVD-ROM drives and hard drives, although some cases offer drive rails only for the 5.25" bays and not the 3.5" bays. The drive rail approach has some disadvantages in comparison to the conventional screw design, in which the drives are physically screwed into the chassis:

- One of the biggest benefits of screws is that they provide a way to conduct heat away from the drive itself and distribute it through the rest of the metal chassis. This isn't too important with CD/DVD drives, but it is relatively useful if you have higher speed (10,000RPM+) hard drives mounted in your case. Plastic drive rails completely eliminate this function of the case, although metal drive rails don't exhibit much of the same problem.

- If you lose your drive rails, you're out of luck because you can rarely go out and purchase more rails for your case from just any vendor. These rails are almost never interchangeable between cases, so if you go down this route make sure that you keep track of your drive rails. Some cases offer a single 5.25" bay that can be mounted using the regular screw method and only provide rails for the remaining 5.25" drives; this is somewhat of a solution to the problem, but then it defeats the purpose of having drive rails in the first place.
- If not designed properly, rails can be a nightmare to deal with when transporting a case. If the drive gets "derailed," removing the dislodged rails can be a pain.

Although I do find drive rails useful, I definitely consider screwless case panels and removable drive cages much more important.

Removable Drive Cages

I just finished mentioning how much I like removable drive cages, so I might as well give you a bit more insight into this facet of the case world. One of the most annoying problems you run into when putting a case together is screwing in all the components—your motherboard, peripheral cards, and drives. Inevitably, screws fall out of your hands while you're working on the case, and the more you drop them, the more frustrated you get.

The introduction of removable drive cages, such as the one shown in Figure 9.7, has been a time saver for many. The name is indicative of its function. A removable drive cage is usually a collection of drive bays (for example, all the internal 3.5" drive bays in your case) that can be removed from the system. This enables you to easily screw in all the drives from both sides, and then just slide the entire cage back into the case with all your drives already installed. Removable drive cages are almost always reserved for internal 3.5" drive bays because for external 3.5" and 5.25" bays you almost always have parts of drives sticking out of the chassis for external access making a drive cage difficult to remove.

The drive cage can be made removable in many ways. The most common, unfortunately, is to have a single screw hold the drive cage in place. This doesn't defeat the purpose of a removable drive cage, but it makes it less useful. By far the most desirable option is to have a removable drive cage that is held in place by a locking mechanism, usually requiring the press of a lever to release it. This is much easier to use and although it takes a bit more work for designers to implement, it's a nice feature to have.

FIGURE 9.7
Removable 3.5" hard drive cages are among the most common in cases.

The Motherboard Tray

Although your drives definitely eat up a lot of screws, your motherboard is the component whose mounting can be the most frustrating. Generally, you have to install around nine screws that almost always happen to slip out of the clutches of your screwdriver. Your motherboard is mounted onto the main part of the chassis, which is known as the *motherboard tray* (see Figure 9.8). Often, this tray is not removable from the case itself. Installing your CPU and memory on the motherboard before mounting it on the tray is usually better, although you run the risk of making one of the screw holes on your motherboard difficult to reach. Removing the power supply from your case can help you get around this. You can also attempt to use an extractor tool like the one described in the section "Other Tools of the Trade" in Chapter 11, "Putting It All Together: Break Out the Hammers and Duct Tape," to get the screw in place and then use a long-neck screwdriver to drive it home.

Not much sets one motherboard tray apart from another. Although some have integrated standoffs, they are all virtually the same. The only time you see any difference is if a case happens to have a removable motherboard tray.

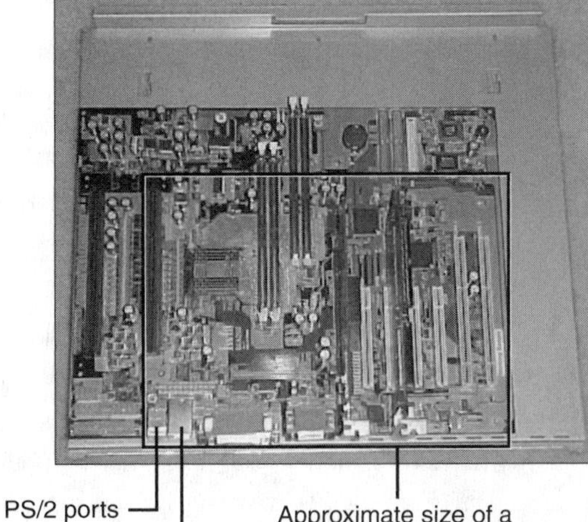

FIGURE 9.8
This motherboard tray from a WTX case is removable. You can also see how a WTX motherboard is wider than a normal ATX motherboard by looking at how far it extends to the left past the PS/2 interface ports.

A removable tray is definitely helpful, although you don't see them too often in cases. Taking the removable motherboard tray concept one step further, some cases integrate the expansion slot part of the chassis onto the tray as well so that you can slide out the motherboard tray and expansion slots at once. As if motherboard trays themselves weren't rare enough, these types of cases are even more exotic.

Chassis Construction

One of the most commonly overlooked features when purchasing a case is the construction of the case itself (see Figure 9.9). Sure, it might look cool and have a lot of drive bays, but if the case isn't well-made then you're going to have a lot of problems. What types of problems am I talking about?

FIGURE 9.9
Palo Alto has always made well-constructed cases. Its cases rarely have sharp edges, are simple to open, and use quiet power supplies and fans.

The most common problem is rough edges inside the case. Remember that these cases are made out of metal, and if the corners of the metal on the inside of the case aren't smoothed out or rounded, chances are that when you're working on the inside of the case you're going to end up with quite a few cuts. If you've ever worked on a computer and afterwards noticed blood and cuts all over your hands, you've experienced a case without rounded or smoothed edges. The easiest way to tell is to obviously run your finger along the inside of the case, feel around for sharp edges and target the areas that you would expect to be most likely to cut you (for example, corners, edges of the case, and so on).

Now let's take a look at gaining access to the case. In the past, the case was covered by a single metal piece that went all around the case. This proved to be far from the best way to gain access to the internals of the case, so manufacturers started using individual panels, usually either two or three (see Figure 9.10). One panel for each side and sometimes a panel for the top of the case, although this one isn't as important because you rarely need to gain access to the top of the case.

FIGURE 9.10
Removable side panels are helpful when you need to get into your case.

Although most case manufacturers insist on attaching these panels to the chassis via screws, a few smarter ones have implemented screwless designs, such as a door handle that unlatches and pulls off the side panel giving you access to the motherboard and drive bays or the use of a thumbscrew. A thumbscrew is preferable to a regular set of screws because you don't have to have any tools to operate a thumbscrew.

The last piece of the construction puzzle is the case's front bezel. This is more aesthetic than anything else, although various case bezels have different types of functionality. Some have integrated cutouts for floppy drives, others can easily be removed, and some just look good.

In general, the case itself should feel solid and all the drive cages, rails, and cover panels should fit well without too much trouble to make sure that they properly align themselves. Keep in mind that excessive force applied during shipping can sometimes warp the case if not packaged properly, so check for any curved surfaces before immediately dismissing the case as being poorly designed.

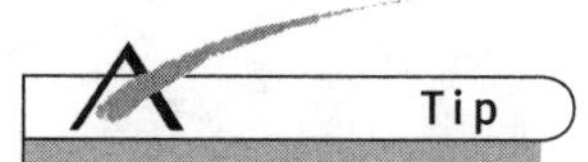

Tip

The flex test is used to measure a case's durability. It involves putting the case on the edge of a table or counter and pressing on opposite corners. This tests the strength of the chassis; stronger cases won't flex as easily, meaning that they don't put additional stress on expansion cards installed in the case.

Case Cooling and Ventilation

Another benefit of having a larger case is that they often have much more elaborate cooling systems. However, smaller cases can sometimes have even more effective ones than their larger counterparts.

The more area you have inside your case, the more air can be moved around and the more space is available for fans to take care of that. The only situation in which you really need to worry about airflow within your case is if you have some very high heat-producing drives (for example, 10,000RPM drives and so on). You also want to have good ventilation inside your case to ensure that the fan on your CPU is pulling in cool air to cool the heatsink attached to your CPU.

Having at least one other case fan in your system is recommended if you're using any of today's high-performance CPUs. The most common place to put this case fan is at the rear of your case, oriented as an exhaust fan that helps get rid of hot air from the inside of your case (see Figure 9.11). If you are going to add another fan to your system to complement this rear exhaust fan, I recommend going with a front-mounted intake fan to bring cool air into the case. The combination of these two helps create an area of low pressure inside the case, thus aiding the cooling process.

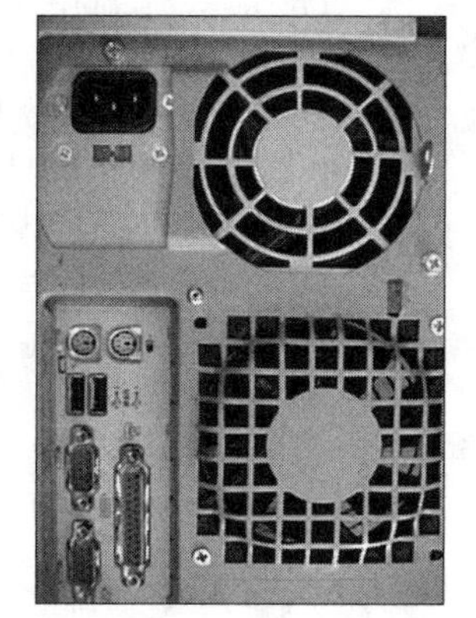

FIGURE 9.11
An exhaust fan at the rear of your case is the best way to add additional cooling to your case. Also, remember that your power supply usually helps exhaust some air with its cooling fan.

The most common misconception with case fans is that the more you have, the cooler your CPU runs and the higher you are able to overclock. Although it is true that having more case fans improves ventilation inside your case, many users go entirely too far with their cooling setups and actually don't help cool their CPU too much. With a good heatsink and fan on your CPU, the addition of multiple case fans don't impact the temperature of your CPU much at all. However, if you have multiple drives running in the case generating a lot of heat, the situation is a bit different. You want to limit the number of fans you have in your system. After all, the more fans you have the louder your setup is.

Power Supply

Although it used to be a convenience that cases were often sold with power supplies, now it can be a one way ticket to an unstable system. The power demands of today's processors and motherboards are so great that a poorly selected power supply could result in system instability. Unfortunately, it took the release of the AMD Athlon to bring this issue to light.

When the Athlon was first released in 1999 it consumed up to 54W of power at 650MHz. This was compared to Pentium IIIs of the day that were only consuming about 34.5W at 600MHz. These power demands were unmet by many of the power supplies available at the time and as the Athlon increased in clock speed, the power demands grew. This unfortunately left many with a bad taste and often they blamed AMD's Athlon for random crashes and problems they had, branding it an immature platform when in many cases the problem wasn't the processor or the platform, but rather the power supply's inadequacies.

The power supply's main function is, obviously, to supply power to your system and it does that by first converting the Alternating Current (AC) it receives from your wall outlet to a more usable form to the computer known as Direct Current (DC). As the name implies, Alternating Current provides an alternating signal while Direct Current provides a current that remains at a constant level.

After converting the current it receives from the wall outlet to DC, the power supply supplies a set of voltages to your system, more specifically +5V, -5V, +12V, -12V, and +3.3V. The capability of a power supply to properly deliver enough power on each one of these voltage rails is what I concentrate on in this comparison, because the under delivery of power to a critical device can result in system instability, which was the case with many of the original Athlon setups.

The Wattage Game

You're used to hearing a power supply defined by a rating such as 250W or 300W, but a power supply has much more to it than whether it's a 250W or 300W unit. You're going to want to know exactly what the power rating is on each one of the voltages described previously, which provides much more information than simply knowing whether you have a 300W unit.

First of all, you're probably not going to pay much attention to the -5V and -12V ratings on a power supply because they aren't of much importance to driving the components in your system.

The rating on the +5V and +3.3V rails is the most important because those are the voltages supplied to the motherboard and the CPU. The combined rating on a power supply indicates the sum of the +5V and +3.3V ratings on the power supplies listed. These two ratings, as well as their combined rating, are very important in choosing a power supply that works well with your system. In the early days of the Athlon, a combined rating of at least 145W was recommended for a 0.25-micron Athlon 650.

The remaining +12V power rail is extremely important if you're going to have any high RPM disk drives in your new system because the +12V rail powers all the hard disks in your system. Also, some coolers run off the +12V rail and often have heavy current demands which is another thing you need to take into account as you look for a power supply that can reliably power your system.

So in the end you want to look for the ratings on the +3.3V, +5V, and +12V rails when looking at a power supply on paper.

Other than the ratings, take into account such issues as cooling and the reliability of the unit itself.

The Fan

The power supply functions as a cooling device as it helps circulate air throughout your case thanks to its integrated fan. From a cooling aspect you want to look for a power supply with large holes through which the fan can pull in hot air from the case and send it on its way out.

From a reliability standpoint, some manufacturers simply produce higher quality products, which therefore last longer under adverse conditions. Companies such as Sparkle Power International LTD. (SPI) and Delta Electronics are well known for making high quality power supplies that aren't prone to failure (see Figure 9.12). The cheaper power supplies often fail under high temperature conditions when under full load, and when a power supply fails during operation. When this happens, the least you see is a crash, however you're also likely to see your system spontaneously reboot or power off entirely.

FIGURE 9.12
The Sparkle FSP300-60GT was one of the most reliable power supplies available for Athlon systems.

Another thing to take into account is the amount of noise the fan in your power supply generates. Delta Electronics has been known for producing very quiet power supplies, but more recently companies such as Enermax have taken it upon themselves to offer quiet units as well. Try turning off your computer in your room one day and note how quiet it gets—kind of nice, isn't it?

The ATX 2.03 Specification—Intel's Solution

When Intel released the Pentium 4 processor, the power demands of the processor with the largest desktop CPU die available at the time were quite incredible. Although the Athlon still dwarfed it in terms of power consumption, Intel did not want to have a repeat of the Athlon power supply fiasco. Because Intel obviously has a bit more muscle in the market than AMD, it introduced a completely new power supply specification known as ATX 2.03.

The main function of the ATX 2.03 specification was to guarantee the delivery of a certain amount of current on the +12V power rail. This additional current is used to ensure that the CPU and motherboard is given enough power to operate properly, thus avoiding the Athlon power supply fiasco. This is done through the use of a new power connector in addition to the conventional 20-pin ATX power block. This connector is a 4-pin (organized in a 2×2 configuration) ATX12V connector that is present on all ATX 2.03 power supplies (see Figure 9.13).

FIGURE 9.13
The new 2×2 ATX12V connector helps to supply power to the CPU.

Although it is true that some power supplies already deliver enough current on the 3.3V, 5V, and 12V rails to run Pentium 4 systems just fine, invest in an ATX 2.03 power supply if you are going down the Pentium 4 route.

You should keep in mind that some Athlon boards also feature the same connector, although in this case it isn't to supply power to the CPU, but rather to enable support for AGP Pro graphics cards (the extra current is supplied to the AGP slot). Remember that AGP Pro50 cards can eat up to 50W of power, and Pro110 cards require 110W for proper operation.

CPU Cooling

Although not necessarily a function of the case, cooling your CPU is key to proper operation of your system. Cooling your CPU is made possible through the combination of two items: a heatsink and a fan. You already know what a fan is, and although you're probably familiar with a heatsink on a conceptual level, do you really know exactly how a heatsink works?

The Physical Effects

To make it simple, a *heatsink* is nothing more than a strangely formed piece of metal. How does it dissipate the heat generated by the CPU?

Well, an object can get rid of heat in three ways: *radiation*, *conduction*, and *convection*:

- **Radiation**—As the name suggests, means that the heat is simply radiated away from the object, through electromagnetic radiation (photon transport). This effect is not bound to gas or other substances surrounding the heatsink. Radiation even takes place in a vacuum. How well an object can radiate heat depends on the material and the color (black is best).
- **Conduction**—The exchange of kinetic energy between molecules. Less energetic (lower temperature) particles gain kinetic energy by colliding with more energetic particles (through physical contact). Because direct contact is required, a heatsink (surrounded by air) cannot get rid of heat using conduction. However, conduction is responsible for the heat transfer from the CPU to the heatsink.
- **Convection**—Heat transfer by movement of a heated substance (gas or liquid). The heat is transferred to the molecules of the gas (or liquid) surrounding the hot object and then transported away through movement of molecules. If the gas or liquid around the object is forced into movement (for example, by a fan blowing air across a heatsink), you're then dealing with *forced convection* (see Figure 9.14).

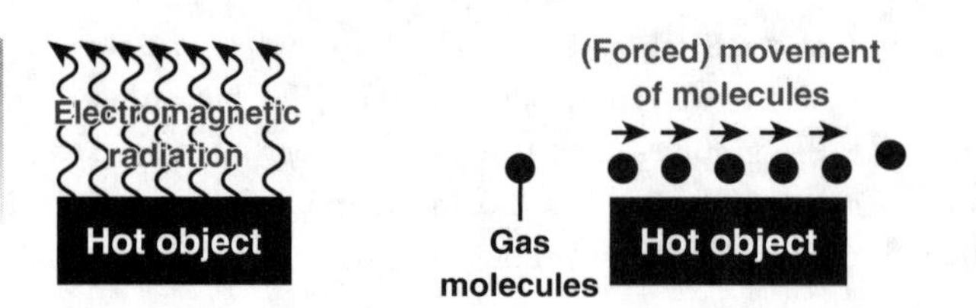

FIGURE 9.14
Heat transfer can occur via radiation or forced convection.

Forced convection is the effect that's mainly responsible for the cooling capabilities of a heatsink-fan combo. When a CPU cooler cools a CPU, most heat is dissipated by forced convection, and only in very, very small part by radiation. The heatsink conducts heat away from your CPU and to the surface of the heatsink and its fans. The fan that is a part of the heatsink-fan combo generally takes in cooler air from the surrounding environment and blows it onto the heatsink, thus moving the heat away from the heatsink through convection.

To be efficient, a heatsink must be designed in such a way that it takes advantage of this effect. This goal can be achieved in two ways:

- Making the surface area of the heatsink as great as possible through the use of larger bases and more/larger fins.
- Providing the best possible amount of air flow across the heatsink through the use of larger and faster spinning fans.

In addition to these two factors, the heatsink must be designed in a such way that good thermal transfer is possible inside the heatsink (meaning that the heat can easily travel from the lower part of the heatsink, that is in contact with the CPU, to the fins, where the actual heat dissipation takes place). The part of the heatsink that is in contact with the CPU must be very flat to enable good thermal transfer. However, even if the surface appears to be perfectly flat, there are still small air gaps in the contact area between CPU and heatsink. Therefore, a thermal interface material, such as thermal compound or a thermoconductive pad must be used.

So, to design an efficient heatsink, a solution would be to make it as big as possible, and add a very powerful fan. Another solution would be to enable it to have very fine fins, and use a clever design that enables the airflow from the fan to travel easily through the heatsink (see Figure 9.15).

FIGURE 9.15
The Thermalright SK6 (right) uses only a 60mm fan yet is a very solid performer courtesy of its fine fins. The Kanie Wing cooler (left), on the other hand, uses two 60mm fans on a very large heatsink base.

An efficient heatsink design avoids turbulence and high air pressures inside the cooler. Of course, the ideal solution is the combination of both solutions.

The Material

It used to be true that almost all heatsinks are made of aluminum. Why? The low cost and great mechanical characteristics make it very suitable for producing heatsinks. Generally, a pure metal has better thermal conductivity than an alloy. However, most heatsink manufacturers use aluminum alloys because of their better mechanical characteristics.

Many people wondered why copper wasn't widely used for heatsinks. Copper has a thermal conductivity that's almost twice as high as the thermal conductivity of aluminum (393 W/mK, as opposed to 221 W/mK). However, the performance of a heatsink doesn't only depend on the thermal conductivity of the material, as the shape and size of the fins do factor in. This means that using a copper heatsink is not automatically twice as efficient as using an aluminum heatsink.

Although not as common with Pentium 4 heatsinks, the incredible cooling demands of the Athlon processors have made some manufacturers rethink the idea of using more copper in their heatsinks. For the 1.4GHz Athlon, most recommended heatsinks use, at a minimum, a copper inlay for the base of the heatsink to aid in thermal transfers between it and the CPU. Many are entirely copper because copper has better cooling characteristics and thus enables heatsink designs to do more, although they're not as large as their aluminum counterparts.

The Color

"A black object radiates the best, so all heatsinks should be black." True? Not really. Remember, most of the heat is dissipated using forced convection and for this effect, the color is irrelevant. When doing a comparison test of two otherwise identical heatsinks with a different color, the measured performance difference is usually negligible. The main reason heatsink manufacturers anodize their heatsinks is to make them look more attractive. Heatsinks exist in a variety of colors—black, silver, blue, green, gold, and red. For the performance, it doesn't make any major difference.

When choosing a heatsink don't let looks alone be your guide as to what is best. Case in point is the earliest Orb heatsinks from Thermaltake. As you can see in Figure 9.16, the heatsink looks rather exotic, and its looks attracted many to it.

I bring this up because the Golden Orb was actually one of the most dangerous heatsinks to use with AMD Athlon (the Orb was never designed to be used with Athlon CPUs, yet many people used it regardless and were met with this unfortunate fate). Because of the method in which the cooler was mounted on the CPU, many users ended up cracking their very fragile Athlon/Duron cores with this heatsink. It just goes to show you that looks don't always translate into functionality.

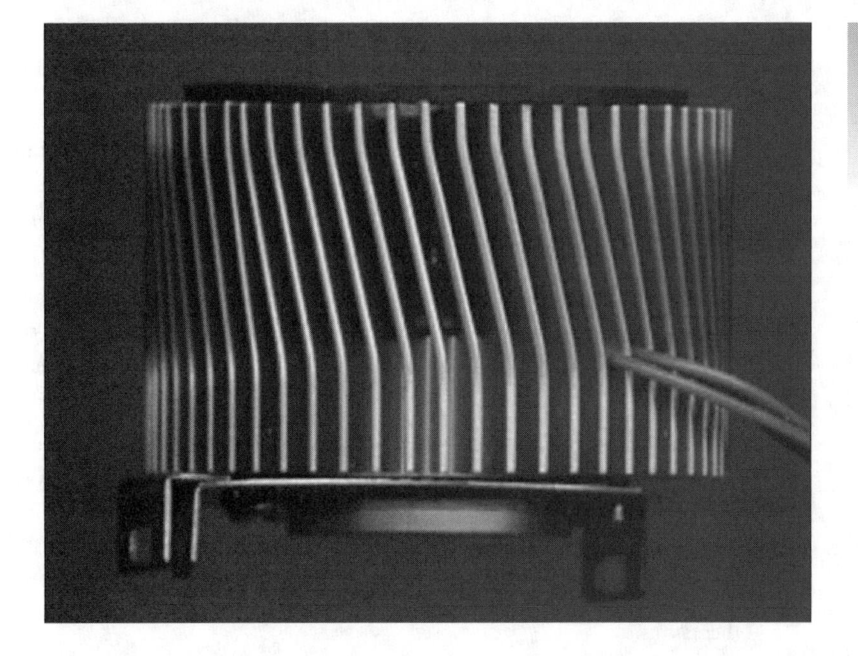

FIGURE 9.16
The Orb pictured here is the Golden Orb which had a yellow color to it, making it even more attractive to some users.

The Production Method

Different heatsink manufacturers have come up with many different production methods. Let's have a look at some of the popular heatsink designs:

- **Extrusion**—The most popular production method for heatsinks. This is inexpensive, and quite fine structures can be created using this production method. The liquid aluminum is pressed through a form so that a long stick with the shape of the heatsink is created. After this "heatsink stick" has cooled down, it is cut into pieces the size of the heatsink. However, this production method has certain limitations. For example, a heatsink shape such as the one shown in the fourth image of Figure 9.17 could not be produced with this method.
- **Folded fin design**—Here, the fins are made of a thin metal plate, which is folded, and bonded onto a base plate. The advantage is that the fins are hollow, so they have a bigger surface and enable better

airflow (and thus better cooling). Using this design, light, compact, and still very efficient coolers can be designed. The disadvantage is that heatsinks with folded fins are more expensive to produce, and therefore only a few manufacturers offer coolers using this design.

- **Bonded fin design**—This design is very similar to the “folded fin design,” except that here, many smaller metal plates are bonded onto the base plate, instead of one large folded plate.
- **Die casting**—This production method gives the heatsink designer a lot of freedom and enables certain heatsink shapes that cannot be produced using extrusion. However, the fins of a die cast heatsink cannot be very fine.
- **Cold forging**—This is a relatively exotic production method. A very popular heatsink, the Alpha PFH6035MUC, is produced using this method. This technology is suitable for heatsinks with many small pin fins.
- **Milling**—Like cold forging, this production method is quite unusual for heatsinks. The heatsinks by HP PolarLogic are produced this way. Milling leaves the heatsink designers a lot of freedom, too, but it is expensive.

In Figure 9.17, you can see an example of each of these various types of heatsinks.

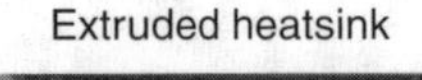

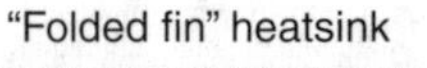

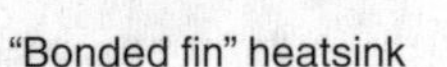

Die-cast heatsink

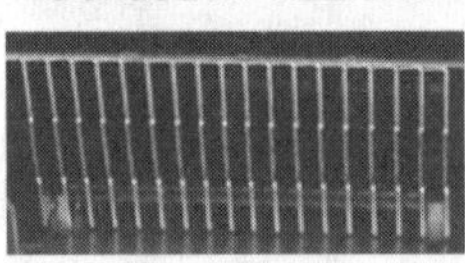

Cold forged heatsink

Milled/cut heatsink

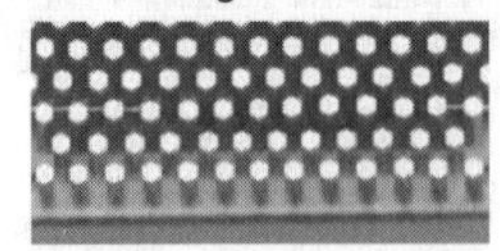

FIGURES 9.17
Common types of heatsinks include: Extruded, folded fin, bonded fin, die-cast, cold forged, and milled/cut heatsinks.

Of course, this is not an exhaustive list, but almost all CPU heatsinks available on the market today are produced with one of the previous production methods.

Today, all CPUs require a fan. Other peripherals such as video cards, memory, and hard drives put out enough heat to require one or more case fans in addition to this. However, when buying a fan, which factors should you consider?

The Bearing System

Two kinds of fans are being used on CPU heatsinks: *ball bearing* and *sleeve bearing* fans.

Sleeve bearing fans are usually less expensive and often quieter, but they are often less reliable. The cheapest kind of sleeve bearing, it simply consists of a ring made of a porous material, dipped in a lubricant. The fan motor's shaft rotates inside this ring and is lubricated by the lubricant stored inside the porous material.

Ball bearing fans are a bit more expensive, and sometimes also louder, but they are generally more reliable (see Figure 9.18). Just in case you're not familiar with bearing types: "Ball bearing" means the rotating shaft is surrounded by tiny balls, which enable smooth rotation with hardly any wear and tear.

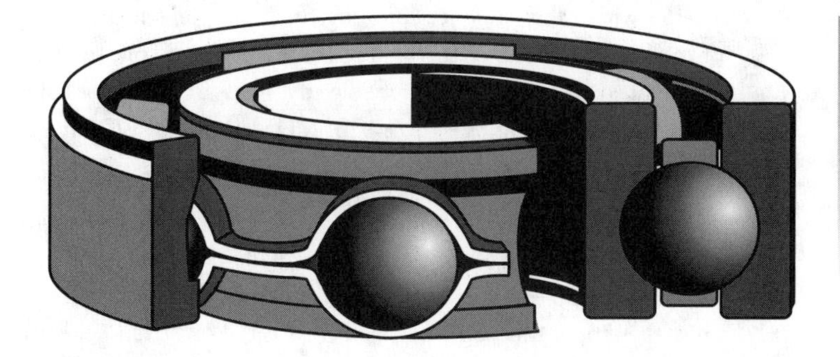

FIGURE 9.18
A ball bearing like the one seen here enables the fan to rotate smoothly. The main benefit of ball bearings, though, is the extended life they offer over sleeve bearing designs.

If you've ever held a ball bearing before, you know that it takes a lot to wear down the surface of the ball. This is why the fan can spin so well without wearing out, even while spinning at 7000RPM+. The harm that can be done by a failing fan could be devastating. Even though the Pentium 4 has always had thermal protection, the Thunderbird core for the Athlon has no built-in thermal protection. If the CPU fan stopped working, the CPU would keep on crunching away until it burned up. The Pentium 4, on the other hand, throttles down in clock speed and eventually shuts off.

Note that if the sticker on the fan says "Ball bearing" you often get a fan that uses both ball bearings and sleeve bearings. A fan needs two bearings, and the popular 50mm×10mm "ball" bearing fans that come with many heatsinks are usually fans with one ball bearing and one sleeve bearing. Larger fans (60mm×5mm and up) sometimes have two ball bearings. These are often referred to as *two ball* or *dual ball bearing* fans.

I highly recommend buying only ball bearing fans (or dual ball bearing fans in the case of larger fans). Cheap sleeve bearing fans usually fail after only six months or less, whereas high-quality ball bearing fans have a very high MTBF (mean time between failure). But some fan manufacturers also offer high-quality sleeve bearing fans with Teflon bearings. These are just as reliable as ball bearing fans; they're also quieter but also expensive.

Some Words on Noise

High airflow always creates noise. For this reason, even a very high quality fan can be quite loud. However, in the case of a good fan, most of the noise it creates comes from the air turbulence, and not from the fan motor. Fan vibrations are a sign of poor quality. If you hold the fan in your hand, you should not feel any significant vibrations. This is why you should never play around with a fan while it's spinning (for example, sticking things in the path of the blades). If one of the blades of the fan breaks off, the fan becomes unbalanced and starts to shake violently. Fans are carefully balanced at the factory and anything that throws off their balance drastically reduces functionality and ends up harming your CPU.

A larger fan that spins at a lower speed is less noisy than a smaller fan spinning at a high speed, even if the two provide the same amount of airflow. So, the rule "bigger is better" also applies to fans. Some of the best heatsink-fan units that apply this principle are Intel's retail or boxed heatsinks. The fans are generally slow spinning, but quite large to make up for it. For example, the retail version of Intel's Pentium 4 2.0GHz processor comes with a very large heatsink that has a fan that spins at under 3000RPM. If you're anything like me, you don't exactly love the sound of 7000RPM fans inside your case, so do a little research before you purchase your fan, especially if you sleep in the same room as your computer.

Fan Performance

The most common unit for specifying airflow is CFM- (cubic feet per minute). In countries where metric system is more widely used, the unit m^3/min (cubic meters per minute) is also common. A conversion table for airflow units can be found at `http://www.heatsink-guide.com/conv.htm`. In addition to this, the air pressure a fan creates can be measured (unlike CFM or m^3/min, this value does not depend on fan size).

50mm×10mm CPU fans usually move up to 10CFM, high speed 50mm×10mm fans with 6000rpm even more. 60mm×25mm fans commonly move 20CFM–30CFM and 80mm×25mm move 30CFM–40CFM—these are becoming more common for coolers. Fans that are 120mm can reach CFM values of more than 100CFM—these fans are mostly used as case fans although sometimes 90mm fans are used instead.

> **Tip**
>
> The type of fan you should have in your PC depends, obviously, on the situation. However, a good heatsink/fan on the CPU itself is your best ally. Larger, slower-spinning 80mm fans (3000—5000RPM) are definitely more desirable than higher-spinning, but smaller fans (6000—8000RPM). Your main goal should be to find a heatsink with more surface area so you can have a slower-spinning fan (keeps things quiet).
>
> In terms of case fans, one that is 90mm–120mm is usually helpful to improve circulation inside your case. This is especially important if you have one or more 10,000RPM hard drives in your case.

Remember, when buying a fan you always have to choose between high performance and low noise. The goal is to find a good compromise.

The type of fan you choose also depends on the application for your system. If you're building a home theater PC that sits in your living room next to your comparatively silent receiver then you want something with very large heatsinks and very slow-spinning but large fans. If you're building a gaming PC for a loud room, however, you probably don't care as much about noise and don't mind going for a smaller heatsink with a faster-spinning fan. Also, remember that when you buy a heatsink, you're not always married to the type of fan that comes on it; heatsink manufacturers rarely sell heatsinks to vendors with a particular type of fan. Vendors pick and choose which fans to pair with the heatsinks. Keep that in mind—especially if you're shopping across multiple vendors and comparing prices and specs. Two heatsinks aren't necessarily identical because they might use different fans.

Chapter 10

Monitors and Input Devices: Your Sense of Sight and Touch Restored

Monitors

Realizing that all these bits and bytes are flying around on the inside of your case, producing some of the most realistic looking games in real time, at 100 frames per second, while providing you with the clearest Dolby Surround sound signals through all 5.1 channels of audio is simply amazing when you think about what kinds of computer games people were playing just 20 years ago. All this is useless, however, if the image you see is fuzzy, grainy, and otherwise pathetic. I'm not talking about your video card, though. What I'm talking about is what your video card connects to—your monitor.

Your monitor or display, as some people like to call it, is the last stop of all the calculations that your computer has been performing. All the AI and collision detection that's in your game has already been calculated, all the texture filtering has already been applied, the appropriate antialiasing samples have been blended, and the grunt your character makes when he attacks his opponent is being transferred to your sound card right now. The combination of all this enables your video card to perform a dump from its frame buffer to its RAMDAC (Random Access Memory Digital to Analog Converter), sending a signal to a connector at the very end of the card. That signal connects to a cable that goes directly to your monitor.

I concentrate on this very device in the first part of this chapter. Too often, gamers skimp on the one component they most likely keep longer than anything else. Your monitor is a very important purchase, not because it improves performance, but because it is what your two eyes must stare at when you're gaming for hours on end.

How a Monitor Works

If you're familiar at all with how a television works, you'd assume that a monitor works in a relatively similar fashion. You wouldn't be too far off, though with one major exception, which I'll get to in a bit. First of all, when I'm talking about a monitor and how it works I'm generally referring to an analog display that uses a Cathode Ray Tube (CRT) to display an image on its screen. I discuss other monitor types later, but for now I'm only going to focus on the most common and most affordable: analog CRTs.

The name Cathode Ray Tube (CRT) is what makes up the majority of your monitor. A CRT is a fairly simple device consisting of one or more electron guns and a screen opposite them. This is the screen that you look at except from the CRT's perspective, you're looking at the screen from the opposite side. These electron guns serve one purpose and one purpose alone: to fire electrons at the screen in front of them. A pretty simple task, but what more did you expect from an electron gun? In computer monitors, three electron guns—one red, blue, and green—are aimed at the CRT screen.

Your screen is coated with Phosphorous, grouped into red, green, and blue phosphor dots. Between these phosphors and the CRT is a mask that makes sure that the electrons only hit one group of these phosphors and not in between groups. The two most popular masks used are either a Shadow Mask or an Aperture Grill (see Figure 10.1). The differences between the two is that a Shadow Mask is a metal mesh that enables the electrons fired from the guns to hit specific dots. So if a red dot (pixel) is needed in the center of the screen, the red electron gun is fired at the appropriate hole in the shadow mask and a red pixel is displayed in the center of the screen.

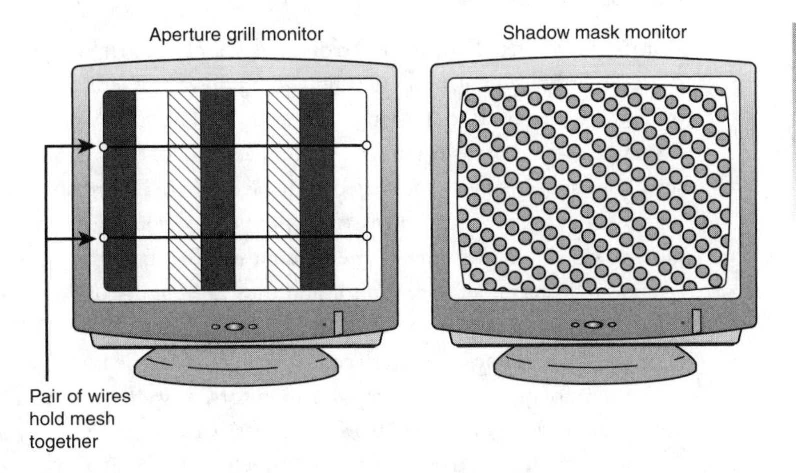

FIGURE 10.1 Illustrating the differences between an Aperture Grill and a Dot Pitch monitor. Notice the slight screen curvature of the Dot Pitch screen.

An aperture grill performs the same basic function as a shadow mask except instead of being a mesh pattern with circular holes for the electrons, a metal vertical line pattern is placed in front of the electron guns and the phosphors are organized into lines instead of a collection of dots. These lines are held in place with a few horizontal wires, which are sometimes visible as faint lines across a monitor. The major benefit of an aperture grill is that the vertical strips enable a much flatter display on a conventional CRT. One of the biggest complaints about traditional CRT displays has been that the curved surface of the screen distorts the picture too much and isn't easy to look at for long periods of time. By using an aperture grill this can be combated and you have monitors such as Sony's FD Trinitron line that boast a "truly flat" screen. Another benefit of the aperture grill is that more electrons are let through generally resulting in a brighter picture, however, the main advantage happens to be the ability to have a flatter screen. The only downside is the faint horizontal lines that are visible because of the metal holding the aperture grill in place.

The path of electrons traveling from these guns to the shadow mask or aperture grill is straight, but that's useless if you want to send these electrons anywhere other than the absolute center of your screen. Keep in mind, though, that electrons are negatively charged particles, which can be knocked off of its set course using magnetism. Using these principles, electron beams can be moved left to right or up and down. This ability enables the electron guns to effectively scan the surface of the CRT, from side to side then up and down, filling the entire screen with "excited" phosphors (those that have been hit with electrons) that create a screen full of pixels. This is where a computer monitor differs from a conventional TV.

With conventional TVs, the electron guns scan left to right and only scan every other horizontal resolution line going down the screen. The guns shut off and are sent back to the top and scan in the lines that were missed the first time around. This is known as interlaced video, because the two sets of scan lines are effectively interlaced with each other. The reason for interlacing video is to offer an inexpensive method of providing seemingly quickly moving video at a low refresh rate without causing discomfort to the viewer (seen as a flickering of the monitor and thus causing discomfort). Because of this conventional interlacing, TVs offer only 30fps of video (NTSC), but because the scan lines are interlaced, your eyes are fooled into seeing a much smoother moving picture. Computer monitors, as well as newer TVs, are non-interlaced (or in the TV world, progressive scan) in that they scan the full screen resolution from top to bottom without stopping.

Note

The rate at which your monitor can redraw the display is its refresh rate. With today's technology this rate applies to how quickly the monitor can redraw the entire display. However, in the future, it will be common for desktop monitors to selectively refresh parts of the screen that are actually updated and leave the rest of it unchanged. Selective refresh enables higher refresh rates in the areas of the screen that are refreshed.

The instructions on what pixels on the screen need to appear as what color are sent to your monitor via a 15-pin cable commonly called a VGA (Video Graphics Array) cable. Calling it a VGA cable is often a misnomer because it can be used to carry much more data than the original 640 × 480 × 16 color VGA standard. The most important pins that make up that cable are the pins that send red, green, and blue data (all colors are formed from a combination of those three colors), the horizontal sync and the vertical sync.

Higher end monitors enable the option of using Bayonet Nut Connector (BNC) cables that split up these five signals into five separate cables, theoretically improving the quality of the picture that is sent to your monitor (see Figure 10.2).

You're generally not going to notice much of an improvement unless you have a really bad VGA cable, a really good monitor, or well-trained eyes. BNC cables don't cost much more than a standard VGA cable if you shop around. However, the problem is that most monitors come with a free VGA cable and if you want BNC cables you have to purchase one yourself.

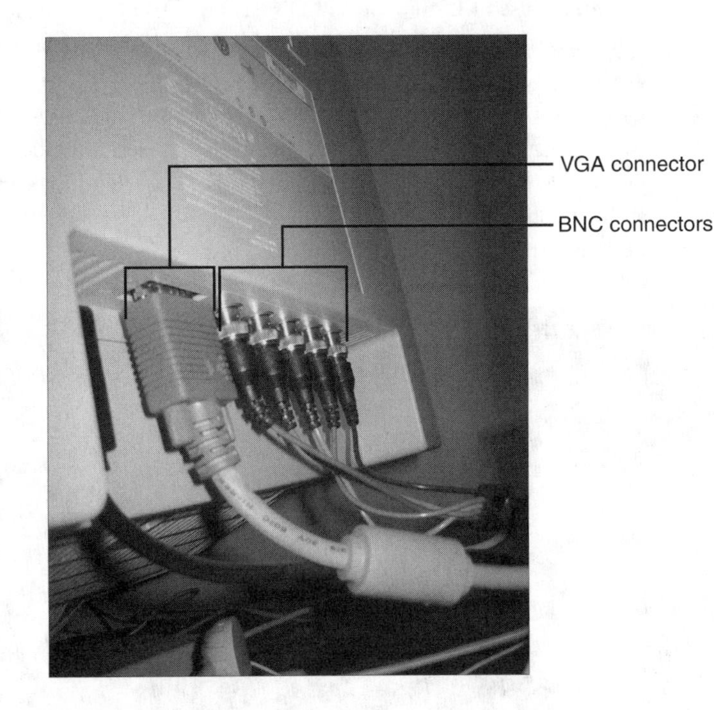

FIGURE 10.2
This Sony Trinitron FD display features both VGA and BNC connectors.

Digital Versus Analog

I mentioned that I would restrict discussion at first to analog monitors alone. However, there has been a trend in recent years toward digital displays. In the early days of computer monitors, they all used to be digital in that they could only operate at a certain frequency and resolution and were often tied down to using only one video card. Obviously this wasn't very practical, so the introduction of more flexible analog displays was met with much enthusiasm.

Unfortunately manufacturers have added to some of this confusion by labeling analog displays as digital monitors. They can get away with this because the circuitry inside of the monitor is still digital while the signals themselves are analog. Manufacturers also claimed that their analog displays were indeed digital because they offered digital controls versus the analog dials that would adjust brightness, contrast, and so on. This is like labeling a car a family sedan because it has cup holders while it only has two doors and two seats.

Today the term digital display has come back, however, this time in a different form. Instead of a display that relies on CRT technology to produce an image, the use of Liquid Crystal Display (LCDs) to produce images offers some appealing benefits (see Figure 10.3). The most popular type of LCDs are Thin Film Transistor (TFT) displays sometimes known as active matrix LCDs. A TFT LCD (the ones I talk about in this section) features a screen with a set number of pixels. Each one of these pixels can take on any color depending on the light passed through them and what filters are used to create that color. The pixels are lit by a backlight that gives LCDs their brightness advantage over conventional CRT displays.

FIGURE 10.3
This 15" Solarism LCD is unique in that it is considerably brighter than other LCDs (and CRTs). This brightness is achieved through the use of components that consume much more power than conventional LCDs.

LCDs can be analog or digital displays. The difference between the two is that an analog display receives an analog signal sent through the RAMDAC of your video card with the potential for a loss in quality. (See Chapter 5, "The Video Card: A Gamer's Heart and Soul," for more information.) A digital display, however, receives a digital signal directly from your video card without passing through a RAMDAC resulting in no loss of image data and thus no loss in image quality.

One of the biggest benefits of an LCD is that the lack of need for a CRT decreases the size of the display considerably, making it easy to create flat panel monitors that are no more than 2" in thickness. These types of displays have been used in laptops for years and today's laptops have LCDs that aren't even 0.25" in thickness. The form factor alone is convincing for many people, but then power consumption is also an issue. LCDs consume a lot less power than CRT-based displays, and thus put off a lot less heat.

As I mentioned before, LCDs are also much brighter than their CRT counterparts. The ability to have a much brighter picture is a positive note for many. Unfortunately, the biggest downside to LCDs, other than price, is that the pixel response rate of the displays are not very good. This isn't an issue if you're just typing in Word, but when playing a movie or even more importantly, when playing a fast moving game, there is a tendency for images to appear to have ghosts on LCDs because of the poor response rate of the pixels. This has improved over time, and most digital LCD displays do work fine for games; however, the issue of price comes into play, and currently prices are simply too high.

Another downside, although not as major, is that the resolution of a LCD is generally fixed because a fixed number of pixels are on the screen. With conventional CRTs you always have ways to adjust to different resolutions, but with LCDs if the monitor was constructed for operation at 1,280 × 1,024, you're stuck with that. Although I don't recommend it because image quality suffers tremendously, you have ways to increase or decrease an LCD monitor's resolution outside of its designed specifications.

Because LCDs are still lacking the degree of market penetration that CRTs enjoy, industry quality standards are few, most importantly in respect to an issue known as dead pixels. Some of the pixels in an LCD might be stuck on one color or fail to change color and this is where the dreaded red, blue, green, or dead pixel syndrome comes from. Unfortunately, each monitor manufacturer deals with dead pixels in a different way. Some exchange the unit if a certain number of dead pixels exist (usually more than 5–8). If you have a couple of dead pixels you're generally out of luck in finding a manufacturer that takes the display back. In my experience I've never had an LCD with more than one dead pixel, although I have seen situations where two or three dead pixels are present. It can be quite annoying, but you can do little about it.

In terms of what sort of digital connection exists between your video card and a digital flat panel or LCD, the standard with the most potential is the Digital Visual Interface or DVI (see Figure 10.4). The interface has enough bandwidth to enable resolutions up to 1,920 × 1,080. If you are familiar with TV resolution standards you realize that this is the 1080i HDTV resolution, offering 1,080 lines of resolution from top to bottom in a 16:9 ratio. Of course the most common resolutions for computer displays are still 4:3 (the dimensions of standard TVs) such as 640 × 480, 800 × 600, 1,024 × 768, 1,280 × 960, and 1,600 × 1,200. Still, the ability to support higher resolutions is important because competing standards generally maxed out at 1,280 × 1,024. The DVI specification uses a Transition Minimized Differential Signaling (TMDS) protocol, and requires that a TMDS transmitter and receiver are present (the transmitter on the video card and the receiver on the monitor) to transfer the signal without any noticeable electrical interference.

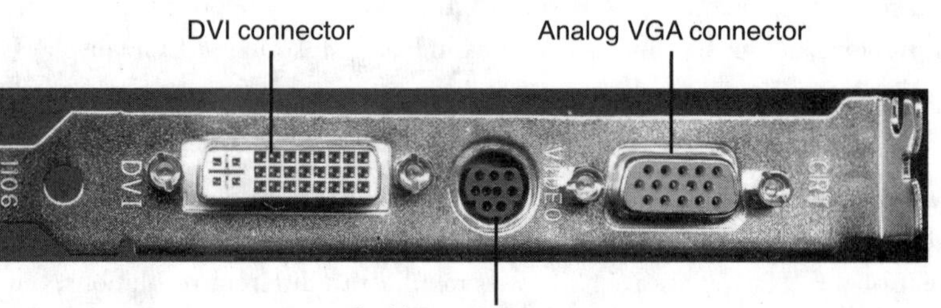

FIGURE 10.4
The back of this Gainward GeForce3 video card features three outputs, including a DVI connector driven by the GeForce3's integrated TMDS transmitter.

The reason that DVI is able to transfer enough data to enable such high resolutions is because it has two interface links, doubling the amount of bandwidth provided between the video card and the monitor. This is compared to competing solutions such as DFP that only have one interface link. The DVI specification is also flexible enough to transfer analog data so that DVI monitors could theoretically be analog monitors with a DVI connector on them. This can easily be used to confuse consumers into thinking that they're purchasing a digital LCD when they're actually getting an analog unit.

What to Look for in a Monitor

When purchasing a monitor, you can look at a few specifications when comparing similar models. The first thing you want to look at is what size monitor you want. Common sizes are 14", 15", 17", 19", and 21". You want at least a 17" monitor for your games, but ideally a 19" is a better choice. Good 21" monitors are still too expensive for most gaming budgets, but if you have the extra disposable income you certainly won't regret the investment.

When looking at monitor sizes realize that these sizes are measured diagonally from one inside corner of the monitor to the opposite. In doing this one thing that isn't taken into account is that not all that space is viewable area, because the electron guns are not always going to be able to scan perfectly at the far corners of the screen. So realistically, the viewable screen sizes are going to be a little less than the monitor sizes that are quoted by manufacturers. The flatter your display is, the larger your viewable screen size is, simply because less curvature is taken into account.

Although it is always good to see a monitor in person first, the honest truth is that most of the big chain electronics and computer stores have some of the worst monitor selections. I don't want to see any of you walking out of a store with a Compaq monitor under your arm unless it's an FD Trinitron made by Sony with a Compaq label on it. Unless you can find a good monitor locally (it is possible, just highly unlikely), you're probably going to end up purchasing a monitor online or from some other mail-order vendor, meaning that you have to figure shipping into your budget for the monitor. Remember that some unscrupulous vendors attempt to make a profit off shipping and handling charges without letting you know, so if the shipping seems even higher than it should be (and it should be pretty high) then you might want to check around for a better deal.

Dot Pitch

The most useful number when comparing two monitors that are relatively similar is a spec known as Dot Pitch. The dot pitch is the distance between two same color phosphors on the screen of the CRT that is measured in millimeters (mm). The smaller the dot pitch, the finer the picture, and the better looking the monitor. When dealing with monitors that have an aperture grill, the dot pitch refers to the horizontal distance between phosphors, but the two numbers are not directly comparable because the type of mask used differs.

In terms of acceptable dot pitch values, I normally like to see the values less than the 0.26mm point. Although going a bit higher isn't unacceptable, anything in the 0.30mm+ range is entirely too high.

Resolution and Refresh Rates

With the size of your monitor and its target dot pitch picked out, now it's time to look at resolutions and refresh rates that are supported. Generally speaking, Table 10.1 holds true in terms of what resolutions are supported by monitors according to their diagonal sizes.

Table 10.1 Typical Maximum Resolutions for Specific Monitor Sizes

Diagonal Size	Maximum Resolution
14"	1,024 × 768
15"	1,280 × 1,024
17"	1,280 × 1,024
19"	1,600 × 1,200
21"	2,048 × 1,536

Although 21" monitors can get pretty high in resolution, very few video cards have RAMDACs capable of driving a clear picture at such a high resolution, not to mention how incredibly small things get on your desktop at 2,048 × 1,536. My pick for a gaming monitor is 19". At this size you can get a pretty good Windows desktop resolution and also a big enough screen to truly immerse yourself in a game when playing at 1,280 × 1,024.

The next consideration is the refresh rate at these resolutions. As a quick refresher (no pun intended), the refresh rate is how quickly an image can be displayed on your monitor. The most common default refresh rate is 60Hz, or your screen is "refreshed" every 16.6 ms. For most people 60Hz is too low of a refresh rate. I prefer 85Hz, but keep in mind that people's eyes vary and what is suitable for one person might be completely unacceptable for another. When buying a monitor, though, make sure that your monitor supports at least 75Hz or 85Hz at the resolution you're going to be running at most of the time (this is your 2D Windows Desktop resolution). Some monitors boast 100Hz refresh rates, and although those are nice to have, at the higher resolutions (for example, 1,600 × 1,200) you're going to be spending big bucks to get that sort of functionality in a monitor.

Other Features

These days monitors don't come with a screen and two cables. They usually have many more functions than just being able to display a good looking image. Obviously, a good-looking image should be your first goal, but second to that you can look for other features.

If you're really short on desk space, try monitors that come with built in speakers, although I am far from a fan of these monitors. Rarely do you find a good monitor with integrated speakers. As I mentioned in Chapter 6, "Sound: Waking Up the Neighbors," a good surround speaker system is key to an immersive gaming experience.

Much more useful in my opinion than built-in speakers, is a built-in powered USB hub that enables you to connect USB devices (usually 2 or 4) to USB connectors normally integrated into the base of the monitor (see Figure 10.5).

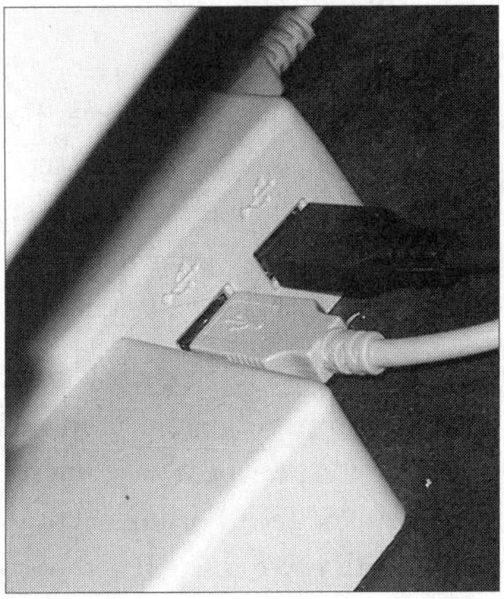

FIGURE 10.5
The base of this 21" monitor has a built-in powered USB hub with four ports; two on each side.

The only downside to a powered hub in your monitor is that if you shut off your monitor, all your devices shut off as well. In this case it's better to tell Windows to put your monitor into sleep mode whenever you leave your desk or after an adequate period of inactivity. With joysticks, gamepads, and camera connections scattered around your desk, it's always easier to plug them into the base of your monitor instead of the back of your computer.

Another feature that is quite useful is short neck CRT monitors. Obviously this doesn't apply to flat panel LCD displays. However, when you get to 19"+ in size, monitors can get pretty big not only in their weights, but in their footprints—meaning they occupy a lot of desk space. Some monitors offer a "short neck" form factor, meaning that the back of the monitor does not extend as far back as other monitors in its size class. However, make sure the quality is there first before going for any short neck monitors. I have seen quite a few good-looking ones in my experience, so they do exist.

Quality, Reliability, and Manufacturer Support

Tip

Ideally, a "good" RMA policy should have a monitor turn-around time of no more than a couple of days and they should cover shipping at least one way, but preferably both ways (this is rare). If you can find a company that cross ships a fixed monitor, you've very likely struck gold in terms of support. However, I have yet to see this happen as monitors are very expensive items.

Unless you're interested in dumping another $300–$800 a year or two after purchasing a monitor, you want to make sure that you pick a quality product. The main reason I stress how important it is that you choose your monitor well is because it is with you through most of your upgrades, for years to come. In the unfortunate event that something does go wrong with your monitor, you want to deal with a manufacturer that has a good RMA (Return Merchandise Authorization) policy and is willing to work with you on problems.

Because of the nature of monitors and because you have to stick with them for so long, I have never been an advocate of purchasing refurbished monitors. Although you can save a lot of money, sometimes the hassles just aren't worth it. Granted in some cases you can find a refurbished product that works even better than a brand new one, but that's like winning the lottery and it's a chance I'm never big on taking.

Do some research, ask around for any good or bad experiences with RMAs and various manufacturers, and do online searches for any positive or negative experiences with the particular brand in which you're interested. The AnandTech Forums (`http://forums.anandtech.com`) is a great place to start with more than 60,000 people waiting to help you out in doing just that.

Monitor Brand Picks

Although it's difficult to recommend that you stick with a particular brand because so many are out there, I can give you an idea of the brands I've had particularly good experiences with:

- **iiYama**—Makes relatively good monitors that are very affordable. I haven't had too much experience with them, but the experiences I have had have been positive.
- **Mitsubishi**—Monitors are often of good quality and reasonably priced. Mitsubishi's tubes are often compared to Sony's quality but are significantly lower priced.

- **Samsung**—Usually has a good balance of price and image quality. A few AnandTech editors either use or have used Samsung monitors in the past and have had good experiences with them.
- **Sony's FD Trinitron**—A favorite of mine. Unfortunately, its monitors are usually priced much higher than the competition for sometimes marginal gains in quality. I've never had any trouble with them, but you can usually find a better deal elsewhere.

Many other good monitors are out there. Your best bet is to ask around. If you're interested in computer hardware, chances are that some of your friends have got some pretty good hardware and potentially good monitors to look at. Ask about their experiences as well.

Input Devices

Now that you know about the biggest output device you're going to have to look at, what about the devices that you use to get input into your system? I often complain about how slow hard drives are when they can only transfer 40MBps of data, but the human hands can only type 60–120 words per minute, so in the end your computer is only as fast as you can give it data. Luckily, that isn't the case for all applications, otherwise there would be no need for 2GHz processors and gigabytes per second of bandwidth between components.

Input devices are one of the few components in your system that aren't directly related to performance, but like monitors, people too often cut corners with input devices. Although these components don't directly relate to performance, in all actuality, they relate to your health and your ability to play games effectively. Anyone who's tried to play a flight simulator game with a gamepad, or had a racing wheel give out in the 495th lap of a 500-lap race can attest to that.

Ergonomics

The ergonomics of your input devices is a very important feature because it affects your health. You've undoubtedly heard of repetitive motion injuries such as Carpal tunnel syndrome. These injuries are caused by overuse of, in this case, your hands for long periods of time. These conditions are worsened by poor posture while typing, poorly designed desks and/or chairs or setups that are too large or too small for you. Even poorly designed keyboards and mice can contribute to such problems.

If any of these conditions develop it is best to get some literature on the condition and see a doctor immediately. The damage that is done by ignoring these repetitive motion injuries can be serious and shouldn't be taken lightly.

This is one of the reasons why you should always get as much experience with the keyboards and mice you're going to be using before you purchase them. Luckily, it's usually pretty easy to find the keyboards or mice you want locally, so you can actually go down to the store to try them out. Don't be surprised if your opinion changes after a few days of actually using the device because even at the store you're not using it in the exact same manner you would at home.

I'm a big fan of the Microsoft Natural keyboards. Their split design doesn't cause a problem if you have proper touch typing technique and the learning curve for the keyboard isn't too steep at all.

Microsoft's optical mice have also been another favorite of mine, although their original Wheel Mouse still feels better in my hand than the newer optical designs.

Interfaces

Your input devices can use many other interface types. In the past, it was common for all keyboards and mice to use PS/2 connectors and all gamepads/joysticks to use the game port on the back of your sound card. With the advent of the Universal Serial Bus (USB) things have changed considerably. These days almost all the input devices you could possibly want are available in a USB version, which is my personal preference.

There are two options in the BIOS that may help USB compatibility: *Enable USB Keyboard Support* and *Enable USB Mouse Support* (the latter being rare in most BIOSes). All these options do is enable USB support in OSes and situations in which you don't necessarily have driver support for your devices (for example, under DOS or at a command prompt). The options are usually found in the Integrated Peripherals menu in your BIOS.

The only thing to keep in mind with adding multiple USB peripherals is that you eventually might need a powered hub. Not all motherboards can supply enough current to their on-board USB ports to power as many devices as you are trying to connect. This is one of the reasons why I am particularly fond of monitors with built-in USB hubs, although you can find keyboards that also include a pair of USB ports for connecting a mouse or other peripheral.

The ease of use with USB peripherals and the ability to hot plug them (add or remove them without shutting off your computer—although you can do this with PS/2 devices it's definitely not recommended) are two main advantages of using USB for your peripherals. And when you're dealing with input devices, you're rarely going to exceed USB's 12Mbps peak theoretical bandwidth (that's a lot of data to be used up by a mere keyboard or mouse).

The PS/2, serial, and game port interfaces used to be popular. With PS/2 you lose any sort of plug and play capabilities as it is always recommended that your computer be off before installing any PS/2 devices. With serial and game port interfaces you're fine installing while your computer is on; you just have to make sure that the ports are enabled in your BIOS (if the game port is on your sound card then you've got to make sure that it has drivers installed under Device Manager).

Other interfaces might be appropriate for you depending on your situation. Wireless interfaces are rare, but those that do exist use RF (Radio Frequency) waves or IR (Infrared) beams to transmit data from the input device, to a receiver that is connected to your PC. These types of interfaces are especially useful in setting up a Home Theater PC or any sort of PC that is connected to a TV, so you aren't restricted by keyboard or mouse cables. For the most part, if you're just running a regular desktop computer you do not need to spend the extra money on wireless input devices because you don't get much benefit from them.

Drivers

Just as is the case with any other device, you want to make sure that your input device has good driver support under the OS you plan on using it. Most of the more well known manufacturers (such as Logitech and Microsoft of course) have drivers integrated into the major Microsoft OSes, and as long as the device isn't brand new, most other devices should have some native driver support under the OS. If they don't, you want to make sure that drivers are available both on CD and for download from the device manufacturer's Web site. A Web-based source for drivers are important if you're anything like me, losing a driver CD isn't too difficult to accomplish.

Keyboards

Many types of keyboards are available, the most common being QWERTY keyboards (indicated by the first six letters across the first row of alphabetic keys). The biggest competing standard keyboard is the Dvorak layout, which is named after the creator of the standard. Although Dvorak is supposed to be theoretically more efficient than the widely accepted QWERTY layout (it places the most frequently used keys in the center of the keyboard), it has never caught on and most likely never will because of the sheer penetration of QWERTY keyboards in the market. In this section, I focus on the most widely available and accepted standard, in this case QWERTY keyboards.

QWERTY keyboards are set apart by their many differences; the biggest difference is the layout of the keys. Although most keyboards have a row of Function keys (F1–F12) at the top of the keyboard, numbers directly below that, and alphabetic keys below them, the positioning and size of keys such as the Enter/Return key, space bar, Windows keys, and so on, can vary tremendously from one keyboard to the next.

With the advent of the Microsoft Natural keyboard, many keyboards began offering a split design where the home row (where your fingers should be located at rest) is split in the middle and the keys angled away from each other to improve ergonomics (see Figure 10.6).

FIGURE 10.6
The Microsoft Natural Keyboard splits the home row in two, offering a more comfortable typing position for some while others find it a hassle to deal with.

Despite the debate over its ease of use, this type of keyboard has improved ergonomics. It appears to be very difficult to master, but its bark is a lot worse than its bite. If you cannot properly touch type, this type of a keyboard might not be right for you. The wrong finger can end up traveling a much longer distance to reach a key that's much closer in normal keyboards.

The type and texture of keys can vary from one keyboard to the next as well. This is where being able to try keyboards before you buy them helps tremendously, so you can decide whether or not you like the feel of the keys and how they respond to being depressed. Also remember to not only see how typing on the keyboard feels, but place your hands in the positions they are in while playing the games you most frequently play and see how the keyboard design works for you then. You are building a gaming computer after all.

Mice

Like keyboards, mice come in a couple different flavors. In the past, mice would use a heavy ball to track along the surface of a pad that would then move two rollers on the inside of your mouse; one controlled movement along the y-axis, and the other controlled movement along the x-axis. This enabled very precise movement, but unfortunately offered a few shortcomings.

The mouse ball would continually pick up dust, dirt, and grime from the mouse pad. The accumulation of this on your pad transferred to the mouse ball that then generally managed to adhere itself to the rollers on the inside of the mouse. This would cause the mouse to lose precision and would make it feel like it was passing over a bumpy surface when moving it around.

Mouse pads offered varying levels of traction and the types of surfaces you could use the mouse on were limited because of the necessity for a mouse pad.

The shortcomings weren't major, but after the technology arrived, there was a demand for a more elegant solution. Thus was the birth of the optical mouse. An optical mouse forgoes the use of rollers and instead uses a small CCD (Charge Coupled Device) to take thousands of pictures or samples per second of the surface it is moving over (see Figure 10.7). By comparing the pictures it tells your computer where, how far, and how fast you moved the mouse. There have been optical mice in the past, but they have never been very efficient nor desirable (most of them requiring placement on a reflective surface). Today's optical mice are much more advanced and are quite useable.

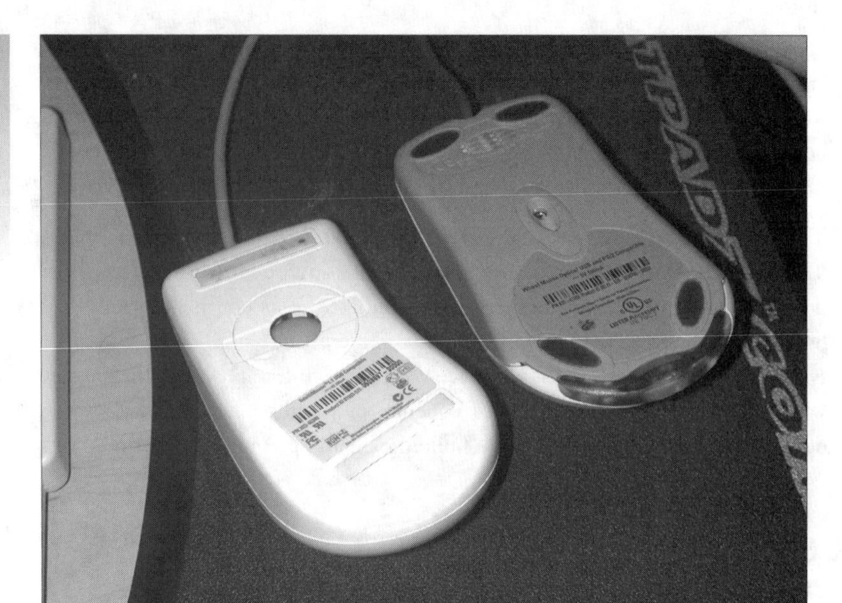

FIGURE 10.7
Maintaining an optical mouse (right) is much easier than doing so for one that uses rollers (left) that collect dirt and hair just through every-day use.

Tip

Even though I use an optical mouse, I still prefer a hard yet smooth surface to track on such as the "Ratpad" created by Kyle Bennett of HardOCP.com.

The benefits of an optical mouse are exactly the weak points of the ball mice. Because optical mice have no rolling balls, you have no chance of them picking up dirt (rollers do not exist) and because they rely on optics to move around you can get good movement on surfaces other than mouse pads. However, some mouse pads often offer the best surface for your mouse to glide on regardless of the technology they're built on (see Figure 10.8).

The biggest downside to optical mice is that the number of samples the CCD takes per second is usually too low. The first optical Microsoft mouse could only take 1,500 samples per second. Although that may seem like a lot, it wasn't enough for some games. One of the most common things that hardcore FPS gamers do is flick their mouse very quickly to spin their character. These flicks are often too fast for the CCD to keep up with, causing the mouse to lose "sight" of where you want to move. Microsoft and other manufacturers of these mice have improved the CCDs in their mice to increase the number of samples taken per second, but the problem still exists. Luckily, you have time to try out the mouse and decide whether you want to keep it or not courtesy of lenient return policies of most larger computer chain stores.

FIGURE 10.8
Mousing surfaces are key to having a responsive mouse, which is very important in fast-paced games.

After you get past the ball versus optical choice, other features to look for are the number of buttons, scroll wheels, and so on. Personally I prefer the standard two button + 1 scroll wheel design, although other designs have buttons such as back and forth buttons for browsing Web pages. The scroll wheel has become very useful in games, especially for quickly switching between your arsenal of weapons in a first person shooter. This is a must have for a gaming mouse.

Of course driver support is another issue to take into account, but for the most part, unless you go with something very exotic, drivers should be included with your OS for most mice.

Joysticks and Gamepads

I don't have much more to say about joysticks and gamepads that hasn't already been said about keyboards and mice. Your best bet is to try out the controller first at a store or through first hand experience with the controller on a friend's computer.

Special concerns to take into account when dealing with joysticks and gamepads include game compatibility and any programs that it ships with to reassign the buttons for games that don't necessarily "see" all of them.

Most older controllers use the game/MIDI port on the back of your sound card to interface with your PC. Again, I'd suggest sticking with USB just for simplicity of the interface if possible.

When it comes to choosing what type of game controller you're going to purchase you have to look at the types of games you play. You don't want to buy a flight stick to play *Unreal Warfare* nor do you want to buy a game pad to get the full experience of *Flight Simulator 2002*.

For racing titles, racing wheels and peddles obviously make the most sense. For flight simulators, flight sticks with accompanying thrust controllers and foot-operated rudder controls can really help immerse you as you cruise those friendly skies. For most sports games and certain action/adventure titles you're best off using a standard gamepad. Using any of these controllers in a first person shooter is difficult, however, because you don't get the flexibility, quickness, or precision of the keyboard/mouse combo. Force feedback controllers are also an interesting bunch in that they attempt to add realism by making the controller vibrate (or provide you with force feedback) as you interact with your surroundings in a game. As to how realistic this effect is, that's really up to you and the quality of the controller you buy. At first the effect can be a bit distracting, but over time it can either improve your gaming experience or become something you get used to and not necessarily enjoy.

Chapter 11

Putting It All Together: Break Out the Hammers and Duct Tape

Building Your PC

If you've been reading this book sequentially, then at this point you are much more knowledgeable about virtually every single component that resides in or around your PC than when you first flipped the page over to Chapter 1, "The Central Processing Unit: The Heart and Soul of the PC." You know about the inner workings of a microprocessor, understand the need for bandwidth, and the word latency actually carries some meaningful explanation. These terms are no longer just buzzwords that manufacturers can throw at you assuming you don't understand them. You are now at the point where you are an educated gaming enthusiast; but the ride isn't over yet.

As you probably know from your experiences in the real world, book smarts can only get you so far. To truly pass the test you not only need book sense, but you also have to have common sense. This is where the next step in building your new gaming PC comes in: putting the system together. It's great if you know that a DRAM cell is capacitor-based, but unless you know how to install a SDRAM module, that knowledge isn't going to help you much in building your PC. So now that you have the book smarts, it's time to give you the practical knowledge of how to start building your computer. Break out the hammers and the duct tape and let's take a look at what you need to complete this job.

Tools for the Job

Contrary to the title of this chapter, you don't really need any heavy-duty tools to build your own PC. Actually when you think about it, you only really need two tools: patience and a screwdriver. However, to make this process as simple as possible, I do recommend having a little more than just those two, but let's take a look at the two basic requirements first.

Patience...and a Screwdriver

The first tool you need is definitely patience. You just spent between hundreds and maybe even thousands of dollars on your hardware, and it takes little more than an impatient soul to ruin some of the most expensive components in your collection. As a kid we've all broken our toys and felt the disappointment when we no longer play with them. You experience the same feeling if you find that you've shorted out your motherboard, or cracked the core on your CPU. The difference this time is that the feeling is 10 times worse and 50 times as costly.

This hopefully makes you understand the need for patience when setting up your system. Often times applying too much force can get you into trouble with your new toys, but even more likely is rushing through something resulting in you either missing a step along the way or actually damaging a component. If you follow the directions in this chapter you should be just fine. Be patient with yourself and the hardware and pace yourself. If you find yourself in an overly excited mood when you're ready to put your system together take a break. Being too fast paced can get you into trouble. Overlooking a minor detail that can result in a cloud of smoke is very easy. Just remember that plugging the power cable in to your floppy drive just one pin off can result in that very cloud of smoke.

During this process it is very easy at times to get frustrated with the hardware, especially if things aren't going exactly as planned. Hopefully, if you've chosen your components wisely, this isn't a problem. However, you can never be fully aware of all the issues that could crop up with various combinations of hardware.

Frustration is the easiest way to land yourself with some broken hardware, and chances are that you are much less productive when you are frustrated. If you do find yourself getting frustrated, it is time for a break. The setup isn't going to go anywhere while you take a break. You are much clearer and level headed when you return to it and hopefully are able to accomplish much more. The frustration element usually comes into play not in the physical construction phase, but in the actual software installation and setup phase where things don't always go as planned. Nevertheless, it's best to keep this in mind now, because when building a PC, if something *can* go wrong, it probably does.

The second basic requirement for the task at hand is a screwdriver. Luckily this tool is much more tangible than "patience" but it is just as important to the job. You can usually get by with nothing more than a Phillips screwdriver. If you don't have one I wouldn't suggest going out and buying the fanciest screwdriver you can. However, if you do have one that enables you to change the bits or heads on it, it is quite useful (see Figure 11.1). Chances are that not all the screws you use will be a best fit by a single Phillips bit, so it's helpful to have multiple bits—some that are larger and some that are smaller.

There you have it, the basic requirements as far as tools go, but you do want to make this process as simple as possible. Let's discuss some of the other tools that you grow very close to during this process.

Note

Using an electric screwdriver when building a PC definitely speeds things up. I've never had a problem using one, but do remember that sometimes too much power can be problematic, especially if your hand slips and the heavy screwdriver finds itself cutting a trace on your motherboard.

When dealing with case, drive, or expansion card screws you're probably okay. However, unless you have extreme confidence in your abilities, don't ever use an electric screwdriver when adding or removing the screws that affix your motherboard to your case.

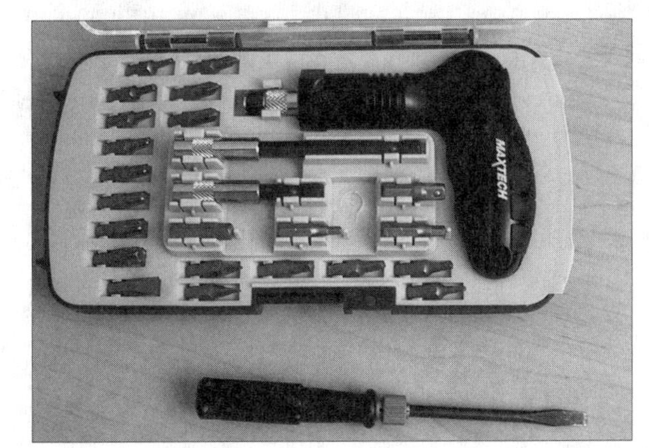

FIGURE 11.1
A Flathead screwdriver and a versatile screwdriver set.

Although you can get by on just a Phillips head screwdriver, it is useful to have a flathead screwdriver as well. This type of a screwdriver, as the name implies, has a flat "head" that is useful for prying things open. For our purposes, it is great for installing the heatsink on your CPU.

Other Tools of the Trade

Needle nose pliers are another unspoken necessity for any hardware enthusiast. Hopefully your first building experience won't require the use of the pliers. However, you might run into a situation where you have to unbend a pin or some other tiny component that has become bent because of a lack of the first tool or simply poor handling later on. Never fear—a steady hand and a set of good needle nose pliers can often solve those issues in which something must be unbent.

Quite possibly the most frustrating thing that can happen during the building process can be dropping a screw into the depths of your case. It happens to the best of us and it happens entirely too often. You're trying to hold a screw in place so that you can screw it in with your driver. The minute you think you have it caught on your screwdriver head and let go, the screw falls and you hear that ever-so-annoying clanging of your screw against the parts in your case. Finding the screw is a science in itself, and you simple can't leave it there because the components in your computer don't like having a piece of metal on them. In fact, this is one of the easiest ways to throw away hundreds of dollars if you're interested. Because it does conduct electricity, metal in contact with a PCB, whether it is your motherboard or one of your peripheral cards, can result in a short that can completely ruin the part. You want to avoid dropping screws in your case because they can be hard to find. Retrieving them after you have located them can be pretty difficult as well.

Luckily a tool accomplishes this very task. The tool goes under a variety of names, but it is essentially a long rod with a set of claws at the end of it (see Figure 11.2). Depressing a button at the top of the rod opens the claws, and releasing causes the claws to close on whatever happens to be caught in them; whether it is your tongue or a screw. You want to use it for picking up screws only. For some reason I always seem to find people that have used it on their tongue at one point or another. Maybe it's something that every true enthusiast must try, but I don't recommend it. This tool is usually found in a lot of the "made for computer" toolkits and can be a very valuable asset.

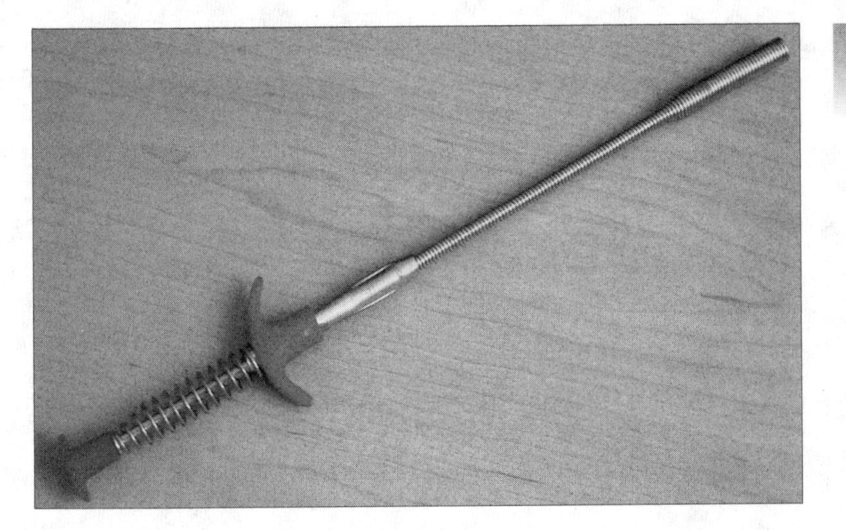

FIGURE 11.2
A four-pronged pickup tool.

Staying Organized

Tip

Although they are a little bulky, empty camera film canisters can make an excellent, and cheap, means of keeping different screws easily accessible.

The more computers you build, the more screws you're going to have leftover. Keeping these screws organized is useful because it helps you when you're looking for a particular type of screw. Organizing screws require very little, outside of containers, for the various types of screws. What you quickly realize is that "one size fits all" does not exist when it comes to the screws that are used in your case. One type of screw is used to mount your motherboard, while another is used for peripheral cards and hard drives, and yet another type is used for CD and DVD drives. The easiest way to keep screws separate and easily accessible is to store them in little bags or plastic containers that aren't too big, but enable you to get to the screws when needed. Although it might seem tedious, you thank yourself countless times if you keep the screws in their place.

Static—Your PC's Silent Stalker

A major problem with computer components is electrostatic discharge or ESD. You've all felt the tingly shock when walking across a carpeted floor on a dry day and reaching out to shake a person's hand only to be met with a spark. This spark can be very bad if the receiving end happens to be your motherboard or a memory module. One of the worst things about ESD is that you don't notice the effects right away. A motherboard damaged by an

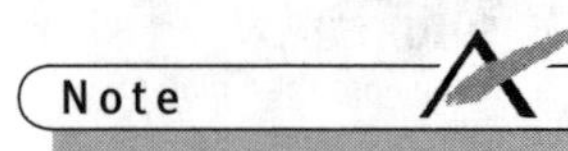

ESD might work just fine for the first few months or even years of operation, but a problem can creep up because of it. Because it is very difficult to diagnose properly (you can't detect physical signs of damage without destroying the PCB and taking a microscope to it), it is best that you take the proper precautions to avoid it the first time around.

Note

Although I know the feeling of excitement when you first get your hands on your new hardware, I'd recommend keeping it in its anti-static packaging until you are ready to install it.

When you're done, store your anti-static bag along with any other PC-related odds and ends you might have. As time goes on, you accumulate a nice collection of anti-static bags, which can come in handy when performing upgrades or troubleshooting hardware.

The easiest way to protect your PC from static is to make sure you are grounded when proceeding with a hardware install. This is done easily by making sure you are in contact with a metal portion of your case, such as the power supply, before proceeding. Another precaution many take is purchasing an anti-static wristband that ensures you are grounded at all times. A small investment in a device like this can definitely help ensure that your components won't develop problems later on in their lives. Nothing is worse than turning on your computer one day and finding out that it doesn't work.

The final unspoken requirement for the tools for the job is just a clean workspace, for example, a tabletop. Just make sure that all your components are within arms reach and your workspace isn't cluttered with junk that isn't pertinent to the install at hand. Keep all food and liquids as far away from your work area as possible. Hard drives don't like roast beef, and CPU's don't know how to swim in the various unhealthy liquids we enjoy so very much. Wiping down your tabletop with an anti-static cleaning wipe can be useful and it keeps things clean.

Now that I've discussed the essential tools necessary for building a PC, it's time to get your hands dirty and put this bad boy together.

Putting It All Together

At this point you should have all your hardware ready. All the pieces should be out of their respective boxes, but it is best if you keep the individual components in their anti-static packaging whether they happen to be in anti-static bags or plastic cases (see Figure 11.3). This keeps them safe until you are ready to deal with them, and, if you have your anti-static wristband on, your handling of them shouldn't cause any problems.

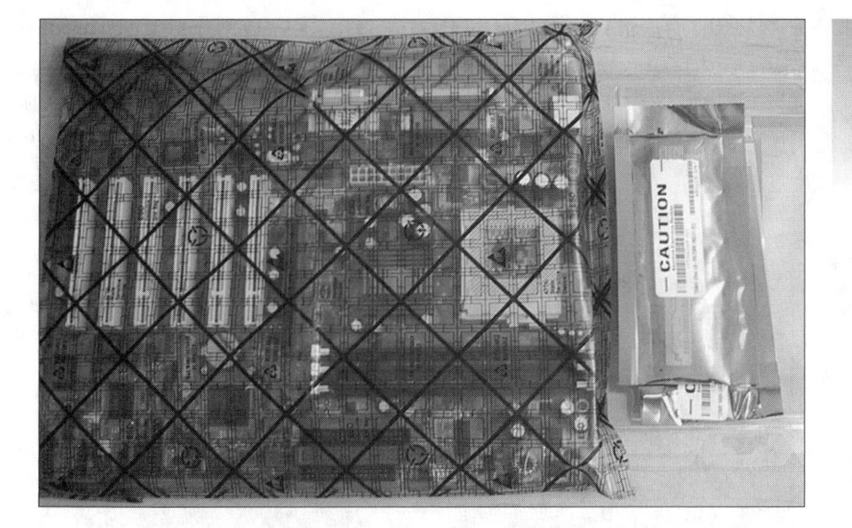

FIGURE 11.3
Anti-static bags help protect components like motherboards and memory modules until you can install them.

Prepping the Case

Definitely the largest component you have to deal with is your case (also referred to as the chassis). Computer cases are generally shipped with all the screws you need for your components as well as a power cord for connecting your power supply to your wall outlet. All this stuff, including the power supply in most cases, is usually found on the inside of the case, so your first task is to open your case.

Depending on the type of case you have, this might require nothing more than removing the left panel from the chassis (or to the right if you're looking at the back of the case) or taking off the entire housing (see Figure 11.4). You know your case best, so find out what is necessary to gain access to the motherboard tray and the drive housings on the inside. After doing that you'll probably find a box with all the screws, cables, drive rails (if applicable), and a set of little components known as standoffs. Take all these components out of your case and lay it on its side. The first thing you need are the standoffs.

As I mentioned before, your motherboard doesn't like being in direct contact with metal. In fact, if you want a quick way to kill a motherboard, then screw it directly onto the motherboard tray in your case. I'm willing to guess that your intention isn't to ruin the $150 motherboard you just bought. Yet you have to be able to screw the motherboard into place or it is going to move around in your computer. If you look at your motherboard you notice that around nine holes are surrounded by metal borders. These are the only parts of your motherboard where you can put a screw in and not short out the board, this is what they are designed for. But we still have the problem of the fact that the bottom of the motherboard can't be touching any metal either. This is where standoffs come into play (see Figure 11.5).

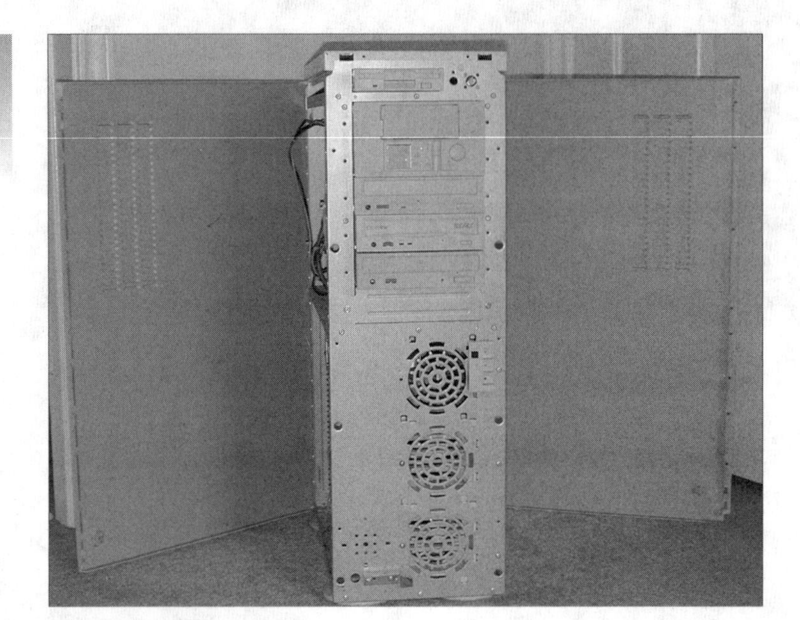

FIGURE 11.4
This tower ATX case has had its side panels and front cover removed.

FIGURE 11.5
Standoffs keep the metal-sensitive parts of a motherboard at a safe distance from the motherboard tray.

A standoff is a little metal object that screws into the motherboard tray in your case and has an open, but threaded top so screws can screw into it. Standoffs used to be predominantly plastic; however most ATX case standoffs today are the metal type that screw into your motherboard tray. Plastic standoffs generally snap into your motherboard tray. The standoff actually raises your motherboard about a quarter of an inch, but this makes sure that the rest of your motherboard doesn't come in contact with the metal motherboard tray in your case.

The first task at hand is for you to mount these standoffs in your case. A couple types of standoffs exist, and some cases actually have the standoffs already mounted on the motherboard tray so you don't have to worry about this step (see Figure 11.6). However, if you do, the easiest way is to look at the holes on your motherboard, line them up with the holes on the motherboard tray, and then put standoffs in all the holes that line up.

Remember that motherboard + metal where it doesn't belong = dead motherboard. So if you screw a standoff into a hole that doesn't line up with a designated hole on the motherboard, your motherboard shorts out. Double and triple check that your standoffs are in the right place during this part of the process.

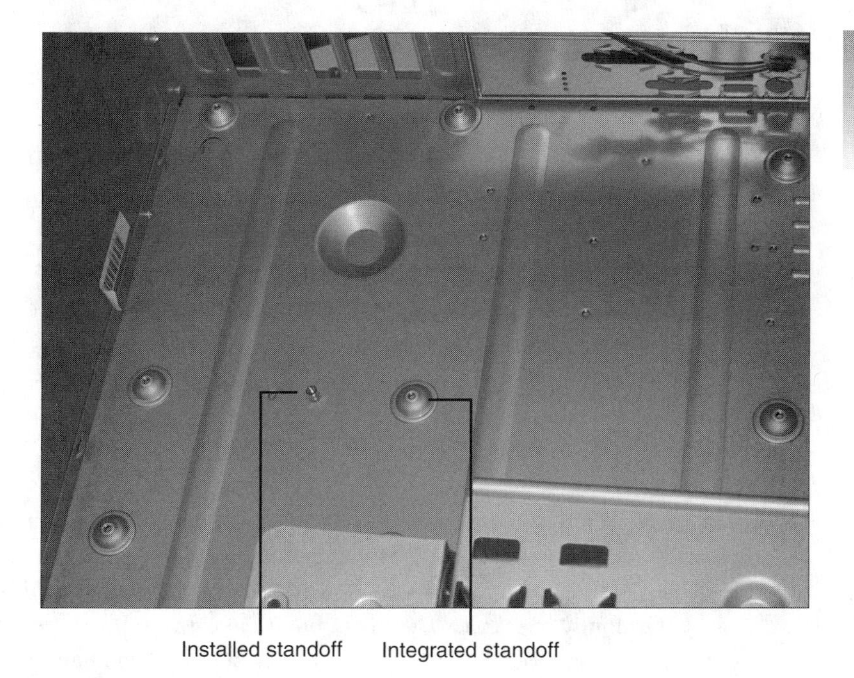

FIGURE 11.6
An installed standoff and a standoff integrated into the motherboard tray.

The standoffs can be hand tightened. They don't require any tools for installation. You want to make sure the standoffs are screwed in well because you don't want them to come out if you have to remove the screw that is screwed into them. If that does happen it's not a big deal. It just means that you have to remove the entire motherboard to reseat the standoff, which is a pain that most of us would rather avoid.

Some motherboards require additional standoffs on which to mount your CPU's heatsink, so make sure that these are in place as well. Your motherboard, not your case, usually comes with these standoffs.

With the standoffs in place, the next job is to install the ATX I/O panel (see Figure 11.7). This is a little piece of flimsy metal that fits in the opening at the rear of your case. It serves two purposes. It enables the only openings at the rear of your case to be for the ports on your motherboard and intakes/outlets for fans. It also provides shielding and a ground for the ports on your motherboard. It is better if you do install this panel, but your computer works just fine if it isn't installed.

FIGURE 11.7
An ATX I/O panel integrated into the case.

The panel installs from the inside of your case by simply pushing it into place. This is one of the relatively few times that some force is required. However, I caution you that it is easy to cut yourself when installing this panel. The flimsy metal seems harmless, but it can cut you. If you feel that you have to push relatively hard to get it to stay in place, you might want to grab a pair of gloves to keep your gaming fingers unscathed. The easiest way to pop the panel into place is to line it up and work from one corner to the next, pushing it in and holding it in as you push in the next to make sure it doesn't pop out.

You might need to remove some of the cutouts on the panel depending on what ports you happen to have on your motherboard. The needle nose pliers can serve a purpose here in removing these cutouts, but your fingers can do the same task if necessary. Make sure you don't bend the parts of the panel that stick out into your case; these make contact with the ports on your motherboard to provide a ground for them.

Once the port is in place you can put your case aside for a moment because you don't need it right away. If your case didn't come with a power supply installed, I'd suggest waiting on installing that after the motherboard is in the case. Doing this gives you some extra room to work with. If the power supply is already installed in the case (which is most common) then don't worry about it; you can work around it.

Prepping the Motherboard

As soon as you get your motherboard inside your case the amount of space you have to work with decreases considerably. Some tasks simply cannot be accomplished while your motherboard is mounted in your case, so it's best to get as much done with the motherboard while it is still out of the case and on your table. While working on your motherboard you can either rest it on your tabletop or rip open the anti-static bag it came in so that you have a single sheet of an anti-static surface for your motherboard to rest on while you work. Because these bags typically have a thin layer of conductive metal on the outside, which is nice for components when on the inside, be sure to rest it on the inside surface of the bag.

> **Note**
> Because these sockets require virtually no force to install a CPU, they were originally referred to as Zero Insertion Force (ZIF) sockets.

The first thing you'll want to do is install your CPU. Depending on the type of interface your CPU uses, the steps necessary to install it varies. For most socketed CPU designs, including Socket A, 370 and 423, a lever must be lifted before you can install the CPU (see Figure 11.8). Lifting the lever enables the socket to accept a CPU. The next step is to line up the pins on the CPU and drop it into the socket.

Lining up the pins properly is critical to not bending them. When the CPU has been properly lined up, it should just slide easily into the socket without any real force. If force is required to get it in, or it doesn't seem to want to go in, double check to see that the pins are indeed lined up.

Today's CPUs don't go in the sockets more than one way, so the pins have to be perfectly lined up in order for the processor to install properly. Flip the CPU over and match the pin pattern with the pattern on the socket to find out the proper orientation of the CPU. If the CPU is properly oriented yet it still won't go in, make sure that none of the pins are bent. Look at them very carefully because a bent pin can easily stop you from installing a CPU. If you've properly handled the CPU and it wasn't poorly packaged, you shouldn't have any bent pins. If a pin is only slightly bent you can try unbending it with your fingernail or with the tip of a flathead screwdriver, but be *very* careful in doing so. These pins are quite delicate and can break easily. With all the pins straight, and the CPU properly oriented, the socket might be a little tight; applying a little more force should get the CPU to install properly. After the CPU is in, close the lever and make sure it is locked in place.

FIGURE 11.8
Lifting the lever on a CPU socket.

If your heatsink requires the use of thermal compound (see Chapter 9, "Cases and Cooling: Living in Style and Keeping Your Cool"), meaning that it doesn't already have a thermal pad in place to aid heat transfers, then you can apply a small amount of it to the surface of your CPU now. Remember that the only place you need to apply it to is the core of the CPU, where the heatsink actually makes contact with the CPU. No more than a thin layer, evenly spread over the surface is necessary. You can apply it with your index finger; just make sure you wash your hands afterwards because thermal grease isn't exactly something you want to be digesting. It might take a few rinses and some good scrubbing before you can get the residue off your finger, but it does come off eventually.

FIGURE 11.9
The pin holes in this Socket 423 (left) are designed to line up with the equivalent pins of a Pentium 4 processor (right).

The final step involving your CPU is the installation of the heatsink and fan. Your CPU gets quite hot so this is an absolute necessity. To help cool today's extremely hot running processors, heatsinks are much heavier and require much more force to install than they once did. Just as the case is with your CPU installation, your heatsink installation varies according to the type of CPU you have as well as the type of heatsink and motherboard you have.

Installing a Pentium 4 Heatsink

The heatsink installation for the Pentium 4 is more complicated than it was for previous Intel processors, but it's not too bad. The first job is to make sure that the heatsink retention mechanism is installed on the motherboard, which should have already been taken care of before you ever got the motherboard. If not, all you do is put the set black retention brackets in place (see Figure 11.10). They later screw into their respective standoffs on the motherboard, unless your motherboard simply uses a plastic retention kit that just snaps into it.

FIGURE 11.10
The Pentium 4 heatsink retention mechanism installed.

With the retention mechanism in place, and your CPU installed, all you have to do is sit the heatsink on top of the CPU. While the heatsink pictured in Figure 11.11 doesn't have a fan on it, most of the heatsinks you purchase already have a fan mounted on it. The next step is to install the brackets, which snap onto the clips on both sides of the retention brackets shown in Figure 11.10.

FIGURE 11.11
The Pentium 4 heatsink brackets installed.

After installing both brackets make sure that the heatsink fan is given power by connecting it to either one of the three-pin fan connectors on the motherboard or to a five-pin power connector stemming from your power supply (after the motherboard and power supply are in the case). Be certain the fan gets power; otherwise it doesn't spin and you can damage your CPU. When this is done, your installed processor and heatsink should appear as shown in Figure 11.12.

Installing an Athlon Heatsink

Installing an Athlon (or Athlon 4 or Duron) heatsink requires fewer steps, but you have to be even more careful not to damage the CPU core when doing so. With an Athlon heatsink the unit has a minimum of two clips that hook onto both sides of the CPU socket. One of the clips should have a little notch in it where you can slide a flathead screwdriver tip into it to give you some leverage in installing the heatsink. This clip should attach to the side of the socket that says, "Socket-462."

FIGURE 11.12
The Pentium 4 heatsink completely installed.

To install the heatsink, lay it flat on the CPU core and firmly hold it there with your finger. Attach the clip furthest away from the Socket-462 label first; it should clip on easily. When you are certain that the first clip is properly attached, slide the tip of a flathead screwdriver into the other clip so that it catches on the notch (see Figure 11.13).

FIGURE 11.13
Using a flathead screwdriver to install the Athlon 4's heatsink.

Now, without shifting the weight of the heatsink, push the clip over the point where it attaches to the heatsink and slide it into place. It might take a few tries to get it right because some of the clips have quite a bit of tension in them. Whatever you do, make certain not to shift the weight of the heatsink to one side or another. Doing this could put too much weight on one corner of the CPU's core, causing it to chip off a bit of the core. As you can guess, this can ruin your CPU; you need to be very careful during the installation of the heatsink.

The Pentium 4 doesn't suffer from this same problem because the heatsink actually comes in contact with a heat spreader and not the core of the Pentium 4 itself. This heat spreader can take a beating without affecting the CPU core. In the case of the Athlon, you are mounting directly onto the core so any damage you do is too much.

Final Touches for the Motherboard

At this point your CPU is physically installed in your motherboard, but you want to make sure that you set any and all jumpers and dipswitches for your motherboard before you put it into your case. Capping jumpers and setting dipswitches in the open is much easier to do than in the cramped quarters of your case.

With today's motherboards, very few jumpers/dipswitches require setting. The main settings to look for are your CPU's FSB and memory bus frequency settings. The CPU clock multiplier and voltage should be autodetected. Leaving them at the auto setting is best. Only change them after you've got everything up and running if you want to overclock. Follow the instructions in your motherboard manual for what jumpers/dipswitches (if any) have to be set.

The final step is to install your memory modules into their slots on your motherboard. These install quite easily. Just open the levers on both sides of the memory slot, line up the module, and it'll snap right into place. Sometimes a little force is required, but luckily you have no danger of bent pins or anything like that. Both DIMMs and RIMMs can only fit in one way because of the way they are keyed (see Figure 11.14).

If you are installing RDRAM remember that CRIMM modules must occupy unfilled banks and also remember that installing RDRAM on a motherboard with a dual channel RDRAM interface requires that RDRAM be installed in pairs.

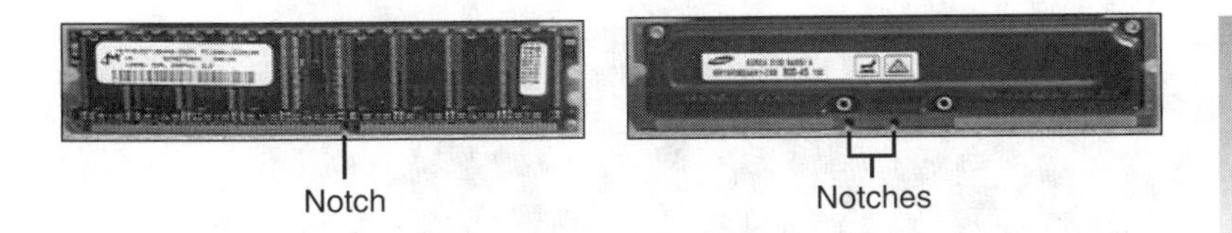

FIGURE 11.14
The notches in this DIMM (left) and RIMM (right) modules prevent the RAM from being inserted improperly.

Motherboard, I'd Like You to Meet Mr. Case

With the CPU and memory installed, your motherboard is ready to be installed in your case. This procedure is actually quite simple. First count the number of standoffs you have installed and pick out exactly that number of screws with which to mount your motherboard. If at the end of that process you have extra screws you either forgot to use one or you used one too many standoffs, which can be devastating, as I mentioned earlier. Simply take the motherboard and place it on top of your standoffs. You want to angle it so all the ports fit through the ATX I/O panel you installed earlier. Make sure that the grounding points from the panel don't actually go inside any of the ports on your motherboard; they should simply rest on or around them. Figure 11.15 shows a motherboard properly fitted into an ATX case with the standoffs lined up to its screw holes.

Next, place screws into each of the standoffs and, using your Phillips screwdriver, tighten the screws until they hold the motherboard firmly in place.

If your power supply wasn't pre-installed with your case, now would be the best time to install it. The unit slides into place at the top of your case and is held in place by four screws with standard positions. You shouldn't have to worry about an ATX spec power supply not properly lining up with the screw holes on the back of your ATX case.

Make sure that your power supply is set to the proper input voltage for your country (in the United States it is 115V) by looking at the status of the switch on the back of your power supply. Leave your power supply unplugged from your wall outlet and connect the appropriate power connectors to your motherboard as shown in Figure 11.16.

There can be as few as one connection to make or as many as four. The connectors just slide and click into place and can only be installed one way, so don't worry about messing up that part of the install.

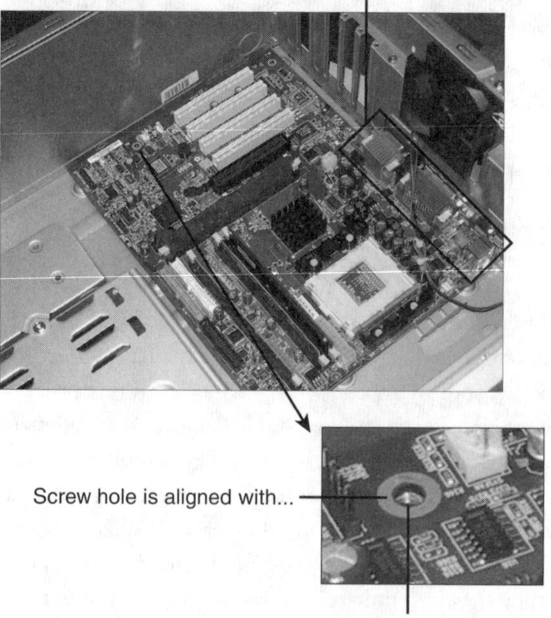

FIGURE 11.15
The motherboard resting on the standoffs.

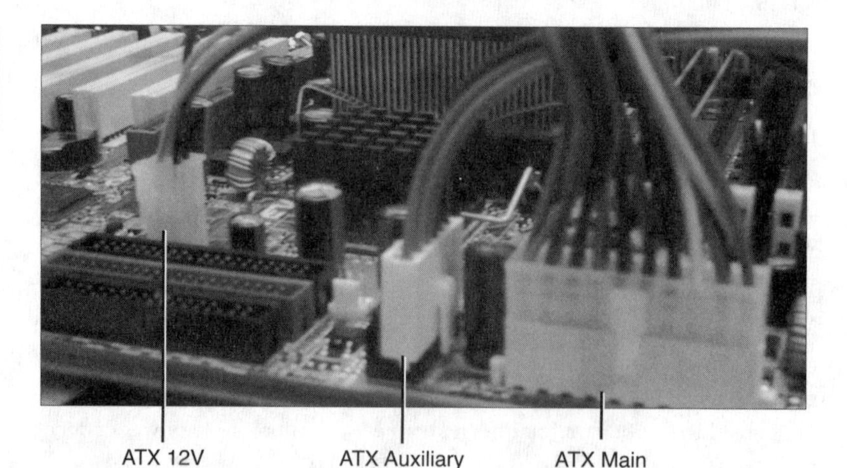

FIGURE 11.16
Three power connectors plugged into your mother board.

Installing the Video Card and Prepping for a Test Run

At this point, you are one component short of having a fully functional system. Granted you can't do much with this system, but it's always a good idea to power it up at this state to test the components that you do have installed to make sure that the install was successful. The only remaining component that you need is your video card.

Installing your video card is even easier than anything else you've done thus far. If you have a system with on-board video, such as an nForce platform, you can skip this section as you're among the few with quality integrated graphics. Simply unscrew one of the brackets at the back of your case that covers the slot where your video card is installed and plug your video card into the appropriate slot (usually the AGP slot) as shown in Figure 11.17.

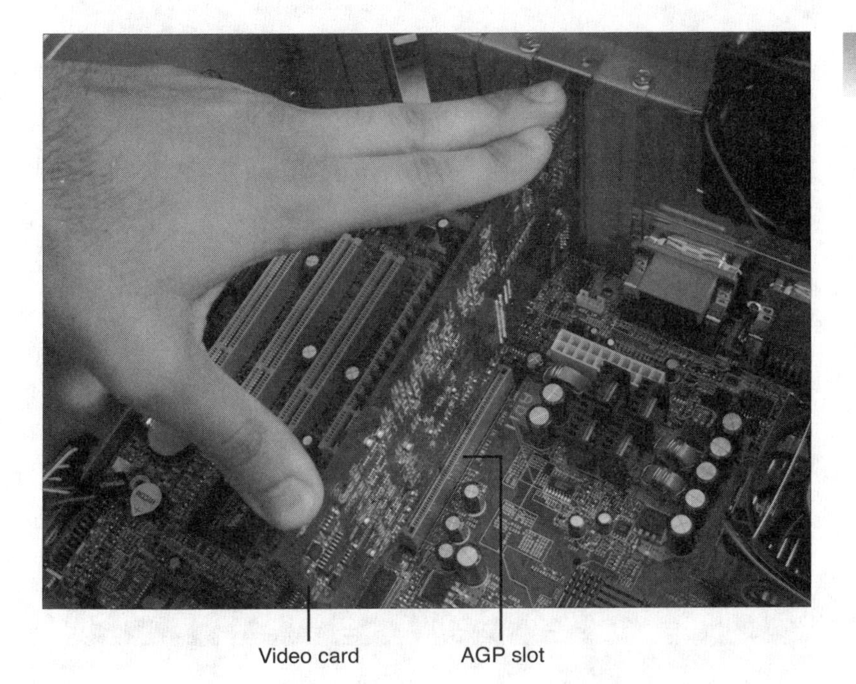

FIGURE 11.17
Installing a video card.

The card should fit snugly in the slot and you install it by applying even pressure across the edge of the card so it sits evenly in the slot (two hands helps accomplish this easier). Screwing the card into the case is the last step, although with some motherboards the AGP slot has a retention bracket that it clips onto your card to prevent it from moving. After screwing in your card, you are almost ready to power up the system. However, first you need to connect the power switch to the motherboard.

Remember that the ATX power switch isn't a mechanical switch. In fact, all it does is connect two pins on your motherboard. This sends a signal to the ATX power supply to begin the power up process. You can find the two-pin power switch connector towards the front of your case, usually with a bundle of other such connectors although this one is generally labeled "Power" or "Power SW," as shown in Figure 11.18. If it isn't labeled, you can usually follow the wire back to the physical power switch itself to confirm that it is indeed the power switch connector. This connector plugs into the motherboard, usually towards the front of the case in a block of pins. These pins are also where your case lights and reset switch hookup. You can find a diagram of which connectors go to which pins in your motherboard manual. The most important one to connect is the power switch, although it is best if you go ahead and connect all of them at once.

FIGURE 11.18
Front panel connectors.

While the layout of this block of pins differs from one motherboard to the next and the color of wires differs from one case to the next, the general rule of thumb is that the negative wire is either black or white and the positive wire is the colored one. For the power and reset switches the orientation of the connector doesn't matter, but for the LEDs (Light Emitting Devices) on the front of your case the orientation of the connector does matter to properly give the LEDs power. The positive/negative orientation of the pins on the motherboard themselves are usually given by a silkscreen printed on the PCB itself and/or are listed in the manual.

The final connections that must be made are your keyboard and your monitor. Your keyboard either plugs into your motherboard via a USB port or a PS/2 mini-din connector (see Figure 11.19).

FIGURE 11.19
Use either the PS/2 connectors (left) or the USB connectors (right) to connect your keyboard.

If your keyboard is a USB keyboard then it can work in any of the on-board USB ports. If it is a PS/2 keyboard, then it only works in the keyboard PS/2 port on your motherboard, which is the lower port that is sometimes colored purple. The remaining PS/2 port is for a PS/2 mouse if you happen to have one. Both of these connectors can only go in one way, so make sure that they are properly lined up before you insert them. Especially in the case of the PS/2 connector, it is quite easy to bend some of the pins out of shape if improperly installed.

Your monitor connects to your video card with either a VGA connector or a DVI (or other digital interface, see Chapter 10, "Monitors and Input Devices: Your Sense of Sight and Touch Restored") connector. Plug your monitor into the appropriate port on your video card; make sure to properly line up the connector. Again, both of these plugs can only go in one way.

Lights, Camera, Action!

With everything connected, the next step is to plug the power cable into the power supply. If you have a power switch on the back of your power supply, make sure it is in the off position (indicated by an O on the switch). Remember that after plugging the power supply into the wall, your entire system has power even though it isn't running yet. Some motherboards default to power on as soon as they receive power. This is why you must make sure that everything is connected and installed properly before you apply power to

Note

The reason I am recommending that you shut the computer off at this stage using the power cable is because the ATX power switch isn't always set to power off the computer after a single touch. Sometimes the power switch must be held down (according to how it is set in the motherboard's BIOS) for a few seconds before the computer powers down. If something major has gone wrong, you want to be able to pull power as soon as possible and the easiest way to do that is by pulling the power cord from the power supply.

the system. This is also why you should never work on your motherboard or any component in your case with the power cable plugged into your power supply.

At this point, after a quick check over all your connections, you can flip the switch on the back of your power supply (if your PSU has one; if not, your PSU already has power).

Assuming that your system hasn't powered up by itself, it is time to give your setup a try to make sure everything works. At this point we haven't tried any of the components and you should never assume that the setup is going to work perfectly. In fact, you should always be prepared for the worst at this point. In doing so, before you hit the power button on the front of your case, you want to keep your hand on the power plug at the back of your case. If, after hitting the power switch, you smell or see smoke, or if your CPU fan doesn't start spinning after, at most, three seconds, you should immediately pull the power from your power supply (it's better to be safe than sorry). Regardless, you'll have to give it a try sooner or later, so with your hand on the power cable, hit the power switch.

The Successful Power-On Test

If everything went properly, you should hear and see your CPU fan spinning up as well as your power supply fan and any other fans you connected. You might hear a single start up beep out of your motherboard's on-board speaker if one is present, but if you hear a string of beeps that don't stop, something has probably gone wrong. After a short while you should begin to see video outputted to your monitor. The amount of time between hitting the power switch and actually getting video depends on several factors including your motherboard and the type of video card. Under no circumstances should the time between hitting the power switch and getting video take over 30 seconds. Even 30 seconds is a considerable amount of time.

If you don't get video within that time period, but your CPU fan and power supply fan are both spinning, something is definitely wrong and you should pull power from the system. What you should see on your monitor is the initialization of your video card BIOS (sometimes your monitor gets the signal too late to display this all the time) and then you get the initialization of your motherboard's BIOS. Your computer begins its Power On Self Test (POST) and starts counting the amount of memory you have in your system (see Figure 11.20). Depending on what the default setting of your BIOS is, the memory counter might count your memory a few times before stopping. You want it to count through once and, actually, you can skip this by hitting the Escape (Esc) key on your keyboard.

```
W6341MS V1.0 022701 17:43:31

Main Processor : AMD Duron(TM) 850MHz
Memory Testing :  262144K OK
```

FIGURE 11.20
A POST screen for a PC using the Award BIOS, AMD's Duron processor, and 256MB of SDRAM.

The amount of memory that it counts up should be the amount of memory you have installed, expressed in Kilobytes. So if you have 256MB of memory installed, the memory counter informs you that you have 262,144KB of memory installed (256MB × 1,024KB in 1MB = 262,144KB).

You should be alarmed if you have 2 × 128MB sticks installed and the POST only indicates 192MB or some other odd number like that. It could mean that one of your sticks of memory isn't working properly. However, if you have 2 × 128MB sticks installed and only 128MB shows up, it could be that only one stick is seated properly in the socket. If 128MB + part of 128MB is reported, then the problem could unfortunately be much more serious. This issue, and many others, are discussed in Chapter 15, "Troubleshooting: Something Is Wrong with My Baby," so I don't go too far into detail here.

Troubleshooting a Failed Power-On Test

At this stage, if everything is spinning and sounds okay yet you get no video on your screen, it is relatively easy to diagnose. You only have four components in your system. Not receiving any video on your screen does *not* mean that you have a bad video card. If you have any major problems with your setup you don't receive video. Not installing any memory results in no video, as does installing a broken CPU; so don't automatically assume it is the video card. The video card can only display whatever data it gets, if it gets no data then it's definitely not going to output any signals to your monitor.

If you don't get any video, try reseating all the components. On most motherboards a jumper can be used to clear all the BIOS settings. Place this jumper in the clear settings state and leave it there (with power applied to the board) for a few seconds. Restore the jumper to its original position and see if that fixes things. If your motherboard doesn't have a clear BIOS (it might also be labeled clear CMOS) jumper then you can clear the settings manually by removing the CMOS battery (it looks like a big watch battery) and unplugging power to your system for approximately 15 seconds (see Figure 11.21).

FIGURE 11.21
To clear BIOS settings for this motherboard you could either set the jumper to clear or remove the battery.

If reseating components and resetting the BIOS doesn't do any good, try booting with the very minimum amount of memory modules you can have installed. This tests for a bad module or two (this only applies if you have more than the minimum already installed). Make sure that nothing is shorting out your motherboard (for example, metal touching the board except for the screws that are used to mount the board). If you have an Athlon 4, Athlon, or Duron, double check that the processor core is not cracked.

Provided that you've tried all the above steps to no avail, and you're certain that you did the install properly, the next step is to either head down to a local repair shop or visit a friend who has some parts you can swap in and out of your system. The goal is a process of elimination. Try using different memory modules that are known to work. Try a different CPU, different video card, or a different power supply. As long as they are known to work in other systems, they are good candidates for helping you diagnose what is wrong with your system. For example, if your system doesn't POST and swapping out the video card with a new one fixes the problem, you either have a bad video card or one that is incompatible with your hardware. At this point you should try it in another system to see if the card is indeed bad or just incompatible with your setup. If the component is bad, send it back. If it's incompatible with your system, you'll want to do some research and find out what the incompatibility is. Sometimes it isn't the component that needs replacing, but the other part of your system that is causing it to act up.

The final piece of troubleshooting advice I can offer you at this stage is related to what happens if you press the power switch and nothing happens. If this happens the first time, don't continue to hit the switch; *immediately* unplug the power from the wall and double and triple check all component installations. For example, a memory stick installed backwards can cause this to happen. If you are persistent enough you can get an incorrectly installed memory stick to emit a pretty glow and produce quite a bit of smoke. The first time this happens you'll want to immediately stop and pull power.

After you're done checking everything and if you're certain that no components are improperly installed, you'll want to make sure the switch is actually making the connection with the right pins on the motherboard; double and triple check that connection. If you are absolutely positive that the connector is properly installed across the right pins on your motherboard, try taking a key or the tip of a screwdriver (or anything that conducts electricity) to the two pins that control power on your motherboard. This does the same job as hitting the power switch. If this fixes it, you might have a bad power switch on your hands. Remember that the ATX power switch isn't a mechanical switch. It simply enables electricity to flow between those two pins on your motherboard.

If all this fails, unfortunately you're in a not so pleasant situation. You might want to have a technician or someone with more experience look at your system.

Installing Peripheral Cards

Hopefully everything has gone smoothly thus far and if so, congratulations. The most intimidating part of building your high performance gaming machine is over. The next step is very easy; it is the installation of your peripheral cards. These cards are your sound, Ethernet, SCSI and other cards that install in the expansion slots in your motherboard.

Which cards go in what slots is not much of an art, although it is important to know what slots share what IRQs. This information is generally available from motherboard manufacturers and in the best motherboard manuals. Generally speaking, when you're dealing with motherboards of a particular chipset (for example, i850 chipset) they all assign and share IRQs in a similar manner. So if you can't find the IRQ mapping for the slots on your motherboard, search for another manufacturer with a board based on the same chipset and see if they provide the information in their user manual. Luckily, most manufacturers do offer on-line user manuals so this information isn't hard to get. ASUS, in particular, is very good about providing this information in their manuals.

The physical installation process works in the same way as the installation process of your AGP video card. Unscrew the bracket at the back of your case. Then, by applying pressure evenly to both ends of the card, push it into the slot and complete the process by screwing the card's bracket into your case.

If you are having difficulty installing a peripheral card, make sure you are installing it in the right slot. Make sure none of the notches present on the card are blocked by anything in the slot. If they are, chances are that you are installing a card in the wrong type of expansion slot. If you're not completely sure about what sort of expansion slots are on your motherboard, consult your motherboard manual.

If applicable, hook up all internal cables to your peripheral cards before installing them. Nothing is more difficult than trying to install a cable between two adjacent peripheral cards.

Some motherboards come with a header for additional USB ports to be utilized. This header is installed in the same way as a regular peripheral card except it isn't plugged into a slot; it is just screwed into the case and a cable is then plugged into the appropriate place on the motherboard (see Figure 11.22).

FIGURE 11.22
Installing a USB header.

Installing Storage Devices

Last but not least when building your PC you must install your storage devices. These include your hard drives, CD/DVD drives, and anything else that occupies either a 3.5" or 5.25" drive bay in your case. This section is broken into two subsections: installing IDE devices and installing SCSI devices. While they are identical physically, the preparation for installing the two types of devices varies enough to warrant separating them. Note that this section only deals with installing internal storage devices; I deal with everything outside of your computer later.

Prepping Your IDE Devices

You should know from Chapter 3, "The Motherboard: Low Rent Housing for the CPU and Chipset," that your motherboard has a minimum of two on-board IDE channels. These two channels are driven by your South Bridge and support two devices each per channel, meaning that you can hook up a total of four IDE devices. The type of devices doesn't matter. As long as they are compatible with the IDE/ATA/ATAPI specifications they physically work with these connectors on your motherboard. Motherboards with an additional IDE controller, such as those with on-board RAID usually feature two more IDE channels in addition to the two that are currently provided through your South Bridge.

The general rule of thumb when dealing with IDE devices is that if you have two or less, each device should be placed on its own channel. This is simply for convenience as it means that you can just plug the devices in without any jumper configuration. When you have more than two devices (and only two channels on your motherboard) is when you have to do a little planning before hand.

IDE devices can be configured in one of two modes, as a Master or as a Slave. A single IDE channel enables a Master device and a Slave device. It doesn't matter what device is made Master and what is made Slave, but there can only be one Master and one Slave per channel. So if you are installing two devices on a single channel, one must be set to Master and one must be set to Slave. Jumpers on all IDE devices control these settings.

IDE devices can have up to three configuration modes: Master (without a slave), Master (with a slave), Slave and Cable Select (CS). The first two modes are self explanatory, while the third is a bit more cryptic. If an IDE device is set to Cable Select, its status (as a Master or Slave) is determined by its positioning on the IDE cable. As I discussed in Chapter 7, "Storage: The

Slowest Part of Your PC," an IDE cable has three connectors on it: the connection to the motherboard and two connectors for devices. The last connector (furthest away from the motherboard connector on the cable) is for Master devices while the middle connector is for Slave devices. This is only true on modern IDE cables (ATA/100 spec); in the past a special cable had to be used for Cable Select operation and the positions of the Master/Slave connectors were switched.

To take advantage of the ATA/66, ATA/100, or the upcoming ATA/133 spec, you need to be sure you have an 80-conductor cable instead of a regular IDE cable. As I explained in Chapter 7, although this 80-conductor cable has the same number of signaling wires (40) as a regular 40-pin IDE cable, it also has an additional 40 grounding wires to cope with the higher peak transfer rates these specifications enable. Everything works okay if you don't have an 80-conductor cable (although all newer drives/motherboards ship with one). You just aren't able to transfer in the faster modes which actually doesn't do much for performance with today's drives.

Generally speaking it is always best to leave your IDE boot drive as the Master device on the Primary IDE channel on your motherboard. The reason is that your motherboard's BIOS is usually configured to boot from this device first, and later when partitioning this device appears as your first drive.

To set the jumpers on your IDE device simply locate them on the drive and cap the appropriate pins. The pins are usually located at the rear of the drive (the end that sticks out into the case) and enough jumpers to properly set the drive (usually one) are provided on those pins already. The various settings are almost always printed on the drive itself but if you can't find them there, consult your drive manual or visit the Web site of the company that manufactures the drive. After that is done, no more "configuration" needs to be done on your drive. It is ready to be installed in your case.

Installing IDE Devices

All modern IDE hard disks are 3.5" devices meaning that they fit in the 3.5" bays of your case. If you are out of 3.5" bays, you can purchase a 3.5" to 5.25" bay adapter. This adapter screws into your 3.5" device and then you screw the brackets into your case as if you were mounting a 5.25" drive.

Be sure you orient the drive with the IDE and power connectors facing the inside of the case, and line up the screw holes on the drive with the open mounts in your case's drive bay. If your case has a removable drive bay it would be helpful to remove it and do this install externally of your case. If your case uses drive rails for 3.5" devices all you have to do is snap on the drive rails and slide the drive into the bay. (You have to do so from the front of the case, so remove any front bezel that is in your way It should pull right off.) While most 3.5" drives feature six screw holes, mounting the device using only four screws is sufficient. However, I would not recommend mounting with anything less. Remember that these screws don't only hold the drive in place, but they also help conduct heat away from the drive and through the metal chassis.

You can start by screwing in the side facing the same direction as the motherboard tray, and then turning the case around to mount the remaining screws on the other side. You might find it easier to lay the case down on its side instead of standing it up to complete this part of the process. Of course, do whatever is easiest for you.

In terms of the screws required, 3.5" hard disks can deal with pretty much any type of screw, where you generally have to switch to smaller screws is when you're trying to mount a 3.5" floppy drive. These drives normally come with a set of four screws that are guaranteed to fit. If you are tightening these screws using an electric screwdriver make sure that you don't break the head off of the screw when you're mounting the drives. This doesn't happen too often, but some case manufacturers provide cheaply made screws. Regardless of what you're using to tighten these screws, make sure that you don't strip the head of the screw as it makes it difficult to remove the screws later on when you upgrade (and trust me, you upgrade eventually). You can avoid doing this by applying a good deal of pressure to the screw when using your driver and making sure that you are using the correct sized bit for the screw you are mounting.

The process is identical for 5.25" devices; the only thing you have to be aware of is that the majority of 5.25" devices (for example, CD/DVD drives) use much smaller screws than what your hard drives use. These screws are usually provided with the drives, so don't lose them.

After the drives are mounted, you'll want to give them power. Most devices take one of the larger four-pin power connectors, which are pretty easy to install. The only common exceptions to this are floppy drives, which usually accept the smaller four-pin connectors (see Figure 11.23). I strongly suggest double checking this connection because it is quite easy to be off by a single pin when installing this connector. This results in a good deal of smoke and a burnt power cable/floppy power connector.

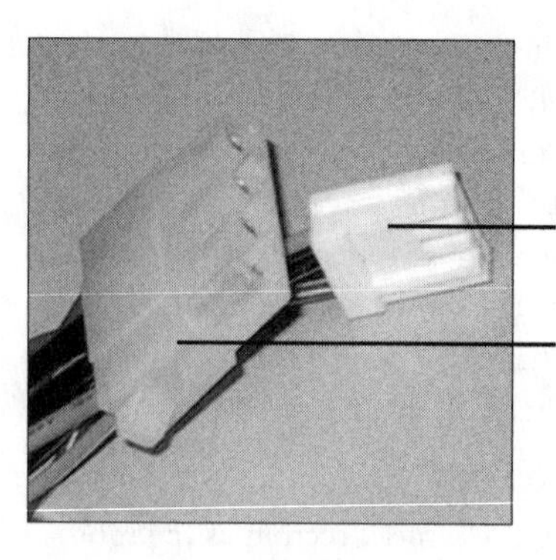

FIGURE 11.23
The two types of power connectors used to power disk drives.

If you do run out of power connectors you can buy a Y-splitter which splits a single connector into two. Extension cables are available for those of you with extremely tall cases. Because you are still limited by the amount of power that your power supply can provide to your drives, don't go overboard with Y-splitters. I discuss in greater detail the power requirements of today's systems in Chapter 9. The main thing to keep in mind is that the power provided on the +12V power rail is what you want to look at because all your drives run off that rail. For the most part, the 300W–400W power supplies you use in your system should be able to adequately power any combination of drives you throw at it. Start taking power consumption into consideration when you get into a 4+ drive array of 10K–15K RPM drives.

The power connector on IDE devices can help you quite a bit in orienting the IDE cable. The rule of thumb to follow is that pin one on your IDE cable (usually denoted by either a red or black coloring) should always be closest to your power connector. If you happen to get this cable backwards don't worry, you aren't greeted with any smoke signals. With that said, you can go ahead and connect this end of the IDE cable to your device(s).

The final step is connecting the IDE ribbon cables to your motherboard (see Figure 11.24).

The location of pin one on your motherboard isn't as easy as lining up the cable with a power connector, but the numbers one and two (indicating pins one and two) are usually printed on the motherboard itself next to where those two pins on the cable belong. If this isn't available, you can look at the notching on your cable and the socket on the motherboard (provided that the manufacturer properly follows the specification). The final resort is to consult the motherboard manual.

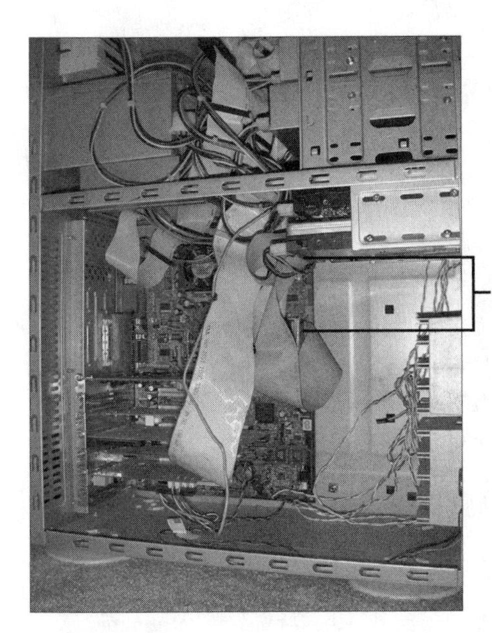

FIGURE 11.24
After you've connected the IDE ribbon cables to both your IDE devices and the motherboard, your case becomes a much more crowded environment.

Prepping SCSI Devices

When you're installing SCSI devices, the process can be more complicated than IDE devices, but the performance benefits are often worth the trouble. One of the biggest advantages SCSI offers over IDE, as you read in Chapter 7, happens to be the number of devices that can be present on any single channel. All modern day SCSI controllers support a maximum of 15 devices per channel (16 if you count the controller itself). Obviously the Master and Slave technique won't work for 15 devices. Instead, the SCSI specification states that each individual device on the channel must have a unique ID number.

This number, known as the SCSI ID, is setup much like the Master/Slave selection is on an IDE device: via jumpers (see Figure 11.25). Because SCSI devices have many more setup possibilities than their IDE counterparts, many more jumpers exist, especially on hard drives (see Figure 11.23). Consult your drive manual for the location and specific jumpers that must be capped to properly set up the ID.

While you can use any SCSI ID for your boot drive, it is often recommended that you set your boot drive to SCSI ID 0 (the default for many hard drives). The reason behind this is that most SCSI adapters are initially configured to boot off of ID 0.

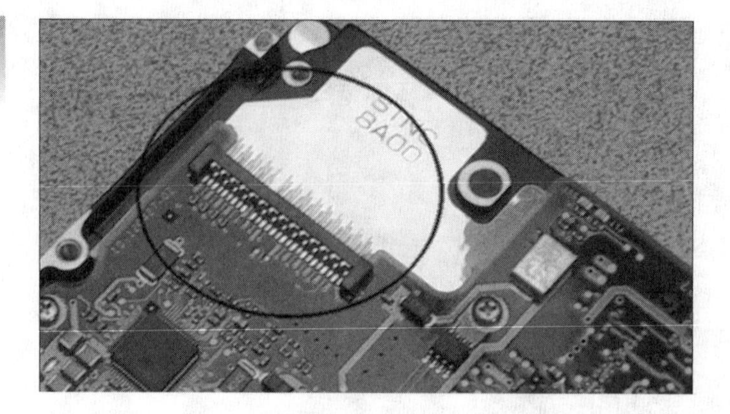

FIGURE 11.25
Jumper pins on a SCSI hard drive.

The biggest quirk that SCSI setups offer users is the concept of termination. A SCSI controller card can offer multiple channels, with each one offering a certain amount of devices that can be chained together on that channel. For every SCSI chain that exists in a system (only a single chain can exist per SCSI channel), both ends of the chain must be terminated. An end can be terminated either through the use of a terminator placed on the cable itself, or through termination logic that is present on the device or card that is doing the termination (see Figure 11.26).

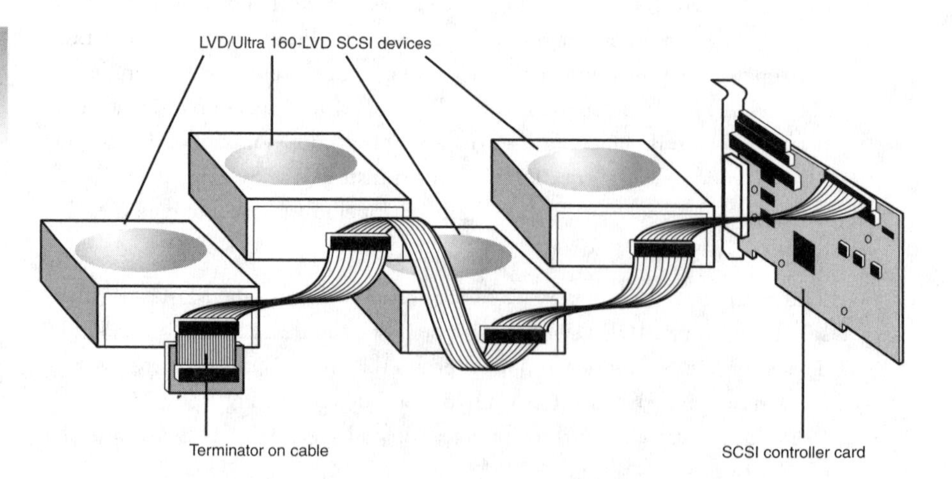

FIGURE 11.26
An internal SCSI chain that has been terminated.

For example, let's take a SCSI controller with a single Ultra160 SCSI channel available via 68-pin LVD connector on the card itself. Let's say I happen to have two SCSI devices that I am connecting to this controller in my system. I call these devices by their SCSI IDs, 0 and 1. On one end of the chain you have the Ultra160 SCSI controller. This controller has an option in its BIOS to enable termination. Enabling termination eliminates the SCSI signal on this end of the chain. Normally this is set to auto, but for this example I manually enable it (you always want to leave it on Auto unless you are having problems with it not detecting your chain properly). Now, one end of my SCSI chain is terminated. Next I connect drive 0 and drive 1, in that order, using my Ultra160 SCSI cable. However, this end of the chain isn't terminated. I do so by placing an Active LVD terminator on the end of one of the connectors on the cable *after* my last drive, drive 1, is connected. Figure 11.27 shows both the SCSI connector and the LVD terminator.

FIGURE 11.27
A 68-pin SCSI connector (left) and an active LVD terminator (right).

Luckily, most new cables come with an active terminator built onto the cable so I could've switched cables and used one of those instead. See how the process works?

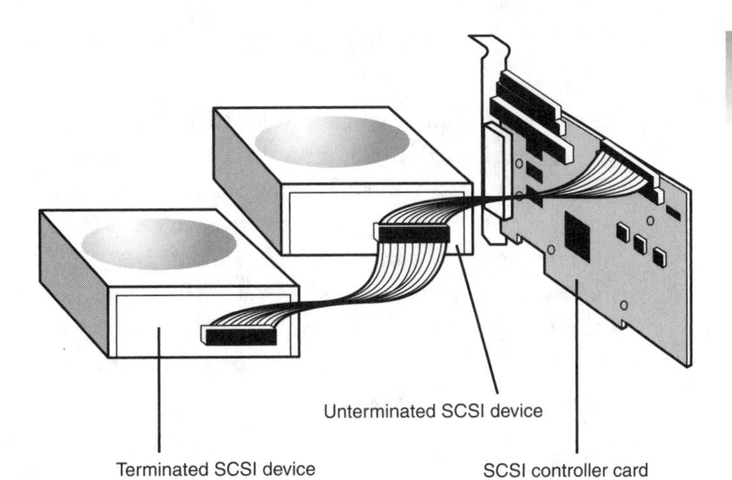

FIGURE 11.28
An externally terminated SCSI chain.

Now if I had an external device on the same channel, I would have disabled termination on the card and put a terminator on the last external device. If two channels were present, both would have to be terminated individually.

After visualizing how your SCSI chain looks, you can mount and install the devices the same way I described in the IDE section. Installing SCSI devices is not different except, in most cases, the data cables connect to your SCSI controller card rather than to the motherboard. When installing the cables, be careful because the pins on SCSI cables are very easily bent. Line up the connector (it only goes in one way) and lightly apply pressure until it pushes into place. If you are feeling resistance, stop immediately and be sure you aren't bending any of the pins on the cable connector. If you have bent pins you can carefully straighten them out with a small flathead screwdriver.

Also make sure that your drives are plugged into the appropriate connectors on your SCSI card. If you have a multichannel SCSI card and multiple devices (especially if they are hard drives) it again helps to move each drive to a separate channel if possible (as long as they are all the same speed), but is it worth it?

For example, if you had two Ultra160 hard drives and an Ultra160 controller with two Ultra160 channels (that doesn't necessarily mean that your card has two channels; check your documentation to be sure), connecting one hard drive per channel would give each hard drive a maximum transfer rate of 160MBps. In this case, it would actually make sense to stick with a single channel because it is unlikely that your two single drives are going to be bursting at over 160MBps and the cost of another cable is going to set you back a few. This is especially important if you are setting up a system with quite a few devices connected in a RAID configuration, but for a gaming system you shouldn't worry about spending the extra cash on making sure each one of your devices is on its own channel. You shouldn't be that disk limited anyway.

Once your machine eventually gets started up you probably want to enter your SCSI adapter's BIOS (it usually lets you know what keystroke combination to hit and when to get into the setup) and configure what SCSI ID you want bootable (if any). At the same time, you can stop the card from scanning for devices on other IDs if you are only going to have one or two devices on your chain. This saves some startup time. Just remember to go back in and enable it to see devices on other IDs if you ever add more drives to your chain.

If you want the HDD LED on the front of your case to blink when activity is occurring on your SCSI hard drive, you have to run that cable to the proper pins on your SCSI card, *not* on your motherboard. If your motherboard has on-board SCSI then the SCSI activity LED pins should be around the SCSI controller chips.

...and You Are Done!

The last thing you need to do is make sure that loose screws are not rattling around in your case (Remember, motherboards don't like coming in contact with pieces of metal; neither do other PCBs in your case). If all looks good, go ahead and hit that power button and listen to that baby purr.

If your baby doesn't come to life immediately, watch for the warning signs: excessive beeping, all red lights on the motherboard's on-board diagnostic LEDs, no fans spinning, smoke, and so on. If any of these happen (especially smoke) then you should pull the plug immediately and double check all your connections.

The only difference between powering up the system this time and when you did it before, is that you have all your peripheral cards installed and your storage devices attached. If your system POSTed before, but doesn't now, remove the components you added one by one. You need to test to see if the computer POSTs after removing each one, until you find the culprit. Another tool you now have is that you should hear your hard disks spinning up during the POST process (IDE disks spins on power-up while SCSI drives may wait until the SCSI BIOS tells them to spin up before doing so). If you don't hear disks spinning up, something is definitely wrong. Check your power and the orientation of your cabling.

I recommend leaving any external components that aren't necessary to the operation of your computer for now. You can plug in your keyboard, mouse, and Ethernet/phone cords, but leave all non-critical devices such as cameras, printers, and other USB peripherals unhooked until you are done with the software setup. After you complete the software setup (the OS in particular if you're using a new primary hard disk drive), add and install these components one by one to ensure that everything works properly. Doing this helps you diagnose any problems later on.

If all is good, congratulations; you just built your first computer. Remember that all you have accomplished is the hardware installation and setup. If your system gets past the POST screen you are most likely greeted with an error reminding you that you have no OS installed. Let's move on to Chapter 13, "Operating Systems and Device Drivers: Making Your Hardware Work," for that.

Chapter 12

Upgrading: Feeling the Need for Speed

I Once Was a King

The inventor of the paper plate would be a computer gaming enthusiast had he been alive today. Every enthusiast's dream is to be able to simply throw away their PCs after they're done with them and find it no less affordable to replace them with new ones. Unfortunately, when reality sets in it becomes very clear that our extremely expensive hobby would become impossible to maintain if we were always throwing away our PCs after they fall a few steps behind the technology curve. This is where the concept of upgrading comes in.

As I mentioned at the start of this book, one of the beauties of building your own PC is that you build it with the knowledge that you are going to upgrade it later on. By paving yourself a nice upgrade path, you can prolong the day when you have to shell out the major cash for a complete upgrade. At the same time you are ensuring that you can always have the highest levels of performance by replacing at most one or two components at a time.

After all, it is much easier to spend $300 on a new video card than it is to spend $1,500 on a new system just because your games are running a tad slow.

In this chapter I deal with the art of knowing exactly what to upgrade in your system and when you need to do it. It is extremely easy to get caught up in the upgrade hype but understanding where the bottlenecks in your system exist and how they are limiting your performance can help save you money while ensuring that you have the best performance money can buy.

Upgrade Paths

The reality that we all must face is that regardless of how much money we spend on our new systems today, within six months our top-notch computers are dethroned by something that is generally faster, cheaper, and offers more features. In just 12 months a new computer is dwarfed by the mid-range systems that are available on the market. In less than 24 months a new system is considered to be slower than the entry-level PCs available at the time. For cost-conscious gamers this is the dark side of Moore's Law.

You might have a system that you are considering upgrading, so before I get into the various methods of determining what needs to be upgraded, let's look at the previous guardians of the performance throne and what upgrade potential they have today.

The Pentium MMX and AMD K6-X Series

The glory days of the Socket 7 processors, shown in Figure 12.1, went out with parachute pants and 2D first person shooters…well, practically, anyway. However, there might be some life you can squeeze out of these systems.

If you're running either the Pentium MMX or a K6-X series of processors in your computer, you are left with relatively few options when it comes to performing a cheap upgrade that's going to boost your performance noticeably. If you do have a K6-X processor (for example, K6, K6-2, or K6-III) the chances are fairly good that you have a motherboard with an AGP slot (see Figure 12.2). This does improve your chances of being able to upgrade your video card to something such as a GeForce2 MX. There are, however, some chipset compatibility issues with older chipsets for the K6-X platform, known as Super7 chipsets, and certain AGP video cards. Provided that you do have the latest drivers from your chipset and graphics manufacturers, the chances are in your favor, but proper operation is in no way guaranteed. If you happen to have a Pentium or Pentium MMX, the chances of you having a motherboard with an AGP slot are very slim. This unfortunately limits your video card upgrade path considerably.

FIGURE 12.1
The Cyrix MII, Intel Pentium MMX, and AMD K6 (clockwise): Three CPUs you don't want in your high-performance gaming system.

FIGURE 12.2
A Super7 motherboard with AGP support.

Regardless of which one of these CPUs you happen to be using, you're going to be CPU-limited regardless of what upgrade you pursue. By CPU-limited I mean that the performance of your entire system in most games is held back by your CPU and not by other portions of your system. In this case, your video card is often waiting around for your CPU to provide it with data. This is why upgrading to an extremely powerful video card with a slow CPU isn't going to provide you with the results you're looking for (see Figure 12.3).

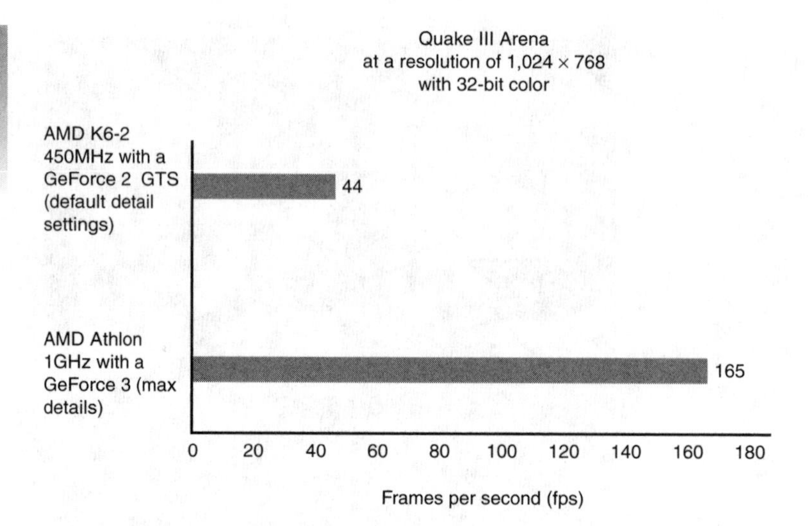

FIGURE 12.3
In this chart you can see that this AMD K6 is severely limiting the performance of Quake III Arena.

One way to alleviate the CPU bottleneck if you do happen to have one of these systems is to see if your motherboard supports the AMD K6-2+ or K6-III+ processors. These two processors are 0.18-micron versions of the K6-2 and K6-III respectively. The K6-2+ received a 128KB on-die L2 cache, while the K6-III+ remained unchanged with its 256KB on-die cache, but runs much cooler than the standard K6-III. These processors were manufactured in low volumes for the mobile market, but with proper BIOS and motherboard support they can work quite well in upgrading your system (refer to Table 12.1).

Table 12.1 Abridged K6-2+/K6-III+ Motherboard Support Table

Brand	Model	K6-2+ / K6-3+ Support
ABIT	IT5H	No
ASUS	P5A	Yes (BIOS AL5I107A)
A-Trend	ATC-5200	No
Epox	MVP3G2	Yes (BIOS VP3C0C21)
FIC	PA-2007	No
FIC	PA-2013	No

Table 12.1 Continued

Brand	Model	K6-2+ / K6-3+ Support
Iwill	XA100	No
Iwill	XA100Plus	Yes (BIOS XAP1027)
Supermicro	P5MMA	No
TMC	TI5VGF	No
Tyan	S1590S	No

Any other performance upgrades outside of adding a faster processor (if supported by your motherboard) and a faster video card are pretty useless for you in this situation. There are a number of upgrade paths for you here; unfortunately almost all of them require replacing virtually all of your components. The easiest thing to do here would be to pick up a cheap Socket-A motherboard, throw a Duron on it, and make that the basis for your new upgrade.

Obviously, if you're still running a Super7 system, you might crave the need for a bit more speed than a simple Duron system would grant you. This is completely understandable. In fact, when I finally left the Socket-7 platform I upgraded straight to the fastest thing out at the time: the Intel Pentium II. Luckily, these days the fastest processor you can buy doesn't set you back $1200 like it did back then. You've got a couple of options if you want to go the fastest platform route. One is to upgrade to a Socket-478 Pentium 4 processor (2GHz or higher) and a Socket-478 motherboard (either based on the Intel 850 chipset or the VIA P4X266 chipset). The other option is to again, pick up a Socket-A motherboard (based either on NVIDIA's nForce or VIA's KT266 chipset) and upgrade to the fastest Athlon 4 you can purchase (or maybe one or two speed grades lower as the highest clocked parts usually carry an unreasonable price premium).

As I mentioned earlier, both of these options require much more of an investment; potentially including new memory, a new power supply/case, and a new video card if you actually want to make use of your upgraded system.

Your new system inevitably needs new memory. All Socket-7/Super7 boards used either Fast Page Mode/Extended Data Out (FPM/EDO) DRAM or Synchronous DRAM (SDRAM). Other than SDRAM, none of those technologies are used in today's platforms. Even when talking about SDRAM, the speeds that Super7/Socket-7 SDRAM ran at were between 66MHz and 100MHz while most of today's platforms that use SDRAM run the memory at 100MHz or 133MHz. More likely, you have to purchase either Rambus DRAM (RDRAM) or Double Data Rate (DDR) SDRAM. A memory size upgrade might be necessary as well with 256MB being a good point to aim for. Having more won't hurt you anywhere, but your bank account.

Caution

If you have an LPX form factor power supply and are adding or removing components from the inside of the case, be very careful with the wires that connect to the power switch. Even when your PC is powered off, these two wires carry a hazardous electric current.

If you have an older system (I know, they're all "old") then you might have a standard AT case with an AT power supply. The quickest way to find out is to see if your power switch is actually a real switch or just a button that connects to a pair of pins on your motherboard. If it is the latter then you *probably* have an ATX case and you should only need a new power supply. However, if it isn't, unless you want to start hacking up your case with a saw, you need a new case and power supply. For more information on cases check out Chapter 9, "Cases and Cooling: Living in Style and Keeping Your Cool."

The reason you most likely need a new power supply is because of increased power requirements of today's CPUs and other components. Most Pentium 4 motherboards require an ATX 2.03 compliant power supply with an ATX12V connector. This connector was not present on power supplies until very recently, although you can purchase an adapter that converts a standard 4-pin Molex connector to the ATX12V.

It doesn't take much of an imagination to figure out why you probably need a new video card. The video cards of the Super7/Socket-7 days were 2D only, 3D only, or very slow 2D/3D combo cards that don't hold a candle to the Radeons and GeForces of today.

A slow/dated hard drive can make your upgraded system feel no faster than your old computer. Remember that your hard drive bottlenecks most of your day-to-day tasks, so if you can't read off your hard drive any faster than you could before, your system definitely isn't performing to its full potential. Unless you've upgraded your hard drive since you purchased your system, you're probably using an older 5400 RPM IDE drive with next to no space (by today's standards). Two years ago an 8GB drive was average. Now 60GB drives that spin at 7200rpm are becoming increasingly more common.

While this can be a lot of work, by the end of the process you pretty much have a completely new system, which is definitely evident in the performance improvement you see.

The Slot-1 Pentium III, Pentium II, and Celeron

If your system currently has a Pentium II or a slot-based Celeron processor, you have a few options depending on what type of chipset your motherboard uses. If you have a 100MHz FSB Pentium II, your motherboard is based on either the Intel 440BX (most likely) or the VIA Apollo Pro chipset. In either case, you have a clear upgrade path to a higher speed Pentium II or even a Pentium III processor with little more than a BIOS update. The specifications of your motherboard dictate whether or not you are able to upgrade to a Coppermine processor. For information as to whether or not your motherboard works with a Coppermine CPU, consult your motherboard manufacturer's Web site.

Slot-1 Pentium III owners can also upgrade to a higher speed grade Pentium III. With proper motherboard support, a Coppermine is a good upgrade path. As I discussed in Chapter 1, "The Central Processing Unit: The Heart and Soul of the PC," there are three types of Pentium IIIs. The first Pentium IIIs used what was known internally to Intel as the Katmai core. The main difference here being that the Katmai core had a 512KB L2 cache located on the CPU card itself and not the die of the chip. Its L2 cache ran at half the CPU clock speed. The Coppermine core moved to a 0.18-micron process and included a 256KB L2 cache on-die running at the full core clock speed (the faster speed more than makes up for being half the size). While the Socket-370 versions of the Coppermine are more common, you can still find versions that use the Slot-1 interface.

The Pentium III Tualatin core, which introduced some architectural enhancements to the core as well as implementation of Intel's 0.13-micron manufacturing process, is for specific Tualatin compatible Socket-370 platforms only. Because it requires a new motherboard/chipset the Tualatin isn't the best choice for an upgrade if you don't want to replace your motherboard.

If the only Coppermines you can find use the Socket-370 interface, there is a way to adapt these processors for use with a Slot-1 motherboard, using a Socket-370 to Slot-1 converter card (see Figure 12.4).

Electrically, the Socket-370 and Slot-1 interfaces are identical; the card simply interfaces with the Slot-1 connector and adapts it to a Socket-370 connector. If you do decide to go this route, remember that your motherboard must still support the CPU you're using. For example, if your Slot-1 motherboard won't work with Coppermine CPUs and you use a Socket-370 to Slot-1 converter, you cannot use a Socket-370 Coppermine CPU and expect it to work. You also have to make sure that the converter card is compatible with the CPU you want to use. The biggest concern you should have here is whether or not the converter works with Coppermine CPUs.

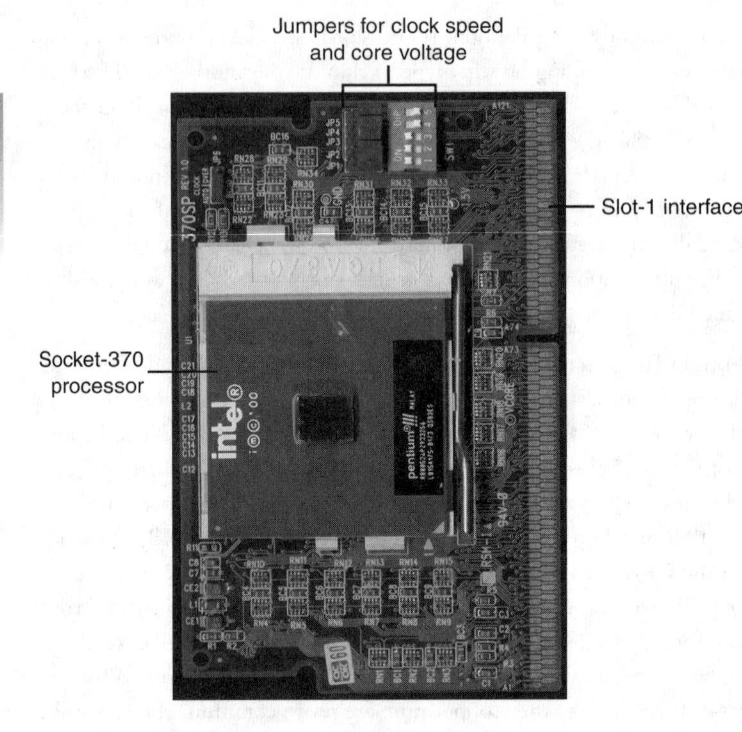

FIGURE 12.4
This converter can be used to adapt a Socket-370 Pentium III to a compatible Slot-1 based motherboard.

If your motherboard uses a 440LX-based chipset, your options become much more limited as the chipset only supports the 66MHz FSB. Provided that your motherboard does have proper voltage and BIOS support for them, your only CPU upgrade options in this case are to a higher clocked Celeron. The problem with this is that you are going to end up being FSB and memory bandwidth limited in the games you play. Investing too much money into an upgrade here isn't wise as you are never able to make your memory bus or your FSB faster.

Because all the aforementioned chipsets are AGP compatible, you are able to upgrade to most of the recent video cards although some older motherboards had problems with delivering enough power to certain graphics cards. Your best bet is to ask around Internet message boards and newsgroups to see if any other users out there can confirm that the combination works. The AnandTech Forums (`http://forums.anandtech.com`) is perfect for this type of question.

In terms of making an easy upgrade, the only trouble you can really get into is if you have a 440FX-based motherboard. This was the very first Pentium II chipset from 1997. It doesn't support AGP and although it supports SDRAM, very few boards came with anything other than 72-pin EDO SIMM slots. The chipset only supports a 66MHz FSB, so you're pretty much stuck with what you got. If you're in this unfortunate situation, it's probably time to build a system from scratch.

Socket-370 Platforms

The upgrade path makes a three-pronged fork in the road if you happen to have a Socket-370 platform. As a quick refresher, remember that the Celeron was the first processor to eventually use the Socket-370 interface, followed by the FCPGA Pentium III. Unfortunately, there are three different types of Socket-370 motherboards.

The first type of Socket-370 motherboard is truly a Celeron-only motherboard that won't accept the FC-PGA Pentium III. With every processor release, Intel also releases a set of guidelines that motherboard manufacturers should follow so that their products are compatible with the new processor. A part of these guidelines is the design specifications that address what voltage regulator module (VRM) implementation needs to be placed on the motherboard. When the Pentium II was released, motherboard manufacturers had to follow the VRM 8.1 guidelines and upon the release of the Celeron processor, the VRM 8.2 specification had to be adhered to. Intel's higher end CPUs and multiprocessor systems also require a different VRM specification—VRM 8.3 for all Xeon motherboards and optional for dual processor Slot-1 Motherboards. How does this apply to the FC-PGA running in older motherboards?

Each VRM specification is generally backwards compatible as long as it applies to CPUs of a similar family. For example, a motherboard with a VRM that meets the 8.2 guidelines has no problem suiting an original Pentium II CPU that required the 8.1 specification. Obviously, this compatibility doesn't work both ways (Intel can't predict the voltage requirements of future processors) and thus, a Pentium III CPU won't work in a motherboard that only meets the VRM 8.1 specification. Make sense? Well, guess what the FC-PGA requires? Compliance with the VRM 8.4 guidelines, which currently, no Socket-370 BX motherboard officially supports.

The FC-PGA has *not changed* the Socket-370 Voltage Identification Definition (VID) pinout that was originally defined with the Celeron. This means that the VID pins on the FC-PGA correspond to the same settings on the Socket-370 Celeron. If this weren't the case older Celeron CPUs wouldn't be able to work on newer Socket-370 motherboards that are FC-PGA compatible.

If you have a Socket-370 BX motherboard whose design hasn't been modified to meet the VRM 8.4 specification, you aren't able to upgrade to anything other than a higher-speed Celeron which, as I mentioned before, ends up giving you diminishing performance returns.

The next type of Socket-370 motherboard you could have would be one that does support the VRM 8.4 specification. This means that it does work with the FC-PGA Pentium III (Coppermine) CPUs. In this case, you are free to upgrade to any Pentium III processor based on the Coppermine core. Provided that you have AGP support on your motherboard, you can also upgrade your video card to pretty much any of today's current cards. If paired up with a high enough speed CPU, you can actually have a pretty high performing system simply by upgrading your current platform.

The final type of Socket-370 platform that you could have leaves you with the broadest number of options. In the second quarter of 2001 motherboard manufacturers began shipping Socket-370 motherboards with support for Intel's Tualatin-based Pentium III (see Figure 12.5). As you remember, this is the 0.13-micron Pentium III.

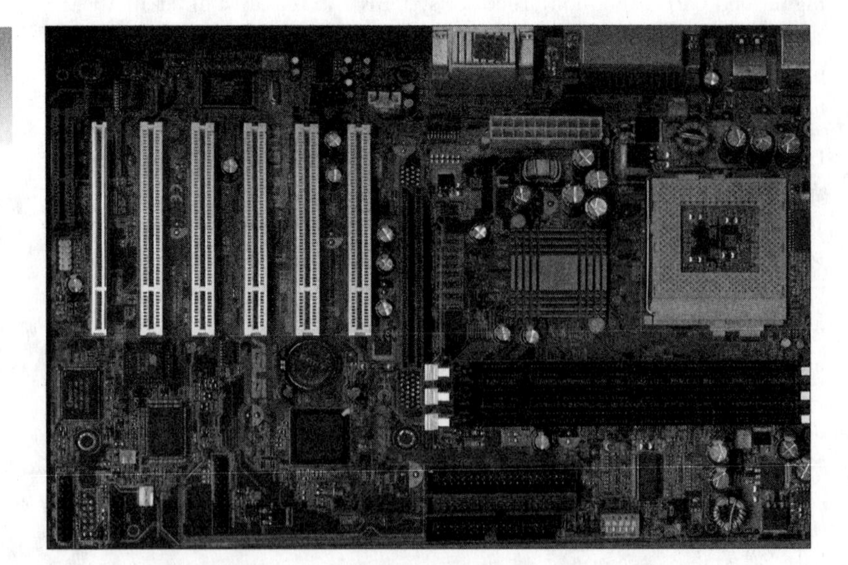

FIGURE 12.5
A Socket-370 motherboard with Tualatin support.

Boards that support this chip work with all Socket-370 processors and provide you with the most flexible upgrade paths. However, if you are using one of these boards, it means that you've purchased your system relatively recently and there shouldn't be much reason to upgrade just yet. If you are looking to upgrade and do not have one of these boards, you're better off upgrading to an Athlon or Pentium 4-based solution.

Slot-A Athlons

When AMD first introduced the Athlon as a Slot-A processor, it was inevitable that the Athlon would go the way of the original Pentium III and get replaced by a socketed version. What the market didn't bank on however was that AMD wouldn't make the Slot-A to Socket-A transition nearly as smoothly as Intel made their Slot-1 to Socket-370 transition. The result of this was a very sudden push towards Socket-A processors at the release of the Thunderbird core that left many major customers, as well as enthusiasts, with no real upgrade path using their current motherboard.

True, AMD did make a very limited number of Slot-A Thunderbirds, but the highest frequency Slot-A processor you can upgrade to is still 1GHz. Still not bad, but the 1GHz barrier isn't nearly as impressive as it was in 2000. Besides that, finding Slot-A processors is far from easy now that Socket-A parts dominate the market.

The good news is that, currently, the chances that you are overly CPU limited in your gaming performance are relatively small with an Athlon. However, when the time comes, don't expect to have too bright of an upgrade future with a Slot-A motherboard in your system.

Socket-A Athlons

One of the most interesting things about AMD's processor roadmap for the desktop Athlon processor is that from the Thunderbird core, through the Palomino, Thoroughbred (0.13-micron), and Barton (0.13-micron and SOI) cores, all the CPUs are using the Socket-A interface. The reason this is so peculiar is because it is the exact opposite from what we have seen from Intel in the past. Since 1997 Intel has gone through four physical connector changes for CPUs: Slot-1, Socket-370, Socket-423, and Socket-478; not to mention the three different types of Socket-370 interfaces for Celerons, Coppermine and Tualatin processors. Clearly, AMD has kept this picture much less complicated. Unfortunately, there are some quirks. The degree to which your motherboard manufacturer followed the specs AMD has set forth determines how far up the processor chain your upgrade path lies.

Provided that your motherboard can deliver adequate voltage to the CPU and it was designed according to AMD's spec, you are able to use any Socket-A processor provided that you have BIOS support for it. The reality of the matter is that not all motherboards were designed with respect to AMD's specification being followed down to the T. The only way to determine your upgrade path, if you do have a Socket-A Athlon platform, is to write your manufacturer and find out exactly which processors are supported and which aren't. The physical interface is the same. Whether or not the processor runs properly is a much more complicated question that cannot be issued a general answer.

Pentium 4s

Since the Pentium 4 line is relatively new, I cannot say much about the upgrade paths you have in the future. The original Pentium 4 made its debut with a 423-pin socketed interface. Pentium 4s based on the Northwood core, which uses the 0.13-micron manufacturing process, replace this interface with a 478-pin PGA interface (see Figure 12.6). However, Intel rarely leaves their larger customers up a creek without a paddle so I would expect to be able to find Socket-423 processors for a little while to come, at least.

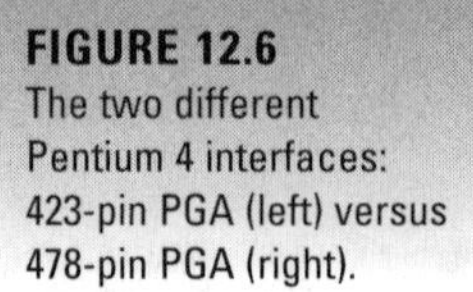

FIGURE 12.6
The two different Pentium 4 interfaces: 423-pin PGA (left) versus 478-pin PGA (right).

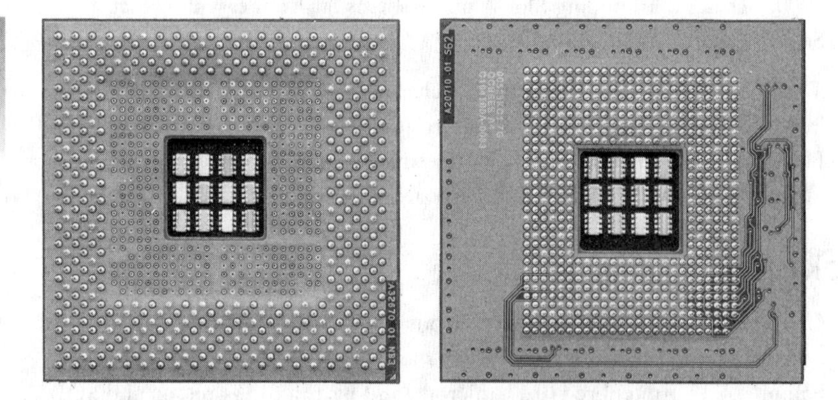

Currently, you won't have to worry about graphics card compatibility with any of the Pentium 4 platforms. Just about anything coming out works just fine. Currently all newer motherboards support AGP 4X cards; however, they use what is known as a universal slot that can accept AGP 1X, 2X and 4X cards. If you plug an AGP 4X card into an AGP 2X slot, the only difference is that the card just runs in AGP 2X mode.

Although it is rare, sometimes a card is specifically keyed for use in a single type of slot. The only modern cards I've ever encountered with this problem were the 3dfx Voodoo4/5 series. These cards do not physically fit into any Pentium 4 motherboards because of a difference in keying (where the notches are located) in their AGP slots. Keying a slot differently has no tangible gain; it's mainly done to force manufacturers to properly adhere to standards.

Help! My Computer Feels Slow

The first time you power up a new computer after building it, the performance hits you immediately. Your OS and games install much quicker, not to mention they run blazingly fast. Everything responds instantaneously and you can barely imagine a system that is any faster than what you are using today.

Yet for some reason, six months down the line, that feeling of excitement is usually gone. Windows are taking an eternity to pop up. When you start your computer in the morning it seems like there's an endless amount of disk crunching before you can actually start using it. And your games don't seem to be running quite as quickly as they used to.

Contrary to popular belief, your PC doesn't get slower with time. Your CPU doesn't slow down, your video card doesn't grow more brittle with age, and your chipset doesn't all of a sudden lose bandwidth or increase internal latencies as it gets older.

Some of the previous complaints are in fact psychological. For many users, when they perform a major upgrade, they are upgrading from an incredibly slow machine to something that is easily 10 or 20 times as fast. Imagine being in a car that can accelerate 20 times as fast as your current ride. Wouldn't you be breathless the first time you got behind the wheel? After you get used to the performance, it seems average and you often develop a craving for more. As silly as that may sound, it is true. This is the reason that Porsche 911 drivers crave the 911 Turbo, and this is the reason that the owners of the fastest systems today eventually crave greater speed later on. It is our nature to want to get things done even quicker as soon as we become used to a new standard of speed to which we have upgraded.

However, psychological games aren't the only story. To a certain degree, your six-month old PC might feel slower than you remember because it actually is slower than you remember. You aren't going crazy; you're simply installing more and more junk on your computer. Every program you install, every game that you play, but don't properly delete after you're done, and every little utility you download that sounds cool, but ends up being a crock, can contribute to an overall slowdown of your system. These applications, games and utilities all leave their files and settings in various places on your hard drive, and the more you have, the more cluttered things get. Sometimes a tune-up is in order to get rid of a lot of this junk and keep it somewhat organized.

In other situations, you are only using a handful of applications and your hard drive is as tidy as can be, but your computer still feels slow. The difference between the first time you built your computer and today happens to be that now you're actually running applications and games on it. With no software, save the operating system, running on your computer, it's going to be performing at its peak. But as soon as you start loading your antivirus, instant messaging, video playback, and other applications that are always resident (present) in memory, your computer has a lot more baggage to carry around while you're playing your games. If you take the fastest track star on the planet and make him run with a sack of bricks thrown across his shoulder he's obviously not going to be posting any new world records. Your computer is.

The final possibility in determining why your middle-aged PC might seem to be performing much more slowly, which is also very likely, is that the games you are running today are much more demanding than what you were playing when you originally built the system. For example, when *Quake III Arena* was released back in 1999, the hardware that was available at the time could run its predecessor (*Quake 2*) at 100fps. Yet that same hardware would have difficulty running *Quake III* at even half that rate. Chances are the games you buy a year from now are much more taxing on your system than those you are playing today.

The real question is, how do you tell if your computer has too much junk on it, if your applications are hogging your resource, or if the games you're running today are just too demanding for your hardware?

Simple Tune-Ups

Without immediately resorting to throwing money at the problem, there are a few relatively easy ways to keep your computer running smoothly. Doing a little spring cleaning or a little defragmenting every couple of weeks never hurts. In this section I take you through a couple of tune-ups that keep your system feeling new.

The messy ones are always making excuses for what a clean desk means. I've heard everything from an empty mind to others I'm not going to repeat here, but regardless of what you have against keeping something clean, forget them when it comes to dealing with your computer. Otherwise, you're going to definitely run into some performance issues.

By clean in this case, I don't mean in a physical sense, although it does help to dust out your computer every now and then. What I am referring to is the removal of unused drivers and programs. Everything occupying space on your computer, especially those applications that tightly integrate themselves with your OS, can contribute to sandbagging your PC.

The first thing to do is to go through Windows' Add/Remove Programs utility and remove any applications, utilities, and games you no longer use (see Figure 12.7). To get to this utility, click Start, Settings, Control Panel, and activate the Add/Remove Programs icon.

When you find a program you want to axe, click the Change/Remove button (or equivalent for your specific flavor of Windows). Very often you find that there is usually a fair amount of stuff in there that shouldn't have been installed in the first place.

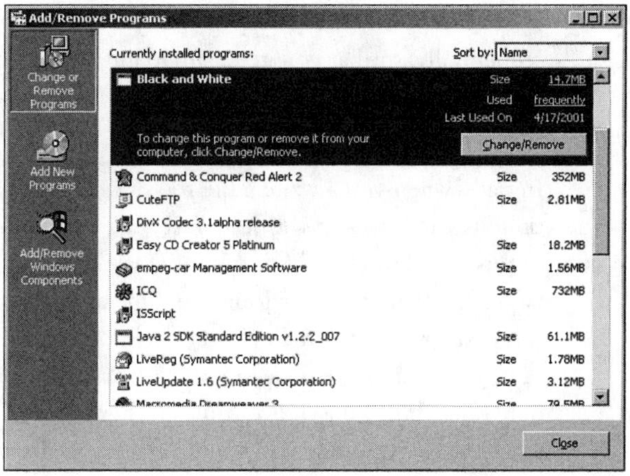

FIGURE 12.7
Use the Windows Add/Remove Programs dialog box to clean up space on your hard disk and speed up your PC.

Caution

When deleting programs from your PC, don't get too trigger-happy. After all, you don't want to remove something that you actually use quite frequently.

Unfortunately, not all programs are created equal, and although most can be uninstalled without a hitch, some might not uninstall properly and even worse, others might not even have their own uninstall utilities. Outside of digging into the black art of registry editing, there isn't an easy way to get rid of these applications. If you are interested in editing your registry (it's not nearly as difficult as I make it sound), there are a number of tutorials and utilities online to help you out. Drop by your favorite search engine and have a look for one or just visit the AnandTech Forums (`http://forums.anandtech.com`) and ask a question or two. Still, although there might not be a simple, sure-fire method for removing programs of this nature, I do suggest that when installing programs you keep things organized into folders with some relative method to the madness. At the very least, you know where to find a program's main folder if you're looking for it.

One of the most commonly overlooked tune-ups is simply defragmenting your hard drive. This does not improve your gaming performance, but it can make your applications and operating system itself feel and act much more responsively.

The reason your hard drive gets fragmented in the first place is simple. When you write data to the hard drive, it is organized in a long chain of clusters. Since the size of an individual cluster is rarely big enough to hold the amount of data you are writing, individual files usually span multiple clusters. Your files can end up spanning thousands of clusters. The ideal way to have these clusters positioned on your disk is to have them positioned sequentially, so that you get a single line of clusters in contiguous fashion that pertains to a single file. If this isn't the case your hard drive has to move all over its platters to read a single file.

Initially when you a write a file to your hard disk, it is stored in a single continuous cluster chain with the next file's chain immediately following the end of this one. However, if the first file is eventually deleted and replaced with a larger file that can't fit within the same area, the file becomes fragmented. In this case, part of the file's cluster chain occurs before the second file and part of it occurs afterwards (see Figure 12.8). Now imagine this happening not only once, but thousands of times to hundreds of thousands of files. See why your hard drive can become quite fragmented?

The reason fragmentation results in degraded performance goes back to the actual construction of a hard disk. Remember from Chapter 7, "Storage: The Slowest Part of Your PC," that your hard disk is one of the only components in your system that is actually made up of moving parts. These moving parts take hundreds and thousands of times longer than system memory to find the data they need. In the best case scenario, the data that must be read from the hard disk lies in a continuous line. Unfortunately, this best case scenario is rarely the case, and its made even rarer if your disk is overly fragmented.

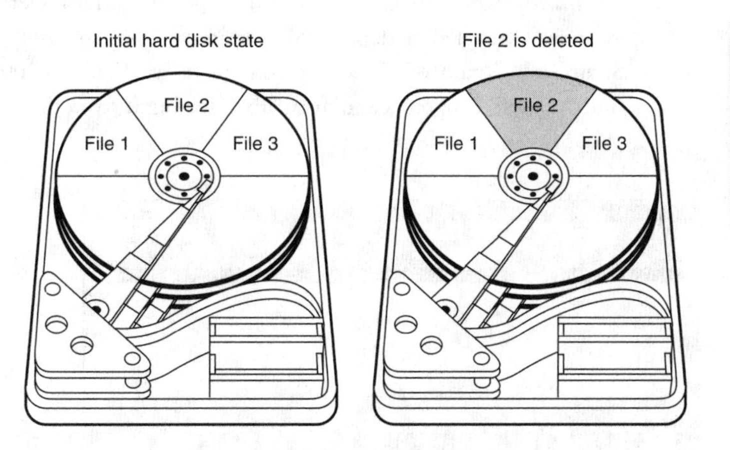

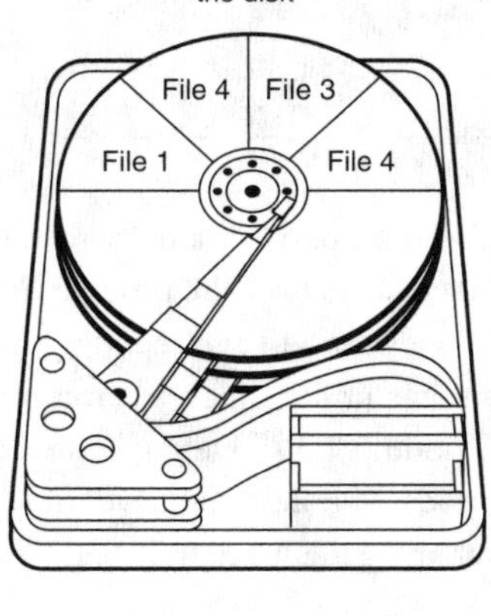

FIGURE 12.8
When files on a hard disk are deleted and new ones are added, the disk fills gaps by any means available to it. This causes fragmentation of data.

Defragmenting your hard disk should be done as frequently as possible. Luckily, the programs available that do it for you often enable you to schedule when you want the program to defragment your hard disk automatically. Because of the relatively intensive nature of the task, you can't really use your computer while its disk is being defragmented. Even owners of a very powerful system shouldn't use their computer while its disks are being defragmented. Performing operations that cause the operating system to attempt to write to your disk while the disk defragmenter is doing its duties can often cause the program to restart its process.

The most basic defragmenter is actually built into all Microsoft Windows 9x, NT/2000, and XP OSes (see Figure 12.9). The program is called *Disk Defragmenter* and is located under System Tools in your Start Menu (usually Start, Programs, Accessories, System Tools). If the Disk Defragmenter program isn't installed by default, you can install it by going to the Windows Setup (Add/Remove Windows Components in Windows 2000/XP) tab of Add/Remove Programs and manually selecting it from the available Windows tools and applications.

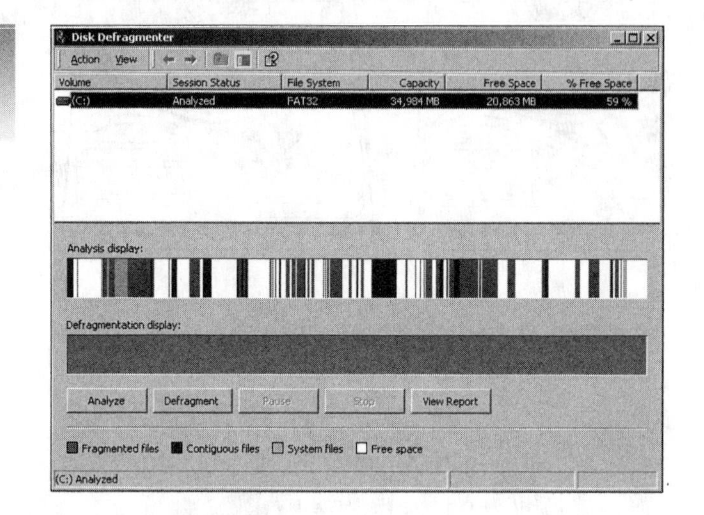

FIGURE 12.9
Disk Defragmenter's analysis of a badly fragmented hard drive.

There are also third party disk defragmenter programs available that often feature enhancements over the program integrated into Windows. You're better off saving your $40 and spending it on a hardware upgrade or a game later on than on a utility, albeit a better one, that you already have built into Windows. Windows' Disk Defragmenter takes care of all your basic defragmentation needs, so unless you have some specialized need, there isn't a reason to go out and get a more fully featured version.

In addition to defragmenting the data on your disk, it is a good idea to scan it for errors and corruption every now and then. It used to be a habit of mine to skip the Windows Scandisk utility whenever it tried to run after an improper shutdown. But one of the most useful tune-ups you can do is a quick scandisk to make sure that there are no file system errors on your disk. This is especially important after an improper shutdown where data may or may not have been completely written to your hard disk.

Another easy to perform tune-up is removing unnecessary programs from loading when you start Windows. These programs may or may not appear in your system tray (the area in the lower right hand corner of your screen where the clock appears). I am far from a fan of applications and drivers that install utilities that run constantly. Ideally all you should have running alongside your basic OS functions is antivirus software, any instant messenger software you might have, and any sort of system/network management software (for example, a software firewall). Things like quick access to Real Player are usually not necessary unless you are constantly having to run that program and would benefit from having it always running.

An easy way to get a listing of these running applications is to look at the 'processes tab' under Windows 2000/XP's task manager (see the section, "My Programs Feel Slow," later in this chapter). In Windows 98 and Me, use the Start menu to navigate to Programs, Accessories, System Tools, and System Information. Then select the Tools menu and click System Configuration Utility. On the Startup tab of the window that appears you can selectively disable any of the applets that load when Windows boots (be careful as some of these are necessary for Windows to boot properly). Unfortunately, this utility is not present under Windows 95, in which case your only resort is to look in the Start Up folder in your Start Menu. You can also consult your registry to remove any programs that shouldn't be running, but if you have to look through there to find them, I'd strongly suggest first making a backup of your registry by clicking the Registry menu and then export registry file.

Tune-Up Programs: Buyer Beware

A few years ago, one of the most attractive utility packages to help "speed up your computer" was RAM Doubler. This program came out during the days when 16MB of memory was an extremely expensive upgrade, so the prospect of doubling your memory size without shelling out $600 was quite attractive. The one thing you always have to remember with products such as this is that software can never replace hardware. Installing a program can never give you more physical CPU power, memory, or hard disk space. What a program can do is compress things or perform some other tricks to make it seem like you have a faster CPU, more memory, or more hard disk space. However, this is almost always at the sacrifice of a performance factor somewhere else.

For example, in addition to RAM Doubler, disk compression was a somewhat popular trend in the late 80s and early 90s when hard disk space wasn't as plentiful as it is today. Disk compression could easily result in twice as much disk space at no cost other than the cost of the program itself. Disk compression software was eventually integrated into Microsoft DOS and it made itself even more prevalent in the market because of that. The problem with disk compression was that the compression and decompression process often slowed down your PC tremendously. Although effectively doubling the size of a 50MB hard disk might sound appealing, the performance hit, especially for gamers, was often too great to make it a viable option for many users.

It is generally recommended that you stay away from programs that make promises that seem very far fetched. I often equate these programs to the things you see marketed at 3:00 a.m. on TV infomercials. Very rarely do they deliver on the promises they make without making some other sacrifice. My suggestion here is to save your money for use on something else that can earn you better PC performance without the sacrifices.

Before you get the impression that all performance "adding" applications are hokey gimmicks, know that there are some tune-up programs that are actually useful. I've already mentioned one type, third party disk defragmenters, but there are many others. There are utilities that can do better cleanups of programs and drivers installed on your computer, as well as sort through and remove unneeded keys from your Windows registry. These programs can be useful, but be careful when running a lot of these cleanup programs, as there is always the possibility that they could end up removing something that Windows needs to start up. To protect yourself, always make backups of your most important files before running any of these utilities.

Tip

Stay away from utilities that keep themselves running at all times. There are very few programs that need to be running all the time, and I usually limit those to mission critical programs such as anti-virus software and software firewalls. Remember, the less you have running in the background the less your system has to worry about when you're running a game.

My Programs Feel Slow

Your computer, just like your car, can often tell you a lot about how it's feeling just by listening to it. No, I don't mean you should put your ear up against your case and ask your computer questions when your programs are running slowly. Just listen to what is happening when the programs that you are running happen to feel slow.

The first and most obvious sign is a lot of disk crunching. You know by now that the weakest link in your PC is your hard disk; it is by far the slowest storage device inside your case. If your CPU is waiting for data to be read off your hard disk, the performance of your entire system is going to suffer tremendously.

Now remember that whenever your hard disk must be read from, you're going to hear it crunching away or if you've got a very quiet drive, your disk access light is constantly blinking. When loading a program, as well as when reading or writing files, your disk is obviously going to be crunching. However, when browsing the Internet or just switching between windows there shouldn't be excessive amounts of disk swapping. The trick to knowing if your performance in a particular application is limited by the performance of your hard disk is by listening to when your disk starts crunching. If it starts crunching away and doesn't stop when you are doing something that isn't disk intensive (for example, no significant amount of data is being written to the disk) then the odds are highly in favor of your PC running out of system memory and swapping to disk. It is useful at this point to take a look at your task manager and see how much physical memory is available on your system. The task manager is made available under Windows 2000 and XP by pressing Ctrl+Alt+Del and selecting task manager (see Figure 12.10).

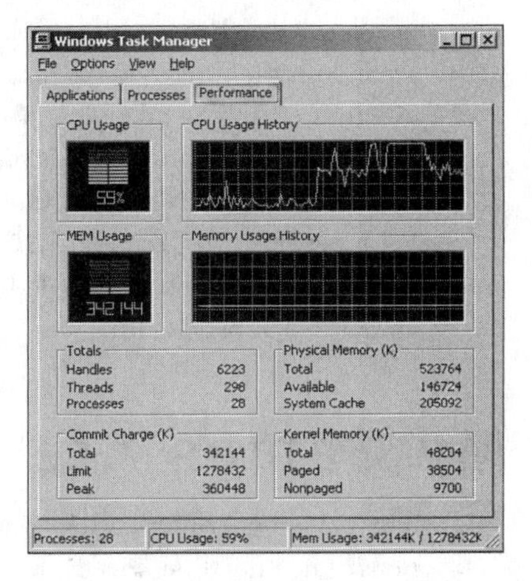

FIGURE 12.10
The Task Manager available in Windows 2000 and XP shows you how much of your system's memory is in use.

If your system is swapping to disk because it is running out of memory, which in turn is slowing down your computer considerably, you have two options. The first, obviously, is to increase the amount of memory that you have. As I mentioned in Chapter 4, "Memory: Your PC's Scratchpad," the ideal amount of memory to have is between 256MB and 384MB for today's applications and games. These days, having 512MB is just about perfect for the power-hungry gamer, but anything more likely goes unused for the current crop of applications and games you're running.

Note

In Windows 9x/Me, Task Manager does not break down your system's memory usage. However, you can right-click My Computer, choose Properties and select the Performance tab to see how much of your system's resources are available. Unfortunately, this won't tell you what programs are actually using up those resources.

The second option is to increase the speed of your hard disk by purchasing a faster unit. By today's high performance PC standards, you almost always want to stick with a 7200RPM drive. For more information on how to dissect the specifications of a hard drive, consult Chapter 7. This is generally only a good solution if you already have a lot of memory and your application load times are simply slowing you down. Remember, though, that if your PC is swapping to disk a lot, your problems extend far beyond having a slow hard drive. Buying a faster drive in that case only helps performance while it is swapping, but it won't stop the disk swapping that is your system's real bottleneck.

If your computer doesn't give you any audible feedback and you are certain that there are no disk accesses when things are slow, the limitation could either be with your CPU or your motherboard's chipset.

To determine whether your CPU or the chipset is the culprit, you have to find out a bit more about the applications being run. If the applications can be classified as bandwidth intensive, it's quite likely that your CPU is waiting around on the various buses that are too slow in feeding it. This situation is even more likely to take place if you have an older setup that is FSB or memory bandwidth limited. This is highly unlikely to occur with most of the newer platforms, such as the Intel i850 or any of the DDR Athlon setups. With between 2.1GBps and 3.2GBps of available FSB and memory bandwidth at your disposal, it would be highly unusual for an application to eat up that much bandwidth.

My Games Are Running Slow

The same types of limitations can arise with games as they can with applications. The only difference is that games that perform badly can also be due to a 3D card limitation and they are often somewhat easier to diagnose.

For starters, if you are swapping to disk at all during your game (thus bringing your game to a halt while you wait for your disk to stop crunching), you definitely don't have enough memory in your system. If it's only a single game that's causing this and you have 512MB of memory in your system, there could very well be something inherently wrong in the game. Anyone who played *Pacific Strike* in the mid-90s or, more recently, the unpatched version of Dues Ex (on a GeForce2 GTS) can attest to this.

Although quite a few programmers are in fact one step away from being godly, not all can make the perfect game. There have been examples where poorly implemented game engines have resulted in games that perform horribly on even the best hardware. Be aware that some of the slowdowns can't be tracked down to hardware limitations. There might be issues with the game.

Because diagnosing the programming of a game as a source of your PC's woes isn't particularly an exact science, I'm going to assume the source of your troubles lies in your hardware. In the following sections I take a look at the other types of limitations you might encounter in your games and how to determine exactly what is slowing down your gameplay.

> **Note**
>
> Unfortunately, there's no simple way to tell if you're using an application that is bandwidth intensive or if your system is CPU limited. Benchmarking can sometimes reveal the answer, but you need to do some extensive benchmarking studies comparing multiple platforms and configurations. You can, if you have the hardware of course, perform this benchmarking yourself. However, obtaining this kind of information is exactly what my AnandTech.com Web site is for, so be sure to check there before you spend many hours (possibly days) compiling your own benchmarks.

CPU and Chipset Limitations

When data cannot get to your video card fast enough, your gaming performance suffers. There are a number of bottlenecks that can be present when dealing with data getting to your video card.

The first and most obvious bottleneck is your CPU. If your CPU can't prepare the data to send to your video card fast enough, your video card is going to be waiting around for your CPU to hurry up and finish.

Other less obvious bottlenecks revolve around FSB and memory bandwidth limitations. Remember that the only way to get data to and from the CPU is through the FSB. If the FSB doesn't make enough bandwidth available to your data, you're not going to get that data in a timely fashion. The same holds true regarding the memory bus. If your memory bus cannot provide data to your CPU or video card fast enough, your performance is limited as well.

Generally speaking, if you increase your resolution and your frame rate does decrease, you are probably bottlenecked by your CPU and/or chipset. Let's look at the performance of a fairly dated platform, the AMD K6-III+ and pair it with a decent video card, the NVIDIA GeForce2 GTS using *Quake III Arena* (see Figure 12.11).

As you can see, under *Quake III Arena*, the K6-III+ is able to average 59 frames per second at 640×480×32-bit color. At 1,024×768×32, the frame rate drops down to 57 frames per second. The difference between the two resolutions ends up being a 3.5% gap; when you compare that to the fact that at 1,024×768×32 your video card has to render 60% as many pixels, it's clear that your video card is not the bottleneck. In this case, the bottleneck is a combination of the CPU and the memory bus. That is known simply by extensive benchmarking, but as you can see it's very easy to narrow down performance bottlenecks by looking at some fairly available results. In cases where you aren't CPU limited the difference in frame rate is much larger. For example, with a Pentium 4 1.8GHz (and much more memory bandwidth) the difference ends up being around 30% between the two resolutions.

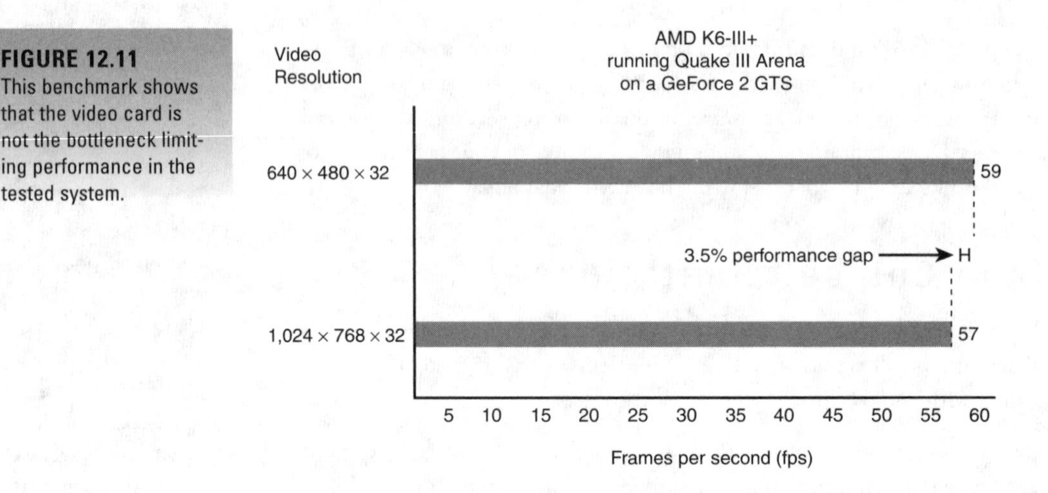

FIGURE 12.11
This benchmark shows that the video card is not the bottleneck limiting performance in the tested system.

A game that scales perfectly with CPU power (for example, one that is not chipset or video card limited) provides a performance increase almost identical to the increase in clock speed. For example, if you upgrade from a 1.5GHz Pentium 4 to a 1.7GHz Pentium 4, you have increased your clock speed by 13%. If doing so results in a 13% increase (or even 10%) in performance, you aren't being held back by any video card or chipset limitations, enabling the game to scale perfectly with CPU performance.

Video Card Limitations

There are three types of limitations with your video card, geometry, fill rate, and memory bandwidth limitations.

When you are geometry limited, the number of polygons that must be processed by your graphics card are much more than what it can handle. This type of limitation is quite rare because game developers design their games to work with the current crop of hardware and very rarely can you heavily manipulate the polygon count in a particular scene. Older video cards with hardware T&L (Transform and Lighting, see Chapter 5, "The Video

Card: A Gamer's Heart and Soul") easily become geometry limited in future games, if their T&L engine is even taken advantage of. The reason for this is that before long the very first hardware T&L engines (for example, NVIDIA's GeForce 256) will no longer be powerful enough for the sheer number of polygons being thrown at them in future games.

One of the most common video card limitations you can run into is what is known as a fill rate limitation. This occurs when the fill rate of your video card has reached its peak and your frame rate suffers because your video card can't render and display the pixels fast enough. At lower resolutions this is difficult to attain because the rest of your system becomes the bottleneck (you are limited by your CPU and chipset). However, as your game resolution increases, the amount of rendering your video card has to do increases as well.

For example, at 640×480 there are only approximately 300,000 pixels on the screen, but at 1,024×768 there are more than twice the number of pixels and at 1,600×1,200 there almost two million pixels on the screen that must be rendered. Fill rate limitations kick in as the resolution increases, but how do you tell if a game is fill rate limited or if it's another type of limitation present (such as a video card memory bandwidth limitation)? The easiest way to do so is crank up the resolution, and then turn on graphics related features (available in the options menu of most 3D games) that eat up memory bandwidth, but not fill rate. The easiest way to do this is by increasing the precision of the pixels being rendered by comparing 16-bit color to 32-bit color and increasing the Z-buffer precision (for example, 16-bit versus 24-bit versus 32-bit). This won't work if your chip renders everything internally at 32-bit color (for example, STMicro's Kyro II). (You should know, however, that it is highly unlikely that you have a situation where you are completely fill rate limited, but if you're curious, that's how you test for it.)

The final video card limitation is being constrained by the memory bandwidth available to your graphics processor. Just like a system memory bandwidth limitation, if your graphics processor can't get the data it needs it waits to render those pixels until it does get it. This limitation is much more common in real-world situations and is much easier to detect. Memory bandwidth limitations kick in as resolution increases, as color depth increases, as more features are turned on, as texture complexity and size increases, and so on. Today's graphics cards are much more likely to be memory bandwidth limited than they are going to be fill rate or geometry limited. Unfortunately, there is no way to increase the amount of memory bandwidth on your card without overclocking or purchasing a new card. I explain overclocking in Chapter 14, "Tweaking and Overclocking: Turbo-Charging Your PC."

Chapter 13

Operating Systems and Device Drivers: Making Your Hardware Work

From MS-DOS to Windows XP: The Role and Evolution of PC Operating Systems

On a purely electrical level, getting your hardware to communicate with its many individual components isn't too hard. Provided that everything was designed and implemented properly this is only a matter of applying the proper voltage at the right points and essentially powering on the system.

However, your system is completely useless if all you can get it to do is run its Power-On Self Test (POST). The games you're going to be running require an environment to run in, and that environment *isn't* your motherboard's BIOS. The environment your applications, games, and utilities run in is known as your computer's operating system (OS).

The operating system is a software layer that communicates directly with your hardware, allowing other applications to install directly within this layer and also communicate with your hardware. The fact that your games run on top of the OS layer means that a poorly designed OS could theoretically impact your gaming performance. The more layers that exist between your game and the hardware that is doing all the calculations, the more performance bottlenecks and compatibility issues can arise.

Luckily (although some may argue otherwise), the process of choosing which OS you want to run on your computer is a much simpler one than picking out your CPU, motherboard or video card. The main reason behind this is that only a handful of OS developers are out there, and of them really only one or two are viable for a gamer's platform.

By far the most popular OS developer is Microsoft, and they produce the only truly viable gaming OSes out there. The Redmond-based corporation originally set forth to simplify the OS scene when the first PCs hit the streets with what was known as the Microsoft Disk Operating System, MS-DOS or just DOS for short. The original MS-DOS was released in 1981 and was heavily used by IBM. This OS was nothing like the screen full of icons that you are used to with Windows; instead DOS was a command-line–based OS (see Figure 13.1). Instead of using icons to represent files and programs, files and programs were accessed by executing text commands at what is known as a *command prompt*, which waited for user input.

The phasing out of MS-DOS has lasted an incredibly long time. Even when Microsoft began releasing OSes with a graphical user interface (GUI) instead of DOS's command-line–based interface, MS-DOS still remained in some form. In the earliest versions of Windows (3.11 and earlier), the Windows interface was just installed over DOS. With the release of Windows 95, Microsoft included a copy of DOS 7 that installed along with Windows 95 but was much less predominant. When Windows NT was released, DOS was absent from the OS. Slowly, Microsoft has continued to eliminate DOS from its operating systems.

FIGURE 13.1
In the Fall of 1995 Microsoft abandoned the use of their command-line–based operating system, MS-DOS.

After subsequent releases of Windows 98 and 98 Second Edition (see Figure 13.2), Microsoft launched Windows Me, which was its first consumer OS that prevented users from booting to DOS without a boot disk.

FIGURE 13.2
Prior to the release of Windows XP Home, Windows 98 Second Edition was the most stable consumer version of Windows available.

Still based off the Windows 9x core, Windows Me didn't completely get rid of DOS, as it is still present in the OS. It was more hidden from users to encourage the full transition to 32-bit 9x/NT/2000 applications. Using the Windows 2000 kernel, Windows XP has completely exorcised DOS from its code (see Figure 13.3).

Although DOS is no longer present, Microsoft has included some tools in their most recent OSes to improve compatibility with older games and applications. These tools help run not only DOS but, as shown in Figure 13.4, Windows 9x applications under Windows 2000 and XP as well.

FIGURE 13.3
In addition to having the most aggressive changes to the look of Microsoft operating systems since Windows 95, Windows XP (like Windows 2000) also completely does away with legacy DOS code.

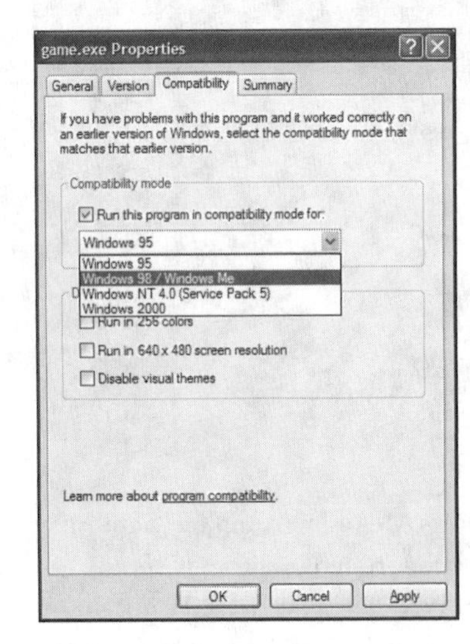

FIGURE 13.4
The use of compatibility modes in Windows XP helps ensure that it can run older Windows software.

The main reason for getting rid of DOS is because it is quite outdated. However, the unfortunate problem associated with doing so, and the reason it has taken so long to phase out, is that when you have an OS that has been in use for a couple of decades, it is difficult to get rid of it just like that. When Windows 95 came out there were far too many applications, especially games, that required support for it. Several types of applications have yet to make the move over to a Windows-based form. Case in point would be a large amount of available BIOS-flashing software for PC motherboards. It wasn't until late 2000 or early 2001 that motherboard manufacturers first really emphasized having a Windows-based flash utility that users could run to upgrade their BIOSes.

Today three main OSes from Microsoft can be considered when making the decision of which OS to run on your computer: Windows 98/Me, Windows 2000, and Windows XP. Various versions of these three OSes exist, and I mention them where appropriate, but these are the three major ones.

Hardware Compatibility

You should know by now that you can't just grab any processor, stick it into a motherboard, and assume it works. You know that the processor must communicate with the rest of the components in your system via buses. If the interface between the CPU and the motherboard doesn't match up, then you're not even going to get it plugged, let alone make it work when powered on. The same types of compatibility concerns have to be taken into account when choosing your OS. The concerns are much less of an issue because most OSes support a broad range of hardware configurations.

All the OSes I discuss here are x86-compatible OSes, meaning that they run on any of the CPUs I discussed in Chapter 1, "The Central Processing Unit: The Heart and Soul of the PC." Each of these processors implement the x86 ISA (Instruction Set Architecture). Motherboard and chipset compatibility can be an issue as well, although not under the three major OSes I cover here. The main reason for this is that because Microsoft Windows is the most widely used OS, it also receives the bulk of the attention from game publishers and hardware manufacturers. If a particular component doesn't work in Windows, the hardware manufacturer has essentially shut itself off from the largest computer-buying body of the industry. It's a big no-no.

Simply being hardware compatible with your OS doesn't mean that you're in the clear. Basic compatibility is necessary to ensure that your hardware can even work under the OS, but it is also up to the manufacturer of your hardware to make sure that the OS knows what it is and how to communicate with it. The manufacturers do this by providing what is known as a *device driver* for the OSes under which they support their hardware. Your OS recognizes this device driver, and it is used to provide information to software about what you have installed in your system and what it is capable of doing.

With that in mind, let's take a look at the operating systems currently available that make for suitable gaming platforms.

Windows 98/Me

Windows 98 is built from the same code base as Windows 95, released years ago, although it has received a few improvements over time. The OS is available only in a 32-bit form and installs a version of DOS when it is set up. Because of the DOS portion of the OS, Windows 98 retains some compatibility with older software titles and games. For the most part, you won't miss compatibility with any of the Windows 3.11 applications because they have long been replaced by much more up-to-date software. The beauty of the OS's DOS support is that if your motherboard manufacturer doesn't provide a Windows-based BIOS flash utility, you can always boot into DOS and use a DOS-based flash utility.

Windows 98 is far from stressing on system resources. Running the OS with 128MB of RAM is definitely adequate. Unfortunately, one of the reasons the OS isn't stressing on system resources is that it is not at all robust. Compared to the NT-based Windows 2000 and XP, Windows 98 is a joke when it comes to stability. For the most part, when running a single application or game at a time, the OS works as expected. However, as soon as you start opening multiple applications that put a decent load on the system, you begin to notice the shortcomings of the OS. Long-time users of Windows 9x have no doubt encountered frequent lockups and crashes of the operating system due to one misbehaving application. In Windows 2000 and XP, you are much more likely to successfully shut down the offending application without shutting down the rest of the operating system.

In the fall of 2000, Microsoft replaced Windows 98 with Windows Me (Millennium Edition), which is geared even more toward the home user who has never used a PC in his life (but still maintained the DOS core at its heart). This trend toward user-friendliness continues. A goal of virtually all companies in this industry is to initiate the uninitiated, to bring computers to those users who still don't have them or don't feel comfortable with them. The more computers that are in the hands of users, the more Microsoft can sell its OSes, the more Intel can sell its processors, and the more ASUS can sell its motherboards. The downside to this is that those users who do have some experience have to suffer (sometimes) through extremely oversimplified UIs (user interfaces) in their OSes.

Windows Me is the perfect example of this at its worst because DOS has one of the scariest UIs to a user who has ever touched a computer. Windows Me did everything possible to ensure that you couldn't get to DOS as easily as you could in Windows 98. When Windows 98 was first starting on your machine, pressing the F8 key on your keyboard would open a menu that would enable you to boot directly to a DOS prompt. Although it is possible to put back in with very little effort, that feature was removed from Windows Me. The Restart in MS-DOS Mode option under the Shut Down Windows menu was also removed.

Obviously, I'm not a fan of Windows Me. The reason is simple: It took the only thing Windows 98 had going for it, the capability to drop to DOS, and killed it. The OS is okay for someone who has never used a computer before, but you just spent all this time and money on putting together a killer system. So you might as well install an OS that can actually do something with it.

One thing that can be said about both Windows 98 and Me is that virtually all games run on them properly. Microsoft positioned Windows 98/Me as its official home/gaming OSes, and software developers heeded its recommendations, for the most part. In spite of this, a much better alternative exists.

Windows 2000

When Microsoft Windows NT was released, it was clearly only for high-end workstations and servers. The code base was entirely 32-bit and ran quite well on the higher-end processors available at the time. Because most of the applications and games at the time were 16-bit, Windows NT was never even thought of as the basis for a gaming OS. However as an operating system, Windows NT was much more reliable than Windows 95 and 98. When Windows NT hit version 4.0, there were some enthusiasts that began dual booting between Windows 9x and Windows NT 4 using the latter for their applications and keeping 9x for their games.

Some shortcomings kept Windows NT out of the gaming community. For starters, drivers for 3D cards were rarely optimized for performance under Windows NT and, unfortunately, Windows NT didn't support USB. I know that kept me from moving to NT immediately since I had quite a few USB peripherals at the time. A lot of the hardware that was deemed to be "consumer" or "for the home" was also rarely supported by manufacturers under the OS. To top it off, there was no support for DirectX 7 under NT that limited game compatibility. But without a doubt, Windows NT was a much more robust and stable platform than the 9x series.

These deficiencies, however, paved the way for Windows 2000, originally known as Windows NT 5.0. Windows 2000 combined a lot of the features that were missing from Windows NT 4, such as USB and DirectX (version 7, at that point) support, to an updated NT code base with a semi-tweaked User Interface.

Windows 2000 removed all traces of DOS with the exception of a command prompt that provides some limited functionality. With Windows 2000, you either make sure that your motherboard manufacturer provides a Windows-based flash utility or keep a DOS boot disk handy.

Although Windows 2000 was targeted at the professional business user, it ended up being the best overall choice for most people in the enthusiast community. It took a few months after the initial launch of the OS before gaming performance was up to par, but things did eventually turn around. The main problem users encountered was very poor 3D drivers under Windows 2000. Microsoft was telling all the video card manufacturers that people weren't going to be running games under Windows 2000 when the exact opposite was true. Currently, very few issues prevent Windows 2000 from being a viable gaming platform. Virtually all game titles are tested under Windows 2000, and drivers are at the point where they sometimes outperform their Windows 9x counterparts.

When video card manufacturers began noticing that gamers were actually using Windows 2000 as their work and game OS, they were forced to spend time developing proper Windows 2000 drivers. The first and only manufacturer to get its Windows 2000 drivers to be capable of offering performance similar, if not better than, its 9x drivers was NVIDIA.

Being a very mature platform that does work wonderfully with the latest games, Windows 2000 is my personal choice for a gaming OS. However, a replacement is just now beginning to show its face.

Windows XP

Originally, Windows 2000 (at that time, still referred to as NT 5.0) was supposed to be the point where Windows 9x and NT would merge, and there would be one code base for the entire product line. This product line would still be segmented according to the needs of the users, but unlike Windows 9x versus NT, the core of the operating systems would be the same. However, although Windows 2000 ended up offering a Windows 98-like interface, it was still directed at basically the same market as Windows NT and faced significant compatibility issues with existing games due to the inadequate hardware driver support mentioned in the previous section.

The OS to fix this is Windows XP, which is based off Windows 2000, yet is available in Home and Professional versions (as well as server versions with the name Windows .Net Server). The Home version has much of the functionality of the Professional version, yet several features are either watered down or removed to make it easier for the average home user to work with. For true hardware and gaming enthusiasts, your choice should be Windows XP Professional, as it boasts improved functionality over Windows 2000 and more features than Windows XP Home. In the end, I believe it most likely replaces Windows 2000 as the OS of choice for enthusiasts.

Microsoft Windows XP is also available in a 64-bit version that accompanies the processor market's transition to 64-bit architectures such as the Itanium from Intel and the x86-64 Hammer line from AMD over the next few years. In many ways, this transition mimics the 16-bit to 32-bit transition that took place during the Windows 3.11 to Windows 9x era.

Microsoft has focused very heavily on the launch of Windows XP. Because of this, hardware compatibility for the XP launch is leaps and bounds above what it was at the 2000 launch. Generally speaking, most of your basic hardware (chipset, audio, drive controllers, and so on) have better out-of-the-box support under Windows XP than under Windows 2000. This is mainly because many more drivers are built into the OS. Windows 2000 was the same way when it was released; the number of drivers supplied with the OS completely shadowed what Windows 98 offered at the time.

Although it is controversial, the new user interface under Windows XP is a point of attraction for many. Unfortunately, with this new user interface a number of performance penalties must be paid to gain all the fancy effects. This puts the burden on you to have a faster overall system to achieve the same performance you had under Windows 2000. The burden is also placed on the video chip manufacturers to provide drivers that are more optimized for these new 2D effects. Both ATI and NVIDIA already have drivers that improve Windows XP 2D performance.

The ones that are truly left out to dry are owners of 3dfx cards. Since NVIDIA's acquisition of the company's IP and the dissolution of the remaining structure, no one has taken the time to develop solid XP drivers for the Voodoo4 and Voodoo5 products (or Voodoo3 for that matter). If you have one of these cards you're better off upgrading your video card or not touching XP at all.

Windows XP does improve performance in a few areas in spite of the 2D performance hit you take. The OS uses some intelligence when writing data to your disk and it does its best to limit the amount of fragmentation created when writing to the disk (see Chapter 7, "Storage: The Slowest Part of the PC"). Windows XP also features some intelligent prefetching that examines application usage patterns and attempts to optimize the loading of most frequently used applications by prefetching the data into main memory. The combination of these features makes XP's disk performance seem much greater than 9x and 2000.

Installing the OS

In the last two chapters, I explained everything you need to know to get the hardware portion of building your computer set up. But at this point you're only half way through the building process. This is where the hardware ends and the software begins.

You can take a couple of approaches to installing an OS on a new computer. Regardless of which one you take, assuming that you are installing your OS on a brand new hard drive, you can only get the OS files onto your computer one way: via another storage device.

That other storage device is usually your CD/DVD drive, as all the major OSes discussed earlier are produced and sold on CD-ROMs. The installation process for these OSes is relatively simple; the first step is to set up your system to boot from your CD/DVD drive. This is accomplished by entering the BIOS setup (usually by pressing DEL or F2) during the POST process and selecting your CD/DVD drive as your boot device. If you have a SCSI CD/DVD drive (Chapter 7) from which you want to boot, simply make sure that the device is bootable. You should go into your SCSI adapter setup when you are prompted (usually by pressing Ctrl + another key, the card tells you what key to press) and make the modifications there. Then make sure your BIOS is set to boot from your SCSI card first, and you should be good to go.

All Windows 2000/XP CDs are bootable, meaning that if you set your BIOS to boot from the CD/DVD drive with the Windows setup CD inside, your computer can boot into the Windows setup directly from the CD. Although this is simplified for you in the installation process, the next step is to create a boot partition and mark it as active on your hard drive.

If you cannot install off a bootable CD, try booting off a floppy. This can be arranged by ensuring that your floppy drive is set to be the first device from which to boot (selectable within your BIOS) and using a bootable disk. One of the most handy tools is a Windows 98 or Me boot disk because it enables you to boot to a DOS prompt with CD-ROM support. Now you can copy the OS installation files from any CD to your hard drive and install the OS from there, or straight off the CD.

As you remember from Chapter 7, your hard drive contains an area of data known as the *Master Boot Record (MBR)*. For data to be stored on your hard disk, the drive must be divided into partitions, and the partitions can be made into volumes. These volumes become your drive letters (see Figure 13.5).

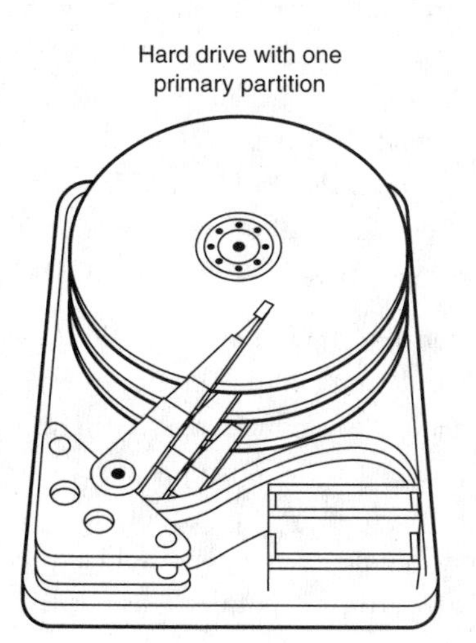

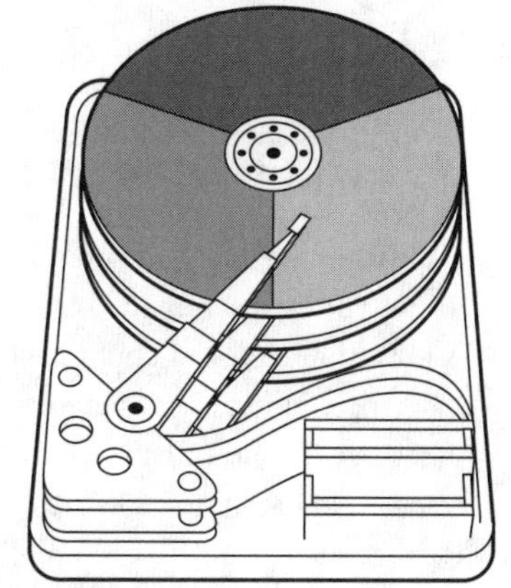

FIGURE 13.5
A hard disk can be partitioned into one or more "logical" drives.

In the "old" days of DOS, a program called F-Disk did the partitioning of your hard drive (see Figure 13.6).

```
MS-DOS Prompt - FDISK
                     Microsoft Windows 98
                   Fixed Disk Setup Program
            (C)Copyright Microsoft Corp. 1983 - 1998

                        FDISK Options

Current fixed disk drive: 1

Choose one of the following:

1. Create DOS partition or Logical DOS Drive
2. Set active partition
3. Delete partition or Logical DOS Drive
4. Display partition information


Enter choice: [1]



Press Esc to exit FDISK
```

FIGURE 13.6
The F-Disk utility allows you to customize the number and size of partitions to use on your hard drive(s).

Although F-Disk has never been officially replaced by a newer version, its necessity has been diminished over the years. The Windows 2000/XP installs enable you to partition your drives during the install process, so having to use F-Disk is avoided. Do keep in mind that when you delete a partition on your hard disk all the data that resided on the drive is lost. If you have two partitions, C: and D: and you only delete C:, all the data on D: is still intact. However if you delete both and recreate them, the data on both is lost.

Utilities, such as Partition Magic, enable you to modify partitions without losing your data. For the most part, having multiple partitions isn't necessary. A long time ago you could have made the argument that it can improve performance. However, when you're dealing with 2GHz processors with gigabytes per second of bandwidth to your PC's system memory and hard disks transferring at above 40MBps, the arguments no longer hold any value. Performance is already too high for partition optimizations to play any role in ensuring high system performance.

Many make the argument that more partitions results in better organization; however, in most situations all that gives you is a bunch of drive letters and less flexibility. Organizing your data into folders makes much more sense and allows the individual folders to get as large as you need. However, if you have a particular partition set aside for games, as soon as your games partition becomes full you have to either delete or populate your program's partition with some of your games, thus defeating the original purpose. Remember, having multiple drives doesn't make your computer any better; it just means that you now have to deal with multiple, rather cryptic drive letters, instead of various folder names, to categorize all your files.

If you need to create more than one partition under Windows 2000/XP install, it is very simple: You just follow the onscreen directions for creating a partition, and it walks you through the various steps. Don't worry if you accidentally create a partition you didn't want—you can still delete it and create it again. But do remember that if you delete a partition with data on it, the data goes away.

If you have to partition under F-Disk, the onscreen instructions can be confusing. The process, however, isn't all that difficult to grasp.

Chances are that you're either running a FAT32 or NTFS file system on your hard drive or you will be, in which case you get a screen upon starting F-Disk that asks if you want to enable large hard disk support. By answering Yes to the question, you enable FAT32 support for your drive under F-Disk.

This brings you to the main F-Disk menu shown earlier in Figure 13.6. You can display existing hard disk partition information for your computer's hard disks by selecting option 4 from this menu (see Figure 13.7).

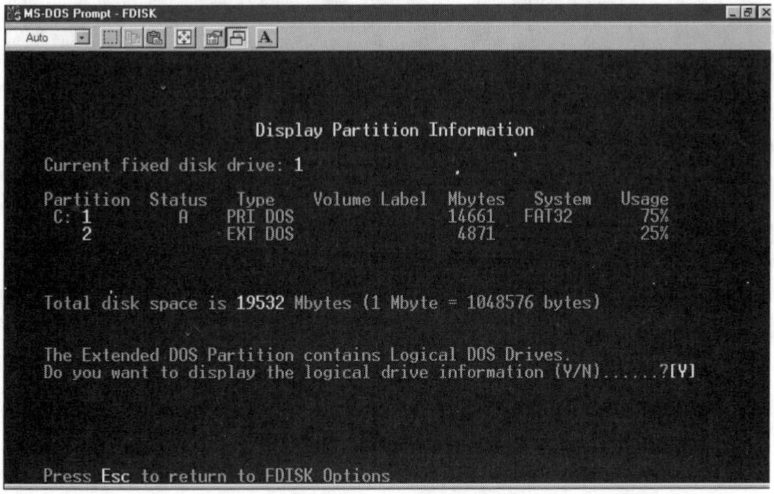

```
MS-DOS Prompt - FDISK

                    Display Partition Information

Current fixed disk drive: 1

Partition  Status   Type    Volume Label  Mbytes   System   Usage
 C: 1         A    PRI DOS                14661    FAT32      75%
    2              EXT DOS                 4871               25%

Total disk space is 19532 Mbytes (1 Mbyte = 1048576 bytes)

The Extended DOS Partition contains Logical DOS Drives.
Do you want to display the logical drive information (Y/N)......?[Y]

Press Esc to return to FDISK Options
```

FIGURE 13.7
The partition information screen in F-Disk lists all of the available drives and any existing partitions.

First, choose which fixed disk (physical hard drive) you want to partition. Creating a primary partition using F-Disk is easier than it seems. Just choose option 1 from the main F-Disk menu, which opens a screen asking you what type of partition you want to create.

The next task is to create your primary partition on the drive, so choose that option. When F-Disk asks if you want the primary partition to occupy the maximum available size (the size of your disk) you can either answer yes if you only want one partition or no if you want to create multiple partitions on the same drive.

If you answer no, remember to mark the partition active (another function in the F-Disk menu) if you want to make it bootable (see Figure 13.8). To create other partitions, you can create an extended partition after creating the primary partition with the space left over on your drive and then create logical drives in the extended partition area. With those steps in mind, you should be able to navigate through F-Disk if you need to use it.

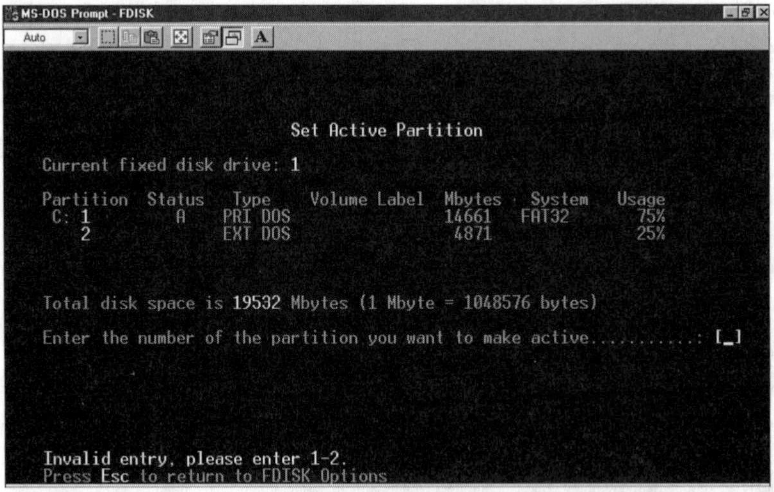

FIGURE 13.8
Never forget to mark your partition as active. If you don't, the drive will not be bootable and you'll get an error or no response when you try to start your OS.

You should keep in mind that if you are installing Windows 2000 or XP to a hard disk connected to a disk controller these operating systems don't directly support, you must provide drivers for the controller before the OS setup can see the hard disk. These drivers are provided by the controller's manufacturer and can usually be found at their Web sites.

If your boot drive is connected to a controller that is integrated into your chipset, you should be good to go. However, if you are booting off a SCSI card or an on-board IDE RAID channel, you most likely have to supply a driver disk during install.

Drivers and OS Updates

A large part of making sure that your computer is running as quickly and as smoothly as possible is keeping up to date with device drivers and OS/application updates. In this section, I focus on those two areas from the perspectives of building a computer from scratch and maintaining that computer with proper driver updates.

Most users have dealt with device drivers at some point, but often they don't know exactly what makes them tick. A device driver is basically a software layer of abstraction between the Operating System and the hardware itself. Because an OS cannot talk to every single piece of hardware out on the market, the hardware manufacturers provide device drivers that bridge the communication gap between the OS and the hardware. As you can probably guess, the more layers of abstraction you have, the greater the chances are for a weak link to form. In the case of device drivers, a poorly written driver could mean loss of functionality of the hardware (for example, a video driver that didn't implement support for the video chipset's antialiasing functions). In this case, although the driver might tell the OS that the video card can perform some sort of antialiasing the driver is not able to actually command the hardware to enable the function.

Device drivers can also be the cause of poor performance. Think of water (data) flowing through a pipe (the driver). The water can flow at a certain speed from the source and it can flow at the same speed at the end of the pipe. However, if something is wrong with the pipe that limits the flow then the end result is a reduced amount of water flow. Such is the case with some poorly made drivers.

> **Note**
>
> Updates and patches to your OS and applications work a bit differently. Like device drivers, they are software additions. However, they are used to work with software applications and not hardware devices. These updates often fix bugs in the software code that were either undetected during the original testing of the OS/application or that have surfaced while interacting with new hardware/software that wasn't available when it was originally being tested.

Paying close attention to both driver and software updates is key to ensuring solid system operation going forward.

Different Types of Drivers

There are many different types of drivers, but they can generally be classified according to a couple of criteria. Drivers are classified according to the hardware they service, then the OS with which they are compatible, and finally, the type of driver they are.

The first classification is fairly straightforward; you don't expect to be able to use video card drivers on your sound card and vice versa. An exception to this is that sometimes drivers for one product work on another because they share common hardware. The best example of this is video drivers. When NVIDIA releases a graphics chip such as the GeForce3 Ti 500, they provide a set of *reference drivers* for the chip itself. Video card manufacturers that use the Ti 500 chip then take NVIDIA's reference drivers and apply their own look to them as well as any additional tools necessary for their product. For example, Gainward might choose to put their logo in the display properties sheet and include an overclocking utility with their drivers while ASUS might include functions for video capturing because their card supports it. If you had a Hercules Ti 500 card then it would work with not only NVIDIA's reference drivers, but Gainward's drivers, ASUS' drivers, and Hercules' drivers as well.

The rule of thumb for video drivers is to stick with the reference drivers from the chip manufacturer because they are usually updated much more frequently than your card manufacturer's drivers. These drivers usually don't have any performance differences because they're all based off NVIDIA's reference drivers.

Remember that your chipset also needs drivers to function properly. A basic set of drivers is usually built into the OS, but you're better off visiting the chipset manufacturer's Web site and downloading the latest drivers for your chipset. You're better off going to the chipset manufacturer than to your motherboard manufacturer for these drivers.

Although drivers can sometimes be used with cards that they don't officially support, the use of drivers across unsupported OSes usually leads to trouble. You can sometimes get away with using Windows 9x drivers under Me or using Windows 2000 drivers under XP because 9x and Me share the same base as do 2000 and XP. However, you are always better off using drivers (provided that they are available) that are intended for your OS.

The final classification is the type of driver with which you're dealing. With most hardware you run into, the only types of drivers you encounter are either beta or unreleased drivers or official releases. Unless your current drivers have a bug that a set of beta or unreleased drivers happens to fix, stick with officially released drivers. The only exception to this rule is video drivers.

With video drivers you can have a few more types such as Windows Hardware Quality Labs (WHQL) certified drivers. WHQL certified drivers are certified by the Microsoft hardware quality labs' specifications to be compatible with Windows operating systems. Having WHQL certified drivers generally doesn't hurt.

Another driver category you run into is what NVIDIA calls Unified Driver Architecture (UDA). This type of a driver works with virtually all chips produced by a manufacturer. For example, NVIDIA's "Detonator" drivers boast a UDA that enables them to work on everything from the Riva TNT through the GeForce3 Ti 500; kind of like a one-size fits all for drivers.

NVIDIA's UDA incorporates another layer of abstraction into the hardware of all its GPUs and its UDA drivers. These abstraction layers don't change from GPU to GPU or from driver to driver and always maintain a certain level of compatibility with past, present, and future products. This enables NVIDIA to perform very few modifications to its drivers and ensure operational and functional compatibility with future products. Later, it can tweak and tune its drivers to extract even more performance from its GPUs.

This type of Unified Driver Architecture is *very* difficult to achieve. NVIDIA has a lab of 4,000 test computers running Linux that test its drivers nightly to ensure ongoing driver compatibility and ever-improving performance. These test machines are upgraded every 6 months to higher-performance models (see Figure 13.9). To date, no competing manufacturer can rival this type of quality control on its drivers, which is evident in the quality of drivers NVIDIA releases.

FIGURE 13.9
Close to 4,000 machines run in this datacenter-like facility every night at NVIDIA's headquarters in Santa Clara, California.

The machines shown in Figure 13.9 continuously test updates to NVIDIA's ever-evolving drivers and automatically reject any driver builds that break functionality over previous versions. This prevents the latest drivers from being any worse in terms of functionality than those they are replacing. This type of aggressive testing and optimization is why NVIDIA generally releases new drivers every 4–6 months, which improves performance tremendously for all its products.

Installing Drivers and Updates on a Brand-New System

After your OS install completes, you have to do a few final steps before your computer is ready for use.

The first step is to update any critical OS files that may be provided by the manufacturer. Microsoft generally releases these in the form of individual updates on their Web site or in large collections of updates known as Service Packs. These updates are found at `www.microsoft.com` in the downloads section. Service Packs are cumulative in that each Service Pack features all the bug fixes contained within the previous Service Pack. To install a Service Pack, all you have to do is download the executable and run it. You are prompted to back up your current configuration if you want to uninstall the Service Pack at a later date. This is usually safe if you're installing a Service Pack you've never tried before. You should always install the latest updates/Service Packs for your OS because they can often fix problems that creep up in the future. However, I wouldn't recommend installing updates/Service Packs that aren't finalized (still in beta stages) or not officially supported by your OS vendor. This is acceptable in some remote situations, but for the most part, make sure all your OS updates come from your OS vendor.

Starting with Windows 98, Microsoft included a little tool in Windows called Windows Update. Windows Update is essentially a link to Microsoft's Windows Update Web site that detects what your current OS/software configuration is and provides you with a list of updates, patches, and Service Packs that have been released and aren't currently present on your system. This is a good way to ensure your OS is indeed up-to-date.

Windows Me and XP take this feature one step further by automating Windows Update in what Microsoft calls "Auto Update." The process remains the same, except instead of forwarding you to the Microsoft Web page, the updating occurs without your intervention (with the exception of reboots, and so on). This can be controlled through the Automatic Updates tab under the System Properties control panel (see Figure 13.10). To access this, press the Windows Key, Pause/Break, and then click Automatic Updates.

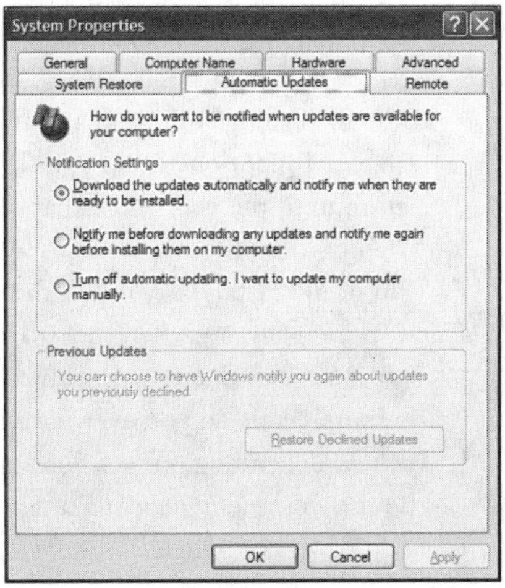

FIGURE 13.10
If you don't want Windows Me or XP going out on its own to fetch operating system updates, use this control panel to adjust how Windows Update works.

The next step is to install all the drivers for your chipset and other critical components on your motherboard. These drivers are available from both the manufacturer of your motherboard as well as the manufacturer of your chipset. Most of the time it is best to go directly to the manufacturer of your chipset for the drivers. The types of drivers you install here enable your OS to properly recognize your North/South Bridges or Hubs depending on what chipset you're using. The drivers also enable proper AGP support. In the end, installing these drivers generally improves performance and compatibility, so you usually have no reason to be without them. When it comes to these drivers it is often best to stick with final releases rather than toy with beta updates. If you have a problem that can be tracked down to these drivers, using a beta version might be advisable, but don't upgrade just because a new beta version has been released.

By this point you are probably getting frustrated with looking at your monitor at such a low resolution; help is on the way because it is now time to install your video card drivers. Similar to chipset drivers, these drivers can be obtained from the manufacturer of your card or the manufacturer of the graphics processor itself. Unless your card has unique features (3D glasses, video input, and so on) that require special drivers, I'd suggest going directly to the manufacturer of the graphics processor for the drivers. These are generally more up-to-date than what your card manufacturer can provide, and although they don't have the unique logo of ASUS or ELSA, they get the job done—which is what counts. Functionality over form is one of the key lessons to take away from this book. Again, stay away from beta drivers unless a specific problem you have with the final release drivers is addressed in the beta release.

The final things to install are the drivers for your peripherals. In the last chapter I mentioned that you should leave the non-critical peripheral installation until the very end. That comes into play here. As I mentioned in that chapter, the proper way to install these peripherals is one at a time. Physically install one, install the drivers, reboot to make sure everything is working okay, and then move on to the next one. This takes up more time, but it ensures that if any problems exist, tracking down the culprit is easy. It definitely helps if you ever have to do any troubleshooting at this stage, which, depending on how long you keep up with your hardware enthusiast hobby, eventually happens to you.

Keeping Everything Up to Date

When it comes to updating drivers, the old adage, "If it ain't broke, don't fix it," applies more than anything. Just as I mentioned in the previous section, upgrading to beta or unreleased drivers should be done only if a serious bug needs to be fixed with the current drivers. These drivers are called "beta" for a reason, and they should be avoided, especially if you value your stability. This might come off a bit precautionary, but I cannot stand an unstable system (and the use of beta drivers can cause just that).

With that said, you want to keep an eye out for updated drivers in a few areas. You definitely want to keep your chipset, video, and audio drivers up to date, although the latter is not updated nearly as frequently as the others. The best place to find these drivers are, as I stated earlier, the manufacturers' Web sites. Beware of drivers that are linked to other sources, especially if the files don't reside on the manufacturers' servers.

The types of drivers you most frequently update deal with hardware that, if the driver update doesn't go smoothly, cause your system to pretty much be hosed.

For this reason you should always keep the drivers you're upgrading just in case you have to revert to them. With Windows XP, the driver rollback feature comes in handy here becuase it enables you to automatically revert to your previous drivers through the Device Manager (see Figure 13.11).

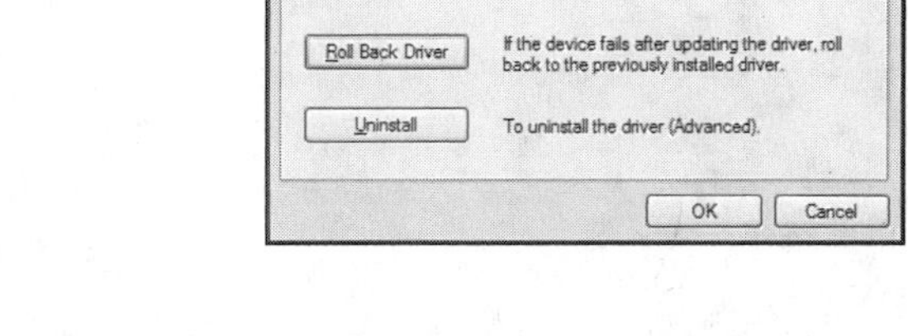

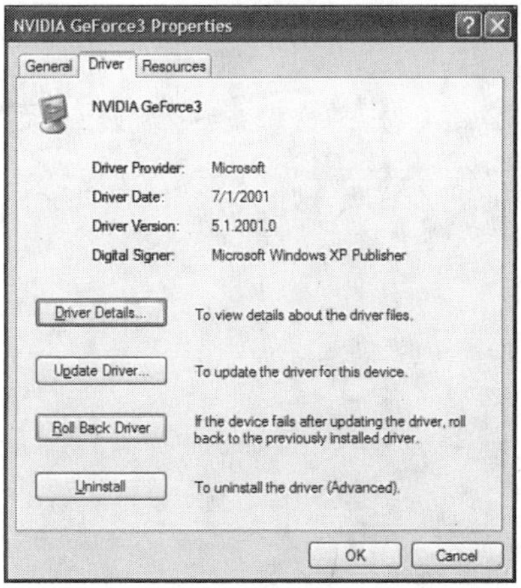

FIGURE 13.11
Use the Driver Rollback button on your hardware device's properties sheet in Windows XP to restore to a previous driver for that device.

Another feature that both Me and XP offer is System Restore, which enables you to restore your system to a previous state by choosing a restore point set by date (see Figure 13.12).

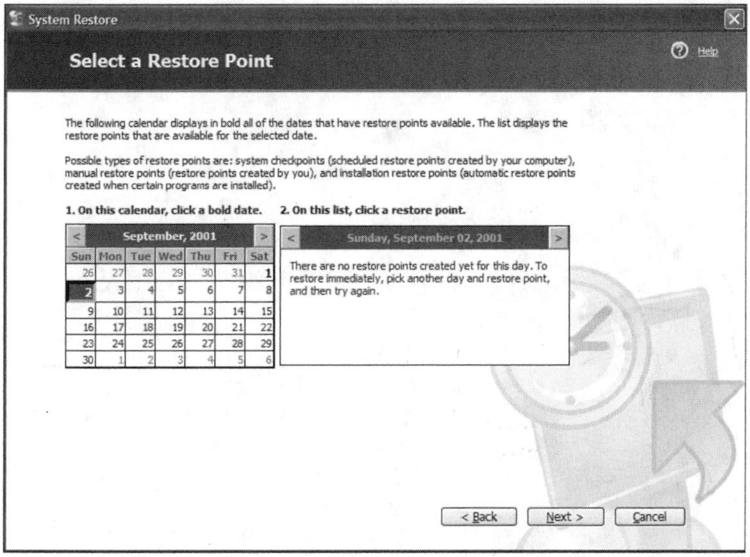

FIGURE 13.12
The Windows System Restore feature gives you an increased margin of error in attempting to recover a corrupted Windows installation.

With application/OS updates, it's a bit more difficult to simply "revert" outside of reinstalling the application. One of the beauties of the way Microsoft releases Service Packs is that they enable you to back up your configuration before applying the Service Pack so you can "uninstall" the Service Pack through the Add/Remove Programs control panel.

Chapter 14

Tweaking and Overclocking: Turbo-Charging Your PC

Overclocking: Getting What You Didn't Pay For

Face it, with bills to pay and the fact that you actually have to eat, it's not always possible to get the highest performing hardware on the block. Maybe you really wanted the 2.2GHz Pentium 4, but all you had the cash for was the 1.8GHz CPU. Granted, you realize that the extra 400MHz isn't the difference in whether you can play *Unreal 2*, but it's always nice to have the extra power (not to mention, bragging rights). Are you at a loss? They say there's no such thing as a free lunch. For the most part that's true…unless you're willing to overclock.

When a piece of hardware is manufactured, it is set to operate within certain specifications. For example, an Athlon 4 1.6GHz CPU is rated to run at a certain core voltage, FSB frequency, and multiplier (in this case 133MHz × 12.0), within a certain temperature range. If any of those specifications are exceeded, you are essentially going above and beyond what the manufacturer originally intended for normal usage of the CPU. This is known as *overclocking*.

You can overclock a lot more than just your CPU. You can overclock your chipset, and in doing so, you can overclock many other components on your motherboard. The VIA KT266 chipset is capable of operating at a 133MHz DDR FSB frequency (effectively 266MHz); the memory bus operates synchronously with the FSB, the PCI bus operates at 1/4 the FSB frequency, and the AGP bus runs at 1/2 the FSB clock speed of 133MHz. By overclocking your FSB (exceeding the manufacturer's original specifications) from 133MHz to 150MHz, you are not only overclocking your chipset/FSB, but you are also overclocking your

- **CPU**—Assuming a 12x clock multiplier, your CPU is now running at 1.8GHz.
- **Memory Bus**—Instead of running at 133MHz, your memory now runs at 150MHz.
- **PCI bus and all the cards on the bus**—Instead of running at 33MHz, they now run at 37.5MHz.
- **AGP Bus**—Instead of running at 66MHz, it now runs at 75MHz.

So by simply overclocking your FSB from 133MHz to 150MHz you get a 12.5% increase in CPU frequency, a 12.8% increase in memory speed, a 13.6% increase in PCI bus speed, and an identical increase in AGP bus speed. So much for there not being such a thing as a free lunch.

Motherboard manufacturers make overclocking even easier because it is almost a prerequisite that they offer overclocking options within their BIOS setups. These options include FSB adjustments, AGP/PCI bus divider manipulation and more aggressive memory timings that enable you to overclock by reducing memory wait states among other things.

However, overclocking isn't always as simple as making a few changes to your BIOS and reaping the benefits. If you notice, from overclocking the FSB I just listed at least four things that were overclocked in addition to the FSB. If even one of those things isn't capable of working out of spec or as far out of spec as your little FSB tweak has placed it, your system's stability could be compromised. For example, if my CPU could handle working at only 1.7GHz, but crashes at 1.8GHz in *Emperor—Battle for Dune*, my overclock would be useless.

That's the first rule of overclocking: If your overclock results in reduced stability, you've gained nothing. But what makes one 1.6GHz CPU work at 1.7GHz, whereas another works at 1.8GHz? If they're based on the same architecture, something else is obviously at work here.

Overclocking Your CPU

If you were to build a bridge that was capable of holding only 10 tons of weight and not a single ounce more, you'd be branded a poor engineer. Why? Because although you might design the bridge for use with no more than 10 tons of weight on it at any time, the bridge shouldn't collapse if an extremely out-of-shape driver happens to tip the scales a wee bit over the maximum. This same principle can be applied to CPU manufacturing. If a CPU is guaranteed to operate at 1.6GHz but fails when running at 1.60000001GHz, the CPU won't be running too well under normal conditions. The fact of the matter is that under normal conditions, variations occur in the operating conditions the CPU is under, and it wouldn't be too surprising to see the CPU actually running a tad above frequency at times.

An extremely healthy and mature manufacturing process is one that produces CPUs that work well at not only their rated clock speeds, but far beyond them as well. So, how does a CPU get a "rated" clock speed?

The initial design phase's calculations are done to figure out exactly what clock speed range a company, such as AMD or Intel, can expect from one of their CPUs. At the start of the manufacturing on a particular line of CPUs, the yields (percentage of usable chips out of those made) are never at their highest. However, they improve as time goes on (provided that all variables remain the same). An understanding of yields helps tremendously in understanding the concept of speed binning.

When a CPU is produced, it is first tested to see whether it is capable of working at its rated speed. Let's take the 1.6GHz CPU I introduced as an example. If AMD tests the 1.6GHz CPU and finds that it doesn't meet their quality/reliability standards for 1.6GHz operation do they simply throw it away? Of course not, that would make very little sense and end up wasting quite a bit of money. Instead they try it at a lower speed, and continue to do so until they find a speed at which that the CPU works. They then package the CPU and label it accordingly, so now the 1.6GHz CPU that was produced will be sold as a 1.4GHz CPU. This is *speed binning*.

At other times yields are so good on CPUs that even the 1.4GHz processors can run at 1.6GHz with no problems, in which case these 1.4GHz processors are just waiting to be overclocked—but how?

FSB Overclocking

Remember from Chapter 1, "The Central Processing Unit: The Heart and Soul of the PC," that the CPU clock speed is obtained by taking a Front Side Bus clock frequency generated on the motherboard and multiplying that by the CPU's clock multiplier. It would make sense that adjusting either of those two parts of the CPU frequency equation would result in a higher speed CPU. In this section, I talk about increasing the FSB frequency (see Figure 14.1).

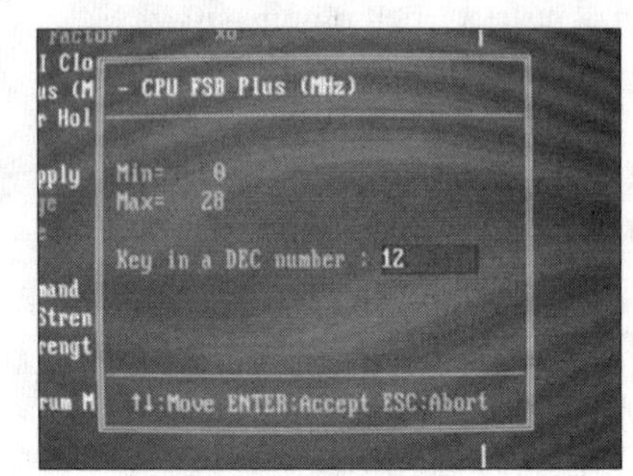

FIGURE 14.1
Most motherboards enable you to fine-tune your FSB frequency in 1MHz increments like this BIOS setup.

In the case of the image shown in Figure 14.1, the motherboard BIOS enables you to add anywhere from 1MHz–28MHz to the default FSB frequency. For example, typing in 12 here would result in the addition of 12MHz to your current FSB frequency. If it were 100MHz, your overclocked FSB frequency would be 112MHz.

The best part about CPU overclocking via increasing your FSB frequency is that your CPU not only gets faster, but so does the rest of your system. Your memory bus runs faster, as does your FSB among other things. Now that your CPU is capable of processing more information, your FSB and memory bus are now able to supply it with even more information. This is why you notice many situations in which a lower clocked CPU with a higher FSB and memory bus is able to outperform a higher clocked CPU with a lower FSB and memory bus. This is also why a CPU running at 2GHz with a 133MHz FSB is going to be faster than the same CPU running at 2GHz with a 100MHz FSB. Remember that a CPU can only process data as fast as it is fed the data to process.

This process is also, however, a double-edged sword. The biggest problem associated with FSB overclocking is that by increasing the FSB you are overclocking not only your CPU, but your chipset, memory bus, peripherals, and many other components of your system. If it all works then great, but if any one of these components isn't capable of handling the overclocked speed, you have nothing to show for your efforts.

The more variables you must tend to when overclocking your system, the greater the possibility that something will go wrong. Luckily, most of the other peripherals in your system are capable of being overclocked, as well. Generally, a 10%–20% increase in FSB frequency doesn't take your components too far out of their operating specifications. Typically, your CPU is the most picky when it comes to being overclockable, so if you can successfully overclock it under normal conditions, most of your other components should be okay.

Multiplier Overclocking

Aside from modifying your motherboard's front side bus speed, the only other way to overclock your CPU is by adjusting the multiplier. However, this is easier said than done. In an effort to combat re-marking Intel initiated a multiplier lock on all their CPUs produced around or after late 1998. Basically, this means that any Intel processor you buy today has had its multiplier set at the manufacturing plant and that setting cannot be changed, regardless of which motherboard or BIOS you might be using. This unfortunately limits all Intel overclocking potential to FSB overclocking.

This is such a big issue with Intel processors for two reasons. First, Intel still has the largest share of the desktop microprocessor market, so if someone is going to re-mark CPUs, the chances of him re-marking Intel CPUs are much higher than for AMD CPUs. Secondly, around the time Intel implemented this policy, it had some extremely high yields on the CPUs it was producing. This made them perfect for overclockers, but even more profitable for re-markers. Re-markers were simply overclocking the CPUs without telling their customers and charging more for them. This is an easy way for unscrupulous vendors to increase profits.

Note

Re-marking of a CPU is when a reseller takes a CPU, clocks it at a higher speed than its manufacturer has rated it for, and then sells it as if it were a higher speed CPU. Because Intel and AMD brand their processors by their rated speeds, this requires those markings to either be erased or redone to indicate the higher operating frequency. This practice is, of course, highly illegal.

AMD, however, implemented a different method to prevent re-marking. On the original Slot-A Athlons there was an interface in the upper-left corner of the CPU card. This interface was used for attaching devices that would internally aid in the testing of the CPU by enabling control over things such as the voltage and clock multiplier. This device gave testers the ability to easily switch between clock speeds and voltages on a single CPU.

FIGURE 14.2
The interface connector at the upper-left of this Slot-A Athlon CPU paved the way for cheap overclocking cards.

When it became known that the CPU's clock multiplier signals could also be sent from this connector, devices could easily be manufactured that would interface with this connector and enable users to adjust the multiplier of their Slot-A Athlon CPUs via dip switches or rotary dials on the interface card. These devices, as shown in Figure 14.3, became known as *gold finger devices* or *GFDs* (a misnomer because the interface pins on the Athlon CPU card are actually copper, not gold). It is useful to note that the Athlon's multiplier could also be adjusted via some resistor hacking on the card itself. However, that was a far more dangerous endeavor.

The Gold Rush GFD shown in Figure 14.3 was one of the more complex GFDs available. It used more complex circuitry to adjust the clock multiplier on the Athlon CPU while competing cards used simpler designs. This resulted in the Gold Rush unit dissipating much less heat than competing solutions.

With the move to socketed processors there was no use for GFDs, but AMD still did not completely lock the CPU. Instead AMD prevented casual re-marking of their Socket A processors by introducing a series of "bridges," as they were unofficially called, on the CPU itself. These bridges controlled things such as the clock multiplier and core voltage supplied to the CPU. A "completed bridge" was one that had both contact points connected via a conductive link, and an uncompleted bridge was one that didn't have any connection between the two contact points.

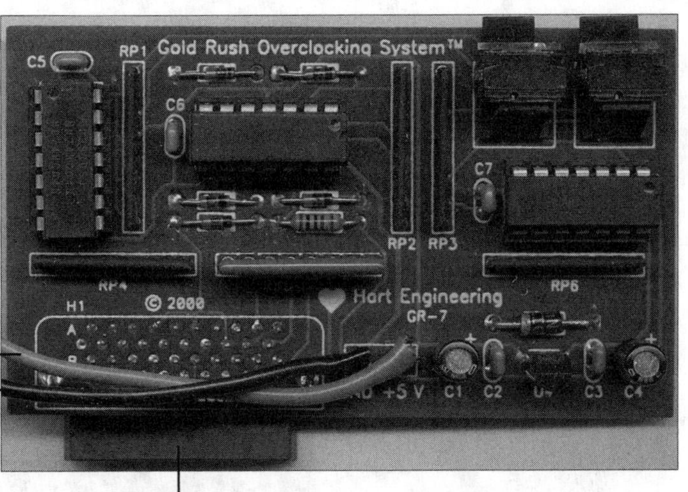

FIGURE 14.3 One of the best GFDs was the Gold Rush unit that never actually made it to the mass market.

Completing a bridge isn't a tremendous problem. Although solder doesn't adhere to the chip's ceramic packaging, conductive epoxy or conductive ink works like a charm. Some users even use pencil lead that contains conductive graphite, but I don't recommend this. Pencil lead doesn't always work, and with conductive pens costing around $10, it doesn't make too much sense to opt for pencil lead unless you want to temporarily try it (conductive pens are usually available at most electronics stores). In Figure 14.4 you can see a listing of the bridge configurations necessary to set the clock multiplier.

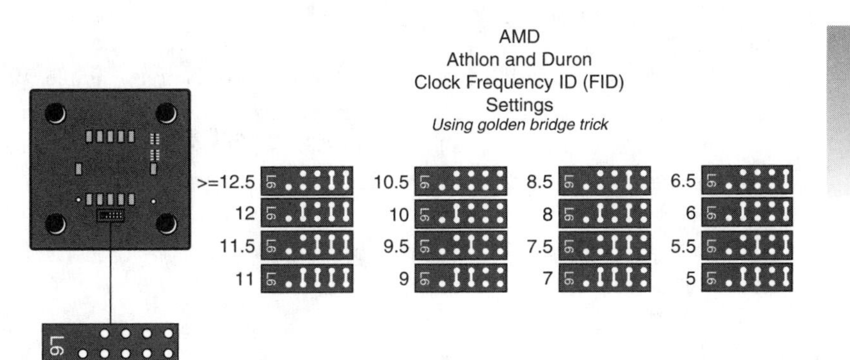

FIGURE 14.4 Enabling various clock multipliers on an Athlon or a Duron is a "simple" matter of connecting the appropriate bridges.

The biggest problem with the bridging technique however, is cutting the bridges. A normal knife isn't capable of cutting through the bridges; although you have many ways to get around this problem, it's usually more of an effort than most people want to undertake. Luckily, another option is unlocking the multiplier and allowing your motherboard to adjust the multiplier of the CPU, provided that it has this functionality (see Figure 14.5).

FIGURE 14.5
The L1 bridges in the upper-left corner of this Athlon CPU are already connected, leaving the CPU unlocked.

Unlocking the multiplier on a Socket-A processor is pretty simple. You just have to make sure that all the bridges present at the L1 marker on the chip are connected. Doing so allows you to adjust the multiplier of your CPU through your motherboard (see Figure 14.6).

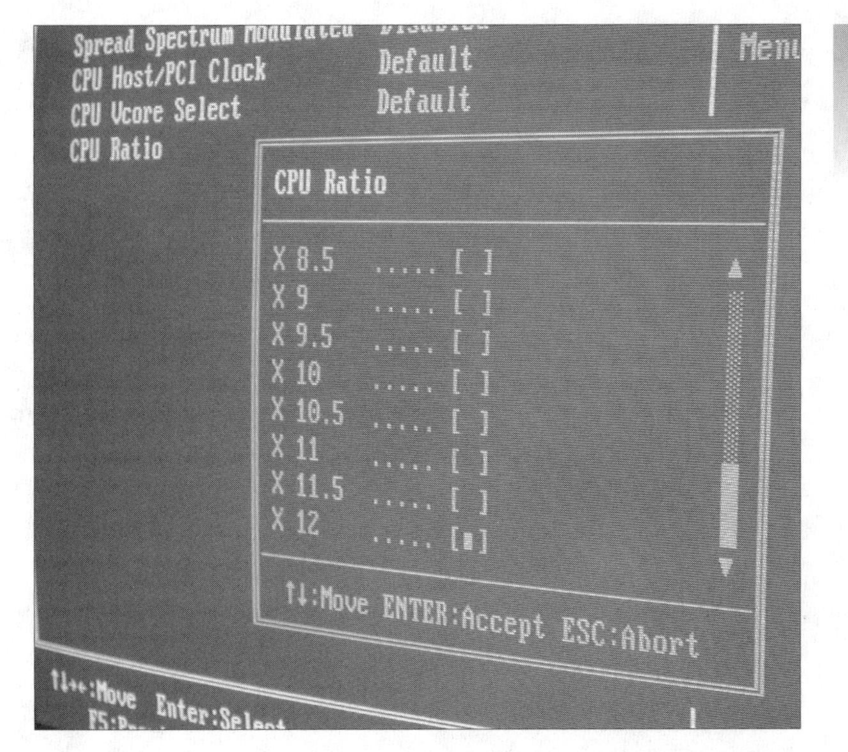

FIGURE 14.6
The BIOS of this Socket-A motherboard allows you to adjust the clock multiplier of the CPU.

In Table 14.1 you'll find an extensive list of the clock multiplier settings for today's processors and the speed ratings they generate. If you divide the clock speed by the clock multiplier, you'll also get the proper front side bus speed.

Table 14.1 Common Processors and Their Proper Clock Multiplier Settings for a Specific Speed

CPU	Clock Speed	Clock Multiplier
AMD Athlon-C 1.4	1.4GHz	10.5x
AMD Athlon-C 1.33	1.33GHz	10.0x
AMD Athlon-C 1.2	1.2GHz	9.0x
AMD Athlon-C 1.13	1.13GHz	8.5x
AMD Athlon-C 1.0	1.0GHz	7.5x
AMD Athlon 1.4	1.4GHz	14.0x
AMD Athlon 1.3	1.3GHz	13.0x

Table 14.1 Continued

CPU	Clock Speed	Clock Multiplier
AMD Athlon 1.2	1.2GHz	12.0x
AMD Athlon 1.0	1.0GHz	10.0x
AMD Athlon 950	950MHz	9.5x
AMD Athlon 900	900MHz	9.0x
AMD Athlon 850	850MHz	8.5x
AMD Athlon 800	800MHz	8.0x
AMD Athlon 750	750MHz	7.5x
AMD Athlon 700	700MHz	7.0x
AMD Athlon 650	650MHz	6.5x
AMD Athlon 600	600MHz	6.0x
AMD Athlon 550	550MHz	5.5x
AMD Athlon 500	500MHz	5.0x
AMD Duron 1.0	1.0GHz	10.0x
AMD Duron 950	950MHz	9.5x
AMD Duron 900	900MHz	9.0x
AMD Duron 850	850MHz	8.5x
AMD Duron 800	800MHz	8.0x
AMD Duron 750	750MHz	7.5x
AMD Duron 700	700MHz	7.0x
AMD Duron 650	650MHz	6.5x
AMD Duron 600	600MHz	6.0x
Intel Pentium 4 2.2	2.2GHz	22.0x
Intel Pentium 4 2.0	2.0GHz	20.0x
Intel Pentium 4 1.9	1.9GHz	19.0x
Intel Pentium 4 1.8	1.8GHz	18.0x
Intel Pentium 4 1.7	1.7GHz	17.0x
Intel Pentium 4 1.6	1.6GHz	16.0x
Intel Pentium 4 1.5	1.5GHz	15.0x

Table 14.1 Continued

CPU	Clock Speed	Clock Multiplier
Intel Pentium 4 1.4	1.4GHz	14.0x
Intel Pentium 4 1.3	1.3GHz	13.0x
Intel Pentium III 1.2	1.2GHz	9.0x
Intel Pentium III 1.13A	1.13GHz	8.5x
Intel Pentium III 1.0EB	1.0GHz	7.5x

Overclocked Stability

When overclocking your CPU by increasing the FSB, clock multiplier, or a combination of the two, the chances that your CPU can handle it and simply not POST are quite high—depending on how far you push the CPU. As long as your CPU has adequate cooling (for example, a heatsink or fan properly installed), you shouldn't have to worry about frying it because the POST failed and it has run for a short amount of time at the out-of-spec frequency (see Chapter 9, "Cases and Cooling: Living in Style and Keeping Your Cool"). If the CPU doesn't POST or your system boots but is clearly quite unstable, the solution is to back down a bit by decreasing the FSB, the multiplier, or both.

However, the following are a few tricks to make your overclocked CPU more reliable. Doing this could shave a few years off your CPU's 10+ year life span (as if you were going to have the same CPU for 10 years!). The first trick is increasing the voltage supplied to your CPU. A big feature of many motherboards is the capability to adjust the core voltage supplied to the CPU. By giving a CPU more voltage (don't go overboard, obviously—nothing more than 10% over your default voltage), you are increasing its tolerances for operation out of spec, which often improves stability when overclocked (see Figure 14.7).

The downside to increasing the core voltage of your CPU is that you are now overclocking two parts of the CPU, the clock speed and the core voltage. Provided that the operating voltage of the CPU is within the manufacturer's specifications (this can normally be found in datasheets provided by the CPU manufacturer on their Web site) then you should be okay. However, your CPU is now going to be generating quite a bit more heat.

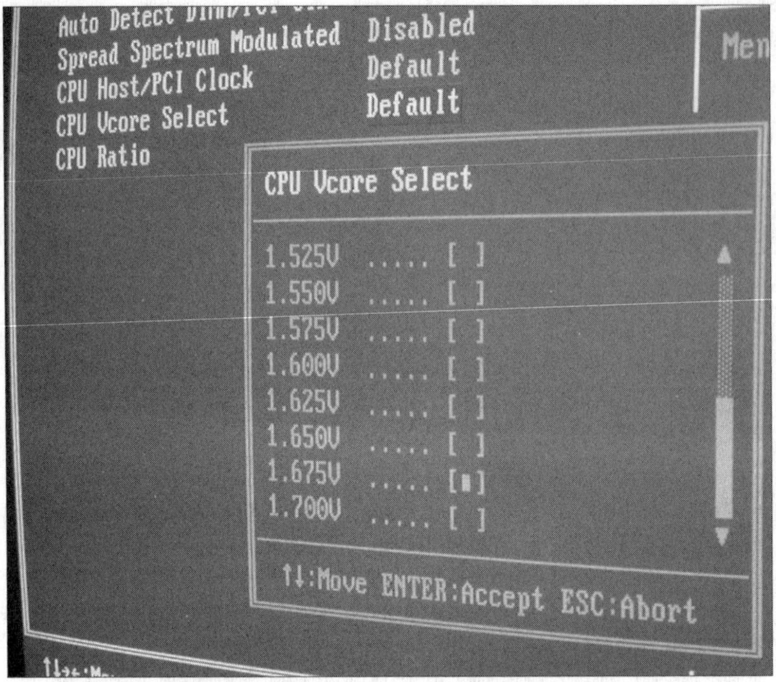

FIGURE 14.7
Finding an enthusiast motherboard without voltage selection options in the BIOS is almost unheard of.

If you have overstepped your bounds and picked a core voltage setting that's too high (I generally prefer to stay in the 10%–15% range for voltages I try above and beyond the default), you actually might decrease the stability of your setup. If done properly, however, you might have just given your CPU enough breathing room to work at the higher frequency.

The other major trick is to get rid of the extra heat generated by using better cooling methods. If you have a well-ventilated case, the heatsink/fan combo sitting on your CPU keeps the temperature of your CPU under control. I recommend using either a thermal pad or some sort of thermal compound between your CPU and the heatsink/fan combo to increase thermal conductivity. For more information on cooling, see Chapter 9.

One thing that can happen is that months or maybe even a year or so go by, and then all of a sudden your CPU doesn't work at the overclocked frequency. This happens every now and then, mainly because when you are overclocking and increasing the core voltage of your CPU, you are running it out of its intended specs. So, there might come a time when it no longer works at the overclocked frequency. However, overclocking is relatively safe for the most part and highly advocated within the community as long as you don't sacrifice stability for a little extra speed. In terms of reliable overclocking ranges, it's very difficult to give you a safe target to shoot for because it varies so much depending on the architecture of the CPU, the manufacturing process, yield, and cooling. Again, the general rule of thumb is that 10% is usually achievable, but in some cases a 20%–30% overclock can be obtained.

Overclocking Your Video Card

Other than your CPU, overclocking your video card can result in some very tangible performance gains. Just as is the case with overclocking your CPU, you can overclock two main things on your video card: the graphics chip itself (referred to as the *core*) and the memory.

Overclocking your video card is almost solely accomplished via driver/software controls. Some drivers provide overclocking utilities in them by default. Others make you unlock them via some registry hacking, and some don't provide any overclocking utilities at all—in which case you should use a third-party utility such as Power Strip (`http://www.entechtaiwan.com`) or NVMAX (you'll find a number of download sites for this utility if you enter this name into a search engine).

Increasing the core speed of your video card doesn't normally improve gaming performance too much because your memory bandwidth is usually limited before you are fill-rate limited. Therefore, you get the most performance increase (generally speaking) by increasing your memory operating frequency.

Increasing core/memory voltage is unusual when overclocking your video card. Although some motherboards do enable you to increase the voltage supplied to your AGP slot, this doesn't improve things too much. In other words, the only way to increase stability when overclocking your video card is to improve cooling of the core or memory using larger heatsinks/fans. The major issue here is that you have space limitations with how big the heatsinks/fans on your video card can be because you're dealing with a horizontally mounted add-in card with very little keeping it in place.

Telltale signs of pushing your core or memory too far are seeing artifacts in your games (and in 2D mode as well), hard locks during gameplay, and any other video corruption you might notice. An investigation done at AnandTech looked at the telltale signs that the core/memory had been overclocked too far. When the core is overclocked too high, improperly rendered images resulted.

Remember that when you're pushing your core to the limits you run into chip heat issues; the hotter your GPU runs, the more difficult it is for the GPU to properly render a scene. As you can see in Figure 14.8, the face to the left is rendered properly while the face to the right has been improperly rendered because of excessive core overclocking. Note the blocky triangle on the character's right cheek.

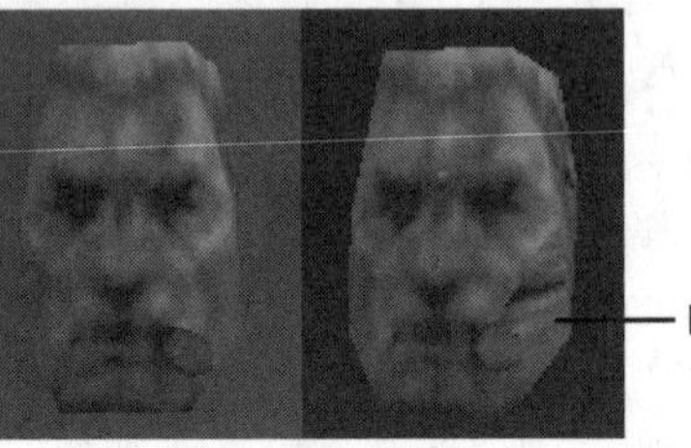

FIGURE 14.8
Overclocking your system too far can result in odd graphical problems as illustrated here.

When dealing with out-of-spec memory speeds, the main results are pixels that are the wrong color or discolored. You get pixels that are incorrect colors, or in many cases, you get what appear to be snowflakes around your screen or random white pixels, as shown in Figure 14.9.

FIGURE 14.9
If you look closely, you can see several miscolored pixels that in the right context might look like snow, but in this case are indicative of memory errors.

Other Tweaks

Overclocking your CPU (and in some cases FSB/memory bus) as well as your video card are usually the easiest ways to get more performance out of your configuration. Other tweaks you can do involve using more aggressive memory timings in the BIOS, as well as the quick tweaks I mentioned in Chapter 12, "Upgrading: Feeling the Need for Speed."

Benchmarks—Grading Your PC

Now that you've overclocked, the real question is was it worth it? How do you know? Of course the system is going to feel faster, but is your mind just playing tricks on you or did you actually increase the performance of your machine? The way to find out is to benchmark your creation, but what do you use? How do you benchmark? And what do the results mean?

Synthetic Versus Real-World Benchmarks

The two types of benchmarks are synthetic and real-world benchmarks. A synthetic benchmark is one that stresses one or more parts of your PC by running a script that targets the functions of that part of your PC (see Figure 14.10). This script isn't necessarily something that you'd do with your computer with a real-world application, but it does adequately stress and measure a part of your computer that you use frequently.

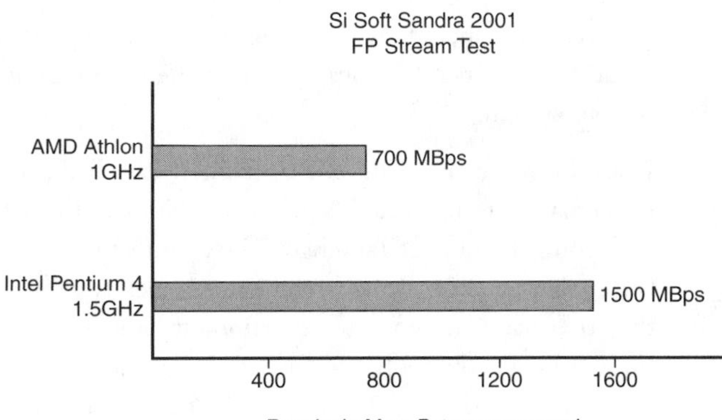

FIGURE 14.10
This benchmark is purely a memory bandwidth test using floating point operations. The Pentium 4 has a clear advantage over the Athlon (the Pentium 4's i850 chipset physically has more memory bandwidth than the Athlon's AMD 760 chipset in this test).

An example of a synthetic benchmark would be a program that performs the calculation 1+1 as many times per second as your CPU can handle and outputs a number of integer calculations per second as the performance of your

CPU. Obviously you're never going to be figuring out 1+1 over and over again for no reason, but this type of a benchmark gives you a clue as to how powerful the integer unit(s) of your CPU happens to be (to a certain extent).

A real-world benchmark however is one that takes an application or game that you commonly use, and measures performance in that situation doing something you would normally do under that program (see Figure 14.11).

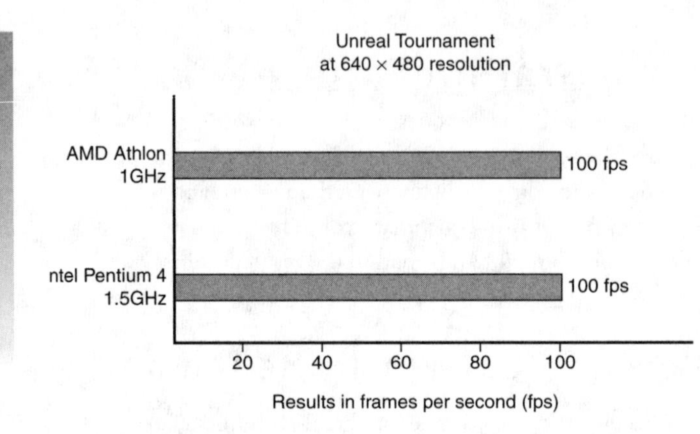

FIGURE 14.11 This benchmark is a real-world test that measures performance within a game. You can easily see that the 115% performance advantage the Pentium 4 had in Sandra did not translate into any performance advantage in Unreal Tournament.

An example of a real-world application benchmark would be one that opens up Microsoft Word, opens a file, edits the file, checks spelling on the file, prints it (albeit to a NULL printer driver so that the file isn't actually printed but the system thinks it is), and then closes down the program—all while measuring the time it took to complete all that. Another example would be running through a level in a first person shooter and measuring the average frame rate while doing that. These are all examples of real-world benchmarks that actually have some meaning for the performance of your system.

Does this mean that synthetic benchmarks are bad and all real-world benchmarks are inherently a god send? Not exactly. Synthetic benchmarks help you get an understanding of the architecture and are quite useful for comparing products on an architectural level. Real-world benchmarks, on the other hand, are good ways to find out how well something performs in the tasks you commonly use, provided that the real-world benchmark you are using does simulate the tasks for which you are interested in improving performance.

How to Benchmark

Although you might hate thinking of it in this way, benchmarking is a lot like performing a lab in a science class. You have to keep a control or baseline to compare to, repeat your tests for reliability, and limit the number of variables you introduce into the equation.

The first requirement is that you understand the benchmark you are running. If you're running a benchmark that runs through Microsoft Word, don't expect it to measure graphics performance very well. Try and find out what sorts of limitations are present in the benchmark script. For example, if you're running a game benchmark at a resolution that is memory bandwidth limited and you want to see the performance increase that your 10% CPU overclock resulted in, chances are that you're not going to see an increase of more than a couple of percentage points in this benchmark. Does that mean that your overclock didn't work well? No, it means that you're limited by the performance of your video card and increasing your CPU speed doesn't help you in this type of a situation.

Some benchmarks do serve as great tests for things other than what you would normally expect. Most gaming benchmarks serve this role very well as they not only stress your graphics card but also your CPU, memory bandwidth, FSB, and many other parts of your system.

I mentioned at the start of this section that you should make it a goal to keep the number of variables introduced to a minimum. Don't compare the performance of two systems if they're using different graphics cards, or different sound cards. By simply benchmarking with sound your frame rate can be reduced by as much as 10% because of all the additional calculations.

Make sure you keep as many variables constant as possible. If you overclock your CPU/video card, don't install a new set of drivers before benchmarking and then compare to your old configuration. At the same time, if you're testing a new driver set don't decide to overclock your CPU along with installing the new drivers and compare performance either. Removing as many variables as you can from the equation helps make sure that your benchmarks are not only telling you something, but they're reliable.

If you want to benchmark how CPU performance has increased by overclocking your CPU while using a 3D game as a benchmark, turn down the resolution and color depth in your game to reduce the dependency on your video card. If you want to benchmark your video card, however, set the game settings at the resolution you normally play at (such as 1,024 × 768) and see how things improve.

Although it is best to benchmark on a clean system without any other devices/drivers installed, I understand that this is not always possible on your personal machine. For this very same reason make sure that you don't get into a benchmark competition with your friends because the chances of you all having an identical configuration (hardware and software-wise) is very low. This is one of the downsides to doing full system comparisons because the hard drives, video cards, drivers, CPUs, and motherboards vary so much between one system to the next that it is difficult to say that system A is faster than system B if the only thing making system A faster is that it has drivers properly installed.

If you take this scientific approach to benchmarking, you are able to actually make some sense out of these numbers.

Chapter 15

Troubleshooting: Something Is Wrong with My Baby

The Mental Game

If you're reading this section for fun, consider yourself lucky and take away from it as much knowledge as you can. However, in all honesty, the only way you learn how to troubleshoot is by experiencing first hand the situations I discuss in this chapter. With that said, if you aren't reading this section for fun and you actually have a problem that needs troubleshooting, it's important to lay some ground rules on how to troubleshoot effectively so that whatever problem you have is solved as quickly and painlessly as possible.

The most important rule of troubleshooting is to have a proper state of mind. If you approach any problem without a clear mind, you may never come to a solution, and even if you do manage to solve the problem, it certainly takes much more effort than necessary. If you get frustrated easily, just as I mentioned in Chapter 11, "Putting It All Together: Break Out the Hammers and Duct Tape," you want to be very careful when troubleshooting, especially when troubleshooting a hardware problem where you have to install or remove any components. Being frustrated with what you're working on can easily cause more damage. So, if you're not getting anywhere and you've got more on your mind, take a break and come back to it later.

You also have to approach troubleshooting as a scientific method; remove as many variables as possible and introduce one at a time until you find the cause for your troubleshooting woes. After all, if you are troubleshooting a problem in your BIOS by making several random changes, and one of them actually works, how do you know which one it was?

Symptoms and Solutions

With the mental part covered, let me explain the format of this chapter. This chapter operates much like a flow chart where I list symptoms and where to go for the potential solutions. Keep in mind that the number of problems that could exist is entirely too vast for me to cover in a single chapter, much less in a single book, but this should provide an overview of where to look for the solutions to your problems.

My System Does Not POST/I Don't Get Any Video

If your BIOS never initializes or your system never POSTs (performs its power on self test), you are normally met with a blank screen that usually leads people to believe that the video card is at fault. That, however, is rarely the case. Before even beginning to diagnose this problem, make sure your PC speaker is connected. That likely helps in diagnosing the problem.

Is Your Monitor/Computer Connected/ Plugged In?

Although this seems obvious, you'd be amazed at the number of times I've seen someone put together a computer only to leave the monitor unplugged from the video card and wonder why his new system isn't POSTing. Make sure all external connections (including power) are made properly. To be very safe you can even try leaving things like keyboards, mice, and any other external devices unplugged until you can get the system POSTing. Remember the goal is to minimize the number of variables in your setup while troubleshooting. The minimum configuration necessary for your system to post is a power supply, motherboard, CPU (with heatsink and fan), video card, the minimum amount of memory, and a monitor.

If you don't get any response at all from pressing the power button, also make sure that your power button is properly connected to your motherboard, the power supply's power switch is on, the CMOS jumper on your motherboard isn't set to clear, and your power switch isn't damaged. You can test for this by using a piece of metal to temporarily make the connection between the two power pins; that is the equivalent of pressing the power switch.

Are You Using the Correct Components?

Make sure

- You're using a CPU that is supported by your BIOS.
- You're using supported memory (for example, don't use Virtual Channel SDRAM, such as PC133 VC SDRAM, in a system that supports only regular SDRAM, such as PC100 SDRAM).
- Your power supply can supply enough power to the motherboard/CPU. If you have a system that requires an ATX 2.03 power supply with an ATX12V connector, make sure the power supply is ATX 2.03 compliant and the ATX12V connector is inserted into the motherboard.

Do You Hear Any Beeps?

If you hear any beeps coming from your PC speaker refer to your motherboard manual, which contains a list of BIOS beep codes that help narrow down the problem to a particular component. If it doesn't, find a way to get to the motherboard manufacturer's Web site and look there. Check the health and status of that particular component to troubleshoot this problem.

Do Your CPU Fan and Hard Drive Spin Up?

If your CPU fan and hard drive don't spin up, you've got a serious issue. Make sure your motherboard is getting power and also make sure that nothing is shorting out. Check to see whether your CPU is installed properly and that the CPU has no bent pins that aren't inserted into the socket (if it is a socketed CPU).

If everything looks okay and your CPU fan and hard drive don't spin up, the problem is serious. Try removing all components (memory, video card, and so on) and see whether your CPU fan and hard drive (leave them plugged in) spin up. If they do, add in the components you removed one by one. When the CPU fan and hard drive refuse to spin again, you've found the culprit.

If removing all those components fails to improve the situation and you're certain you don't have a short, you might have a dead motherboard, CPU, or power supply. Test each one of those components individually (preferably in another computer) to determine which one is causing the problem. Many motherboard manufacturers are including LEDs and other diagnostic tools on motherboards that help identify the component causing the failure.

Are All the Components Installed and Seated Properly?

The best way to diagnose this problem is by removing all the components except for the bare minimum, meaning that the only things mounted on your motherboard are

- The CPU and its heatsink/fan
- The minimum number of memory sticks
- A video card

The power supply should be the only other component that's connected in your case. Applying power to this setup should result in your system POSTing. If not, there could be a problem with one of those components. Make sure everything is disconnected except for what I have explicitly stated here. Sometimes things such as an IDE cable installed backwards can prevent a system from POSTing.

Is the CPU's FSB and Core Voltage Set Properly?

Double-check any jumpers or dip switches on the motherboard to ensure that your CPU's clock multiplier, FSB, and voltage are properly set according to the manufacturer's specifications. If you happen to be overclocking, back down off your overclock and run at the default clock speed and core voltage.

Also check AGP/PCI dividers and memory bus frequency settings. A lot of these options might be offered only in the BIOS, in which case you should try resetting the CMOS values by either using the jumper on the motherboard or unplugging your system and removing the CMOS battery for 10–15 seconds minimum.

Are There Any Faulty Components?

Unfortunately, the only way to tell whether any faulty components exist is by testing them in a setup that is known to be working. This is a luxury few have, so you might have to give a friend a call and convince him to let you swap a few components to see whether you can get to the bottom of this problem.

If you have more than one memory stick installed and your setup can operate with only a single stick installed, try each memory stick individually. You might have a faulty memory module, or a combination of the two might be preventing your system from POSTing because of an incompatibility between them and the chipset or motherboard.

My System Hangs After POST/During OS Install

A system that crashes or refuses to complete the earliest steps of booting/OS installation still has some serious problems; just having video on your screen doesn't put you in the clear. The problems at this stage can be related to faulty hardware, incompatibilities, or—many times—timings or frequencies that are too aggressively set.

Remove All Unnecessary Components

You can install your OS with no more than your primary hard drive (and CD/DVD drive if you're installing off a CD), video card, memory, CPU (with heatsink and fan), and keyboard plugged in. That should be your first attempt at diagnosing this problem. Remove and unplug everything else. If that fixes the problem, add in the components one by one, testing after adding each component until you find the culprit.

Tip

Note that underclocking your CPU can sometimes help diagnose problems that otherwise keep you from booting properly or operating your PC normally. For example, if you have an 133MHz/1GHz Athlon, you can slow down the FSB to 100MHz, lowering the core processor speed to 750MHz in the process.

If that doesn't fix the problem, you have to try swapping out individual components until you can find the culprit. As long as your CPU isn't overclocked, that's usually *not* the cause of common problems like this. If it is a hardware problem and not a BIOS setting problem, the most likely candidates are the motherboard and the memory, but don't rule out the others.

Check BIOS Settings

Try resetting your BIOS settings either by using the jumper on your motherboard or by selecting the Load BIOS Defaults or Fail Safe option in the BIOS setup. Disable all on-board audio, Ethernet, and modem controllers. Set all memory timings to their lowest performance levels, and make sure your processor isn't overclocked.

Also use your BIOS' built-in hardware monitor to ensure that the proper voltages are being supplied on all your power rails. Being off by a bit is not unusual for these values, but they shouldn't be off by much more than 10%. For example, only getting 2V on the 3.3V line is cause for alarm.

Finally, try disabling Quick Boot in your BIOS so that the system can run through a full set of tests before completing POST. This might narrow down the problem to bad memory.

Check OS Installation Media

If you've copied your OS installation files onto your hard drive, make sure the files aren't corrupt. Try installing off the original CD. Try the CD in another computer to ensure it does in fact work if you have reason to believe the CD would be bad (this is very rare unless it's a copy of the original CD).

Check Cooling

Make sure your CPU is getting adequate cooling. You can monitor its temperature as well as the temperature of the rest of your system within the BIOS usually in a section labeled "PC Health" or something to that effect. Take note of any temperatures that rise too quickly. Do keep in mind that your CPU runs well into the higher temperatures, seeing 50°–60° Celsius isn't uncommon with some of the higher-speed Athlon CPUs.

Check the Drive

Although this is rare for a brand new drive, make sure that no significant bad sectors or any other forms of corruption exist on your drive. If so, run a tool such as Scandisk to fix them.

My System Hangs When Booting the OS

If this is the first time your system is booting and it hangs during the OS initialization process, chances are that some component in your system is causing the problem—in which case you should remove all unnecessary components as I've described in the previous two sections. If your computer was working properly before, but just started crashing while booting the OS, you have a few options to consider.

Note

Safe Mode is a diagnostic mode of Windows (9x/Me/2000/XP) that is useful for uninstalling drivers and so on when your system cannot boot normally. You can enter Safe Mode by pressing F8 at the Starting Windows text screen before you see the Windows logo. This opens a menu that has Safe Mode as an option to start your computer. If the computer has repeatedly failed to boot properly, Windows might run in Safe Mode automatically.

Have You Installed Any New Hardware?

If the last thing you did before you rebooted was install a new piece of hardware, try removing that hardware and see whether that helps. Sometimes you have to enter Safe Mode and uninstall the hardware from Windows's Device Manager first, and then reboot the system.

The cause of this could be a driver incompatibility that could be fixed by an updated driver from the manufacturer, or it could be something more serious, such as a hardware incompatibility with something in your system.

Also see if any flags are in Device Manager that would help you narrow down which component is at fault.

Another option is to enable resetting configuration data in the BIOS, which sometimes helps in situations where your OS fails to boot after a new hardware install.

Have You Installed Any New Software?

If the culprit is software, your best bet is to enter Windows's Safe Mode and attempt to correct the problem or uninstall whatever software you installed. If you can get into Safe Mode with Networking enabled, you might want to check both Microsoft and the software developer's Web site to see whether your problem is noted in their knowledgebases.

Have You Overclocked/Tweaked Any BIOS Settings?

If you've overclocked your CPU, try backing down off the overclocked frequency a bit. Remember that even though your CPU worked fine at the overclocked frequency initially, things do change over time when overclocking.

If you've changed any BIOS settings try changing them back to their original values. If you don't remember their original values, try resetting the BIOS to its fail-safe defaults to undo any harm that might have been caused.

If you just upgraded your BIOS, try downgrading to the previous version that works fine. Then check with other online resources to see whether anyone has had any trouble with the BIOS revision to which you were trying to upgrade.

Is Your System Running Too Hot?

Make sure all your fans are still working, and make sure your CPU's heatsink/fan is rated for use with your CPU at whatever clock speed it happens to be running. If you suspect that heat is the issue, try underclocking your CPU by using a slower FSB or a lower clock multiplier if possible. If that solves the problem, it could be heat related, and upgrading your cooling would be the appropriate solution there.

My System Hangs When in the OS

If your system crashes when in the OS, your problem can usually be solved by going through the same steps as if your OS wouldn't boot. Just because you're at your desktop doesn't mean that the problem changes; it just means the issue still enables your OS to boot.

Sometimes tracking down a culprit months after you have set everything up can be difficult, especially when it's a software issue. A program you had installed left its mess and has unfortunately degraded your system's stability.

When diagnosing instability in the OS, try to minimize the number of applications running at once to eliminate them as potentially causing your stability problems. Remember that not all applications are written well. It's quite common for applications to use too many resources and when another application or your OS tries to regain those resources, problems can arise.

In the event that something you've installed has degraded the stability of your system, sometimes your best bet is to back up your documents, e-mail, and other important files and just reinstall your OS. See Chapter 13, "Operating Systems and Device Drivers: Making Your Hardware Work."

Heat is another issue. I discussed what options you have in that event earlier in the chapter.

My System Randomly Reboots/Crashes

One of the most common problems I've seen throughout the years has been the random reboot or crash where you're working on something or playing a game and all of a sudden your system randomly reboots or crashes. This can happen for a couple of reasons.

Resource Encroachment

Sometimes when one component is using a particular set of resources and another component in your system requests the same resources, if your OS and hardware do not properly arbitrate the transfer of resources, an error occurs. Sometimes this results in a Windows crash (for example, Blue Screen of Death—BSOD), and other times Windows simply reboots your system. Generally speaking, Windows gives you some sort of access violation error. In the case of 2000/XP you get a BSOD. Luckily, it tells you a bit about the problem that occurred. An error such as "IRQ is less than or equal to" lets you know that the issue you just encountered was indeed a resource sharing issue. Look at the devices involved, and what you were doing when it happened. See if you can find any resolution to the problem. Sometimes no resolution exists, and the problem occurs only once in a blue moon. Other times updating drivers or simply moving the device to a different expansion slot helps.

Heat

When your CPU is gradually getting too hot and eventually reaches its threshold, it either underclocks—if it has the capability to—or reboots. Most newer CPUs (such as the Pentium 4) decrease their operating frequencies until the temperature is back into the normal operating range. Older CPUs aren't that intelligent.

Remember, heat is often a culprit when random reboots occur.

Memory Errors

When an error occurs in either reading from or writing to memory, the results can be devastating. If your CPU gets bad data or doesn't get the data it needs to continue, things can get ugly and your system might end up rebooting. Check to ensure that all your memory modules are good. You might want to try installing the minimum number of modules to see whether any one module is causing the problem.

Overclocking Too Far

When you push your CPU, chipset, FSB, memory bus, or any other part of your system beyond its limits, you might have gone too far. When overclocking, just because you can make it past the initial POST screen doesn't mean anything. If you lose stability, the overclock loses its purpose. Try backing down on your overclock or going back to your original stock settings to see if that changes things.

A Device Run Astray

Every now and then you install a device that either has some poorly written drivers or just has poor compatibility with your current configuration. These devices usually aren't the major devices, such as your motherboard, video card, and so on. However, little things like compact flash card readers or wireless networking devices usually come from smaller companies that don't necessarily have the best resources to focus on driver/hardware compatibility testing.

This is where you've got to apply a bit of common sense. Try to examine the problem at hand and think about what components are involved with the process that leads to the reboot.

A Damaged Component

In Chapter 11, I described the importance of preventing any sort of electrostatic discharge. An unfortunate consequence of ESD is that the tiny traces in or on the PCB of your motherboard, video card, or any other peripheral card can sever over time as a result of the ESD. With ESD, the problems don't arise on day one (unless they're really bad). Instead, they crop up three to six months later. If after months of use, reinstalls and swapping out major components don't work, you could have a bad motherboard or another bad component. That's what warranties are for, and now you see why I suggest you take proper care when handling static-sensitive equipment.

My System Won't Run a Specific Application or Game

If the only problem you have is that you can't run one application or game, consider youself well off. There have been numerous cases throughout the history of PC game development in which games have been released with major compatibility problems with specific pieces of hardware or operating systems. The most recent case is *Anachronox* not working properly on many Windows 2000 systems, although ION Storm never claimed support for the OS. Because so many gamers do use the OS, it doesn't make sense to not support it.

The first thing to do in this case is figure out where the application or game is crashing. If it doesn't load, it could be a hardware initialization problem, especially with 3D games. Make sure other OpenGL or Direct 3D games work (depending on whether it is an OpenGL or a Direct3D game). If they don't, the problem could be related to your video card's drivers, the OpenGL ICD being used for the game, or your installed version of DirectX.

If the application or game crashes during the middle of the game, the issue could be any of those I listed in the previous section. Again, if it is a 3D game, ask around and search knowledgebase articles about any incompatibility with your video card's drivers. In the end, it's likely a bug in the game is causing the problem. PC hardware setups have more variations than a game developer can possibly test, so a situation in which a game crashes constantly on your machine but runs flawlessly on a friend's is not uncommon.

If the problems are within the game, check periodically for any patches available for this application or game. If the problem is widespread enough, developers often devote a good chunk of their time to fixing it. Often, one of the best places to look for support in situations like this is the forums or knowledgebases for the particular application or game on its own Web site or the developer's Web site.

My System Performs Slower Than It Should Be

System performance can relate to a number of things, but look in the following areas for solutions to this problem.

BIOS Settings

While it is rare that a BIOS setting (unless you disable cache or something of that magnitude) can offer a 20%–40% reduction in performance, you have cases in which large performance increases can come from an optimized BIOS. Many BIOS setup utilities feature a Load Optimized Defaults setting, which makes this task much easier. Otherwise, you should decrease memory timings wherever possible and ask around for the impacts of enabling and disabling other features. Some very good FAQs about BIOS settings specific to certain motherboards are online, so a quick search should turn up a lot of results.

Tip

For some useful tips, check out Adrian's Rojak Pot's BIOS Optimization Guide at `http://www.rojakpot.com/Speed_Demonz/BIOS_Guide/BIOS_Guide_Index.htm`.

Drivers

Unlike BIOS settings, drivers can really change the picture. Be sure to install the latest chipset drivers from your chipset manufacturer, the latest IDE drivers from your chipset manufacturer, the latest video card drivers, and just about any other drivers for which you have hardware. These drivers should always be kept up-to-date, but don't worry about upgrading them unless you have a serious reason to do so. Many configurations that were otherwise working perfectly have been disturbed by users upgrading drivers for no reason. If it ain't broke, don't fix it.

Benchmarking Tool

As I discussed in Chapter 14, "Tweaking and Overclocking: Turbo-Charging Your PC," make sure the performance tool you're using and the numbers you're comparing to are putting your system and everything else on a level playing field. Just because your benchmark score is lower than your friend's doesn't mean that your system is underperforming. Remember, you want to make an apples-to-apples comparison whenever possible; otherwise, the comparison loses meaning.

Index

Symbols

A

B

E

F

I

N

O

P

Q-R

S

T

Z

Hey, you've got enough worries.

Don't let IT training be one of them.

Get on the fast track to IT training at InformIT,
your total Information Technology training network.

www.informit.com | **SAMS**

■ Hundreds of timely articles on dozens of topics ■ Discounts on IT books from all our publishing partners, including Sams Publishing ■ Free, unabridged books from the InformIT Free Library ■ "Expert Q&A"—our live, online chat with IT experts ■ Faster, easier certification and training from our Web- or classroom-based training programs ■ Current IT news ■ Software downloads ■ Career-enhancing resources

InformIT is a registered trademark of Pearson. Copyright ©2001 by Pearson.
Copyright ©2001 by Sams Publishing.